The Development of Working Memory in Children

SAGE has been part of the global academic community since 1965, supporting high quality research and learning that transforms society and our understanding of individuals, groups, and cultures. SAGE is the independent, innovative, natural home for authors, editors and societies who share our commitment and passion for the social sciences.

Find out more at: **www.sagepublications.com**

The Development of Working Memory in Children

Lucy Henry

Los Angeles | London | New Delhi
Singapore | Washington DC

First published 2012

SAGE Publications Ltd
1 Oliver's Yard
55 City Road
London EC1Y 1SP

SAGE Publications Inc.   *10 0730713 2*
2455 Teller Road
Thousand Oaks, California 91320

SAGE Publications India Pvt Ltd
B 1/I 1 Mohan Cooperative Industrial Area
Mathura Road
New Delhi 110 044

SAGE Publications Asia-Pacific Pte Ltd
3 Church Street
#10–04 Samsung Hub
Singapore 049483

Library of Congress Control Number: 2011937258

British Library Cataloguing in Publication data

A catalogue record for this book is available from the British Library

ISBN 978-1-84787-328-6
ISBN 978-1-84787-329-3 (pbk)

Typeset by C&M Digitals (P) Ltd, Chennai, India
Printed in Great Britain by Ashford Colour Press Ltd

This book is dedicated to my husband and children.

Contents

Preface

How to use the chapters in this book effectively

Working memory encompasses a number of skills that underpin thinking, reasoning, remembering and perhaps even consciousness. It is not only everyday activities that are supported by working memory skills, more demanding tasks requiring concentration and effort draw particularly strongly on working memory resources. It is, therefore, no surprise that working memory abilities are closely linked to educational achievement. The purpose of this book is to examine how working memory develops in children with a range of abilities, including those with typical development and those who have developmental disorders.

This book has been written primarily for students, teachers and researchers interested in working memory development in typical and atypical populations of children, but it should also be accessible to anyone with an interest in this area. The book is structured such that the 'working memory model' is explained first, and then details are given on how working memory can be measured in populations of children with and without special needs. This provides a background for the other chapters that deal with working memory development in typical children, and working memory development in six populations of children with atypical development.

Therefore, there are three distinct parts to this book: (1) the working memory model and how to measure working memory; (2) working memory development in typical children; and (3) working memory development in children with atypical development. In order to use this book effectively and to target your specific interests, brief descriptions of what will be covered in each chapter are now presented.

Two chapters outline the working memory model and how to measure working memory:

- *Chapter 1* If you are interested in learning about the working memory model in general, together with some key evidence supporting the model, you will find this information in Chapter 1.

- *Chapter 2* This chapter considers methods of measuring working memory that are suitable for children and special populations. It is included because the focus of this book is partly on methodology, and understanding the exact demands of particular tests helps in interpreting the results appropriately.
- A brief 'Aide Memoire' to the working memory model and how to measure working memory is provided at the end of Chapter 2.

If you are interested in the development of working memory in typical children, this is dealt with in Chapters 3 and 4:

- *Chapter 3* This chapter focuses on the 'phonological loop', one of the four key components of the working memory model. The working memory model makes a series of very specific predictions about typical development in relation to the phonological loop, and these are presented and later questioned. The greater part of this chapter is devoted to the difficulties with the working memory account. It also covers research that has led to significant modifications to the working memory model and its application to typical development. This is the most theoretically demanding chapter.
- *Chapter 4* Here, working memory development in typical children is discussed with respect to the other three components of the working memory model: the 'visuospatial sketchpad', the 'central executive', and the 'episodic buffer'. Finally, we touch on whether the overall structure of working memory is the same in adults as it is in typically developing children.

If you are interested in atypical development, Chapters 5, 6, 7 and 8 discuss working memory in individuals with a range of developmental disorders. In essence, a straightforward question is posed for each developmental disorder: is there good evidence that this population of children has difficulties with working memory, and, if so, which component/s of the working memory model are affected? A brief breakdown of each chapter is given below:

- *Chapter 5* This chapter is devoted to working memory in children with general intellectual disabilities. It includes an introduction to the concept of intellectual disabilities and an explanation of how to choose suitable comparison groups when carrying out research in this area.
- *Chapter 6* This chapter deals with working memory development in children who have dyslexia and specific language impairment. The profiles of working memory abilities for children with these two related disorders are discussed and compared in relation to all four components of the working memory model.
- *Chapter 7* This chapter considers children who have Down syndrome and Williams syndrome. The somewhat contrasting profiles of working memory abilities in each of these disorders are considered in relation to the four components of the working memory model.
- *Chapter 8* The penultimate chapter considers children with autism spectrum disorders (ASD). Working memory profiles in respect of each component of the working memory model are assessed, with an emphasis

on evaluating whether having intellectual disabilities and ASD adds to or alters the relative patterns of strength and weakness.

- *Chapter 9* This chapter summarises the overall conclusions and offers some final comments about working memory in typical and atypical development.

General points about the structure of each chapter

Most of the chapters are structured largely in terms of the four components of the working memory model (the phonological loop, the visuospatial sketchpad, the central executive, and the episodic buffer). The exceptions to this are Chapter 3, which focuses on the phonological loop in relation to typical development and Chapter 4, which focuses on the other three components of working memory in relation to typical development.

At the beginning of every chapter a list of the section headings relevant to that chapter are specified, together with a set of learning outcomes. Short summaries are provided for every section and each chapter is also summarised overall. Suggestions for further reading are given at the end of each chapter, which should be useful for essays, dissertations or further research. Some suggested exam questions are also provided; and additional ideas for 'extended essays' are given in some chapters.

Three key questions about this book

Next, we consider three key questions about this book that will hopefully give useful background information and guide readers to the parts that are of most interest.

1 Which populations of typical and atypical children will be covered and why?

Seven populations of children are included in this book and the following sections give brief descriptions of each one, along with a rationale as to why each particular group of children has been included.

Typically developing children (Chapters 3 and 4)

These are children who are developing at broadly the rate we would expect them to for their age. If we were to measure their intellectual abilities using an IQ test, these children would all be in the typical range with IQs of 80 or above. Typically developing children do not have identified developmental disorders. In other words, they do not have developmental problems such as autism, Down syndrome or dyslexia that would impact on their cognitive, emotional or social development. There will be considerable variation in terms of overall development within a group of typical children. However, theoretically, we feel justified in assuming that the mechanisms underlying this development are broadly the same for all individuals in this group.

Why include typically developing children? This group acts like a baseline, providing a reference point to which we can compare all of the other groups. If we can understand working memory development in typical children, it is possible to assess whether working memory development is fundamentally different in groups of children with developmental disorders.

Children with general intellectual disabilities (Chapter 5)

These are children who are not developing as rapidly as we might expect, based on their chronological age. They will have IQs in the 'intellectual disability' range (i.e. IQs of less than 70/80) and probably also some difficulties in coping with mainstream schooling and/or other aspects of daily living. However, children who have known developmental disorders associated with intellectual disabilities such as Down syndrome would not be included in this group.

Why include children with general intellectual disabilities? These children have low intellectual ability (i.e. low IQ), but they do not have a specific developmental disorder. This group allows us to evaluate whether having an intellectual disability on its own has a detrimental impact on working memory development.

Children with dyslexia and specific language impairment (Chapter 6)

These are children who have intellectual abilities in the typical range (i.e. IQs of 80+, particularly for non-verbal abilities), but who have a very specific developmental disorder that affects particular aspects of their cognitive functioning. We cannot explain their difficulties in terms of a poor environment growing up, a low IQ or some form of specific brain injury that has occurred during childhood. Instead, we assume that they have a developmental disorder that has affected the development of one particular area of their functioning from birth or even earlier. In this book, we will look at two such examples: (a) dyslexia, which is a specific deficit in reading and/or spelling; and (b) specific language impairment, which is a specific deficit in language.

Why include children with dyslexia and specific language impairment? These disorders are regarded as being related to each other in recent theories, which makes comparing them particularly fruitful. These groups are also interesting because they allow us to assess whether having a developmental disorder, in the absence of an intellectual disability, has particular implications for working memory development.

Children with Down syndrome and Williams syndrome (Chapter 7)

These are children who have both an intellectual disability (low IQ) and a developmental disorder. Most of these individuals have abilities in the moderate to severe intellectual disabilities range (we will discuss this range in Chapter 5), together with a specific, genetically determined, developmental disorder.

Why include children with Down syndrome and Williams syndrome? These disorders are interesting, because they allow us to look at the potential 'double' effects of having both an intellectual disability and a developmental disorder. Development may be constrained by all of the factors relevant to having an intellectual disability, as well as additional factors associated with the developmental disorder itself. In other words, it is possible that having an intellectual disability and a developmental disorder places additional constraints on working memory development. These two disorders have been chosen because there are very clear differences in the memory abilities of children in each of these groups which make comparing individuals with Down and Williams syndromes theoretically and practically valuable.

Children with Autism Spectrum Disorders (Chapter 8)

Individuals with Autism Spectrum Disorders (ASD) have a developmental disorder that affects their cognitive, social and emotional development. However, there are several variants of this disorder (which is why it is described as a 'spectrum') and one of the key things that varies along the spectrum is intellectual ability. Some individuals, perhaps up to 50%, have intellectual disabilities such that their measured IQ would be less than 70/80. However, many 'high-functioning' individuals with ASD do not have intellectual disabilities.

Why include children with ASD? This is a developmental disorder that encompasses those with and without intellectual disabilities. This means that we can look for potential differences between those who just have the developmental disorder and those who have the developmental disorder with an additional intellectual disability. This approach has the potential to elucidate different effects on development caused by intellectual disability on the one hand, and a specific developmental disorder on the other.

Summary

Several different populations of children will be covered in this book, and they vary in terms of whether they have typical or atypical development. In addition, we contrast those with and without intellectual disabilities; and those with and without developmental disorders. All of the groups included are summarised in Table P.1 below. The key features which distinguish each group of children are also indicated, namely, do they have intellectual disabilities, a developmental disorder, both, or neither?

2 Why is the book structured around the working memory model?

The working memory model has had an enormous influence on the fields of cognition and memory, both for adults and children. For example, over the past four decades the working memory model has provided a clear and testable set of predictions regarding the development of several aspects of memory in typically developing children. A large body of literature has emerged to test many of these predictions and the model retains the ability to account for a

Table P.1 Summary of the groups of children with typical and atypical development covered in this book

Group	Intellectual disability?	Developmental disorder?
Typically developing	No	No
Intellectual disabilities	Yes	No
Dyslexia/specific language impairment	No	Yes
Down/Williams syndrome	Yes	Yes
Autism Spectrum Disorders	Yes and No	Yes

range of interesting developmental changes in working memory. That is the first reason for structuring this book around the working memory model.

The working memory model has also motivated much research on memory development in children with intellectual disabilities and developmental disorders. This means that typical and atypical populations can be directly compared using the same theoretical rationale and the same types of tests. This compatability of theory and method makes drawing comparisons between groups much more straightforward, and is the second reason for structuring the book around the working memory model.

Finally, recent revisions to the working memory model allow it to take a much broader view of memory processes and to include areas of current and historical research interest such as the impact of long-term memory knowledge on memory development, the development of episodic memory and the development of executive control. This inclusivity, taken together with the advantages of a unified and clearly structured theoretical approach which the working memory model offers, constitute the third reason for adopting the working memory model as a basis for presenting the research covered in this book.

3 What is one key feature of this book that should make it useful for those wanting to have a critical understanding of working memory in children with typical and atypical development?

In order to have a critical understanding of research evidence (and to be able to write good essays) it is vital to focus on critical evaluation. This means knowing enough about the strengths and weaknesses of the methodology of an experiment to judge properly whether the experiment adequately tests its hypotheses. Critical evaluation also means drawing out clear implications from results, and placing these in theoretical context. In order to do this, it is crucial to understand how the results of research studies are only as good as the methods that have been employed to obtain them. For example, in the study of developmental disorders one key issue is the importance of comparison groups. In particular, how should we choose suitable comparison groups; and how do comparison groups limit the conclusions that can be drawn?

Therefore, one key feature of this book that will be particularly useful for those wanting a critical understanding of working memory development in typical and atypical children is its focus on methodology. Most studies/ methodologies are described in enough detail such that readers are able to really understand what the strengths and weaknesses of particular experiments are and can comment on how these strengths and weaknesses impact on the conclusions that can be drawn.

Writing good essays

Reading research papers is an excellent way to gain an even deeper understanding of methodology and important details. Many are tempted to just read introductions and conclusions of research papers, but focusing on the methods and results sections enhances appreciation of experimental findings. For example, looking carefully at such issues as the way participants were selected, the matching criteria used (if relevant), diagnostic criteria, the exact nature of the experimental tasks used, the adequacy of the sample sizes, and the precise details of the results is very important. This information helps to give a critical and evaluative view of research, rather than relying on 'headlines', which is the foundation for proper, informed critical evaluation (and writing good essays). It is very difficult to offer sound and convincing critical evaluations without reading at least some experimental papers. In many cases, extra reading prevents naive or unsophisticated comments or appraisals that can be a very direct 'giveaway' of imperfect understanding.

The papers at the end of each chapter under Further reading represent a recommended selection of the research covered in each chapter and have been chosen to represent the area; they are neither exhaustive nor compulsory and can be used according to need. A full selection of references is also provided in the reference section at the end of the book. Suggested 'test yourself' exam-style questions are given at the end of each chapter for those that find them useful. These can be a helpful way of checking that important concepts and issues have been thoroughly understood. Providing 'practice' answers to these questions in your own words can act as a useful revision aid and expose areas that need further attention.

Overall summary

This brief introduction has outlined how this book can be used most effectively and emphasised that three distinct areas are covered: (1) working memory and how it is measured; (2) working memory and typical development;

and (3) working memory and atypical development. Brief outlines of each chapter have been given together with short explanations as to why particular populations of children have been chosen for discussion. The rationale for using the working memory model as a theoretical framework has also been presented.

We will now consider research and theory relevant to the development of working memory in typical and atypical populations of children. You may find it useful to read the chapter on the working memory model (Chapter 1) if you are not familiar with this model already. Similarly, if you are not familiar with the types of tests used in this area, the chapter on measuring working memory (Chapter 2) should be read before embarking on Chapters 3 to 8, which consider working memory in typical and atypical development. In other respects most of the chapters can be read relatively independently, but signposting will indicate if this is not the case.

1

The Working Memory Model

Learning outcomes

At the end of this chapter, you should have an understanding of the original and revised versions of the 'working memory model' (Baddeley, 1986, 2000, 2007; Baddeley & Hitch, 1974). This has been a dominant model of memory in recent decades and represents a key approach to understanding the development of memory in children with and without developmental disorders. Once you have read this chapter, you should be able to: (1) describe each of the four components of the revised working memory model; and (2) outline some of the key evidence supporting the structure of each component.

Introduction to the working memory model

The working memory model is a very influential theory of memory designed to account for how we temporarily manipulate and store information during thinking and reasoning tasks. The model helps us to understand how memory processes are used during day to day familiar activities, or during more demanding tasks that require greater effort and new thinking (perhaps a problem-solving task that has not been encountered before). One way of understanding working memory is to consider the types of memory we need while we read, plan future activities, do the crossword/Sudoku, or follow the news headlines.

One of the important concepts to understand about working memory is that it is limited in capacity, which means that we cannot store and manipulate endless amounts of information. Therefore, the types of thinking and remembering tasks we can undertake will be constrained by working memory resources. Working memory also limits, to some degree, the types of things we can handle concurrently. Whilst there are some types of tasks that can be carried out at the same time, other types of tasks compete for the same resources within the working memory system and, therefore, interfere with each other.

Working memory is vital because it underpins abilities in many other areas such as reasoning, learning and comprehension. In the most recent description of the working memory system, Baddeley (2007) even attempts to use his model to account for consciousness!

The working memory model is used in this book as the theoretical underpinning for our discussion of memory development in typical and atypical children. There are three major reasons for choosing the working memory model for this purpose. First, the working memory model has become a major explanation for memory and thinking in recent years and has received wide support. Secondly, using one unified theoretical framework makes it much easier to compare memory development in children with typical development to those who have various types of developmental disorders (i.e. atypical development). The final reason for using the working memory model as the theoretical foundation in this book is its comprehensiveness and clear four-part structure, which accounts for many different types of remembering. The four-component structure of the working memory model provides not only theoretical sophistication, but an organisational template for every chapter in this book. Each chapter is organised around the four components of the working memory model, making it easier for readers to navigate through the research and see how development differs in typical and atypical children.

This chapter provides a description of each of the four main components of the revised working memory model and covers some of the key psychological evidence presented to support the model. However, this is not an exhaustive account of the working memory model, but rather an overview, covering the main points in enough detail so that you can understand the rest of the book. If you would like more information on the working memory model, including evidence concerning neuroimaging and neuropsychological studies, please look at the Further reading section at the end of this chapter.

Note that the next chapter (Chapter 2) provides detailed descriptions of the most common ways in which working memory has been measured in typical and atypical children/populations. Chapters 3 and 4 are devoted to the development of working memory in typically developing children. Chapters 5 to 8 go on to consider the development of working memory in children with atypical development. As already noted, every chapter adopts the same general structure. Each area of working memory is discussed in turn with respect to the population of children under discussion.

For now, however, we return to the central issue of the current chapter, providing an introduction to the working memory model.

Key features of the working memory model – an overview

This section provides a brief overview of the key features of the 'original' working memory model (Baddeley, 1986; Baddeley & Hitch, 1974) and the 'revised' working memory model (Baddeley, 2000, 2007). In most respects, the revised working memory model simply adds to the original, but there are some changes to individual components that will be pointed out. The sections following this overview will describe each component of the model in more detail, and present some key experimental evidence to support the proposed structure of working memory.

To start to understand what working memory is, it is useful to examine a quote from Baddeley (2007), in which he describes working memory as follows:

> ... a temporary storage system under attentional control that underpins our capacity for complex thought. (p. 1)

There are several important points even in this one short sentence. First of all, the system deals with temporary storage and so deals with things we are doing right now. Secondly, the system is under attentional control, indicating that, in most instances, we choose where to direct our attention. Finally, the system underpins our capacity for complex thought, making it fundamental for any type of higher order thinking or reasoning task. In this way, working memory can be viewed as the bedrock for virtually all thinking processes (often described as 'cognitive' processes) that rely on temporary memory storage. We will not go into the history of why this model was proposed as this is readily available in any of Baddeley's very readable books about working memory (see Further reading at the end of the chapter).

The original working memory model (Baddeley & Hitch, 1974) consists of three components. The most important component is a system for controlling attention, known as the 'central executive'. This is used to ensure that working memory resources are directed and used appropriately to achieve the goals that have been set. There are also two temporary storage systems. One of these is for holding speech-based information and it is known as the 'phonological loop'. The second storage system is for holding visual and spatial information and it is known as the 'visuospatial sketchpad'. These two storage mechanisms are regarded as 'slave subsystems', because they do not do anything beyond holding information in a relatively passive manner. The real 'brains' of the working memory system is the central executive. Figure 1.1 below illustrates the original working memory model.

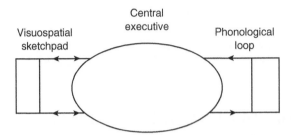

Figure 1.1   The original conceptualisation of the working memory model

Source: Reproduced with permission from Oxford University Press (Baddeley, A.D. & Hitch, G.J. (1974). Working memory. In G.A. Bower (Ed.), *The psychology of learning and motivation*, Vol. 8 (pp. 47–89). New York: Academic Press)

Although the original working memory model was very successful in accounting for a large body of experimental research, various criticisms of the model led to some significant revisions. For example, it became clear that there was a need to account for the effects of long-term knowledge (all of the stored information that we know about the world) on working memory, something that the original model did not take into account.

Therefore, Baddeley added a fourth component to the working memory model, the 'episodic buffer' (Baddeley, 2000). This new component of working memory provides a number of important new features. First, a link to long-term memory; second, a way of integrating information from all of the other systems into a unified experience; and third, a small amount of extra storage capacity that does not depend on the perceptual nature of the input. Figure 1.2 illustrates the new version of the working memory model, which takes account of the episodic buffer.

Now we will turn to each of the four components of the revised working memory model, looking at each in more detail. We will also consider some of the more important evidence that has been used to support the proposed structure of the working memory model. The relationships between the components illustrated in Figure 1.2 will become clearer as we continue our discussion.

The phonological loop

The phonological loop component of working memory is proposed as a specialised storage system for speech-based information, and possibly purely acoustic information as well. The phonological loop is described as a 'slave' system as it is not 'clever' in any way; it does not have any capacity for controlling attention or decision-making. The phonological loop is merely a temporary store for heard information, particularly speech. It represents the storage system responsible for 'phonological short-term memory' (PSTM), the ability

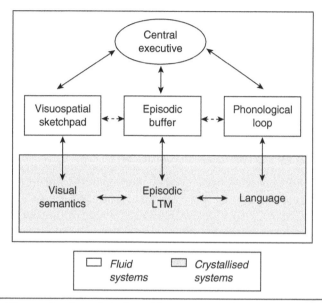

Figure 1.2 The revised model of working memory (Baddeley, 2000)

Source: Reproduced with permission from Elsevier (Baddeley, A.D. (2000). The episodic buffer: A new component of working memory? *Trends in Cognitive Science*, 4(11), 417–423)

of individuals to remember small amounts of heard information over short periods of time. This type of memory has been closely studied in adults and children for many years and a large part of this book will be devoted to discussing how PSTM develops in children. Please refer to Chapter 2 for details on how PSTM is measured in typical and atypical populations of children.

The phonological loop is divided into two further subcomponents, both believed to be located in the left hemisphere of the brain according to neuroimaging evidence (Jonides et al., 1998; Paulesu, Frith & Frackowiak, 1993). These two subcomponents are now described.

The phonological store

The first subcomponent of the phonological loop is the phonological store. This is the area of the system in which speech material is held for short periods of time. The phonological store is described as 'passive', because it simply holds the information; and 'time-limited', because the information fades rapidly. The information in the phonological store is often described as the 'memory trace', and the phenomenon of rapid fading is often called 'trace decay'. Trace decay reflects the fact that representations held in the phonological store are temporary, rather than completely accurate, long-lasting representations of the things we encounter. Trace decay is so rapid in the phonological store that only around two seconds' worth of speech-based material can be held, perhaps just long enough to hold a telephone number in mind before dialing it.

Although there are long-standing arguments over the whole notion of whether trace decay (or interference) accounts for forgetting in phonological short-term memory (PSTM), we do not have time to go into the detailed arguments here. You can read more about this issue in Chapter 3 of Baddeley (2007) referenced at the end of this chapter.

The articulatory rehearsal mechanism

The second subcomponent of the phonological loop is the articulatory rehearsal mechanism. We have already mentioned the two-second limit on the phonological store. The articulatory rehearsal mechanism is used to recite the information in the phonological store, in order to prevent this very rapid decay. The recitation of the material re-enters it into the phonological store, where it immediately starts to decay again. Baddeley describes the articulatory rehearsal mechanism as like a tape loop or a tape recorder with a two-second duration. The recitation processes can prevent the material decaying, by constantly refreshing it. The process of recitation is called 'articulatory rehearsal' or 'verbal rehearsal' and is a major strategy used to improve or enhance the capacity of PSTM.

Verbal rehearsal is usually done internally (i.e. you can't hear a person doing it) by adults, but there are interesting changes in verbal rehearsal in children throughout their development, which we will consider in Chapter 3. There are also arguments over the exact form that verbal rehearsal takes and these revolve around whether real articulation is taking place. However, most researchers would agree that verbal rehearsal involves some form of covert verbalisation (i.e. internal speech) which uses the same speech planning mechanisms that we use for real speech, even if it does not always require actual speech output.

We will consider the issue of verbal rehearsal and articulation further in Chapter 3, when we discuss the development of working memory in typically developing children. For now, Box 1.1 gives an example of how verbal rehearsal may be useful in real life, when good PSTM could prove vital.

Box 1.1   Remembering a car number plate

Witness A has just seen a hit and run driver knock down an elderly pedestrian at a controlled crossing. Knowing that providing a description of the vehicle, and better still the car number plate, is vital, Witness A attempts to remember as much as possible. The car was relatively small, royal blue in colour and had blackened windows and spoilers. Witness A thinks that she could probably remember this information using a visual image.

The number plate is more difficult. She thinks she saw it as LY06 VGC. There are a number of ways Witness A could aid her memory for the number plate. She could write the number down on a piece of paper, although in this particular instance it takes her at least a few seconds to locate a pen and paper in her handbag. So what does she do to keep the number in mind? She repeats the letters and numbers over and over again in order, using the process of verbal rehearsal, until she finds her paper and pen.

'LY06 VGC, LY06 VGC, LY06 VGC, LY06 VGC....'

Note that a Police Officer may wonder whether Witness A was accurate in her recall of the 'VGC' portion of the number plate. Why? Because these letters all rhyme. Rhyming items cause confusion in the phonological store, as we shall see later. It might be prudent in this case to check these letters in different orders (and perhaps with rhyming substitutions) against relevant databases, just in case any confusion has occurred.

Note also, that it is possible to 'chunk' various portions of the number plate together. The first two letters can be chunked together as one unit (denoting the area in the country the car was first licensed, making it easier to recall if Witness A recognises 'LY' as denoting London). The second two numbers can be chunked together as a second unit representing the date of licensing, and the third three letters can be chunked together as a unit. These final letters are visually distinct, as a space occurs in the number plate just before them, making chunking easier.

Obligatory and optional access to the phonological store

The articulatory rehearsal mechanism does not just carry out verbal rehearsal; it has a second function. This is known as 'phonological/verbal recoding' (or 'phonological/verbal coding'), a process by which information presented in a visual form (printed words, printed letters/numbers, pictures) can be converted into speech. Obviously, this can only be done if the visual information has a verbal label, e.g. a picture of a 'house' can be labelled as 'house'. Verbal/phonological coding is often advantageous, because remembering visual information can be more difficult than remembering speech (phonological) information. The benefits of remembering information in a phonological form are particularly marked for lists of separate items that must be recalled in order; and also when there is a delay between encountering information and recalling it (verbal rehearsal can be used to keep the information in mind).

Phonological/verbal coding, therefore, is carried out by the articulatory rehearsal mechanism. Items presented in a visual form are simply named or labelled, and the phonological information produced from this naming process is entered into the phonological store. Hence, the articulatory rehearsal mechanism 'converts' visual information into verbal (phonological) codes via an articulation process. Clearly, if visual items are recoded in this manner, this can change a visual remembering task into a test of PSTM.

One further point to make is that auditory information gains obligatory access to the phonological store: we do not have to do anything to create a phonological record. However, nameable visual inputs such as pictures, written letters or written words, must first be 'recoded' into a phonological form in order to gain access. Their access to the phonological store is, therefore, optional.

Figure 1.3 provides a simple schematic diagram illustrating the differences between obligatory and optional access to the phonological store. On the left, auditory inputs proceed directly into the phonological store. On the right, visual inputs must proceed via the articulatory rehearsal mechanism, before entering the phonological store. Once in the phonological store, however, all items can be recirculated between the phonological store and the articulatory rehearsal mechanism using verbal rehearsal. Verbal rehearsal operates in the same manner, regardless of how the information has entered the phonological store, i.e. via the optional route or the obligatory route. Verbal rehearsal keeps the items refreshed so long as it is continued.

Hence, the two roles carried out by the articulatory rehearsal mechanism are: (1) converting visual input into a phonological code; and (2) rehearsing the contents of the phonological store.

Summary

The phonological loop is one component of the multi-component working memory model (Baddeley & Hitch, 1974) and its structure remains largely unchanged in the revised working memory model (Baddeley, 2000, 2007). The phonological loop is a specialised storage system for holding sound-based material, particularly speech, but its contents decay rapidly (within two seconds) unless refreshed using verbal rehearsal. The phonological loop is

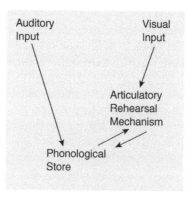

Figure 1.3   Diagram illustrating how auditory input gains direct access to the phonological store (obligatory access), whereas visual input must proceed via the articulatory rehearsal mechanism (optional access)

divided into two components, the phonological store (for storage) and the articulatory rehearsal mechanism (for verbal rehearsal and phonological coding). The basic capacity and duration of phonological short-term memory (PSTM) can be increased by using verbal rehearsal. Information we hear goes directly to the phonological store (obligatory access), whereas information that is presented in a visual form can be phonologically recoded and reach the phonological store via an optional route (optional access).

Evidence in support of the phonological loop

In the next sections, evidence in support of the main features of the phonological loop, as well as its structure (the division into a phonological store and an articulatory rehearsal mechanism), is briefly outlined. Note that this evidence concerns adults, but we will consider similar evidence in respect of children later in Chapter 3. For more detail concerning the adult evidence reviewed below see Baddeley (1986).

The phonological similarity effect

Why can we assume that the phonological loop is specialised to hold speech-based material? A classic piece of research by Conrad and Hull (1964) gave adults a test of PSTM, which involved asking them to recall short lists of letters in the correct order. Some of the lists contained letters that were all rhymes (e.g. B, G, V, P, T), whereas other lists contained letters that did not rhyme (e.g. Y, W, H, K, R).

Conrad and Hull (1964) found that rhyming lists were much more difficult to remember in the correct order than non-rhyming lists. This finding demonstrated that PSTM was affected by sound similarity, and led to the conclusion that memory for speech material utilises some kind of sound-based storage system. The logic for this conclusion is that similar sounding letters create similar sounding (and, therefore, confusable) memory traces in the storage system used to support PSTM. The phonological store of the working memory model is just such a storage mechanism, designed to hold small amounts of speech-based material. Memory traces for speech items that all sound the same have very similar features and this makes recall difficult, because the discrimination between separate items is poor.

This effect of sound confusability in PSTM is very robust and has been found many times since. For example, Baddeley (1966) found that rhyming words were also more difficult to recall in order than non-rhyming words. The effect of sound confusion is described as the 'phonological similarity effect', the 'phonemic similarity effect' or sometimes the 'acoustic similarity effect'. This is illustrated in Box 1.2.

Box 1.2   The phonological similarity effect

Read out the following list of words and then close your eyes and try to recall them in order:

ring   bus   owl   cake   frog   clown

Now try the same with this list:

hat   cat   bat   sat   fat   pat

Which list was easier to remember?

Most people find the words that are rhymes to be much more difficult, because they become confused. This is evidence that the way we store auditory information for short periods of time is based on *sound characteristics*, supporting the theoretical notion of a phonological or sound store.

Interestingly, words do not have to be exact rhymes for this effect to occur, the most important feature is that the middle vowel sound is the same (Nimmo & Roodenrys, 2004).

The word length effect

Next, we consider the evidence to support the existence of some type of verbal rehearsal mechanism that operates in 'real-time'. The evidence to support the proposed articulatory rehearsal mechanism comes from another important result, known as the 'word length effect'. This effect was described in detail by Baddeley, Thomson and Buchanan (1975) and a reference to this paper is provided at the end of the chapter under Further reading.

Baddeley et al. (1975) presented adults with a test of PSTM that required them to recall lists of five words in the correct order. Some of the lists contained short words that were all one-syllable in length, whereas other lists contained longer words of two, three, four and even five syllables. As the number of syllables increased, something interesting happened to levels of performance. Box 1.3 illustrates the 'word length effect'.

Box 1.3   Remembering lists of short words and long words

Read the following list of words once clearly to yourself out loud or inside your head, then close your eyes and see if you can recall the words in the correct order.

university   refrigerator   tuberculosis   periodical   hippopotamus

---

Now read this list of words, close your eyes and see if you can recall these in the correct order.

stoat   **mumps**   **school**   **zinc**   **scroll**

Although the words in both of these lists are equally familiar, most people find the longer words much more difficult to recall in order than the short words. This is known as the 'word length effect'.

Baddeley et al. (1975) found, in a series of experiments, that recall was always better for shorter words than longer words, and called this phenomenon the 'word length effect'. They argued that word length effects occur because verbal rehearsal for long items takes longer in real time than verbal rehearsal for short items. This word length disadvantage for longer items allows more time for decay of the memory trace within the phonological store. Short items, on the other hand, can be rehearsed rapidly, so that more words are maintained within the two-second time limit of the phonological store. Remember, once information has entered the phonological store, only those items that can be verbally rehearsed (i.e. repeated over and over again in the internal 'tape loop' known as the articulatory rehearsal mechanism) will be remembered after the critical period of two seconds.

The word length effect findings are very robust and are attributed to real-time rehearsal differences. If you want to read about word length effects in more detail please refer to the papers referenced at the end of the chapter (Baddeley et al., 1975; and Baddeley, Lewis & Vallar, 1984). We will come back to evidence concerning word length effects when considering the development of working memory in typical children in Chapter 3.

The relationship between speech rate and memory span

There are further predictions that can be made, based on the proposed structure of the phonological loop and the articulatory rehearsal mechanism. In particular, the working memory model predicts a close relationship between the rate at which a person can carry out verbal rehearsal (usually measured by assessing their speech rate) and the number of items that can be recalled in tests of PSTM (often described as 'memory span'). People who use verbal rehearsal very quickly should be able to maintain more items in the phonological store than people who use verbal rehearsal more slowly.

This prediction led to the experimental approach of measuring individual people's rates of speaking (to get an approximate measure of rehearsal rate), and then measuring the capacity of their PSTM (using measures of memory span – how many words could be recalled immediately in the correct order).

This was exactly what Baddeley et al. (1975) did. Fourteen adults were asked to remember lists of words that were either of one, two, three, four, or five syllables. This created five separate measures of PSTM, each one for a different length of word. Next, participants were asked to read aloud lists of these words as quickly as they could and their reading times were measured. This gave five separate measures of reading rate, again one for each different length of word.

The final stage was to take the mean memory spans for each type of word and plot them against the mean reading rates for each type of word. Remember that the decay theory, which is part of the working memory model's account of the phonological loop, predicts that for shorter words, reading rates and memory spans should be higher, because more short words can be rehearsed verbally within the two-second time limit of the phonological store. However, as the number of syllables increases both reading rate and memory span should decline.

As you can see in Figure 1.4, there was a consistent relationship between memory span (percent correct recalled, on the vertical axis) and reading rate (on the horizontal axis). One-syllable words with the highest speech rates and memory spans are at the top of the line, and each data point consecutively below represents, respectively, two-, three-, four-, and five-syllable words. With every unit decrease in reading rate, there was a corresponding decrease in memory span, such that a straight line (linear function) could describe the relationship between the two variables over a range of words with different syllabic lengths.

In summary, these results supported the proposed structure of the phonological loop system in working memory. Baddeley et al. (1975) concluded that individuals 'are able to remember as much as they can read out in 1.8

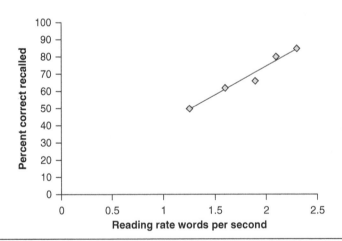

Figure 1.4 The relationship between reading rate and memory span for words of one, two, three, four and five syllables in a sample of adults

Source: adapted from Baddeley et al., 1975

seconds' (p. 583). These results have been replicated many times. For example, Schweickert and Boruff (1986) followed up Baddeley et al.'s findings by measuring memory span and reading rate for a variety of different materials, finding the same results. Similarly, articulation rates for different languages are related to memory spans in those languages (e.g. Ellis & Hennelly, 1980; Stigler, Lee & Stevenson, 1986). We will return to the relationship between articulation rate and memory span when we consider the development of memory span in typically developing children in Chapter 3.

The effects of articulatory suppression

Looking back at the diagram in Figure 1.3 and comparing it with the diagram in Figure 1.5 will help to illustrate an experimental technique known as 'articulatory suppression'. Articulatory suppression is a method of 'knocking out', or blocking, the use of the articulatory rehearsal mechanism. Figure 1.5 shows the predicted effects of blocking the articulatory rehearsal mechanism, according to the working memory account of the phonological loop. These effects are as follows: (a) visual inputs should not be able to enter the phonological store (phonological coding is blocked); and (b) verbal rehearsal of the contents of the phonological store should be impossible.

Using articulatory suppression allows the predictions of the phonological loop model to be tested. How do we bring about articulatory suppression? You simply ask the participants in your experiment to repeat an irrelevant sound or word over and over again while they are carrying out the remembering task (e.g. 'blah, blah, blah', 'the, the, the', or 'one, two, three, one, two, three...' etc.). By 'filling up' the articulatory rehearsal mechanism with an irrelevant task that requires minimal attention and resources, the articulatory rehearsal mechanism becomes unavailable for either phonological coding or verbal rehearsal. In practice this means that visual inputs cannot be entered into the phonological store (they cannot be phonologically recoded) and the contents of the phonological store cannot be rehearsed. However, auditory inputs can still be registered in the phonological store, because they have direct access (see earlier section), although they cannot be rehearsed.

To test the role of articulatory suppression, researchers present participants with PSTM tasks whilst at the same time requiring them to engage in articulatory suppression. We will take one example of such research: comparing the recall of words that rhyme (i.e. are phonologically similar) and those that do not rhyme. Some lists are presented as spoken items, whereas other lists are presented as printed words. All participants use articulatory suppression, so this experiment tests between optional and obligatory access to the phonological store in relation to visual and auditory materials.

The specific research question is whether the words have been registered in the phonological store. How do we tell? If there is a phonological similarity effect, i.e. worse recall for rhyming items, this indicates that the words have been stored as sounds, despite using articulatory suppression. Phonological

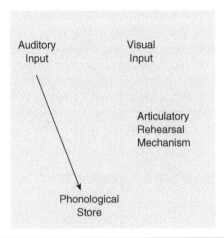

Figure 1.5   Diagram illustrating what happens in the phonological store when the articulatory rehearsal mechanism is blocked by articulatory suppression

similarity effects are regarded as evidence for registration in the phonological store (see earlier section).

Looking at Figure 1.5, the predictions according the working memory model are clear. Spoken words will reach the phonological store, even when the articulatory rehearsal mechanism is blocked, because spoken items have obligatory access. Therefore, effects of phonological similarity should be expected. However, if we present lists of words in a printed form, no effects of phonological similarity should be observed, because the items cannot be phonologically recoded and entered into the phonological store via the optional route. Therefore, we do not expect a phonological similarity effect.

This is exactly the result that is found (e.g. Baddeley et al., 1984; Murray, 1968), supporting the predictions of the working memory model and the structure of the phonological loop being divided into a phonological store and an articulatory rehearsal mechanism. (Although see recent debates, for example, Baddeley & Larsen, 2007a, 2007b; Jones, Hughes & Macken, 2007.)

Similar logic is used to account for the data when articulatory suppression is used in combination with the word length effect. Looking at Figure 1.5, it is clear that blocking the articulatory rehearsal mechanism should block all forms of rehearsal, regardless of how the items are presented. Without rehearsal, we would not expect word length effects.

Baddeley et al. (1984) found results to support this prediction. They showed that word length effects disappeared when articulatory suppression was used, regardless of whether the presentation of memory items was auditory (heard items) or visual (printed items). This was because the articulatory rehearsal mechanism was blocked and unable to carry out any form of verbal rehearsal, regardless of how the items had been presented. Articulatory suppression simply prevented all verbal rehearsal from occurring. However, although the method of input was irrelevant, as predicted by the phonological loop model, it is important to note that articulatory suppression needed to continue throughout the presentation and recall of a list to totally eliminate verbal rehearsal (Baddeley et al., 1984).

In this book we will be using the framework of the working memory model to try to understand memory development in typical and atypical populations. One of the key strengths of the phonological loop model is the explicit link between how material is encoded and stored on the one hand and how strategies for enhancing that encoding and storage (such as verbal rehearsal or phonological coding) can be used on the other.

There is a great deal of research on PSTM in typical children, as this area of memory development has received detailed attention. We will consider this research in Chapter 3. We have also touched upon the strategy of verbal rehearsal and will consider this and other verbal strategies in Chapters 3 and 4, as these strategies are central to understanding the development of PSTM. Where adequate research exists in atypical children, these issues will also be covered in Chapters 5 to 8.

Finally, it is useful to consider more broadly what the phonological loop may be for. In other words, what biological function has it evolved to serve? Baddeley (2007) argues that the purpose of the phonological loop is for learning language. There is quite a lot of convincing evidence for this and the best place to read about this in some detail is in a paper by Baddeley, Gathercole and Papagno (1998), which is listed in the references at the end of the book.

Summary
The 'phonological loop' component of the working memory model was designed to accommodate a great deal of experimental evidence concerning phonological short-term memory (PSTM) in the most parsimonious manner possible. In order to do this, Baddeley and Hitch (1974) proposed a two-part phonological loop system, comprising a phonological store (to hold speech input temporarily) and an articulatory rehearsal mechanism (to refresh this information as necessary). A range of experiments exploring the properties of the phonological loop has supported this structure, which remains largely unchanged from the original working memory model.

We will now move on to considering the next 'slave' storage system in the working memory model, the visuospatial sketchpad.

The visuospatial sketchpad

The visuospatial sketchpad is the other 'slave' storage system proposed in the working memory model. This component is responsible for holding visual and spatial information for short periods of time, so that it can be used during thinking, remembering and processing tasks (Logie, 1995). Therefore, this is the component of working memory responsible for supporting visuospatial short-term memory (VSSTM). Please refer to Chapter 2 for details on how VSSTM is measured in typical and atypical populations of children.

One of the first questions to ask about the visuospatial sketchpad is whether it is completely distinct from the other slave storage system we have just discussed, the phonological loop. In fact, a range of experimental evidence has indicated that VSSTM is very much distinct from phonological short-term memory (PSTM), such that we really do need two separate short-term stores for each of these types of information (e.g. Baddeley, 1986; Logie, 1995).

Like the phonological loop, the visuospatial sketchpad has been described as a 'slave' storage mechanism (Baddeley, 1986). Again, this means that the system is not in any way 'clever'; it is not responsible for the overall control, allocation or switching of attention. It is simply a repository for holding information temporarily.

The visuospatial sketchpad is believed to be located in the right hemisphere of the brain (the hemisphere that is most often specialised for dealing with visual and spatial information), as opposed to the phonological store, which we saw earlier is believed to be located in the left hemisphere of the brain (the hemisphere that is most often specialised for language).

One distinction that is helpful in understanding the visuospatial sketchpad is that between remembering 'what', i.e. the visual features of an object such as form and colour, and remembering 'where' i.e. where in space an object was located. Broadly speaking, these two types of remembering can be referred to as visual versus spatial short-term memory. Although the visuospatial sketchpad deals with both types of information, visual and spatial, several authors have argued that there are likely to be separate mechanisms within the sketchpad to deal with each of them (e.g. Vicari, Bellucci & Carlesimo, 2006). There is also some evidence for a third subsystem that stores sequences of actions in a kinaesthetic code (e.g. Smyth & Pendleton, 1989). Figure 1.6 illustrates the three types of information it is proposed that the visuospatial sketchpad can store, coordinate and manipulate.

Like the phonological loop, storage in the visuospatial sketchpad of working memory is subject to very rapid trace decay. The details of exactly how rapidly this occurs are far less clear than they are in the proposed phonological loop model. However, it is assumed that some form of rehearsal (i.e. keeping information in mind by refreshing or repeating it before it fades) does take place.

Although there are few interpretations of the nature of rehearsal in the visuospatial sketchpad, one exception is the model of Logie (1995). He proposed a passive 'visual cache' that is responsible for the storage of visual information like form and colour, and may be closely linked with activity in the visual perceptual system. Logie (1995) describes a second component, the 'inner scribe', as a more active system designed to hold information about movement sequences and also to carry out rehearsal, which will refresh the contents of the visuospatial sketchpad and reduce time-related decay. The inner scribe may also be responsible for image manipulation and is regarded as being more directly involved in the spatial component of the system.

Figure 1.6 The visuospatial sketchpad is hypothesised to deal with three types of information

Overall, the details of the visuospatial sketchpad are not so carefully worked out as those of the phonological loop. In his more recent writing, Baddeley (2007) has somewhat extended the role for the visuospatial sketchpad, describing it in the following terms:

> The sketchpad is a subsystem that has evolved to provide a way of integrating visuospatial information from multiple sources, visual, tactile and kinaesthetic, as well as from both episodic and semantic long-term memory. (p. 101)

This somewhat more complex system requires further research to distinguish it clearly from other components of the working memory model. Baddeley (2007) points out that there is a surprising lack of research on VSSTM, probably because memory researchers have focused on verbal materials that are somewhat more tractable in terms of experimental manipulation.

We will now look at some evidence for splitting the visuospatial sketchpad into at least two separate subcomponents that deal with information about visual appearance (colour, shape, pattern) and memory for spatial location (locations or movements between locations). This evidence concerns adults, but we will review evidence relevant to typical children in Chapter 4.

Separate visual and spatial components?

One way of examining whether there are separate components dealing with visual/spatial information is to examine neuropsychological patients with particular cognitive difficulties arising from brain damage. For example, Della Sala, Gray, Baddeley, Allamano, and Wilson (1999), among others, have found evidence that some patients show specific difficulties with visual information, whereas other patients show specific difficulties with spatial information. A second way of looking at the potential separation between visual and spatial components in the visuospatial sketchpad is to consider how these components might develop in children. This will be considered in Chapter 4.

A third way of assessing whether there are separate visual and spatial components in the visuospatial sketchpad, is to ask people to remember visual or spatial information and then try to interfere with their recall. This experimental procedure involves asking people to remember either visual or spatial information, but with the additional handicap of an interference condition in each case.

The interference is carefully designed to be either visual or spatial in nature, so that four experimental conditions are created as follows (see Box 1.4).

Box 1.4   Four relevant conditions in an 'interference' study of visuospatial working memory

1   a visual memory task with visual interference
2   a visual memory task with spatial interference
3   a spatial memory task with spatial interference
4   a spatial memory task with visual interference

The predictions are as follows. If there are separate mechanisms for visual and spatial short-term memory, visual interference should affect only visual memory and spatial interference should affect only spatial memory. This prediction is based on the assumption that if there are separate storage areas for visual and spatial information, they will be able to deal with interference of the opposite type of material, but not of the same type of material. Two visual inputs or two spatial inputs (the memory material and the interference), on the other hand, will compete for the same storage capacity and interfere with performance.

This method aims to provide evidence for a 'behavioural double dissociation' between visual and spatial memory. Several studies using this method have been reported in the literature (e.g. Della Sala et al., 1999; Logie & Marchetti, 1991), but we will look at just one to illustrate.

Darling, Della Sala and Logie (2007) employed the four conditions described above by asking adults to look at a display of 30 small boxes on a contrasting background. All were empty except one, which contained the letter 'p', in any one of over 400 different fonts. Some participants were asked to concentrate on the location of this letter (i.e. which box did the letter appear in), which aimed to assess memory for spatial location. By contrast, other participants were asked to concentrate on the appearance of the letter 'p' (i.e. focus on the font), which aimed to assess memory for visual appearance. Figure 1.7 illustrates a similar display, albeit using only 14 boxes instead of 30.

Following the presentation of the original display participants received 'interference' for either five or 15 seconds. This took the form of another display of distracting visual information (flickering black-and-white randomly placed dots) or the requirement to do a distracting spatial task (pressing keys on a 3 x 3 key pad in a figure of eight pattern). A final set of participants had 'no interference' as a control condition. The flickering dots were argued to interfere selectively with visual short-term memory; the spatial task was

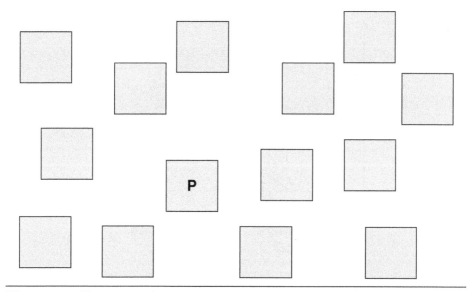

Figure 1.7 Illustration of type of display used by Darling et al. (2007) in their study of location and appearance memory (note that this does not correspond to the actual experimental materials)

argued to interfere selectively with spatial short-term memory. Finally, a 'memory' display containing the 30 squares was presented again, with the letter 'p' in one of the boxes. Participants had to judge whether the letter 'p' was in the same location in the 'location memory' task, or of the same appearance in the 'appearance memory' condition. The features of spatial location and appearance were varied systematically on each trial.

The authors looked at how quickly participants responded: i.e. how fast could they remember location or appearance information? Results were in line with predictions: spatial interference had a stronger negative impact on memory for spatial location; whereas visual interference had a stronger negative impact on memory for the appearance. Figure 1.8 illustrates reaction times after five seconds of 'interference'. Note that long reaction times imply the task was more difficult.

These findings support the proposal that visual and spatial aspects of VSSTM are reliant on separate mechanisms that do not selectively interfere with each other.

One potential criticism of these general findings is that spatial tasks are often sequentially presented (for example remembering a series of spatial locations), whereas visual tasks are often simultaneously presented (for example, looking at one visual image). Some have argued that the apparent separation between visual and spatial short-term memory may simply reflect differences between sequential and simultaneous presentation (Pickering, Gathercole, Hall & Lloyd, 2001).

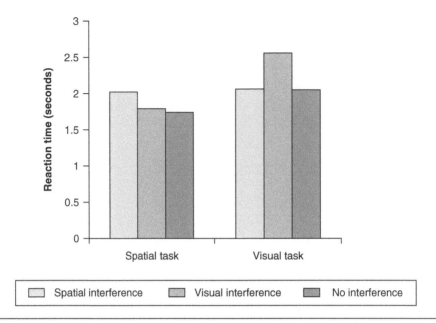

Figure 1.8 Mean adjusted reaction times to illustrate the relative effects of visual interference, spatial interference or no interference on a visual short-term memory task and a spatial short-term memory task

Source: data adapted from Darling et al., 2007

However, some evidence supports the view that the visual/spatial distinction is more important than the sequential/simultaneous distinction. Darling, Della Sala and Logie (2009) used a similar method to the one described above and found that it made no difference whether the visual and spatial information was presented simultaneously or sequentially. In either case, spatial interference had a greater detrimental effect on recalling spatial information and visual interference had a greater effect on recalling visual information. This supported the original distinction between visual and spatial mechanisms.

However, others have argued a 'middle way': that there are distinctions between visual and spatial mechanisms, yet spatial information is further subdivided into sequential spatial information and static spatial information (Mammarella, Pazzaglia & Cornoldi, 2008). This issue has not yet been resolved, but further research on the proposed visuospatial sketchpad of the working memory model will offer more insights in the future.

Increasingly, links are being made between research into visual memory, visual attention and visual working memory, which will no doubt increase the level of theorising in this area. However, the treatment of visuospatial working memory development in children is not always so sophisticated, and usually does no more than compare memory for visual materials with memory for spatial materials. Accordingly, the research that we discuss in later chapters will generally focus on this somewhat more simplistic level of analysis.

Summary

The visuospatial sketchpad is a specialised 'slave' storage system for holding visual and spatial (and perhaps kinaesthetic) information for short periods of time; hence, it supports visuospatial short-term memory (VSSTM). Information in this store decays rapidly unless rehearsed. Compared to the phonological loop, there is less experimental evidence to flesh out the details of the visuospatial sketchpad, but this is changing rapidly. For example, measures of dynamic (moving) versus static (still) visuospatial recall are now believed to reflect the operation of different submechanisms within the visuospatial sketchpad.

We will now move on to considering the intellectual powerhouse of the working memory model, the central executive.

The central executive

The central executive is the component of working memory that has overall attentional control of the working memory system. It was originally described as: (1) having some capacity for storage; (2) having the possibility of interfacing with long-term memory; and (3) allocating resources between the components of working memory by focusing, dividing and switching attention.

The current view of the central executive has changed somewhat. First, the central executive is now not regarded as having any capacity for storage, rather, it is only responsible for the control and allocation of attention (Baddeley, 2000, 2007). Secondly, the link between the various working memory components and long-term memory is now via a new component known as the 'episodic buffer', which will be discussed more fully in the next section.

Therefore, the core role of the central executive in the revised working memory model is in allocating attention within the working memory system, and this is done via focusing, dividing and switching attention. Baddeley (2007) argues that there may be separate subcomponents for focusing and dividing attention, but he considers the evidence for a separate component for the switching of attention to be limited at present.

When the model of working memory was first presented (Baddeley & Hitch, 1974) little detail was given about the central executive. Baddeley (1986) fleshed out the central executive by adopting the model put forward by Norman and Shallice (1986) of a supervisory attentional system (SAS). The SAS was responsible for intervening to direct behaviour when new thought and planning was required. In other words, this attentional system came into play when it was not possible to rely on well-learned patterns of responding. New ideas, new strategies and new plans to deal with new situations required a more demanding degree of attentional control, and this was provided by the SAS (Shallice, 1990).

Therefore, the central executive provides the higher levels of executive control that are required for carrying out novel tasks requiring new behaviour or new approaches. Box 1.5 provides an example to illustrate how central executive resources may be used in novel situations.

Box 1.5 Using executive resources when things go wrong

Think about driving to work using a well-known route on a day when nothing unusual happens. This probably does not require much in the way of central executive resources to focus, divide or switch attention. The route is familiar, driving is a routine process and nothing untoward occurs during the journey.

However, imagine that, on a particular day, the usual route is blocked because of a burst water pipe. In this circumstance, the central executive must intervene to *inhibit* the well-learned behaviour (i.e. following the familiar route) and work out a new plan that achieves the same goal of reaching the desired destination.

Central executive resources may also be required to change the plan if other upsets occur such as traffic jams, to monitor progress, to check that the goal is being reached, and focus attention on negotiating an unfamiliar route.

Note that satellite navigation systems remove much of the central executive burden from such tasks, which probably accounts for their popularity!

Baddeley (1986) described the SAS as a 'potential framework' for the central executive because the job it does is very similar to his conceptualisation of the role of the central executive. Executive processes are likely to be strongly dependent upon frontal lobe functioning (Kane & Engle, 2002). For example, there is a large body of evidence from patients with frontal lobe damage showing that they often have difficulties with inhibiting well-learned patterns of behaviour and arriving at new ways of solving problems. They become trapped in repetitive cycles of well-learned behaviour (known as 'perseveration') and lack the flexibility to change their behaviour when novel situations arise. Baddeley refers to these general difficulties as the 'dysexecutive syndrome' (e.g. Baddeley & Della Sala, 1996), although those who work in neuropsychological settings might use the term the 'frontal syndrome'.

Therefore, it is increasingly helpful to view the central executive of working memory as a broad attentional control space. This type of system is likely to resemble very closely what many authors mean when they refer to 'executive functions'. If we take a current definition of executive functions, 'processes that control and regulate thought and action' (Friedman, Miyake, Corley, Young, DeFries & Hewitt, 2006: 172), it becomes clear that the concepts of 'central executive' on the one hand, and 'executive functions' on the other, are very similar.

It is beyond the scope of this book to provide a theoretical synthesis and comparison of these two concepts. However, the striking point is the similarity between them both in practical and theoretical terms. Therefore, in order to provide a full and comprehensive account of 'central executive' processing in typical and atypical children, we will consider research on 'executive functioning' rather broadly. In every section on the central executive throughout this book, the research will be discussed in two separate subsections: one dealing with 'executive-loaded working memory' (ELWM); and one dealing with 'other aspects of executive functioning'.

Summary

The central executive component of working memory is responsible for focusing, dividing and switching attention. It provides the overall regulation and control of the working memory system and coordinates activity between all of the components. Defining the types of activities undertaken by the central executive has led us to conclude that the broader concept of 'executive functioning' is very similar to the working memory model's proposals regarding what a central executive might do. Therefore, research evidence concerning both central executive-loaded working memory and executive functioning more generally will be considered in this book.

We will now go on to explore the different areas of skill that can be regarded as requiring 'central executive' resources. In order to do this, it makes most sense to draw on the more general literature pertaining to 'executive functioning'.

Different types of executive functioning

Research in the area of executive functioning has grown rapidly in recent years, both in the adult and developmental literatures. One of the key issues to emerge is the belief that executive functions represent not just a single type of skill, but a number of related skills (e.g. Miyake, Friedman, Emerson, Witzki, Howerter & Wager, 2000). Therefore, within the broad domain of executive functioning there are, nevertheless, separate abilities that can be distinguished.

A recent twin study has provided support for this viewpoint. Friedman, Miyake, Young, DeFries, Corley and Hewitt (2008) showed that executive functions draw on a common factor that is highly heritable, arguing that this is why different measures of executive functioning are related to each other. These authors also suggested that executive functioning is not simply another ability that can substitute for 'intelligence'. They have provided evidence that executive functions are not uniquely related to measures of intelligence, despite the fact that they are, nevertheless, responsible for much of what we might describe as 'intelligent' behaviour (Friedman et al., 2006).

One of the sub-skills in the executive functioning 'family' of abilities has been identified as 'working memory', but the meaning of this term is rather specific. For example, Swanson (2006) defines working memory as:

a processing resource of limited capacity, involved in the preservation of information while simultaneously processing the same or other information. (p. 61)

There are several other skills believed to belong to the executive functioning family of abilities, and these will all be described in the next section, together with further details about executive-loaded working memory (ELWM). However, an important point to reiterate before we do this relates to what brings together and unifies all executive functioning skills. This is that executive skills, regardless of their exact type, are used to deal with tasks that are novel; tasks that require new solutions outside routine behaviour. As we have already pointed out, this is what the central executive is designed to do, so the concepts of 'executive functioning' and 'central executive' are at the very least highly overlapping, although there are uncertainties about exactly how these concepts interrelate.

In the literature on executive functioning, some authors (e.g. Pennington & Ozonoff, 1996) have suggested that executive functioning can be divided into five or six discrete sub-skills. This division is often referred to as the 'fractionation' of executive functioning. Box 1.6 describes the main areas of executive functioning identified in the literature.

Box 1.6   Different sub-areas of executive functioning

1 *Planning/problem-solving*: this type of skill refers to the preparation of future actions to achieve goals and the generation of solutions for difficulties.
2 *Set shifting/switching*: this refers to the ability to change responses/strategies when necessary, or after feedback indicates that the original plan is not working.
3 *Fluency*: this refers to the ability to quickly and efficiently search for and generate new information (sometimes called generativity).
4 *Inhibition*: often it is as important to *stop* doing certain irrelevant actions that get in the way of achieving goals as it is to execute relevant actions.
5 *Working memory*: in the executive functioning literature, this refers to the ability to keep in mind goals, current performance and future actions.
6 *Self-monitoring*: the ability to check on progress towards goals.

Other authors have suggested that there is good evidence for three sub-skills of executive functioning: inhibition, working memory and set shifting. There is a reasonable amount of evidence in children and adults for the existence of these factors (Anderson, 2002; Fisk & Sharp, 2004; Garon, Bryson & Smith, 2008; Huizinga, Dolan & van der Molen, 2006; Lehto, Juujärvi, Kooistra &

Lulkkinen, 2003; Miyake et al., 2000; van der Sluis, de Jong & van der Leij, 2007). However, not all of the evidence is entirely consistent, particularly for children, and this issue will be returned to in Chapter 4. Another point to emphasise is that several of the aforementioned studies did not look for more than three factors, so this figure may be arbitrary.

Another key point that has emerged from the literature is that, whilst we can divide executive functioning into a number of distinct sub-skills, these skills are still loosely related to each other. Again, the evidence is not entirely consistent, but there is reasonable consensus that the sub-skills of executive functioning measure broadly the same types of abilities in relation to the control and regulation of behaviour during complex, novel tasks (Miyake et al., 2000). This evidence will be considered in more detail in Chapter 4.

In this book, we will look at a wide range of tasks that have been used to assess executive skills to keep our discussion as inclusive as possible. These areas include executive-loaded working memory, inhibition, set shifting, planning, fluency, dual-task performance and random generation. Some of these tasks have traditionally been used to study executive skills within the working memory domain, whereas others have been regarded as measuring executive functioning more broadly. This comprehensive approach has been taken to try to gain a greater understanding of executive control in typical and atypical development. However, please bear in mind that there are still uncertainties with respect to the relationships between the central executive and executive functioning in its widest sense. There is also the issue of exactly how these systems might be limited in terms of capacity, although it is clear that such capacity limitations do exist (e.g. Swanson, 2006).

In the next sections brief overviews will be given of each sub-skill of executive functioning discussed in this book. Please refer to Chapter 2 for details on how they can be measured in typical and atypical populations of children.

Executive-loaded working memory

This aspect of executive functioning captures our ability to manipulate and store information at the same time. A good way of understanding executive-loaded working memory (ELWM) is to think about situations in which you must process some information (perhaps adding two numbers together) and then store the results of that processing while you move on to something else (perhaps performing another mathematical calculation). Sometime later, you are asked to remember the results of your various processing tasks. This is a bit like memory 'plus' in that you must keep in mind ever increasing amounts of information, whilst carrying out other tasks. Mental arithmetic is a good example of a task that requires ELWM resources.

We will look at exactly how ELWM is measured in the next chapter. However, it is worth briefly describing the historical background for one of the more important working memory tasks in the literature known as 'reading span'. In a now classic study, Daneman and Carpenter (1980) asked participants to read a sentence, make a judgement about the sentence, and then recall the final word from the sentence. This, of course, is trivial with only one sentence, but becomes increasingly difficult as the number of sentences is increased. Daneman and Carpenter (1980) noted that performance on this reading span task was more strongly related to reading aptitude than performance on simple word span tasks.

There followed, in subsequent years, an enormous degree of interest in this task, which saw it being developed in many different ways. Tasks of this nature are often described as 'complex span' tasks and all have the same basic requirements, although they can be designed to incorporate different skills or domains of processing. There is a remembering component, as well as a processing component. These two requirements, storage plus processing (at the same time), place a load on executive resources. In terms of the working memory model, one of the slave subsystems may be used to store interim information, i.e. the phonological loop in a verbal ELWM task (for evidence that the phonological loop is implicated in verbal ELWM tasks, see Lobley, Baddeley & Gathercole, 2005) or the visuospatial sketchpad in a visuospatial ELWM task. However, it is also necessary for this information to be continually updated, and for real-time processing to be carried out on new information being presented.

Hence, complex span tasks require a combination of updating, processing and overall monitoring, which all necessitate input from the central executive. This is why complex span measures are regarded as assessing ELWM, and, more broadly, executive functioning.

However, a set of related tasks, collectively known as 'updating' measures, are also described by many authors as assessing ELWM resources. The Debates and Issues box below considers whether there is evidence that updating and complex memory tasks are closely related or not.

Debates and Issues 1.1   Complex memory and updating tasks – do they measure the same underlying construct?

St Clair-Thompson and Gathercole (2006) assessed whether measures of complex memory span and updating were, in fact, assessing closely related constructs. This is an important issue, because if they are, we are justified in thinking about both of these types of tasks as measures of executive-loaded working memory (ELWM). Much of the literature is rather vague on this issue, making assumptions that many different types of tasks assess 'working memory'.

Around 60 11-year-old children were given four complex memory tasks (listening, backwards digit, odd one out and spatial span) and two updating tasks (letter memory, keep track task). They were also assessed on two measures of inhibition (refer to Chapter 2 for further details on these tasks).

St Clair-Thompson and Gathercole (2006) used 'principal components analysis' to see which of these eight tasks would cluster together. Tasks that clustered together on the same 'component' were likely to be measuring similar abilities.

In fact, the complex span and updating tasks all loaded together on the same component (i.e. clustered together), giving reassuring evidence that these two types of measures were assessing the same underlying construct of ELWM.

Set shifting/switching

There are several names for this ability in the literature and they include switching, mental flexibility and set shifting. These terms all describe the following skill: how readily can a person switch from one strategy or behaviour to another, when they receive feedback that their original strategy has not been successful in achieving their goals? In other words, the executive skill of switching captures the ability to adapt behaviour to changing task situations, and to do so quickly and flexibly (Davidson, Amso, Anderson & Diamond, 2006).

In order to switch strategies, a person must be able to monitor how successful they are being in achieving their goals. This monitoring function is assumed to be carried out by the central executive. Once feedback is received that the current strategy is not successful, a new strategy must be generated. Finally, the current strategy must be inhibited and the new strategy adopted. Therefore, mental flexibility is required in order to switch from one strategy to another, in a timely manner, in response to feedback. The central executive carries out this switching; in fact, one of its three key features is the 'switching' of attention.

Many patients with frontal lobe damage find this type task very difficult, preferring to carry on with their original strategy. This inflexibility is often described in the literature as 'perseveration'.

Planning/problem-solving

Planning and problem-solving refer to the ability to generate solutions to overcome difficulties in achieving goals, and to plan how these solutions might be carried out. Planning and problem-solving are at the heart of successful goal-directed behaviour, particularly when achieving goals is not straightforward, or there is no well-known method of proceeding. In some instances, it might be necessary to do one thing before another in order to reach a target goal; in these circumstances, planning ahead is clearly an advantage.

As we stressed earlier, executive skills are not essential for routine tasks, for which we have established ways of proceeding. The central executive is required for generating potential solutions for more unusual or novel tasks. As we will see in the next chapter, measures of executive functioning must contain an element of novelty. The central executive is required for planning and problem-solving precisely because there are no automatic methods of dealing with novel situations.

Inhibition

Inhibition refers to the ability to ignore information or strategies that are not relevant to the current task goals. Davidson et al. (2006) describe mature levels of inhibition in the following terms; they allow a person:

> to act on the basis of choice rather than impulse, exercising self-control (or self-regulation) by resisting inappropriate behaviours and responding appropriately. (p. 2037)

For inhibition to require executive resources, most authors believe that the irrelevant information/strategies must be very salient. In other words, the person may be drawn strongly to particular information (which may be automatically processed) or towards strategies that represent the typical way of responding. For example, you may be familiar with the yes/no game. A person asks you a series of questions and you must answer them without using the words 'yes' or 'no'. This is a good example of executive inhibition, because the central executive must intervene constantly to inhibit the powerful tendency to respond with 'yes' or 'no'. It requires continual monitoring of every response and intervention to change behaviour where relevant. Interventions of this kind are believed to be controlled and executed by the central executive.

Fluency

Fluency describes the ability to generate new instances of a particular class of information. For example, generating as many different types of 'animals' as possible, as many different uses for a 'brick' as possible, or drawing as many different 'sketches' as possible within a certain time period (often one minute). Executive control is required in tasks such as these to facilitate search processes through long-term memory, to use strategies for accessing the relevant information, and to monitor the output to avoid repetition. A degree of inhibition may also be required in order to inhibit responses that have already been given.

These comments illustrate clearly that many of the sub-skills of executive functioning we have just described are not entirely distinct from each other.

Although these five areas are often regarded as separate executive skills, there is, nevertheless, overlap between them. In fact, it is acknowledged that executive skills have some areas of overlap and other areas of distinctiveness. Therefore, we would expect to find relationships between different sub-skills of executive functioning, yet we should also expect that each sub-skill broadly measures a somewhat distinct ability (Miyake et al., 2000).

In this book, we will make an assumption that it is possible to measure different areas of executive functioning using tasks that are largely measures of the skill in question (further details in Chapter 2). However, it must be stressed that few measures of executive functioning are totally pure, although many authors have attempted to draw distinctions between 'pure' measures, which are less likely to require a range of skills, and 'complex' measures, which are acknowledged to draw on more than one type of executive resource (e.g. Miyake et al., 2000).

Dual task performance

Dual tasks are relatively rare in the literature on child development but are sometimes used. This is an approach that has developed out of the working memory literature and was designed to test theoretical predictions of the working memory model. Dual task performance involves asking a participant to do two things at once, and looking at the 'cost' to performance of combining the two tests together. For example, a participant may be asked to hold a list of digits in mind by reciting it over and over again, whilst at the same time judging whether two words rhyme.

The role of the central executive in dual task performance is to coordinate performance on both tasks and allocate appropriate amounts of attention when and where required. Often, the instructions for dual task performance require participants to focus more on successfully carrying out one task (primary task) than the other (secondary task), and executive control can be used to allocate more attention to the 'primary' task. On the whole, the participant must decide to focus attention on one task at the expense of the other or switch attention between tasks. These higher-level decision processes relevant to the overall conduct of the task are believed to be carried out by the central executive.

Random generation

This task was also developed as a theoretically effective way of assessing the types of skills believed to be carried out by the central executive. The participant is asked to generate sequences of numbers or letters, but they are instructed to ensure that the sequences are in a random order. In other words they must avoid non-random sequences such as '123', '999', 'MSN' or 'SOS'. This task is often used as a central executive-loaded secondary task, as it would be expected to interfere with the attentional control of complex tasks where executive input is necessary. Again, it is rarely used in the developmental literature on executive functioning.

Final comments

One difficulty with the concept of the 'central executive' is that many of the tasks developed to assess executive processes reflect them rather than directly measure them (see next chapter for examples). We can infer that central executive resources are required in order to carry out the task, but one cannot measuring central executive processing on its own with no other working memory (or other cognitive) components involved. This is almost inevitable, because the central executive allocates attention between all of the relevant components of the working memory system, and complex tasks are almost bound to involve more than one component of working memory.

This is why it is often useful to describe executive tasks as 'central executive-loaded' or 'executive-loaded'. The reading span task described earlier offers a particularly clear example of how the various components of working memory interact. The storage of the final words from each sentence and the processes involved in reading the sentence will most likely involve the phonological loop and possibly the visuospatial sketchpad (e.g. Baddeley & Logie, 1999), but this will be in combination with the central executive, which is responsible for the allocation of attention to the processing and storage components of these tasks.

A second difficulty with the concept of a central executive is that in Baddeley's most recent work he describes complex working memory span tasks as reflecting the episodic buffer and its interface with the central executive. This is a somewhat new way of looking at these tasks and will require further study and theorising to flesh out the full implications. Whether the episodic buffer is involved in other executive-loaded tasks is currently unclear, but it would seem a reasonable guess to expect that it would be heavily involved in tasks such as fluency, where searching lexical long-term memory is explicitly required, and in random generation, to help identify non-random series of numbers and letters.

Summary

The central executive is the key component of the multi-component working memory model (Baddeley, 2000, 2007; Baddeley & Hitch, 1974). It controls the allocation of resources within the working memory system by focusing, dividing and switching attention as necessary. The central executive has no storage capacity; the other components of the model store information. Although this component of working memory was historically little understood (e.g. Baddeley, 1986), the wider literature on executive functioning is adding to our understanding of the types of functions that may be carried out by the central executive. There is a growing consensus that executive skills are 'fractionated' into several areas that are nevertheless linked together. In this book a broad perspective on executive functioning will be taken in order to provide a more comprehensive overview of the area.

The episodic buffer

The episodic buffer is the most recent addition to the working memory model and represents the greatest change to the original model (Baddeley, 2000). The episodic buffer is an entirely new component, described as a 'multimodal' temporary store. This means that it does not just store information in one modality (e.g. auditory or visual or spatial or kinaesthetic), but deals with information from many different modalities. This makes it unlike the phonological loop or the visuospatial sketchpad, which are both specialised to hold particular types of information and nothing else.

The other main characteristic of the episodic buffer is that it 'binds' together information from different sources within the working memory system. For example, information about a scene may comprise visual information, speech sounds and movement. It is the episodic buffer that is hypothesised to join this information together into a coherent memory episode. Binding may be relatively automatic for visuospatial information and coherent language inputs such as prose, but more active, resource-demanding binding requiring additional executive resources cannot be ruled out (Baddeley, 2007).

The capacity of the episodic buffer is not clearly specified, but is believed to be limited and to reflect the number of chunks or episodes of information that can be maintained simultaneously. Presumably, the more the information can be bound together in a coherent fashion, the greater the capacity of the episodic buffer. The idea of a chunk is not precise, but probably reflects a single unit of information. See Box 1.7 for an example of chunking.

The notion of a capacity limitation in terms of chunks may be similar to the conceptualisation put forward by Cowan (2005) in his alternative model of working memory. He argues convincingly that adults are able to cope with only three to five chunks of information in our 'focus' of attention, regardless of how these chunks are measured.

Box 1.7   Chunking

A single numeral could reflect one chunk of information. For example, 5.

However, in many cases, several numerals grouped together in a meaningful manner can also reflect one chunk. For example, 911, or the area code for a local telephone number.

Whenever discrete pieces of information (whatever they are) can be *grouped together* into a meaningful 'bundle', this is called chunking. Cowan (2005) argues that human memory never really exceeds four chunks of information.

For example, the following digits can be chunked together to make the series more memorable. Can you make these 14 digits fit into *four* chunks?

9 1 1 1 4 9 2 8 8 6 5 4 3 2

Baddeley (2007) describes the episodic buffer as:

> ...a temporary storage system that is able to combine information from the loop, the sketchpad, long-term memory, or indeed from perceptual input, into a coherent episode. (p. 148)

Thus, the episodic buffer integrates information from a variety of sources into a meaningful unit or 'episode'. However, it also acts as a link between the central executive and long-term memory so that we can access and utilise our stored knowledge during ongoing memory and processing tasks. This explicit link to long-term memory is one of the key theoretical advances associated with the episodic buffer, as this was missing from the original working memory model.

In the episodic buffer, information is represented in a single 'multidimensional' code. This makes it a flexible interface for integrating information deriving from different sources and in different formats. Central executive resources may be required to control attention while retrieving long-term memory knowledge and/or binding together information from slave storage systems when these processes are effortful and attention-demanding (Allen, Baddeley & Hitch, 2006). Conversely, some binding and long-term memory activation may be relatively automatic.

More dramatically, the episodic buffer is potentially what gives us our experience of consciousness. To experience consciousness we must be able to keep track of our current experience, but also be able to reflect on this experience in real-time. Baddeley (2007) points out that the 'keeping track' and the 'reflecting' could be regarded as storage and processing respectively, something that the working memory system as a whole is specialised to do. Figure 1.2 (earlier in this chapter) shows how the episodic buffer is integrated into the working memory system and how various long-term memory storage systems (visual semantics, episodic long-term memory, language) are linked together and to other components of working memory.

What does the episodic buffer offer? Baddeley (2007) notes that the episodic buffer can act as a 'backup store' to supplement the phonological loop or the visuospatial sketchpad, as well as providing a link to long-term memory. For example, the recall of sentences and paragraphs is considerably better than would be expected on the basis of how many unrelated words can be recalled. We might be able to recall only five or six unrelated words at a time, whereas most adults could recall many more words if they were part of a sentence. Performance might be even better in terms of numbers of words recalled if we were asked to remember an entire paragraph. The episodic buffer, therefore, does two things: (1) it provides extra storage capacity; and (2) it accesses long-term knowledge about language, grammar and the structure of sentences to bolster phonological short-term memory in the phonological loop.

Several research studies support the notion of an episodic buffer, which provides such access to long-term memory knowledge. To take one example, Hulme, Maughan and Brown (1991) found that remembering lists of non-words was much more difficult than remembering lists of familiar words.

They went on to show that if participants learnt the 'meanings' of nonwords (in this case, Italian words), memory for them improved. These results illustrated the role of 'semantic' information, i.e. knowledge of the meanings of the words, on short-term recall. The mechanism through which this information can improve recall is hypothesised to be the episodic buffer (see Chapter 3 for further discussion of this, and related, research).

The episodic buffer also deals with a number of other problems that arose from confining short-term memory storage to just the phonological store and the visuospatial sketchpad (see Baddeley, 2000). For example, why did articulatory suppression not reduce memory for lists of words as much as would be expected, given that it 'knocks out' access to the phonological store and prevents verbal rehearsal? How is it that we can integrate visual and verbal information into a coherent whole, without even thinking about it? The answers to these questions can be provided by the inclusion of an episodic buffer in the working memory model. It provides extra storage capacity; and binds together information from different slave storage systems.

The full set of roles performed by the episodic buffer can, therefore, be summarised as follows in Box 1.8.

Box 1.8   Summary of the roles performed by the episodic buffer

1   Allows long-term memory knowledge to be utilised in the working memory system
2   Offers an extra storage mechanism to back up other storage areas
3   Blends together or 'binds' information from different sources/modalities into a coherent memory experience

---

The interrelationships between all of the components of working memory continue to be refined and specialised. The debate summarised in the box below illustrates that there may be other roles carried out by the episodic buffer, as yet to be determined by future research.

Debates and Issues 1.2   Item and order information

According to the working memory model, remembering *item* information (which items were in a list) and *order* information (which order these items were in) is carried out

(Continued)

by the slave systems of working memory (the phonological loop and visuospatial sketchpad). This means that memory for serial order is *modality specific*; in other words, there are separate mechanisms for remembering the order of verbal information (the phonological loop) and visuospatial information (the visuospatial sketchpad).

However, this is an area of considerable debate, and the working memory view has recently been challenged by Depoorter and Vandierendonck (2009). These authors found evidence that *verbal* serial order memory tasks interfered with *visuospatial* serial order memory tasks and vice versa. This is not predicted by the working memory model, as these two tasks should be carried out by separate slave systems, so should not interfere with each other. Depoorter and Vandierendonck (2009) suggested that memory for serial order is not *modality specific* as previously thought, but carried out by a modality *independent* system.

Interestingly, Depoorter and Vandierendonck (2009) argued that the episodic buffer may be 'the ideal medium to maintain a modality-independent order code'. Therefore, research continues to reveal new ways in which the episodic buffer may contribute to the working memory system.

Summary
The episodic buffer is the newest component of the multi-component working memory model, having been added relatively recently (Baddeley, 2000, 2007). It binds together information from different sources and integrates new material with information we already know (in long-term memory) so that our experiences and memories are unified and coherent. The episodic buffer has a small storage capacity, which does not depend upon the type of input (i.e. it is not visual, spatial or phonological in nature, but 'multi-modal').

Overall summary

The working memory model was developed to account for how we temporarily manipulate and store information during thinking and reasoning tasks in everyday life. It consists of four components: the *phonological loop*, specialised for holding speech material for short periods of time; the *visuospatial sketchpad*, specialised for holding visual, spatial and, possibly, kinaesthetic information for short periods of time; the *central executive*, responsible for the overall control of the working memory system via focusing, dividing and switching attention in a flexible manner; and the *episodic buffer*, responsible for binding or integrating information from the other components together into a coherent whole. This final component also helps us to make sense of conscious experience by allowing long-term knowledge to be used in tandem with current experience.

The working memory model has had an enormous impact on the field of cognitive psychology over the past four decades and has shaped a great deal of research on memory development in children with typical and atypical development. This chapter has given an overview of the main features of the model, to help provide a foundation for understanding the remainder of this book. It is important to emphasise that this is not the only model of memory, but because it has been so influential across the UK, North America and Europe, we are using it as a unified basis for understanding memory development in both typical and atypical populations of children.

Before we move on to considering the development of working memory in children with typical and atypical development, Chapter 2 first describes how all of the components of the working memory system are measured. In this book, there is a strong focus on methodology in the treatment of experimental evidence. A sound understanding of the tasks that are used to assess working memory in children is the foundation for understanding experimental methods. One of the goals of this book is to encourage a critical and evaluative approach to research evidence, vital for understanding the field as a whole, drawing reliable conclusions and writing good essays.

Further reading

Working memory model

Baddeley, A.D. (1986). *Working memory*. Oxford: Oxford University Press. Still very useful on the original model of working memory.

Baddeley, A.D. (2000). The episodic buffer: a new component of working memory? *Trends in Cognitive Sciences, 4*, 417–423. An excellent outline of the original working memory model and introduces the new episodic buffer component.

Baddeley, A. (2007). *Working memory, thought, and action*. Oxford: Oxford University Press. The most recent book on the working memory model, but fairly demanding.

Experimental papers on the phonological loop

Baddeley, A.D., Gathercole, S.E. & Papagno, C. (1998). The phonological loop as a language learning device. *Psychological Review, 105*, 158–173. What is the phonological loop for?

Baddeley, A.D., Lewis, V. & Vallar, G. (1984). Exploring the articulatory loop. *Quarterly Journal of Experimental Psychology, 36A*, 233–252. Another classic experimental paper.

Baddeley, A.D., Thomson, N. & Buchanan, M. (1975). Word length and the structure of short-term memory. *Journal of Verbal Learning and Verbal Behaviour, 14*, 575–589. Experiments on the word length effect. A classic paper.

Experimental papers on the visuospatial sketchpad

Darling, S., Della Sala, S. & Logie, R.H. (2007). Behavioural evidence for separating components within visuo-spatial working memory. *Cognitive Processes, 8*, 175–181. A clear introduction and a great experimental technique to separate visual and spatial working memory.

Papers relevant to executive functioning more generally

Miyake, A., Friedman, N.P., Emerson, M.J., Witzki, A.H., Howerter, A. & Wager, T.D. (2000). The unity and diversity of executive functions and their contributions to complex 'frontal lobe' tasks: A latent variable analysis. *Cognitive Psychology, 41*, 49–100. Already a classic paper on executive functioning, but fairly demanding.

Pennington, B.F. & Ozonoff, S. (1996). Executive functions and developmental psychopathology. *Journal of Child Psychology and Psychiatry, 37*(1), 51–87. A more accessible outline of executive functioning in the context of four developmental disorders.

Papers relevant to the episodic buffer

Allen, R.J., Baddeley, A.D. & Hitch, G.J. (2006). Is the binding of visual features in working memory resource-demanding? *Journal of Experimental Psychology: General, 135*, 298–313. Suggests that binding visual features is relatively automatic.

Hulme, C., Maughan, S. & Brown, G.D.A. (1991). Memory for familiar and unfamiliar words: Evidence for a long-term memory contribution to short-term memory span. *Journal of Memory and Language, 30*, 685–701. Demonstrates the impact of long-term memory on short-term memory processes.

Potential exam questions

1 Critically discuss each of the four components of Baddeley's revised working memory model, using experimental evidence where relevant to support your arguments.

2 Compare and contrast the original and revised working memory models. What significant advantages does the revised model offer?

2

How is Working Memory Measured?

Learning outcomes

At the end of this chapter, you should have an understanding of how working memory is measured in groups of children with typical and atypical development. You should be able to describe examples of the main tasks used by psychologists to measure each of the four components of working memory (phonological loop, visuospatial sketchpad, central executive, episodic buffer). You should also be able to comment on the suitability of these tasks for use with typical and atypical populations of children.

Introduction

In this chapter, methods of assessing the four components of working memory in children with typical and atypical development will be described and evaluated. This chapter can be read in conjunction with Chapter 1 (see the 'aide memoire' to the working memory model at the end of this chapter for a quick reminder), which outlines the characteristics of each component of working memory, together with some of the key evidence relevant to each component.

The purpose of this chapter is to give you a clear understanding of the tasks used in this area. This is helpful when reading papers or discussing experimental evidence in essays, as you will find that your understanding of the area is greatly enhanced by having a thorough understanding of the methodology. There are many different methods of assessing the different components of working memory and these can become confusing. You may find it useful to refer back to this chapter when reading subsequent chapters on research studies, to remind yourself about the particular tasks used.

The phonological loop

The usual way of measuring the phonological loop in children with typical and atypical development (or indeed adults) involves using tests of phonological short-term memory (PSTM). In other words, tests of the ability to recall speech-based information. These tasks have the advantage of being simple to describe, easy to score and very straightforward to adjust to ability level.

Memory span

Most tests of PSTM boil down to asking participants to recall lists of words, letters or digits. The person must repeat back, immediately and in the correct serial order, the exact list that was presented.

The digit span task is the most often-used measure of PSTM in the literature and forms part of several well-known intelligence tests (e.g. the Wechsler Intelligence Scale for Children III-UK or British Ability Scales II). Standardisation of digit span test procedures is usually achieved by presenting digits at a steady and even pace, at a rate of one item per second. Most instruction manuals also suggest dropping the voice inflection on the last digit in a series to signal the final item (Pickering, 2006a).

Digit span is described as a 'span' test because the length of the to-be-recalled lists is gradually increased to determine the longest list that can be recalled reliably, entirely correctly. In most tests, once the child has made a certain number of errors at any particular list length the test ends. Assessments of PSTM which use this incremental method can be referred to as span tasks. For example, 'digit span', 'letter span' or 'word span'. The term 'memory span' refers to the largest number of items that can be recalled in the correct order consistently.

Although digit span and other measures of span for speech-related items are very straightforward, reliable and easy to administer tests, they do have some disadvantages. The use of digits or familiar items (usually words or letters) means that it is unlikely to be a pure measure of PSTM, with no contributions from long-term memory. The revised working memory model explicitly acknowledges these links and we have seen how the episodic buffer is the mechanism through which long-term memory is accessed. However, if the purpose of an experimental study is to obtain a pure measure of PSTM, without the contribution of long-term memory, unfamiliar items must be used. We will come to such methods in the next section on nonword repetition.

Similarly, assessments of memory span will inevitably reflect verbal rehearsal strategies in children over the age of 7 or 8 years, as this is a strategy that emerges with development (Gathercole & Hitch, 1993; Henry & Millar, 1993; Henry, Turner, Smith & Leather, 2000). Again, this means that, for older children, we are not obtaining measures of pure PSTM if we use memory span. In fact, many of the studies that will be discussed in the next chapter on typical development explicitly acknowledge the role of verbal rehearsal in the development of memory span. Indeed, verbal rehearsal is a central feature of the working memory model's account of the development of memory in children.

A similar viewpoint is taken by Cowan (2005), who argues that, despite the fact that memory span improves markedly with age, much of this improvement, particularly after the preschool years, reflects the use of memory strategies. Cowan (2005) believes that there is a basic structural limit on the number of individual units of information we can all maintain. This number ranges between three and five, but can be increased using strategies such as chunking, rehearsal and grouping items together. Long-term knowledge or specific learning can also be used to improve the apparent capacity of working memory, but the underlying structure of the information retained will inevitably reduce down to between three and five chunks or units of information.

Pickering (2006a) has pointed out several other issues to bear in mind when administering memory span tests to children, particularly those with developmental disorders (indeed, these points are relevant for all working memory tasks):

1 Does the child have a hearing impairment (particularly important to assess in children with Down syndrome)?
2 Was the child paying attention when the memory task was presented (a key factor to bear in mind when testing children with attention difficulties, in particular)?
3 Can the child recall the information verbally or do they have difficulties with spoken output (can be a problem for children with Down syndrome and some other developmental disorders)?
4 Is the child able to use additional strategies (apart from verbal rehearsal), such as chunking items together?

There are a number of standardised tests available to assess PSTM. For example, the Working Memory Test Battery for Children (WMTB-C, Pickering & Gathercole, 2001) includes measures of word span and digit span (and nonword span, which we will come to shortly). The theoretical underpinning of this test battery is the working memory model, so all of the tests in it assess well specified aspects of working memory. For a thorough discussion of the WMTB-C, please see Pickering (2006a), referenced at the end of this chapter.

Span tests with gradually increasing list lengths are not the only way of measuring the ability to recall speech-related information in the phonological loop. Alternatively, participants can be presented with lists of items that are all at the same list length, but at a level somewhat above their comfortable span performance (e.g. on every trial the person is asked to recall four-item word lists). The memory score is calculated as the percentage of correct responses at each serial position (i.e. item 1, item 2, item 3 and item 4). The number of items in each list varies somewhat, but is generally much lower for young children and children with developmental disorders (three items), than older children (four or five items). These methods are 'fixed list length' procedures, because everyone gets the same list length. In many developmental studies with large age ranges, researchers choose different fixed list lengths for different age bands to ensure that, for any particular age group, the lists are neither too easy nor too difficult.

Both span and fixed list length methods are often used in research with children and atypical populations and each has different advantages. For example, sometimes we are very interested in the threshold at which span breaks down; in other words, what is the longest list a particular individual or group of individuals can remember (i.e. memory span). This type of data is particularly helpful when looking at how memory span increases with age. It is also useful for comparing memory span levels between groups of individuals with and without developmental disorders.

On other occasions, we might prefer to use measures of PSTM that are based on fixed list length procedures. Often, this is because we are interested in analysing what are known as serial position curves (the level of performance at each position in the list, for example, item 1, item 2, item 3 and item 4 in a four-item list). In order to compare serial position curves directly, all participants must receive the same list lengths. Serial position curves have often been used to draw conclusions about how children (and adults) carry out PSTM tasks, and the mechanisms that might underlie performance (e.g. Engle, Fidler & Reynolds, 1981; Spring & Capps, 1974).

Figure 2.1 gives an example of fictional serial position curves for two children who have been tested using a list length of four items. These curves show the pattern of performance across each of the different serial positions in the list and can be used to make inferences about strategy use. For example, children using verbal rehearsal would be expected to show better performance on early list items that receive more 'rehearsals'. This is known as 'primacy' and, in our example, Child A shows this pattern, whereas Child B does not. These data could be interpreted as indicating that Child A uses rehearsal, and Child B does not. Another noteworthy feature is that both children show 'recency', which refers to better performance on the final list item. This is often interpreted as reflecting the rather good acoustic recall of the final item presented in a list. We will return to the important issue of strategy use in more depth during subsequent chapters, particularly Chapters 3 and 4.

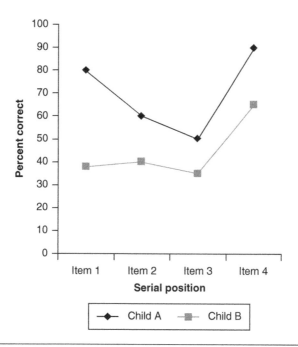

Figure 2.1 Two fictional serial position curves using a serial span task with a list length of four items

Finally, we will briefly consider how memory span scores are useful in practical terms. They are measures of absolute performance, so it makes sense to talk about children who have memory spans of two words, or three words, and so on. Knowing how many words a child can remember in the correct order provides helpful information for teachers when they structure learning tasks. Many children with developmental disorders or special needs can only remember very small numbers of words in PSTM tasks, and this has implications for the types of learning they can tackle successfully and whether they can retain instructions (Gathercole & Alloway, 2008; Gathercole, Lamont & Alloway, 2006; Minear & Shah, 2006). In our research on children with intellectual disabilities, for example, 12-year-olds with memory spans of three or less showed marked difficulties with reading and spelling (Henry & Winfield, 2010).

There are several recommendations for reducing memory demands when teaching children with significant delays in PSTM (see Gathercole & Alloway, 2006; 2008; Gathercole et al., 2006). These include:

1 Using memory aids or supports that can be designed specially for an individual child's needs (e.g. personal boards or 'keyrings' on desks with key information or visual reminders).
2 Reducing verbal demands by phrasing instructions in very short simple subject-verb-object sentences, bearing in mind that many

children with special needs may only have a memory span of two words.

3   Managing processing loads (i.e. how many tasks have to be carried out at once; and how complex each task is) in classroom activities. For example, in a writing task, one could reduce processing loads overall by reducing vocabulary demands, shortening lengths of sentences, and providing a clear task structure and order to reduce planning demands.

There are also methods of remediation that have been used for children who have various developmental disorders that are associated with weak working memory skills, particularly training in working memory skills. For a discussion of these see Minear and Shah (2006).

Nonword repetition

A further measure of the phonological loop, or PSTM, is nonword repetition. Nonword repetition tasks are based on the premise that asking a child to repeat a complex series of sounds (that do not correspond to a real word) is a test of how accurately they can store unfamiliar sound sequences. Children with better PSTM are more able to store and repeat these complex nonwords, particularly the longer ones.

As mentioned earlier, tests of PSTM that use familiar items are unlikely to reflect pure phonological storage. There will inevitably be contributions from long-term memory. One of the key advantages of nonword repetition tasks is that they ask children to recall unfamiliar items with no long-term memory 'backup'. In this way, many researchers argue that they are much purer measures of PSTM.

There are several versions of the nonword repetition test in the literature, but a useful and well-established, standardised UK measure is the 'Children's Test of Nonword Repetition' (CN-Rep: Gathercole & Baddeley, 1996). This test measures a child's ability to repeat complex nonsense words, which are between two and five syllables in length, and contain sound patterns that are legal in English. Box 2.1 gives you some examples of the types of nonwords children are asked to repeat.

Box 2.1   Examples from the Children's Test of Nonword Repetition (Gathercole & Baddeley, 1996)

Children hear 40 nonwords, one at a time, and are asked to repeat each one exactly as they have heard it. Words vary in terms of how many syllables they contain; here are some examples of four and two syllable words.

Four-syllables:

- 'woolgalamic'
- 'loddernaypish'

Two-syllables:

- 'prindle'
- 'ballop'

This test is particularly challenging for young children. It is regarded as a test of phonological short-term memory because, in order to repeat words correctly, clear and distinct phonological memory representations for the sounds in each nonword must be retained.

The CN-Rep task has been particularly helpful in identifying children with specific language impairment, an area that we will cover in Chapter 6. The other interesting thing about nonword repetition is that children who are good at nonword repetition are also likely to have good vocabularies and be good at learning new words (e.g. Gathercole, Hitch, Service & Martin, 1997; Gathercole, Hitch, Service, Adams & Martin, 1999; Michas & Henry, 1994). It is beyond the scope of this book to go into detail about this issue, but you can read a very good summary of the area in Baddeley et al. (1998).

Nonword repetition has two potential advantages over digit, letter or word span. First, none of the nonwords are known to children already. Nonwords do not have what are known as 'lexical entries', because they have no already established meanings; so it is not possible for the participant to use backup from long-term memory/semantic representations via the episodic buffer to aid their recall. This makes long-term memory support during the task far less of a factor in performance (this is an issue we will also come back to again, when we discuss memory span development in typical children in Chapter 3). Of course, the fact that nonwords resemble real words to some extent means that at least some relevant information is available, and those with a greater knowledge of legal combinations of sounds in English will clearly have some advantage in nonword repetition. However, this level of long-term memory 'help' is much reduced when we use nonwords in comparison to real words.

The second advantage of nonword repetition is that children cannot use verbal rehearsal to increase their recall in this task. There is only one word to remember, so using rehearsal is regarded as irrelevant. Nevertheless, it is still possible that rehearsal style processes may be used to repeat elements of the nonwords. However, there is little direct research available on this issue, so it is difficult to draw definitive conclusions.

Both of the above advantages mean that nonword repetition should largely assess only PSTM, without the potential additional factors of long-term knowledge or strategy use. For some researchers, this makes it a better measure than word, letter or digit span.

However, the nonword repetition task has been criticised on at least four grounds:

1 The child may still use knowledge of language rules, what is legal in English and existing vocabulary to help pronounce the nonwords, so long-term memory effects are not absent entirely.
2 The task does not impose the memory for order requirement found in traditional measures of PSTM, which means it may not assess exactly the same skill.
3 Nonword repetition may measure far more than PSTM (principally language skills).
4 The task is unsuitable for individuals who have speech output difficulties.

One can get around the second of the above points by measuring PSTM using memory span for nonwords, i.e. the longest list of nonwords that can be recalled in the correct order. Generally, single syllable nonwords would be used for a test of nonword span, as the task becomes extremely difficult for participants to carry out if each individual item is in itself a complex nonword. However, not all researchers would agree that span tasks for nonwords are functionally the same as nonword repetition tasks, so care needs to be taken in substituting these measures. Nevertheless, there is some evidence that nonword span and nonword repetition are very similarly related to vocabulary development in young children, suggesting that they are not dissimilar measures (Michas & Henry, 1994).

It would also be possible to get around point 4, by presenting two nonwords and asking children to indicate whether they were identical are not. Point 1 has also been addressed in some studies that manipulate the 'word-likeness' of the nonwords that are presented (Gathercole, Willis, Emslie & Baddeley, 1991).

Matching span

One further way of measuring PSTM is to use 'matching span'. In this task, the child hears two very similar lists of items and is asked to say whether they are identical or slightly different from each other. This can be made more fun by using 'characters' to present the two lists. In most versions of this task, the order of just two items from the middle portion of the list is swapped around and the participant's job is to notice when these order changes are made. Order changes from the beginnings or ends of the lists would be too easy to spot.

Matching span tasks can be very useful for testing PSTM in children who have difficulties with speech output, because they remove any requirement to report a list verbally, yet still retain the emphasis on ordered recall. However, they are not often reported in the literature, possibly because they do not produce a threshold span score; and, in order to obtain reliable results, quite large numbers of trials need to be presented. One version of a matching span task is illustrated in Box 2.2.

Box 2.2   The matching span task

The participant hears pairs of lists, one after the other, such as the following:

Leaf	**chair**	**clown**	**ring**	**boot**
Leaf	**chair**	**ring**	**clown**	**boot**

He or she is asked whether the two lists were *identical* to each other or *not identical*. In the above example, they are *not* identical, as the order of items three and four has been changed.

However, on approximately half of all trials, the two lists that the participant hears are, in fact, identical as follows:

drum	frog	bus	cake	kite
drum	frog	bus	cake	kite

The tasks proceeds with participants hearing several pairs of these lists, some of which are identical and some of which are not, randomly occurring. For each pair of lists, the participant's task is always to say (or indicate nonverbally) whether the lists were identical or not.

The difficulty of this task can be adjusted by altering the length of the two lists. The longest list lengths that a participant can manage to distinguish successfully equates to the level of their 'matching span'.

Note that making *order changes* that include either the first item or the final item in the list would make this task considerably easier, because of two phenomena in memory known as primacy and recency. Primacy refers to the fact that the first (or early) items are easier to remember; recency refers to the fact that the final item in a list is easier to remember. Generally, order changes in matching span tasks concern *middle* items only.

Summary

Psychologists have used many tasks to measure phonological short-term memory (PSTM) in children including the classic digit span task. The phonological loop has received a great deal of research attention, hence we have a relatively sophisticated level of understanding about PSTM tasks. We have discussed the advantages and disadvantages of several relevant measures.

The visuospatial sketchpad

There are many visual, spatial and imagery tasks that have been used to examine visual perception and short-term visual memory. However, we will confine ourselves to a relatively small number of tasks that have been commonly used in the literature to assess visuospatial short-term memory (VSSTM) in children with and without developmental disorders.

A key detail that will be of concern here is whether VSSTM tasks assess largely spatial or visual short-term memory. This is because the visuospatial sketchpad is believed to be divided into at least two areas, one specialised for storing spatial information, and one specialised for storing visual information. For evidence supporting this 'split' please refer to Chapter 1.

Spatial short-term memory

Measures of spatial short-term memory are generally based on the 'Corsi Block Tapping' task, and are sometimes described as 'spatial span'. The participant is shown a set of nine or ten identical blocks, arranged randomly in different spatial locations. The experimenter points to a series of blocks, one at a time, and the participant must point to the same blocks in the same order.

Box 2.3 shows an example of this task using black-and-white line drawings of blocks; although note that this task is more often presented using a set of real blocks arranged in a spatial array (for example, the Working Memory Test Battery for Children, Pickering & Gathercole, 2001). Span is measured as the longest sequence that can be correctly reproduced in the correct order, in the same manner as the word, digit and letter span tasks described in the previous section.

Performance on this task is believed to reflect the ability to remember a series of spatial locations presented in sequence. The information to be recalled in the spatial span test is presented sequentially/dynamically, in other words, there is an element of movement to the presentation.

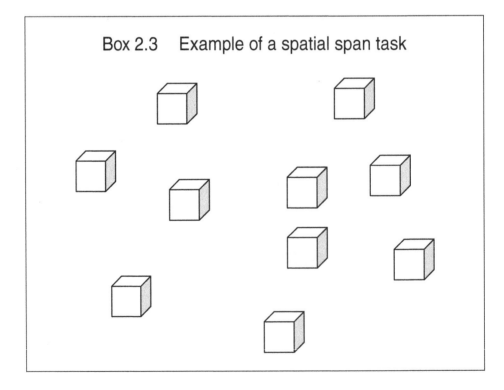

Box 2.3   Example of a spatial span task

Visual short-term memory

Other measures of VSSTM have been designed to assess memory for visual details. In these, information is presented 'all in one go' or simultaneously. One such measure is the Visual Patterns Test developed by Della Sala, Gray, Baddeley and Wilson (1997). This task involves presenting grids that have some of the internal squares filled and others left blank. Grids can be manipulated to be more or less complex by increasing their size and the number of filled squares. Box 2.4 gives some examples of the types of grids that can be used for a visual span test (adapted from the Visual Patterns Test).

In the first example, the grid is relatively simple (3 × 3) with only three filled boxes. The child is shown this grid for a short period of time, often two to five seconds, and then an empty grid of the same size is shown. The child is asked to point to the boxes that had been filled. In the second example, the grid is larger (4 × 3) and there are more filled boxes (four), hence, this is a more difficult grid to remember.

Visual span tasks proceed from smaller grids with fewer boxes filled in to larger grids with more boxes filled in. Although this task is not directly analogous to a span task, where increasingly long lists of discrete items or locations have to be recalled, there are many similarities. Difficulty level can be raised gradually by increasing the size of the grids and the number of filled boxes; and the task proceeds for as long as the participant is able to recall the items correctly. Like the more traditional span tasks, the participant's score reflects the threshold at which their performance breaks down.

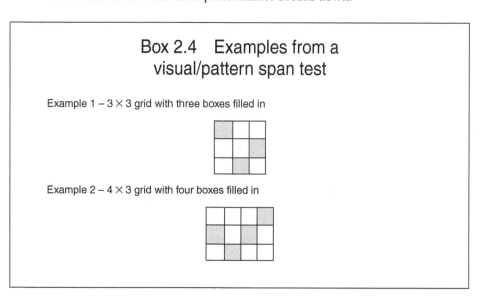

Box 2.4   Examples from a visual/pattern span test

Example 1 – 3 × 3 grid with three boxes filled in

Example 2 – 4 × 3 grid with four boxes filled in

Note that, in the literature, this task is often called 'pattern span'. It is generally regarded as a measure of visual as opposed to spatial memory, because there is visual detail to recall, and, perhaps more importantly, there is no spatial change in the information. Many papers we consider in later chapters compare Corsi span with pattern span, assuming that these two tasks measure spatial and visual elements of VSSTM respectively.

However, it may be that the pattern span task is more correctly viewed as a measure of simultaneous/static spatial memory (Mammarella et al., 2008). If it is true that there is a distinction between static and dynamic measures of spatial memory, this argument would be quite persuasive. Finally, some have even argued that it is possible to 'name' some of the patterns, so that there may be a verbal element to the task (Brown, Forbes & McConnell, 2006). However, even if this is the case, the contribution of any potential verbal component is likely to be small.

Measuring visual span can also be done using a series of visual items that are not easily nameable. It is always difficult to produce visual items that cannot be given a verbal label, even if they are nonsense pictures. A squiggly picture that looks like nothing in particular can often be likened to some real object and then named. In order to ensure that we are measuring visual memory and not the ability to apply and remember verbal labels, it is very important to choose materials carefully.

Provided one can find nonsense pictures that are not easily nameable, they can be presented rather like the 'matching span' task described in the previous section on PSTM. In matching span tasks two 'lists' of pictures are presented, which may or may not be identical. Usually, about half of the lists are slightly different from each other (often with one order change to middle items). The participant must assess whether both lists were exactly the same, or slightly different. Alternatively, a list of nonsense pictures can be presented, followed by an array of all list items in jumbled order, which the participant must put in the correct order via pointing or physically moving the jumbled items via cards or a touch screen computer. In both of these types of tasks, longer list lengths are used to increase the difficulty of the task. There is a test of visual 'nonsense' picture span in the Test of Memory and Learning (a standardised memory battery for children), called 'visual sequential memory' (Reynolds & Bigler, 1994).

Another short-term visual memory task requires remembering the details of a nonsense figure presented for a few seconds, then picking it out from an array of six very similar items. This task becomes more difficult as the figures differ less and less from the foils. This task has no serial order requirements, however.

The essence of a visual short-term memory task is the requirement to recall visual detail, without undue emphasis on spatial information or spatial sequencing. Clearly, visual and spatial tasks are somewhat overlapping in many cases, so that researchers can often only claim that they are broadly tests of each function. However, given the evidence for a theoretical division between visual and spatial memory (see Chapter 1), it is important that assessments of VSSTM include both of these elements.

Summary

Psychologists have used a number of tasks to measure visuospatial short-term memory (VSSTM), and these tasks are often broken down into measures of visual (sometimes referred to as static) versus spatial (sometimes referred to as dynamic) storage. These two aspects of VSSTM are believed by many to reflect the operation of different mechanisms within the visuospatial sketch-pad component of working memory.

The central executive

Much of the theorising about the central executive component of working memory has been based on tasks specifically developed for this purpose, such as random generation or dual task performance. Other tasks have been developed in parallel literatures, which have seemed eminently suitable to assess the form of working memory that requires executive control (complex span tasks). Still other tasks have been developed in the neuropsychological literature to assess patients who have difficulty with executive control, often because they have damage to the frontal lobes of the brain. These measures also seem to get at something important to do with executive control. Therefore, in this section, we will consider all of these types of tasks, focusing in particular on the measures that are suitable for children with and without developmental disorders.

It is also important to note, as we saw in Chapter 1, that central executive abilities are increasingly regarded as 'fractionated'. This means that we cannot regard the central executive as reflecting the operation of one simple and straightforward type of skill. The role of the central executive is to focus, divide and switch attention where necessary, and these skills will be necessary for many different types of tasks. Therefore, several sub-skills seem to be involved in executive control. These sub-skills may fall into somewhat different categories, yet all share similar attributes. The types of skills that are relevant to executive functioning were described in Chapter 1. Here, we take each of these sub-skills and describe how they can be measured in typical and atypical populations of children.

The first point to make is that all tests of executive control or executive functioning should include novelty, complexity and the need to integrate information (Anderson, 1998; Shallice, 1990). Therefore, measures must not be routine, everyday tasks, but rather novel and complex tasks requiring new schema, new strategies and constant monitoring.

We will consider methods of assessing executive functioning that are suitable for children and special populations in seven different areas:

- Executive-loaded working memory
- Switching/set shifting
- Planning/problem-solving
- Inhibition
- Fluency
- Dual task performance
- Random generation

Executive-loaded working memory

A common way of assessing executive-loaded working memory (ELWM) is by using complex span tasks. We touched on these tasks in Chapter 1, and will now revisit exactly why they are regarded as 'executive-loaded', as opposed to straightforward measures of storage in short-term memory.

In order to qualify as a measure of ELWM, a complex span task must include a central executive load. In practice, this requires the task to involve processing and storage of information at the same time. The participant must perform some type of processing on the information (such as reading, counting or arithmetic) before attempting to store and remember it. The central executive must focus attention on the appropriate part of the task, whilst retaining information that will be needed later on. This is much easier to understand with reference to a concrete example.

Box 2.5 illustrates the 'listening span task' (e.g. Henry, 2001; Leather & Henry, 1994; Siegel & Ryan, 1989), which was based on the original reading span task developed by Daneman and Carpenter (1980). This is probably the most commonly used measure of complex memory in the developmental literature and there are standardised versions available (e.g. the Working Memory Test Battery for Children has a 'listening recall' test, Pickering & Gathercole, 2001). The listening span task is a measure of threshold span, in that the task continues until the participant cannot comfortably recall the lists of 'sentence-final' words in the correct order.

Box 2.5   The listening span task
(e.g. Henry, 2001)

A participant is told that he or she will be listening to some sentences, some of which are silly and some of which are sensible. He or she must say whether the sentence is true or false, then try to remember the final word of the sentence.

For example,

'Children go to SCHOOL'

The response here is 'true' (the processing part of the task) and the word that needs to be remembered is SCHOOL (the storage part of the task).

This is quite a trivial task when only one sentence is presented. However, the task moves on to presenting two or more sentences at a time and requiring the participant to remember the final words from each sentence in the correct order, after carrying out the true/false processing task.

For example,

Trees are covered in LEAVES...........'True'
People live in a NEST.......................'False'
Recall..'LEAVES, NEST'

This task is directly comparable to a standard memory span for words task, in terms of the storage requirement and the output requirement. The difference is that the listening span task requires processing of the sentences together with storage of the sentence-final words. Measures can be taken of processing and storage performance, although the measures of interest are more often the storage measures.

There are alternative measures of complex span, including those that measure complex span in the visuospatial domain. An example of such a measure is the 'odd one out' span task (Henry, 2001; Hitch & McAuley, 1991; Russell, Jarrold & Henry, 1996). Here, participants are shown three visual items that cannot be readily named in a 3 x 1 array/grid. They are asked to point to the item that is slightly different from the other two. This is the processing part of the task, i.e. choosing the 'odd one out'. The storage part of the task is to remember the spatial location of the odd one out (to the left, middle or right in the grid). Carrying out this task with only one array of visual items is relatively trivial. However, the task can be made more difficult by presenting increasingly longer lists of arrays (two or more) before asking the participant to recall the spatial locations, in order, of all 'odd ones out'. Box 2.6 gives an example of the odd one out task at a list length of two. Threshold span reflects the longest set of lists that can be successfully recalled in order.

Box 2.6   The odd one out task (e.g. Henry, 2001)

Example at a list length of two.

The participant is presented with the following array and asked to point to the odd one out:

The first array is removed and the participant is presented with another array and asked to point to the odd one out:

(Continued)

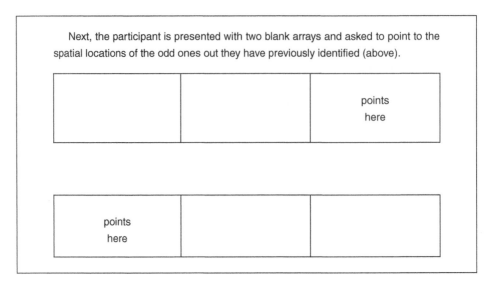

A further well-known complex span task is 'counting span', developed in a classic study by Case, Kurland and Goldberg (1982) (see Figure 2.2). In the counting span task, participants first count the number of dots on a card. Often the card will contain dots of two colours (e.g. red and green) and the participant is asked to count, for example, just the red ones or just the green ones. Counting is the processing part of task, and the storage portion of task is to recall the number of items counted on each presented card. Like the previous two complex span tasks, lists of two or more items can be presented up to the level of the participant's threshold span. Some variations on this task are known as 'operation or sums span'. These are slightly more demanding, where the processing might involve calculating a simple sum or series of sums (e.g.3 + 6; 4 + 1) and the storage involves recalling the answers for each sum calculated.

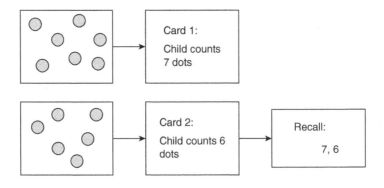

Figure 2.2 An example of a counting span task

A standardised version of this test is available in the Working Memory Test Battery for Children, WMTB-C (Pickering & Gathercole, 2001), and this test is suitable to use with children who have mental ages of 5 years or greater.

Therefore, complex span tasks share several features. They are generally presented as threshold measures of span and they all require both processing and storage at the same time. Complex span tasks are regarded as measures of ELWM, because the combined requirement for processing and storage places direct demands on the central executive component of working memory. In administering complex span tasks to developmentally young participants, great care must be taken to explain the tasks in simple, clear language, and give plenty of opportunity for practice. It is also a very good idea to have a relatively large number of trials at very low list lengths, in order that perform-ance can be discriminated between children who will achieve lower span scores.

Complex span tasks have been used in research for over three decades. They are particularly interesting measures, because performance on them is related to many areas of school achievement such as reading, spelling and mathematics (e.g. Alloway, Gathercole, Adams, Willis, Eaglen & Lamont, 2005; Bayliss, Jarrold, Gunn & Baddeley, 2003; Bull & Scerif, 2001; Bull, Espy & Wiebe, 2008; Gathercole & Pickering, 2000; Gathercole, Pickering, Knight & Stegmann, 2004; Hitch, Towse & Hutton, 2001; Leather & Henry, 1994; St Clair-Thompson & Gathercole, 2006). Executive-loaded working memory seems to tap skills and competencies that are strongly implicated in academic success. These references represent a selection of an exten-sive literature documenting relationships between ELWM and academic achievement. Some further reading on this topic and a proposed 'extended essay' on this topic is suggested at the end of Chapter 4. In the meantime, the Debates and Issues box below provides further insights into complex span tasks.

Debates and Issues 2.1   How complex is the 'complex' span task?

The complex span task is particularly interesting because it appears to involve many com-ponents of the working memory system. Baddeley (2007) suggests that complex span might reflect both the storage capacity of the episodic buffer *and* the efficiency of central executive processing. However, it also seems that phonological storage (in the case of verbal complex span measures) and visuospatial storage (in the case of visuospatial complex span measures) will be implicated in complex memory performance as well.

Cowan et al. (2003) further noted that for *linguistic* complex span tasks such as reading span or listening span, the use of 'episodic information along with the prior knowledge base' (p. 130) is used to help reconstruct items during recall. In other

(Continued)

words, the episodic buffer may be involved in using relevant long-term knowledge to support recall. Cowan et al. (2003) found *very long response times* for reading and listening span, as opposed to *short response times* for counting span. These differences support their suggestion that lengthy processing takes place *during recall*, but only when complex span tasks are 'language-heavy'.

In addition, Towse, Cowan, Horton and Whytock (2008) suggested that reading span is more closely related to academic achievement in children when the task is relatively *novel*. Once children have had some practice with reading span, it is less able to predict their performance on reading and mathematics. This underlines the importance of executive measures assessing performance on complex, non-routine tasks that require 'new' thinking.

In short, the complex span task is *very complex* and this is both a great strength and a theoretical challenge for researchers in the area.

Another commonly used measure of ELWM is the 'backwards' span task. For example, a digit span task can be presented in the normal manner, but participants can be asked to recall the digits in backwards order. This is a demanding task, because it is very difficult to select and output digits in reverse order. It is assumed that such processes require executive input. Similarly, the Corsi/spatial span task can be presented for backwards recall; again, providing a demanding measure of ELWM in the visuospatial domain.

Finally, other tasks that have been regarded as measuring executive-loaded working memory are the self-ordered pointing task (Petrides & Milner, 1982) and the 'N-back' task (e.g. Im-Bolter, Johnson & Pascual-Leone, 2006).

For 'self-ordered pointing', participants are shown a set of items (abstract designs, representational drawing, or words – all presented together on a sheet of paper for example) and are asked to point to one of the items. On subsequent trials, participants are shown the same set of items again, in different random arrangements each time, and asked to point to a different item on every trial. This task requires the person to continually update the group of items that have already been chosen, so that repetitions are avoided (for a study using this task with children, see Archibald & Kerns, 1999). This constant updating is regarded as requiring ELWM.

The 'visual N-back task' (e.g. Im-Bolter et al., 2006), requires children to look at configurations of three dots presented on a computer screen. In this particular study there were nine separate configurations, which were all slightly different, and the purpose of the task was to state whether the current stimulus was the same as the previous one (a '1-back' condition), or whether the current stimulus was the same as the one previous to that (a '2-back' condition). There is often also a '0-back' condition, which simply involves looking for a particular configuration on each trial; this can be used as a control condition, not requiring ELWM. The 'N-back' task is an updating task, because the child must keep in mind the details of several stimuli at once in order to compare them. Additionally, on every trial, the oldest stimulus needs to be 'deleted' and updated with the current stimulus. The task can be carried out with other stimuli such as letters, digits or words.

The 'letter memory task' (e.g. St Clair-Thompson & Gathercole, 2006) is another measure of updating, as it requires participants to look at a series of letters (5, 7, 9 or 11 items long) and recall the final four letters presented in each list. Importantly, participants do not know in advance the length of the list, so must continually keep the final four letters in mind, updating the memory items as each new letter is presented. A further variation of an updating task was used by Carretti, Belacchi and Cornoldi (2010), which involved hearing two lists and recalling the 'smallest' objects from each list (e.g. list 1 – 'pillow, ladder'; list 2 = 'pen, tree'; answer = 'pillow, pen').

As we saw in Chapter 1, there is good evidence that complex span and updating tasks measure the same underlying construct (St Clair-Thompson & Gathercole, 2006). However, Chein, Moore and Conway (2011) have recently argued that 'the most valid and reliable measures of WM capacity are CWMS [complex working memory span] tasks' (p. 551). We finish this section with another debate concerning whether ELWM tasks assess *domain-general* capacity or *domain-specific* capacity in relation to verbal versus non-verbal skills.

Debates and Issues 2.2   Domain specificity and the complex span task

When Daneman and Carpenter (1980) developed their complex span task (the 'reading span task' whereby participants read a series of sentences aloud and attempt to recall the final words from each sentence), they argued that it was a good predictor of performance in *reading and reading-related tasks* because of the shared domain of the relevant skills. However, many researchers prefer to conceptualise complex span tasks as assessing *domain-general* concurrent processing plus storage capacity, i.e. supporting the view that these tasks require 'general' executive resources (e.g. Kane, Hambrick, Tuholski, Wilhelm, Payne & Engle 2004).

This debate, therefore, concerns whether there are *separate* executive-loaded working memory resources for different types of ELWM tasks (domain-specific view), or whether all such tasks draw on the *same* resources (domain-general view).

Chein et al. (2011) tested adult participants on verbal and spatial complex span tasks and used functional magnetic resonance imaging (fMRI) to assess which brain regions were involved in each version of the task. For both the verbal and spatial complex tasks, the *same brain regions* (including prefrontal and anterior cingulate cortex) were activated, suggesting that both tasks recruited the same

(Continued)

domain-general executive resources. Chein et al. (2011) argued against the notion that there were separate pools of verbal and spatial resources for verbal and spatial ELWM tasks.

However, in this book, we will nevertheless consider *both* types/domains of ELWM tasks separately, because it is not clear whether such results also hold for populations of typical and atypical children.

Switching/set shifting (mental flexibility)

This executive skill refers to how readily a person can switch from one strategy or behaviour to another, when they receive feedback that their original strategy has not been successful in achieving their goals. The Wisconsin Card Sorting Test (WCST) is probably the best-known test of switching. It was developed as an adult test in neuropsychological settings and requires the person to match a set of cards with very little instruction. The participant is given a deck of cards, each of which has a different representation of shape, colour and numerosity information in a visual form. For example, a card may contain one green triangle, four yellow circles, or two red squares as illustrated below in Figure 2.3.

Participants are asked to match each card from the deck to one of four possible comparison cards, and feedback is given by the examiner as to whether each match is correct. No mention is made of the dimension that the cards must be matched by and this can change apparently randomly throughout the task. The measure of interest is how well the person can switch from one matching dimension to another when given feedback that the previous matching criterion is no longer correct. Those with poor executive skills will tend to keep sorting by the old rule – this is known as 'perseveration'. The task can be used with children and many authors have used simplified versions of the WCST with younger or developmentally disordered participants (e.g. WCST-64, Kongs, Thompson, Iverson & Heaton, 2000). Other simpler sorting tasks have also been developed (e.g. the Weigl Colour-Form Sort

 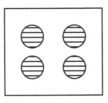 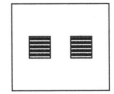

Figure 2.3 Examples of the types of cards used in the Wisconsin Card Sorting Task

Test, Goldstein & Scheerer, 1953, which uses only two dimensions, colour and shape).

The Trail Making Test (Reitan & Wolfson, 1992) is another measure of switching, but also assesses aspects of speed of visual search, attention and visuo-motor function. Part A requires participants to draw a connecting line between letters in sequence that are randomly placed on a sheet of paper (for example A to B; B to C, C to D etc.). Part B involves the same requirements, but the sheet of paper now contains letters and numbers, and requires the participant to alternate between the letters and numbers in order (for example A to 1; 1 to B; B to 2; 2 to C; C to 3 etc.). Only Part B is regarded as a test of executive function as it requires 'switching' between letters and numbers. Scoring reflects how much slower the person is at Trails B compared to the non-switching version, Trails A.

A standardised version of this test, with excellent controls for the component skills required (speed of sequencing letters and numbers), suitable for children down to a mental age of 8 years is available in the Delis-Kaplan Executive Function System (D-KEFS, Delis, Kaplan & Kramer, 2001). Box 2.7 below illustrates a 'mini' trails test.

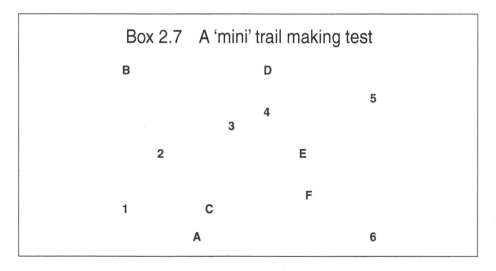

Box 2.7   A 'mini' trail making test

One other commonly used measure is the Intra/Extra Dimensional Shift Task (from the CANTAB battery of tests), which is presented on a touch screen. This test of rule acquisition and reversal involves simple stimuli made of coloured shapes and/or white lines: complex stimuli involve both. Initially, two coloured shapes are presented, and by touching one, the child learns from feedback which was 'correct', and follows this rule. Later, the second dimension, an irrelevant white line (initially adjacent to the coloured shape, but then overlaying it) is introduced. More complex 'intradimensional shifts' introduce new shape and line stimuli, yet the child still must respond to the original shape stimuli to solve the problems. Later still, the complex stimuli are changed and the child has to switch attention to the previously irrelevant dimension, to learn the 'correct' new response ('extradimensional' shift).

Planning/problem-solving

Planning and problem-solving refer to the ability to generate solutions to overcome difficulties in achieving goals. These skills also tap the ability to organise and plan how these solutions might be carried out. Maze Tasks (see Porteus Mazes, WISC-III, WPPSI-R, WMTB-C) have often been used to assess planning ability in children. These resemble puzzles. The child makes a line along a maze route without encountering 'dead ends' and without going outside the lines (procedures vary somewhat).

Maze tasks require forward planning to avoid making poor decisions along the route. They are simple to administer and enjoyable for children, and there are standardised versions available (e.g. WISC-III; WMTB-C). However, maze tasks can cause scoring difficulties among individuals with intellectual disabilities or developmental disorders, as performance may be affected by poor fine motor skills, visual perception or speed of response (many maze tasks are timed). There is good evidence that children with intellectual disabilities, for example, are slower at carrying out a range of tasks (Anderson, 2001), and they will score more poorly for slow responses. In addition, children who have poor pencil control will also lose points for going over the lines.

The Tower of Hanoi (see also Tower of London and Tower Test in D-KEFS) is a measure of problem-solving, developed in order to minimise the contributions of other skills such as perceptual and motor abilities, short-term memory and sustained attention. It requires the rearrangement of different sized discs (or coloured balls for the Tower of London) from an initial starting point on three laterally placed 'posts', to a specified end point. The participant is given the starting point and shown the end point required, and must rearrange the disks in the minimum number of moves. For example, one might

Figure 2.4 Illustration of the Tower of Hanoi task

be asked to move all of the disks to the third post (retaining the same order) in the lowest number of moves. Other rules such as 'larger disks cannot be placed over smaller disks' can be introduced. See Figure 2.4 for an illustration of the materials used for a Tower of Hanoi task.

Some argue that tower tasks measure more than planning, as they require the inhibition of 'obvious' or impulsive moves that are unhelpful for the longer-term solution. Miyake et al. (2000) argued that if participants use a demanding 'goal management' strategy involving setting up subgoals, maintaining them in short-term memory and executing them sequentially, this task is a measure of planning . However, if participants use a simpler 'perceptual' strategy, making successive moves which lead to the display 'looking' more like the desired end state, this task is more a measure of inhibition.

However, despite the theoretical difficulties, tower tasks are frequently used in the literature; and simple versions can be suitable for developmentally young participants.

The Water Test from The Behavioural Assessment of the Dysexecutive Syndrome in Children (BADS-C, Emslie, Wilson, Burden, Nimmo-Smith & Wilson, 2003) is argued to be an 'ecologically valid' test of planning, requiring children to remove a cork from a tube using an array of physical objects and materials (water, plastic tube, screw top, cork); five correct interim steps are needed to succeed. Similarly, the Key Test looks at how well children can plan an efficient and systematic search of a 'field' in which they have lost their keys. The 'field' is an A4 piece of paper and the 'search' must begin from a particular point and be marked out by drawing lines with a pen. Thinking ahead in both tasks is essential, hence, they should reflect planning. Lack of research, however, makes these tests hard to compare with similar measures, and poor reliability is also a problem (Henry & Bettenay, 2010).

Inhibition

Inhibition refers to the ability to ignore or suppress salient information, responses or strategies that are not relevant to the current task goals. The Stroop Test (Stroop, 1935; see also D-KEFS) is a commonly used measure of the ability to inhibit a habitual response. Colour words (e.g. 'blue', 'red') are presented in different coloured inks and the participant must name the colour of the INK rather than name the word. The name of the word often intrudes and this 'habitual' response must be inhibited. Clearly, children must be able to read to carry out this task, so it is unsuitable for developmentally younger individuals.

However, many simpler measures of inhibition suitable for younger children have also been developed. The Conflicting Motor Response task (Shue & Douglas, 1992) involves the examiner showing the child two different hand gestures that they are asked to copy. Next, the examiner shows one of the gestures to the child, but asks the child to make the other gesture as his/her response. These 'inhibition' trials require the child to suppress the copying response. Similarly, the 'Day/Night' task requires participants to say 'day' when they see a picture of the moon and stars (illustrated on a black card); and to say 'night' when they see a picture of the sun (illustrated on a white card). Control conditions require these responses but using two abstract nonsense patterns. As before, inhibition trials require the child to inhibit the obvious response in favour of the opposite response.

Other tasks have been developed that test verbal inhibition (see Box 2.8). Inhibition tasks such as these are straightforward for children of varying ages and cognitive abilities, and have been extensively used in the literature.

Box 2.8   A verbal inhibition task (taken from the VIMI, Henry, Messer & Nash, 2011)

The child is first asked to say one of two words after the examiner says it. 20 *copying* trials are given.

| Examiner | 'doll' | .... | Child | "doll" |
| Examiner | 'car' | .... | Child | 'car' |

Next, the child is asked to say the *other* word instead of copying. 20 of these *inhibition* trials are given.

| Examiner | 'doll' | .... | Child | 'car' |
| Examiner | 'car' | .... | Child | 'doll' |

An indication of inhibition is derived from the number of *errors* the child makes, particularly on inhibition trials.

This task can be repeated with two other words, 'drum' and 'bus' in order to obtain an additional set of inhibition trials.

There are several measures of inhibition in the Test of Everyday Attention for Children (TEA-Ch, Manly, Robertson, Anderson & Nimmo-Smith, 1999). For example, in the 'Opposite Worlds Test', children see a stimulus sheet with a snaking pattern of digits, like a board game (1s and 2s semi-randomly presented). In the congruent condition (Sameworld) children read out the digit names as quickly as possible. In the incongruent condition (Oppositeworld), children read out the opposite name for each digit as quickly as possible. This task requires inhibition of prepotent 'correct' digit names and this is the dependent measure of interest. In the 'Walk Don't Walk Test', children move along a path made up of 14 squares by 'dotting' each square with a marker pen. The signal to make a move forward and place a dot in a square is an auditory tone. The signal to not make a move forward is an identical tone to start with, but one with a different ending. This requires the child to listen to the full tone to decide whether to go forward or not.

Inhibition is one of the simpler measures of executive functioning to assess, and many tasks suitable for developmentally young children are available in standardised test batteries or research papers.

Fluency

All measures of fluency ask participants to generate items around a particular theme or based on a set of arbitrary rules, to see the extent to which they can come up with a range of alternatives.

Many fluency tasks require individuals to generate words, for example, the Controlled Oral Word Association Test (COWAT), and these are referred to as measures of 'verbal' fluency. The Thurstone Word Fluency Test (Milner, 1964) is a similar measure, with participants being asked to generate as many words beginning with the letter 's' as they can in five minutes, and, subsequently, as many four-letter words beginning with 'c' in four minutes. Those with better verbal fluency will generate larger numbers of appropriate words (without repetitions). Another simpler version of this fluency task, often known as 'letter fluency', is to ask participants to generate as many words as they can in one minute starting with the following letters: 'F', 'A' and 'S'. For this reason it is often called the 'FAS' test.

For younger or less able children without established reading and writing skills, an even simpler task is 'category' fluency. Here, the examiner asks the child to generate as many names from one conceptual category, such as animals, as they can in one minute (see Box 2.9). Other examples of conceptual categories would be foods or boys' names. Those with weaker verbal fluency skills will tend to produce fewer correct responses, and possibly repeat some of their answers (perseveration).

Box 2.9   Example of a category fluency test

'Name as many different animals as you can without repeating yourself. You have one minute.'

Example response: 'cat, dog, sheep, goat, elephant, tiger, frog, fish, horse, etc ...'

There are also non-verbal measures of 'design' fluency. One example, developed to partner the Thurstone Word Fluency Test, is the Design Fluency Test (Jones-Gotman & Milner, 1977). Here, the participant must invent as many different 'nonsense' drawings as possible in five minutes. No scribbling is allowed, and nor can real objects be drawn. The instruction is then repeated, but this time the participant invents as many different FOUR LINE drawings as possible in four minutes. Those with poor executive processing produce very similar drawings over and over again (perveseration), or very few drawings. More child-friendly versions of the design fluency test are available in the

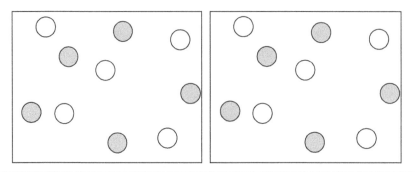

Figure 2.5   Example of two trials from a design fluency task. Instructions: *'Make different "four-line" drawings by connecting the empty dots with straight lines'*

Delis-Kaplan Executive Function System (Delis et al., 2001) or the NEPSY II (Korkman, Kirk & Kemp, 2007). Figure 2.5 illustrates the materials for a similar task based on these measures. The child must make different drawings on each trial, and new 'boxes' are presented after each drawing is completed.

Finally, measures of ideational fluency involve showing participants ambiguous nonsense drawings and asking them to generate ideas as to what they might depict (Pattern Meanings Test), or asking individuals to generate uses beyond the obvious for everyday objects such as a newspaper or a brick (Uses for Objects Test).

Dual task performance

This involves asking a participant to do two things at once, and looking at the 'cost' to performance of combining the two tasks (the participant must decide to focus attention on one task or switch attention between tasks). For example, participants can be asked to remember chess positions or judge the grammatical acceptability of sentences, whilst at the same time engaging in secondary tasks. In some studies, the secondary tasks are carefully chosen to engage particular components of working memory. Articulatory suppression could be used to occupy the phonological loop, or a task requiring the participant to tap two or more spatial positions in sequence, known as 'spatial tapping', could be used to occupy the visuospatial sketchpad. Dual task paradigms vary enormously, as there is virtually no limit to the types of tasks that can be combined. This type of methodology has been used successfully in developmentally young children, but care must always be taken to make sure that the tasks are well suited to ability levels.

A standardised dual task measure is available in the TEA-Ch. In the Sky Search Dual Task, children carry out a relatively realistic and interesting visual search task (searching for identical pairs of spacecraft on a large laminated sheet containing over 120 pairs of spacecraft, most of which are not identical pairs), while silently counting identical auditory tones over ten trials, and relaying the total counts on each trial. Scores reflect the decrement produced by carrying out the two tasks simultaneously, hence, this task measures dual task interference.

Random generation

This task is commonly used in the adult literature, but seldom used for children and those with developmental disorders, probably because it is rather difficult and requires the understanding of the concept 'randomness'. Tests of random generation require the participant to generate sequences of numbers or letters, but they are specifically instructed to ensure that the sequences are in a random order. Participants must avoid non-random sequences such as '123', '999', 'MSN' or 'SOS'. This task is more difficult than it looks as one must continually inhibit familiar patterns of numbers or letters, and monitor the output for signs of non-randomness.

Summary

There are many measures available to assess executive control, all of which may be relevant to the central executive component of working memory. This section has reviewed several areas of executive functioning and described commonly used measures. In particular, some measures assess what we have termed executive-loaded working memory (ELWM); and some assess 'other' aspects of executive control (switching, planning, inhibition, fluency, dual tasks, random generation). In subsequent chapters, these distinctions between ELWM and 'other' aspects of executive functioning will be maintained in our discussions of typical and atypical development, although please bear in mind that this is likely to be an oversimplification, as many tasks and areas may overlap.

The episodic buffer

There are no widely agreed upon methods of measuring the episodic buffer, but some literature is now developing. For example, one approach is to consider how we measure 'binding' of information in episodic memory. Episodic memory refers to the ability to remember a specific event and binding reflects the processes 'involved in establishing connections between items, within items, or between items and their contexts' (Lloyd, Doydum & Newcombe, 2009: p. 1321). This type of memory was not really addressed directly in the original version of the working memory model (Baddeley, 1986; Baddeley & Hitch, 1974), however, it is clearly a very important part of the memory system (see Chapter 5 in Baddeley, Eysenck & Anderson, 2009).

In his latest account of working memory, Baddeley (2007) considers the episodic buffer to be a link between working memory and information kept in long-term memory. He believes that the episodic buffer is of central importance in our experience of consciousness, binding information from different parts of the working memory system with long-term knowledge, to form our experience of the here and now. Measures of the episodic buffer, therefore, could be viewed as requiring an individual to integrate, store and retrieve information over a slightly longer timescale than would be appropriate for the slave subsystems, the phonological loop and the visuospatial sketchpad (merely one or two seconds).

For the purposes of this book, we will investigate the likely operation of the episodic buffer by looking at various binding tasks. These can require a participant to bind visuospatial information into a coherent unit or to bind verbal information such as connected prose into a coherent and meaningful episode (Baddeley, 2007).

We will look at tasks that require the binding of verbal information first. The key example is the recall of connected prose, which will inevitably draw upon long-term memory and language knowledge. Several relevant areas of knowledge are likely to be involved: vocabulary; grammar; understanding of the structure and meaning of typical narratives; and understanding the subject matter of the passage. Information held temporarily in the phonological loop will also be relevant in this task. Others have suggested that memory for sentences, similarly, requires episodic buffer resources, because recalling sentences draws on phonological loop resources plus links to grammatical, semantic and language knowledge (Alloway, Gathercole, Willis & Adams, 2004). In addition, learning associations between pairs of words (paired associate learning) requires the person to establish connections between the words, another example of binding. This task is likely to involve resources such as the phonological loop and a contribution from long-term semantic knowledge (Henry, 2010).

Although it is beyond the scope of this book to consider the attentional demands of various binding tasks, generating new links between items such as in paired associate learning tasks may be more attentionally demanding than recalling connected prose. Baddeley (2007) suggests that there may be distinctions between binding that takes place in a relatively automatic manner versus binding that requires more attentional (i.e. executive) resources. Box 2.10 gives two examples of possible binding tasks in the verbal domain.

Box 2.10   Examples of binding tasks in the verbal domain

Story recall. The participant hears a short story (usually a paragraph, the length and content will vary depending on age) and is asked to recall as much as they can from the story. Often a second delayed recall condition takes place an hour later. Note that information and knowledge from long-term memory and general knowledge about story structures can be used to help interpret and understand this story, all of which support memory.

Paired recall. The participant tries to learn associations between pairs of words such as:

---

dog – table

car – garage

swing – lamp

clock – time

Some words are already associated, others are not. The participant hears the full list of word pairs once, and then hears just the first word and attempts to remember the other one in the pair. This procedure is repeated, often about four times, to give the child a chance to learn all of the word pairs. Note that information from long-term memory can be used to support learning in this task, particularly for the words that are already associated.

These tasks require a person to continually utilise information from long-term memory and integrate it with representations that are active in working memory. Information that is active in working memory could be 'modality specific' material (most likely in the phonological loop); or 'modality free' information held in the episodic buffer itself, which has a small amount of storage capacity. The types of information from long-term memory that may be useful in verbal binding tasks could include:

- language knowledge (imagine how hard it would be trying to memorise either pairs of words or a short speech in an unfamiliar language)
- knowledge about similar events in the past (this helps us to interpret new events and place them in context)
- knowledge about existing links between certain items (for example that clock are used to tell the time)
- for some tasks, knowledge about how to construct a narrative (e.g. in describing an event or a story)

These are complex remembering tasks because they utilise many different processes. We are not yet in a position to break them down into component processes, based on a detailed model of the episodic buffer. Nor can we say that any particular task measures *just* the episodic buffer, as several components of working memory are likely to be recruited in carrying out these tasks. However, by using the overall proposed structure of the working memory model, we can at least begin to think of these tasks as assessing how well individuals access and use information from long-term memory together with active information in working memory.

Another point to emphasise is that, to date, psychologists have used many of these remembering tasks in contexts other than research on the working memory model. For example, many assessment batteries designed to measure memory functioning in clinical contexts include several examples of 'episodic' remembering tasks, as well as a variety of other short- and long-term memory measures (e.g. Test of Learning and Memory, TOMAL, Reynolds & Bigler, 1994). These varied tasks may be used to examine the functioning of different aspects of short- and long-term memory, related in many cases to particular types of brain damage. Psychologists have also been interested in memory for events in the context of looking at developmental differences in eyewitness recall and suggestibility (Lamb, La Rooy, Katz and Malloy, 2011). These approaches have not generally been brought together under the same theoretical umbrella, although all of them have much to contribute to our understanding of childhood memory development.

Another way of measuring the episodic buffer, which has been explored in some detail, is to use visuospatial binding tasks. These require the participant to combine two features into a whole segment of information. Figure 2.6 gives an example of a binding task that might be suitable for children (loosely based on Allen et al., 2006). The participant is shown a black and white line drawing of a shape, followed by a colour swatch and must combine these two features to produce the response.

Other researchers have looked at how well children can remember figures in backgrounds. Sluzenski, Newcombe and Kovacs (2006), for example, used relatively realistic photographs of animals and city surroundings. Children were presented with figures on their own, backgrounds on their own, or figures in backgrounds. The test of binding was to see how well children were able to remember the 'separate' information and the 'blended' information. We will come back to this study in Chapter 4.

In this book, we will consider some verbal and visuospatial binding tasks to try to understand how the proposed episodic buffer component of working memory operates in integrating information from different working memory systems and long-term memory to create coherent memories. However, please note that the use of these tasks is at an early stage of development, so conclusions in this area are necessarily speculative.

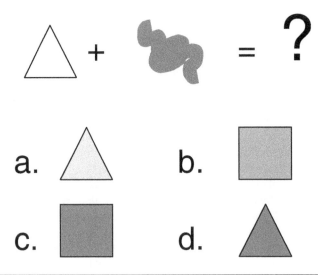

Figure 2.6 An example of a binding task requiring two features to be combined to arrive at a blended response

Summary
Psychologists have developed a few visuospatial and verbal 'binding' tasks that may measure the functioning of the episodic buffer. The important feature of these tasks is that they require information from different sources (e.g. long-term memory), modalities and/or working memory systems to be integrated into coherent memory representations.

Overall summary and 'aide memoire' to the working memory model

In this chapter, we have considered tasks that have been widely assumed to measure each of the four components of working memory (the phonological loop, the visuospatial sketchpad, the central executive and the episodic buffer), in children with and without developmental disorders. Hopefully, this will provide a useful resource to aid and deepen appreciation of the experimental research evidence, as it is much easier to understand and critically evaluate experiments when the tasks that have been used are clearly understood. Therefore, you may find it useful to refer back to this chapter when reading subsequent chapters on different populations of children, to remind yourself about the different types of working memory and executive functioning tasks that are discussed.

Before moving on to consider the development of working memory in typical children (Chapters 3 and 4), we finish this chapter with an 'aide memoire' to the working memory model and how working memory is measured in children. This brief summary can be referred back to at any point in the book for a quick reminder, if required.

Overview

The working memory model was developed to account for how we temporarily manipulate and store information during thinking and reasoning tasks. The revised version of this model (Baddeley, 2000) consists of four components, which are described below.

The phonological loop component of the working memory model is specialised for holding speech material for short periods of time (up to two seconds). Therefore, it is usually assessed by asking children to remember as many words or digits, in order, as they can manage immediately after hearing them. The type of memory supported by the phonological loop is usually called phonological short-term memory (PSTM).

The visuospatial sketchpad is the component of working memory specialised for holding visual, spatial and, possibly, kinaesthetic information for very short periods of time. It is usually assessed by asking children to remember a series of spatial positions in order, the location of several shaded squares in a grid/matrix, or the order of a series of nonsense pictures. The type of memory supported by the visuospatial sketchpad is usually known as visuospatial short-term memory (VSSTM).

The central executive component of the working memory model is responsible for the overall control of the working memory system. It focuses, divides and switches attention flexibly in order to carry out goals, make sense of current experience and allocate resources to competing cognitive demands. There are many ways to measure central executive resources and we have divided them into two main areas. First, memory tasks that have a central executive load, by requiring both processing and storage at the same time (executive-loaded working memory, ELWM). Secondly, 'other' measures of executive functioning that include inhibition, switching, planning and fluency (plus measures of dual task performance and random generation, where relevant).

The episodic buffer is the component of working memory responsible for binding or integrating information from the other components together into a coherent whole. It helps us to make sense of conscious experience by allowing long-term knowledge to be used in tandem with current experience. This produces understanding and memories of coherent 'episodes', facilitated by a limited amount of 'modality free' storage which allows the process of binding/integration to take place. Measuring the episodic buffer is somewhat complicated as there are few clearly agreed methods, but one way is to look at how well people can merge information from different sources or recall short stories.

Further reading

Measuring working memory and executive functioning

Alloway, T.P. & Gathercole, S.E. (2006). Short-term and working memory impairments in neurodevelopmental disorders: Diagnosis and remedial support. *Journal of Child Psychology and Psychiatry, 47*, 4–15. An excellent overview of working memory/ assessment in several developmental disorders.

Anderson, P. (2002). Assessment and development of executive function (EF) during childhood. *Child Neuropsychology, 8*, 71–82. A very useful and accessible paper.

Henry, L.A. & Bettenay, C. (2010). The assessment of executive functioning in children. *Child and Adolescent Mental Health, 15*(2), 110–119. A review of test batteries for measuring executive functioning in children of different ages.

Pickering, S.J. (2006a). Assessment of working memory in children. In S.J. Pickering (Ed.), *Working memory and education* (pp. 241–271). London: Elsevier Academic Press. A thorough review of The Working Memory Test Battery for Children.

Potential exam questions

1 Critically discuss at least SIX measures of phonological short-term memory and visuospatial short-term memory. What are their advantages and disadvantages for use with atypical populations?

2 How do we assess the functioning of the central executive and the episodic buffer in children with developmental disorders? Critically evaluate at least FIVE suitable measures.

3 Extended essay idea: 'How does working memory relate to children's academic achievement?'

3

Working Memory and Typical Development: Part 1

Learning outcomes

At the end of this chapter, you should have an understanding of the working memory account of memory development in typically developing children. You should understand that this model was designed to describe the mechanisms underlying the development of phonological short-term memory in particular (the phonological loop component of the working memory model). You should also have a critical understanding of seven key problems with this account; and the research that has led to important modifications to the model.

Introduction

Typically developing children do not have known developmental disorders (for example, autism, Down syndrome, or dyslexia) and are developing at broadly the rate we would expect (they have a 'typical' range of intellectual abilities, usually measured using an IQ test, i.e. standardised scores of 80+). Therefore, these are children with no general intellectual disabilities and no specific developmental disorders. We will be looking at different atypical populations in later chapters that vary in terms of whether they have intellectual disabilities and/or developmental disorders.

The working memory model has been used to explain the development of working memory in typically developing children, with a particular emphasis on the phonological loop component. This chapter will outline the key evidence in support of this position. We will go on to consider problems with the working memory account of typical development, discussing revised versions of the model where appropriate. If you need a reminder about any of the components of the working memory model, refer to Chapters 1 and 2 or look at the 'aide memoire to the working memory model' at the end of Chapter 2 for a summary.

The phonological loop – relations between speech rate and memory span

The proposed phonological loop component of working memory is a temporary store specialised for holding speech or speech-like materials for short periods of time. It supports a form of memory known as phonological short-term memory (PSTM). In the literature on memory development, this type of memory has often been described as 'memory span' and we will adopt this term in the following discussion to maintain consistency with the research papers. However, the term memory span almost always refers to the same skill as PSTM, when the materials to be remembered are verbal items such as words or digits.

In the early 1980s, researchers were interested in the issue of why memory span increased with age in children (see Dempster, 1981 and Henry & Millar, 1993 for reviews). There is no doubt that memory span for verbal materials does increase with age. For example, children can repeat back around three words in the correct order at age 5 years; four words by age 9 years; and five words by 11 years (Henry, 1991a; Hitch, Halliday, Dodd & Littler, 1989).

Memory span was regarded as an important ability, because it was closely related to a number of academic skills (e.g. vocabulary development, reading), as well as being related to general intellectual ability (IQ). Two broad hypotheses were proposed to account for the clear developmental improvements in memory span that occured with age: (1) basic capacity increased such that the mechanism responsible for storage simply became able to hold more information; and (2) some aspect of processing speed or efficiency that affected memory span improved with age, which meant that the same amount of capacity could be more efficiently utilised (e.g. Case et al., 1982; Dempster, 1981).

In this context, the suggestion emerged that developmental increases in articulation rate might be a key factor in accounting for developmental increases in memory span. This hypothesis was in the spirit of the processing speed hypothesis, but conflicted with most current interpretations, which argued that improvements in 'item identification time' accounted for improvements in memory span with age (Case et al., 1982; Dempster, 1981). As we shall see, the articulation rate hypothesis became central to the working memory account of 'typical' PSTM development.

However, first, we need to understand exactly what is meant by item identification time and articulation rate, and how they are both measured.

Item identification time is the speed at which a person can identify a stimulus item, often measured as the 'gap' between presentation and response in a simple naming task (the Experimenter says a word and the child must repeat it), as illustrated in Figure 3.1 below.

Articulation rate is the speed at which a person can repeat single words, pairs or triads of words over and over again, as illustrated in Figure 3.2. In adults (see Chapter 1), this is usually measured using 'reading rate', or how quickly a set of words can be read aloud, but reading rate would not be suitable for young, non-reading, children.

As discussed in Chapter 1, a key feature of the working memory account is the fact that when we remember speech material temporarily (i.e. in PSTM tasks), this is hypothesised to take place in a specialised speech storage

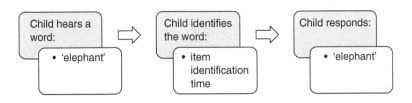

Figure 3.1   Illustration of 'item identification time', i.e. the time between presentation of a word and the child's response

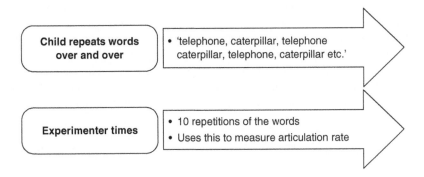

Figure 3.2   Illustration of how articulation rate is measured in children

mechanism called the phonological store. This store is assumed to decay rapidly, in fact, within a critical period of just two seconds. In order to keep information 'live', one uses verbal rehearsal to continually refresh the memory trace in the phonological store.

Baddeley et al. (1975) found evidence that memory span (the number of items, in this case words, that could be recalled in serial order) was closely related to reading rate in adults. Adults were able to recall as many words as they could read in about two seconds. Reading rate was assumed to reflect the speed at which internal verbal rehearsal of the words was carried out (reciting the list sequentially e.g. 'University, hippopotamus, periodical..., University, hippopotamus, periodical...' etc.). Additionally: (1) those adults with faster reading rates had higher memory spans; (2) long words were harder to recall than short words because they took longer to rehearse; and (3) spans were higher in languages with faster articulation rates (e.g. Ellis & Hennelly, 1980).

The proposition that reading rate is closely related to memory span was later applied to the development of memory span in children. The basic argument was that children have slower reading/articulation rates than adults, so they rehearse more slowly. With age, increases in reading/articulation rates allowed faster rehearsal rates and, hence, higher memory spans (Baddeley, 1986; Halliday & Hitch, 1988; Hitch & Halliday, 1983). This remarkably simple explanation for the development in memory span (i.e. PSTM) with age received a considerable amount of support as we will see in the next section.

Evidence supporting the working memory position

Nicolson (1981) followed up the work by Baddeley et al. (1975) in a sample of children, looking to see whether memory span would be related to reading rate. He examined three groups of ten children who were 8, 10 and 12 years old, using the 1, 2, 3 and 4 syllable words from the original Baddeley et al. study (the most difficult 5-syllable words were omitted). Measures of memory span and reading rate were obtained for each word type at each age level.

Nicolson (1981) reported a number of interesting results. Firstly, all groups showed word length effects, providing initial evidence that all three age groups were using verbal rehearsal which, of course, is a necessary starting point for the articulation rate hypothesis (for details see Chapter 1). Secondly, all groups showed faster reading rates for shorter words, again, providing evidence in favour of the articulation rate hypothesis. Finally, Nicolson (1981) went on to look for relationships between articulation rate and memory span in each age group, and these were all significant. In fact, when he plotted each age group's memory span scores for words of each length (1–4 syllables) against their mean reading rates for words of each length (along with the adult results from Baddeley et al., 1975), one linear function described all of the data. This is illustrated in Figure 3.3. Each data point represents one word

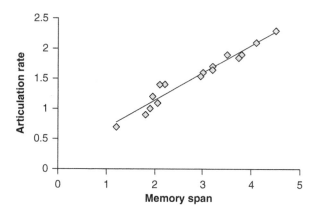

Figure 3.3 Mean articulation rates (words per second) plotted against mean memory spans for words of four lengths (one to four syllables) at four age levels (8, 10, 12, Adult)

Source: data adapted from Nicolson (1981)

type (e.g. one, two, three and four syllable words) for one age group (8, 10, 12, adult). Hence, there are four word types for four age groups, giving 16 data points plotting articulation rate against memory span.

This evidence supported the articulation rate hypothesis and implied that developmental changes in memory span were entirely accounted for by increases in reading rate (hence faster rehearsal rates). For every increase in articulation rate, there was a corresponding increase in memory span, and this was true across a wide age range. Nicolson (1981) believed that reading rate was an index of 'processing speed' and concluded that developmental increases in processing speed caused developmental increases in memory span.

There were, however, some difficulties with this study. The words taken directly from Baddeley's original work with adults were not very familiar to children. Secondly, the measure of reading rate required children to read these unfamiliar words, which may have been a disadvantage for younger children with weaker reading skills. Finally, the youngest children in the study were 8 years old and it would have been instructive to have data for somewhat younger children to test the generalisability of the model.

Therefore, Hulme, Thomson, Muir and Lawrence (1984) carried out a similar study with 4-, 7- and 10-year-olds, as well as adults (n = 9 in each group), using sets of more familiar words that varied in spoken duration (words of one, two and three/four syllables such as 'egg', 'tractor' and 'kangaroo'). In this case, the measures of 'processing speed' were the rates at which children could repeat pairs of words of each syllable length continuously as fast as possible. These measures of articulation rate removed the requirement for reading.

Hulme et al. (1984) replicated Nicolson's (1981) findings. Articulation rate increased with age and was highest for words with fewest syllables. Similarly, memory span increased with age and was, again, highest for words with fewest syllables. When articulation rates were plotted against memory span scores for all age groups, one linear function described the data (see Figure 3.4). The slope of the function relating recall to articulation rate did not change with age (it was 1.5 seconds on average). In other words, individuals from the age of four to adulthood recalled as much as they could articulate in about 1.5 seconds.

These results were interpreted as support for the working memory model account that developmental increases in articulation rate were responsible for developmental increases in memory span (i.e. PSTM). Several other studies replicated these findings (for example, Henry, 1994; Hitch, Halliday, Dodd & Littler, 1989; Hitch, Halliday & Littler, 1989, 1993; Hulme & Tordoff, 1989; Standing & Curtis, 1989), so they did appear to be robust. Interestingly, Hitch, Halliday and Littler (1989) and Hitch et al. (1993) failed to find similar relationships between identification time and memory span, arguing that this provided further evidence in support of the working memory position and against alternative views that identification time was a key factor in the development in memory span (Dempster, 1981). However, Hitch, Halliday and Littler (1989) did suggest that there may be a role for item identification time in the absence of rehearsal (see Further reading).

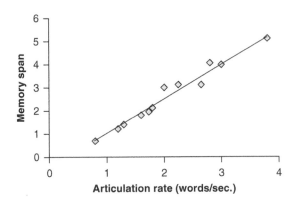

Figure 3.4   Mean articulation rates (words per second) plotted against mean memory spans for words of three lengths (one, two, three/four syllables) at four age levels (4, 7, 10, Adult)

Source: data adapted from Hulme et al. (1984)

Summary
The working memory account of the development of phonological short-term memory (PSTM) in typical children is very straightforward. Developmental improvements in articulation rate are responsible for developmental increases in PSTM.

Problems with the working memory account of typical development

Despite the simplicity and elegance of the 'articulation rate' account of the development of PSTM, there remain several problematic issues. The remainder of this chapter looks at each of these in turn. In some cases, revised explanations were arrived at by considering the intersections between adult and developmental data; in other cases, the developmental data proved somewhat more problematic for the working memory model. Again, please note that the term 'memory span' is used in the following discussion (instead of 'PSTM') as this is the term used most commonly in the literature.

Issue 1: Correlational evidence

If we look at Figures 3.3 and 3.4, for any particular age group, the average memory span is closely related to the average articulation rate. However, some authors began to wonder about similar data at the level of individual children. In other words, was each individual child's memory span related to their articulation rate? If a strong version of the working memory hypothesis is correct, we should find correlations between articulation rate and memory span at the level of individuals, as well as at the level of group averages for different age levels. Box 3.1 gives brief details on how to interpret correlations.

Box 3.1 How do I interpret correlations?

Correlations measure links or relationships between two variables. They can range from perfectly positive (i.e. +1: positive changes in one factor are perfectly mirrored by positive changes in a second factor); to zero (changes in one factor are not the slightest bit related to changes in a second factor); to perfectly negative (i.e. −1: positive changes in one factor are perfectly mirrored by negative changes in a second factor).

Kail (1992a) examined the relationship between articulation rate (measured by asking participants to repeat sets of three words as quickly as possible) and memory span (for both digits and letters) in samples of 9-year-olds and young adults (n = 24 in each group). The correlations at the individual level between articulation rate and memory span ranged from moderate (letter span: r = .36; digit span r = .37), to large (using a composite measure of memory span combining letter and digit span: r = .69). Therefore, Kail (1992a) proposed a framework that was consistent with the working memory model, incorporating the following three key features: (1) processing time generally speeds up with development; (2) this increase in general speed leads to faster articulation rates; and (3) faster articulation rates lead to higher memory spans.

However, Kail (1992a) was careful to point out that one important limiting condition of his study was that only a very small range of ages had been included (9-year-olds and adults). Another potential problem was that memory span was assessed for digits and letters, whereas articulation rate was assessed by measuring speeded repetition for words. It could be argued that both memory span and articulation rate should be assessed for the same materials in order to obtain reliable results.

Kail and Park (1994) remedied both of these issues by including larger samples of 8-, 11-, 13- and 20-year-olds (n = 72 at each age level), and by measuring articulation rate for digits and letters. In all other respects the study was the same. Kail and Park (1994) found correlations between articulation rate and memory span that were modest: letter span, r = .32; and digit span, r = .32. Therefore, not all of the variation in memory span could be explained by articulation rate – if this were the case, the correlations would have been close to 1. Kail and Park (1994) speculated that knowledge of the memory items and efficiency of strategy use could also be relevant factors in the development of memory span with age.

Overall, Kail's position supports the working memory model in emphasising the link between articulation rate and memory span across a wide range of ages and by ascribing to articulation rate a major role in the development of memory span. However, one drawback with this work was that the correlations between articulation rate and memory span were not presented for each age group separately. This makes it difficult to assess whether these relationships were equally strong for children of different ages and, indeed, adults. It is possible that the working memory account may be more relevant for older children and adults. Why? Adults and older children might make more use of *verbal rehearsal* than younger children, who may not even use this strategy (an issue explored in a later section).

Therefore, Henry (1994, Experiment 2) examined relationships between articulation rate and memory span in children of 5, 7 and 10 years (n = 20 per group), focusing on individual level correlations for each age group. Articulation rates and memory spans were measured for four different types of words that varied in terms of length and frequency. When the data were plotted in the same manner as Figures 3.3 and 3.4, using group means for articulation rate and memory span within each age level and for each word type, a very similar result was found. There was a linear relationship between articulation rate and memory span; and the correlation between the group means for these variables was high (r = .83).

When overall correlations between articulation rate and memory span were calculated at the individual level (for the 60 participants), they were somewhat lower (r = .60). However, Henry (1994) noted high correlations between age and articulation rate and between age and memory span (r's = .70/.76 respectively). She, therefore, suggested that correlations between articulation rate and memory span in mixed age groups might largely be accounted for by age. In other words, because children become better at speaking rapidly with age and their memory spans increase with age, we obtain relationships between articulation rate and memory span that could be caused by changes that relate to virtually any cognitive or information processing mechanism that becomes more efficient with increasing age and development. This is the essential problem with correlations; a correlation between two variables does not rule out the fact that a third variable could be the relevant causal factor.

One way of controlling for the effects of age in correlations between articulation rate and memory span is to use a partial correlation. In this procedure, the effects of age are removed statistically from the correlation, and the remaining relationship is examined. When the effects of age were partialled out, Henry (1994) reported that the relationship between articulation rate and memory span was no longer significant (r = .15). Similarly, when the relationships between articulation rate and memory span were looked at for individuals in each age group separately (another method that minimises the effects of age on the relationship, by looking at only one age group at a time), none of these correlations reached significance (see Table 3.1).

These results were broadly replicated by Ferguson, Bowey and Tilley (2002) using considerably larger samples (n = 39–58 per group). The correlations between articulation rate and memory span within each age level were very similar to previous studies (.28, .03, .41, .21 respectively for 5-, 7-, 9- and 10/11-year-old children. (Note that one correlation was significant – .41). Furthermore, Gathercole, Adams and Hitch (1994) examined this issue in 4-year-olds. In one study, 71 participants were included, and no significant correlation between digit span and articulation rate (r = .19) was found. In a second study, 40 of these children were tested again, and there was no relationship between articulation

Table 3.1 Correlations between articulation rate and memory span for 5-, 7- and 10-year-old children

Age	5 years	7 years	10 years
Correlation	.18	.24	.21

Source: data adapted from Henry (1994)

rate and memory span for words (r = -.09) or digits (r = .04). Nevertheless, this relationship was significant in a sample of adults (r's = .43 and .45 for digits and words respectively), implying that relationships between articulation rate and memory span are found for adults but not young children. Finally, Gathercole and Adams (1993) found no correlation between articulation rate and memory span in very young children (2/3-year-olds).

Overall, the findings imply that a very strong version of the working memory model that assumes articulation rate to be the only driving force behind developmental improvements in memory span is not supported.

Ferguson et al. (2002) have summarised the key findings: (1) when we use group means for memory span and articulation rate at a range of age levels, strong associations between the two variables are found; (2) using individual data points, correlations between articulation rate and memory span are found when different age groups are combined; and (3) associations between articulation rate and memory span within particular age groups are inconsistent (Cowan, 1999; Jarrold, Baddeley &,Hewes, 2000) or non-significant, particularly for very young children (Gathercole & Adams, 1993, Gathercole, Adams & Hitch, 1994). In order for a strong version of the working memory account of memory span development in children to be supported, evidence for high correlations at the individual level at all age levels should be found.

Although such high correlations are certainly not found with any reliability, it is important to note that the relationships are often positive and in some cases significant. It is still feasible, therefore, that articulation rate plays some role in the development of memory span; just that it may not be as large a role as originally speculated.

In fact, Kail proposes a slightly revised articulation rate hypothesis. We have already seen his argument that general improvements in processing speed lead to increased speed and efficiency of articulation rate, which, in turn, improves memory span. Kail (1997) replicated and extended these findings in a further sample of 6- to 10-year-olds (correlations between articulation rate and memory span ranged from .39 to .48), but brought in an additional factor, that of phonological skill, arguing that this was important in addition to articulation rate. The logic was that being fast at accessing phonological representations of items in long-term memory is helpful during recall if the memory trace has begun to decay. Many have suggested that it might be possible to guess or reconstruct the correct word, based on some remaining phonological features of the memory trace. This guessing process is easier and more efficient if accessing relevant long-term information proceeds rapidly. Figure 3.5 illustrates the relationships between these various variables. We will return to the issue of guessing in a later section (Issue 4).

Kail (1997) also pointed out that simple measures of speeded articulation rate for groups of words involve several relevant skills (e.g. time to initiate a response, time to articulate each item, time to identify the next item, etc. – derived from detailed work by Nelson Cowan and colleagues). Therefore, it might be worth breaking down articulation rate into some finer grained

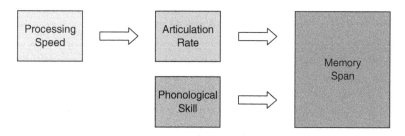

Figure 3.5 Possible relationships between processing rate, articulation rate, phonological skill and memory span

Source: based on Kail (1997)

measures in order to probe potential relationships in greater detail. We will address this point in a later section (Issue 7).

Finally, it is worth considering a detailed test of Kail's (1997) model that was carried out by Ferguson and Bowey (2005) on large samples of children between 5 and 13 years of age. Measures of memory span, processing speed, articulation rate, and phonological skill (this was assessed using two types of measures, phonological sensitivity and vocabulary knowledge, and described as 'availability of long-term phonological representations') were collected for 220 children.

Using structural equation modelling, these authors found results that broadly supported the key proposals of Kail's (1997) model. In particular, Ferguson and Bowey (2005) noted that measures of processing speed directly contributed to: (1) the 'availability of long-term phonological representations' (phonological sensitivity and vocabulary); and (2) articulation rates. In turn, long-term memory representations and articulation rates both contributed independently to memory span. However, Ferguson and Bowey (2005) argued that the link between articulation rate and memory span was very weak, whereas the link between long-term representations and memory span was strong and significant. These authors argued that articulation rate was only weakly related to memory span (here the simple correlation was .44), offering little strong support for the working memory position. Although these findings supported Kail's (1997) position, it is important to note that the structural equation model accounted for only 34% of the total variance in memory span, so other 'unknown' variables that were not tested and included in the model must also be important.

Summary

A very strong version of the working memory account of PSTM development in typical children is not supported. We cannot assume that articulation rate is the only relevant factor responsible for improvements in PSTM with age. Articulation rate may, however, play some role in the development of memory span; although there are authors who have suggested that its contribution may be, at best, minor.

Issue 2: Causality

As we have seen, the articulation rate model was based on evidence in the form of correlations – i.e. relationships shown between two variables. Such data cannot prove that faster articulation rates cause higher memory spans, because correlations cannot prove causality. In the previous section, we noted the essential problem with correlations, which was that some additional factor could cause the increase in both skills. Some researchers, therefore, have attempted to assess whether or not there is a *causal* link between articulation rate and memory span. We will discuss two such studies.

Hulme and Muir (1985) hypothesised that one test of whether higher articulation rates cause higher memory spans, would be to train children to speak more quickly, then look to see if this increased their memory spans. Hulme and Muir (1985) tried to increase articulation rates for three sets of 'to be remembered words' (six short words such as 'egg' and 'pig'; six medium words such as 'monkey' and 'tractor'; and six long words such as 'elephant' and 'helicopter') in a sample of 12 7-year-olds. These children were compared to one comparison group (n = 12) with no exposure to the words, and another comparison group (n = 12) with equal exposure to the words, but no requirement for speaking quickly.

Three sessions of training aimed to teach children to say groups of three words as quickly as possible, using a fun computer game format. Children with equal exposure to the words simply named the words with no emphasis on speed. Unfortunately, the articulation rate training produced only small improvements in speech rate that were no larger than those seen for the 'equal exposure' group, even when the experimenters markedly increased (tripled) the amount of training given. Similarly small improvements in memory span emerged as a result of articulation rate training, but, again, there were no group differences. Therefore, the results were not able to answer the causality question posed by the experimenters, because it was not easy to separate articulation rate training from simple increases in familiarity with the words that resulted from the 'equal exposure' condition. Both of these factors may contribute to improvements in memory span.

Henry and Millar (1991) also attempted to determine whether articulation rate directly affected memory span. They gave groups of children, aged 5 and 7 years (n = 12 in each group), words to recall for which they had the same speaking rate. This necessitated measuring articulation rate for a relatively large pool of words and choosing words for the memory span tasks such that younger and older children did not differ in the speed at which they could say them. Some of the words were familiar, high-frequency items (e.g. one-syllable: bed, girl, house, ball; and three/four syllable: hospital, policeman, bicycle, elephant). Some of the words were unfamiliar, low-frequency items (e.g. one syllable: bait, plough, cane, dock; and three/four syllable: audience, dictionary, artichoke, dowager).

If the articulation rate hypothesis is correct, matching children of different ages on their articulation rates should result in their memory spans being matched too. This matching was done separately for the one- and three-syllable words; and also for the high- and low-frequency words. The matching process was repeated in two separate experiments, one in which the measure of articulation rate was based on one repetition of each word, and another in which the measure of articulation rate was based on three repetitions of each word.

Henry and Millar (1991) found results that were partially in support of the articulation rate hypothesis, as illustrated in Figure 3.6. Once articulation rates were matched between the age groups, the usual age difference in memory span reduced to non-significance (look at the third set of columns, marked 'High: 3'). However, there were two important qualifications to this result. First, the matching only succeeded in equating memory span between the two ages when it was done for high-frequency words. Memory spans for the low-frequency words, even when matched for articulation rate, still differed between the two age groups. Secondly, the matching only succeeded when the measure of articulation rate used derived from repeating groups of words (i.e. repeating a word three times over) rather than individual words (i.e. repeating a word once). When articulation rates were matched based on speed of repeating individual words, significant age differences in memory span remained (see first two sets of columns marked 'High: 1' and Low: 1'). Finally, it is important to note that the size of the change after matching, although significant, was not particularly large.

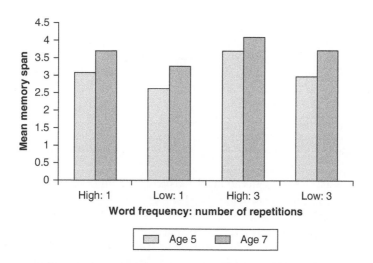

Figure 3.6   Mean memory spans for children of 5 and 7 years. High = 'high-frequency words'; low = 'low-frequency words'; 1 = articulation rate based on one repetition of the word; 3 = articulation rate based on three repetitions of the word

Source: data adapted from Henry and Millar (1991)

Therefore, in some circumstances, matching older and younger children for articulation rate did match their memory spans – implying that there was some explanatory power to the working memory account, that articulation rate was causally related to memory span.

There were two other implications of these results, however: (1) how articulation rate was measured seemed to have important implications for its relationship with memory span; and (2) there were differences in the relationship between articulation rate and memory span depending upon whether words were high- or low-frequency. We will take up these points in the next two sections below (Issues 3 and 4).

Summary

Causal tests of the working memory account of PSTM (memory span) development in typical children have been partially successful in providing supporting evidence. In some circumstances, articulation rate may account for developmental improvements in memory span, but it does not represent a complete explanation. Other factors must be relevant to the development of PSTM in addition to articulation rate.

Issue 3: How to measure articulation rate?

We have seen different results in the previous study, depending upon how articulation rates were measured, i.e. repeating groups of words or single words. The differences between repeating individual words and repeating groups of words may reflect the contributions of speech planning and execution time during the repetition of sequences. Saying a series of items could involve more processes than simply saying individual words. In fact, Sternberg, Monsell, Knoll & Wright (1978) reported that articulation times for longer sequences were longer than the sum of the individual word times, and that this discrepancy became even larger as the list lengths were increased.

This finding implies that articulation rates for groups of words may differ in terms of supporting mechanisms from articulation rates for individual words. Subsequent research has supported this conclusion and we will shortly consider several relevant studies. First, however, look at Figure 3.7, which illustrates two methods of measuring articulation rates. In one case, we measure articulation rate for single words, and in the other case we measure articulation rate for groups of three words.

Henry (1994) suggested that measuring articulation rates by asking children to repeat groups of two or three words runs the risk of exceeding comfortable memory span levels for younger children. For example, the average memory span for 5-year-olds is about three words, which means that rapid repetition of a three-item list would represent a full span load. Even a two-item list represents a significant memory load for a substantial number of younger children. Hence, articulation rate measures based on repetitions of pairs or triads of words might confound articulation rate with memory span,

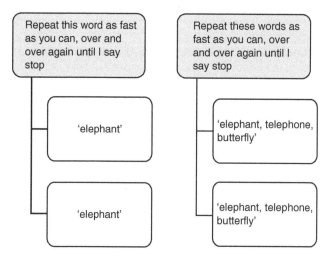

Figure 3.7 Measuring articulation rates from single words and word triads

because carrying out the articulation rate repetition task requires the words to be remembered.

Henry (1994, Experiment 1) found evidence to support this view. Significant correlations between articulation rate and memory span were present when articulation rate was measured using repetitions of pairs or triads; but not when articulation rate was measured using individual words (see also Cowan, Wood, Wood, Keller, Nugent & Keller, 1998). This finding implied that relationships between articulation rate and memory span could be based on a memory component shared by both tasks.

Ferguson et al. (2002) took this argument a stage further. We have already mentioned (see above) that these authors tested articulation rate and memory span in relatively large samples of 5-, 7-, 9- and 10/11-year-olds. Although not all participants were administered every measure, full data were available for 7- and 9-year-olds and we will consider these findings. Ferguson et al. (2002) included long and short words that were either familiar or unfamiliar (the word sets were very similar to those used by Henry and Millar, 1991, described above) as well as digits. Children either repeated individual items over and over again (single words) or they repeated groups of three words.

The first question concerned how these variables would be related to each other. One way of answering this question is to use 'factor analysis' to see which measures of articulation rate and memory span form coherent subsets (the technique is based on how well different measures correlate with each other and the analysis produces groups of related variables that can be interpreted as 'factors').

We might expect that if it does not matter how we measure articulation rate (single words or groups of words), all of the measures should be equally related to each other and form one factor. Conversely, if articulation rate for single items requires different mechanisms than articulation rate for groups of items, we would expect measures of articulation rate for single items to group together; with measures of articulation rate for groups of words forming a separate factor. We might also expect all of the memory span variables to group together in a further separate factor. Table 3.2 illustrates the data for 7- and 9-year-olds, showing which measures loaded on each of the three independent factors they found.

Factor 1 in Table 3.2 represented articulation rate for triads of words, but, importantly, it also represented articulation rate for single long words. Why were single long words included in this factor? The authors suggested that repeating more than one syllable over and over again was important; it did not matter whether these syllables were from the same word or from different words. Therefore, this was a factor reflecting articulation rate for multi-syllables. Factor 2 represented the memory span variables, so can best be interpreted as a PSTM memory factor. Factor 3 represented articulation rate for single one-syllable words, so can be interpreted as articulation rate for single syllables.

The important result was that there were two independent factors representing articulation rate, one for multi-syllables and another for single syllables. Therefore, it does seem to matter how we measure articulation rate. Measures for multi-syllable items and single syllable items represent different constructs.

Ferguson et al. (2002) made two further arguments: (1) articulation rate for single-syllable items explained a significant 4% of the variation in memory span, which means that articulation rate plays a small role in the development

Table 3.2 Factor groupings for memory span and articulation rate variables in children of 7 and 9 years. SR3 = articulation rate for triads; SR1 = articulation rate for single words; MS = memory span

Measure	Factor 1	Factor 2	Factor 3
SR3 digits	Yes		
SR3 common short words	Yes		
SR3 common long words	Yes		
SR3 uncommon short words	Yes		
SR1 common long words	Yes		
SR1 uncommon long words	Yes		
MS digits		Yes	
MS common short words		Yes	
MS uncommon short words		Yes	
MS common long words		Yes	
MS uncommon long words		Yes	
SR1 digits			Yes
SR1 common short words			Yes
SR1 uncommon short words			Yes

Source: data adapted from Ferguson et al. (2002)

of memory span; and (2) articulation rate measures based on repeating multi-syllable items were contaminated by memory load, particularly for younger children. This means that when we measure articulation rate using multi-syllable words, our measure is partially a reflection of the child's memory span and partially a reflection of the child's articulation rate.

Summary

How we measure articulation rate is very important. In particular, single-syllable measures are more appropriate, because they do not confound a child's memory span with their articulation rate. Articulation rates measured using single syllables account for a small amount of variation in memory span, giving partial support to the working memory account of the development of PSTM in typical children.

We now move on to consider other factors that may be relevant to the development of PSTM in typical children.

Issue 4: The role of long-term knowledge

The role of long-term memory and existing knowledge in the development of PSTM had been put to one side in the working memory account. Nevertheless, research with children and adults had recognised the role of long-term knowledge in remembering. For example, Watkins (1977) pointed out that memory span for common words was higher in adults (5.82) than span for uncommon words (4.24). He noted that this indicated PSTM must be more complex than was believed at the time. As we have seen, Henry and Millar (1991) argued that the familiarity of items to be recalled was an important factor in the development of memory span. Other authors concluded that there was a need to incorporate a role for long-term or semantic/lexical knowledge (see also Chi (1978) for related work). In other words, stored knowledge of the meaning and phonology of words was relevant to any explanation of the development in memory span. However, what might be a convincing theoretical mechanism behind these effects?

The general argument is that when we are asked to recall lists of words in PSTM studies, we use speech perception and production skills to support our storage and recall of the information. Recognising and repeating high-frequency words is much easier than recognising and repeating low frequency words or nonwords. This is because familiar items have more detailed and easily accessible phonological representations – stored knowledge about what the word sounds like – and semantic representations – stored knowledge about what the word means. How does this impact on PSTM?

Think about what is required in recalling an auditory list of words. The participant hears the list, which is then registered automatically in the phonological store (see Chapter 1). The phonological store is assumed to hold information about the phonological forms of each word, yet has limited capacity and decays within two seconds. In attempting to recall longer lists of items, participants are most likely faced with partially decayed traces of phonological forms for at least some items in the list. This is where existing knowledge of the phonological forms of words comes in useful. Partially decayed memory traces can be reconstructed from incomplete information. In other words, the participant guesses the correct word based on their knowledge of known word forms (e.g. 'neighbours' that sound similar to the actual word) and the remaining information left in the phonological store. This process is known as 'redintegration' and is argued to represent the mechanism by which long-term knowledge has an impact on PSTM.

Figure 3.8 gives an example of how redintegration might work for a highly familiar word. This is followed by a further example indicating how this process does not generally apply to unfamiliar or nonwords. Hence, redintegration will be of use only for known items (although see later in this section for an alternative view).

We will now look at some key findings concerning long-term knowledge effects on memory span in adults and children.

Long-term knowledge: Adults

We first consider evidence in favour of the concept of redintegration, by looking at studies with adult participants. Hulme et al. (1991) examined memory span for words compared to nonwords with 12 participants. They included short, medium and long words and nonwords, but were careful to match the articulation rates between the words and nonwords. This was done in several ways. First, they used short words that were unfamiliar and included consonant blends such as 'st' or 'scr', which made them longer to articulate (stoat, mumps, scroll, zinc); as opposed to using very simple nonwords (fot, zog, pid). Secondly, medium length words of three syllables (gorilla, botany, calcium) were included, as opposed to medium length nonwords of just two syllables (taffost, giffol). Finally, long words of five syllables (physiology, refrigerator) were included, as opposed to long nonwords of just three syllables (tushebon, arellum).

Having successfully matched the two types of items for articulation rate, one would expect that memory span should also be matched, if articulation rate were the only relevant factor. However, Hulme et al. (1991) found that nonwords were still more poorly recalled than words, clearly indicating that whether the items were words or nonwords made a big difference to how well they could be remembered. Hulme et al. (1991) also found that there were orderly relationships between articulation rate and memory span for words and nonwords, but that these were slightly different; words had an inbuilt advantage, which could not be attributed to articulation rate.

This advantage reflects the fact that known words have long-term memory representations (i.e. what they sound like – phonological forms) that make recall more straightforward. It is, therefore, possible to generate the correct response from a degraded memory trace using redintegration.

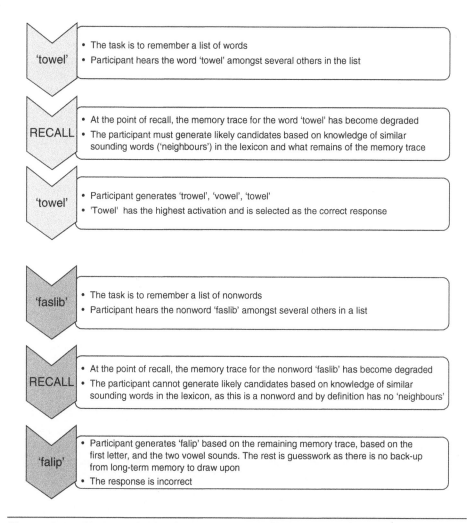

Figure 3.8 Diagram illustrating how redintegration may operate for a known word. The second example illustrates how redintegration fails to contribute during recall for a nonword

Hulme et al. (1991) also argued that teaching participants English translations for previously unfamiliar words (e.g. Italian words), should improve memory span. Therefore, in a second study with nine English young people (unfortunately, they did not report whether any could speak Italian), they measured memory span for three lists of Italian words. Following this, participants were asked to spend ten minutes per day, for three days, learning the English translations and correct pronunciations for the words (24 words in total, e.g. LAGO – lake; PRETE – priest; STELLA – star). On the fourth day, span was measured again for the Italian words. Another nine participants carried out the same experiment, but using English words and learning their Italian translations, as a control condition.

Hulme et al. (1991) reported significant increases in memory span for Italian words in the first group of participants; but no change in memory span for English words in the second group. These results reinforced the view that learning new long-term memory representations for the previously unfamiliar Italian words helped support recall in the PSTM task.

However, in teaching English translations, both semantic and phonological information was gained: i.e. the meanings of the words as well as the sound characteristics of the words. Hulme, Roodenrys, Brown and Mercer (1995) went on to provide another causal test of their hypothesis. Their argument was that if participants were familiarised with the sounds only of nonwords prior to a memory span test, this should also increase recall. The logic was that the familiarisation process would start to develop representations of the phonological forms of nonwords (i.e. start to build up long-term memory representations), even without information about meaning.

To achieve this, participants read three pools of nonwords aloud (short words, 'gug'; medium words, 'crepog'; and long words, 'gossikos'), to gradually get to know their precise phonological forms. They did not learn anything about meaning as they had done in the previous study using Italian words. The question was, would this familiarisation procedure with 'sounds only' have an impact on memory span? In line with predictions, Hulme et al. (1995) found that memory span for all types of familiarised nonwords showed improvements. Figure 3.9 illustrates these results.

This study demonstrated that knowledge of the sound forms of nonwords was enough to improve recall in a memory span task, without any need to learn the meaning of the item. This does not rule out a positive contribution from semantic long-term memory as well (i.e. a 'meaning' contribution), but illustrates that phonological knowledge is enough on its own to improve PSTM.

Hulme, Roodenrys, Schweickert, Brown, Martin and Stuart (1997) looked again at this issue using high- and low-frequency words, arguing that word frequency should affect recall in a similar manner. Their premise was that, although there might be some stored knowledge of phonological forms (and semantic information) for low-frequency words, this should be less elaborate and less easily accessible than similar information for high-frequency words. Therefore, one would expect memory span to be higher for high- than low-frequency words, and that these differences would not be accounted for by differences in articulation rate.

Hulme et al. (1997) carried out this experiment with 18 adults, measuring memory span and articulation rate for six separate lists: short, medium and long high- (e.g. game, religion, professional), and low-frequency words (e.g. truce, bequest, contamination). The results were exactly as predicted. High-frequency words were better recalled than low-frequency words. However, it was possible that these differences could be accounted for by differences

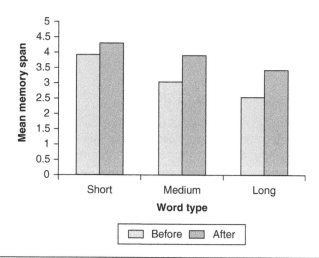

Figure 3.9 Differences between memory span for nonwords *before* a familiarisation procedure versus *after* familiarisation

Source: data adapted from Hulme et al. (1995)

in articulation rate between these two types of words, given that articulation rates (and, hence, rehearsal rates) were significantly slower for low-frequency words. Therefore, Hulme et al. (1997) used a statistical technique to remove the effects of articulation rate from their analysis (using articulation rate as a 'covariate' in an analysis of covariance). Articulation rate did exert a significant influence on memory span, but when this influence had been removed statistically, memory spans for high-frequency words were still higher than memory spans for low frequency words.

Hulme et al. (1997) concluded that at least two independent factors were important in explaining memory span: one related to articulation rate; and the other related to long-term memory representations of the sound characteristics (phonological forms) of words. Hulme et al. (1997) argued that we use the long-term representations to help generate items when their phonological memory traces have begun to decay:

> ...automatic pattern completion processes operate to clean up decayed traces, possibly as a by-product of the mechanisms that exist for the perception and production of speech. (p. 1220)

They went on to refer to Schweickert's (1993) proposed model of this 'red-integration' process. Schweikert suggested that some items will be recalled staightforwardly from the phonological memory trace; whereas for other items, the memory trace will have decayed. Whether a participant can recall item/s from these decayed memory traces will depend on whether long-term memory representations are available of the phonological forms of these words. In this way, knowledge of the language, and in particular the sounds of known words, supports PSTM.

Long-term knowledge: Children

We have looked in some detail at these important papers on redintegration and long-term memory effects on memory span, because they have been critical in shaping theory in this area. There are, however, some developmental findings that suggest redintegration processes are also used by children.

Turner, Henry and Smith (2000) examined the influence of item familiarity on memory span in adults and children of ages 5, 7 and 10 years (n = 32 children in each group and 36 adults). They asked half of the participants to recall words (familiar items) and the other half to recall nonwords (unfamiliar items). For everyone, a 'probed recall' method was used. This involved presenting lists of heard words/nonwords via a computer, with a simultaneous visual representation of one empty box per word on the computer screen (see Figure 3.10). Children's recall was then probed for one item in each list. They were either asked to recall the name of one of the items (which was signalled at the end of the list by the relevant box flashing on the computer screen); or to indicate the correct serial position of the items (one list item was repeated after the list had been presented and the empty boxes re-appeared). In this way, item recall and position recall were tested separately.

Turner et al. (2000) found different effects of familiarity on item versus position recall. The effects on item recall depended on age: there were no effects in the 5-year-olds, but there were significant effects in the older children and adults. By contrast, no effect of familiarity was found at any age when recall of position was required.

Turner et al. (2000) argued that when precise phonological information was required (e.g. for item recall a participant must produce the name of the word or nonword), familiarity effects were found in older children and adults, because redintegration could be used strategically to support recall for known words. By contrast, redintegration could not be used for nonwords, because there are no lexical/semantic representations for nonwords. However, when position recall was required, there was no need to produce a detailed phonological specification for the word or nonword, it was necessary only to remember where that particular item had been located. In other words, redintegration was not needed, because the name of the item did not need to be generated. Turner et al. (2000) concluded that: (1) redintegration was used when the phonological specifications for items had to be generated; and (2) this process developed with age, emerging between 5 and 7 years.

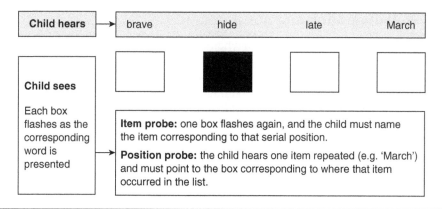

Figure 3.10 Probed recall task used by Turner et al. (2000). Example gives a word recall condition; but half the participants received identical conditions employing nonwords

Why might the use of redintegration increase with age? One possibility is that as the network of lexical information becomes richer and more elaborate during the course of development, its ability to complete patterns (and to exhibit redintegration) increases. In other words, children gradually learn large numbers of new words, so their representations for existing words become more specific to accommodate minor differences between members of this ever expanding 'dictionary' of word knowledge. Another possibility is that redintegration is a voluntary strategic approach, which develops gradually in children alongside other key memory strategies after the age of 5 years. We will return to this issue in the next chapter.

Turner, Henry, Brown and Smith (2004) went on to look at redintegration in more detail, in children from 5 to 10 years of age. They predicted that the emergence of a lexicality effect, whereby familiar words are recalled more accurately than unfamiliar words, would depend upon the nature of the memory task. They found that the use of redintegration increased with age for tasks requiring spoken item recall, but decreased with age when position information but not naming was required. In a second experiment, redintegration was found in a recognition task when some of the foils rhymed with the target. Older children were able to profit from a rhyming foil, whereas younger children were confused by it, suggesting that the older children made use of sublexical phonological information in reconstructing the target. It was proposed that redintegrative processes in their mature form support the reconstruction of detailed phonological knowledge of words. For further discussion of this issue, and some methodological comments, see Jarrold, Cocksey and Dockerill, 2008).

Redintegration and nonwords

Several authors have wondered whether long-term memory knowledge could still be helpful in recalling unfamiliar or nonwords. So far, we have made an assumption that redintegration is unhelpful for items that have no lexical representations. In other words, redintegration is only useful for known words where the sound characteristics of that particular word (and other information such as meaning) are stored. However, long-term memory representations about the general properties of words, which types of sound combinations are 'legal' in a particular language, the usual rhythm and accent of words and the likelihood of certain sounds coming before or after each other is likely to be of benefit when recalling nonwords. Think of it as a language knowledge effect; the more knowledge we have of a language, the more flexible we might be in dealing with new instances of potential words within that language. Another way of describing this is to refer to 'sublexical' representations: information that is not at the 'word' level, but is nevertheless relevant to words.

For example, Gathercole, Frankish, Pickering and Peaker (1999) found that 7 to 8-year-old children were better able to recall nonwords that were made from combinations of sounds that were common in English, as opposed to nonwords made from combinations of sounds that were uncommon in English. They argued that recall was supported at least to some extent by children's knowledge of the language, even in relation to nonwords (see also Gathercole, Pickering, Hall & Peaker, 2001).

However, Thomson, Richardson and Goswami (2005) suggested an alternative. Children might be using their knowledge of parts of real words to support the recall of nonwords. For example, the nonword 'vack' contains a sequence of sounds 'ack', known as the 'rime'. This is a common sequence (rime) in English and perhaps a child may be able to compare the nonword 'vack' to all of the similar real words that they know ending in 'ack'. These items with the same rime (e.g. 'back, tack, pack, rack' etc...) are known as 'neighbours' and common rimes are said to come from 'dense' neighbourhoods. By contrast, a nonword such as 'geb' has very few neighbours ('deb' perhaps?), so less detailed knowledge about the rime is available to support recall. Children are known to have particularly detailed knowledge about rime units in dense neighbourhoods (De Cara & Goswami, 2003), so it is plausible that they use this knowledge to support PSTM.

In fact, Thomson et al. (2005) found evidence to support their view. Seven- and 9-year-olds found nonwords with larger numbers of neighbours easier to recall than nonwords with smaller numbers of neighbours. Thomson et al. (2005) concluded that word knowledge, about rimes in particular, was used to support nonword recall via redintegration.

Of course, the amount of useful information available to support nonword recall is likely to be far less than for real words. Therefore, any effects of redintegration will still be relatively minor for nonwords. One could also make a prediction that these effects will be much stronger for one-syllable items, as short words are much more likely to share discrete rime units with real words than longer words with two or more syllables (see also Majerus & Van Der Linden, 2003; Majerus ,Van der Linden, Mulde, Meulemans & Peters, 2004).

Summary
Long-term memory knowledge is used to support recall in PSTM tasks. This knowledge can be phonological (sounds of words) or semantic (meanings of words). There is good evidence that (at least) older children and adults use such information to help reconstruct partially decayed memory traces from the proposed phonological store, a process known as 'redintegration'. Our understanding and knowledge of language may also help us to recall nonwords, although the exact mechanisms underlying these processes are more controversial.

Issue 5: Assumptions about the role of verbal rehearsal

The development of rehearsal

The first problem regarding assumptions made by the articulation rate hypothesis about verbal rehearsal was as follows. If speed of rehearsal was the key factor accounting for developmental improvements in memory span, then preventing children of different ages from using rehearsal should equate their levels of memory span.

Unfortunately, this is not the case. For example, Hitch, Halliday and Littler (1989) assessed memory span in two groups of 17 children (8- and 11-year-olds) using a very reliable incremental memory span procedure (three estimates of span were averaged in each case). The critical comparison was to compare span in 'normal' conditions with span under 'articulatory suppression'. As we discussed in Chapter 1, articulatory suppression is a procedure whereby the participant must continuously repeat an irrelevant word or phrase during presentation of the list items (in this case '1, 2, 3, 4, 5') to prevent them using articulatory rehearsal.

Although suppression reduced recall for both groups of children, it did not eliminate age differences (see Figure 3.11). This suggested that although 8- and 11-year-olds seemed to use rehearsal, this could not be the only factor responsible for developmental improvements in memory span, otherwise, age differences should have disappeared. These findings have been replicated (e.g. Henry, 1991a; Hitch et al., 1993), so appear to be reliable.

A second problem with the articulation rate hypothesis was that it assumed all children must be using verbal rehearsal. This directly implied that children as young as 4 years (these were the youngest children tested) used verbal rehearsal in memory span tasks. Such a view contradicted previous evidence regarding the development of verbal rehearsal in children. The strategy had been regarded as developing gradually between the ages of 7 and 9 years. For example Flavell, Beach and Chinsky (1966) observed children performing remembering tasks and looked for evidence of lip movements or verbalisation

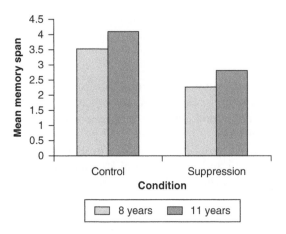

Figure 3.11   Mean memory spans for 8- and 11-year-old children in conditions with and without articulatory suppression

Source: data adapted from Hitch, Halliday and Littler (1989)

which might imply the use of verbal rehearsal. Most 5-year-olds showed no such evidence, whereas most 10-year-olds showed at least some instances of verbalisations. These results were replicated by Bebko (1979) and Bebko and McKinnon (1990), so were robust, and have been used by many researchers since as evidence for the gradual development in verbal rehearsal with age.

This type of evidence seemed to contradict the extensive data collected by researchers on word length effects in young children's recall (Henry & Millar, 1991; Hitch, Halliday & Littler, 1989; Hulme & Tordoff, 1989; Hulme et al., 1984; Nicholson, 1981). All of these experiments reported clear and robust effects of word length in PSTM tasks with children as young as 4 years. According to the working memory model, the presence of word length effects should indicate the use of verbal rehearsal. How could these two conflicting perspectives be reconciled?

Hitch, Halliday, Dodd & Litter (1989) presented evidence that offered a partial explanation for this puzzle. Their key argument revolved around whether children heard the lists as spoken words, or saw the lists as pictures.

Hitch, Halliday, Dodd et al. (1989) looked at groups of 18 children who were 6, 8 and 10 years of age in one study; and groups of 18 children who were 4, 5, 7 and 11 years of age in a second study. Memory spans for words of one, two or three syllables were tested. Critically, the authors compared both visual presentation (picture span) and auditory presentation (spoken word span). The results of Experiment 2 are illustrated in Figures 3.12a (picture span) and 3.12b (word span). The important result was that for picture span, there were only word length effects for the oldest children; whereas for auditory word span, word length effects were present at all age levels.

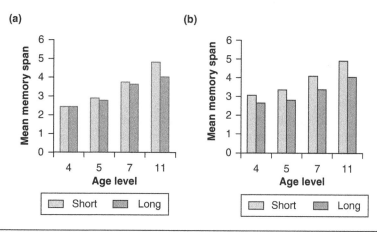

Figure 3.12(a) and 3.12(b)   Mean memory spans for children of ages 4, 5, 7 and 11 years for one- and three-syllable words. (a) = data for picture memory span; (b) = data for auditory span

Source: adapted from Hitch, Halliday, Dodd et al. (1989)

Therefore, Hitch, Halliday, Dodd et al. (1989) replicated previous findings of word length effects at all age levels using auditory presentation of word lists. However, with picture presentation of lists, only the 11-year-olds showed significant word length effects. The authors concluded that all children used verbal rehearsal for auditory material, but only the 11-year-olds used it for visual material. Why might this be so? Repeating a heard item may be a more 'compatible' response (McLeod & Posner, 1984) than repeating/ naming a visual item. It is also the case that rehearsing visual items requires two steps: first, producing a verbal label for each item (naming); and second, verbally reciting these labels (rehearsal). Hitch, Halliday, Dodd et al. (1989) suggested that the younger children had relatively slow rates of information processing and, hence, did not have time to carry out both of these steps.

Johnston, Johnson and Gray (1987) replicated the finding that 5-year-olds did not demonstrate word length effects with visual presentation of pictures. However, they also included groups of children who were trained to use a verbal rehearsal strategy. Clear word length effects *emerged* for children trained to rehearse. These results supported the view that verbal rehearsal was responsible for word length effects. Further, it was not necessary for children to rehearse covertly (whispering was equally effective); and nor was it necessary for the children to repeat the list over several times (one repetition was sufficient).

It was still a strong claim to make that children under 7 years spontaneously used verbal rehearsal with auditory presentation, but did not do so with visual presentation (see also Henry et al., 2000). Two potential explanations emerged to account for the 'pro-rehearsal' findings with auditory presentation. We will consider each in turn.

Speech output delays

Several authors wondered whether word length effects might reflect processes other than verbal rehearsal, such as speech planning and output. Henry (1991b) examined word length effects in 5- and 7-year-old children using auditory presentation, but took care to use a recall method that avoided full verbal output of the list. Hence, one could test whether the process of preparing and outputting a sequence of speech may in itself produce a word length effect, because long words take longer to prepare and say than short words.

Henry (1991b) included 32 children in two age groups, 5 and 7 years. The method involved presenting spoken lists of words, but with accompanying pictures that were simultaneously shown to the child together with the relevant spoken word and then placed face-down in a horizontal row from left to right on a table. Once the list had been presented and all pictures were face down in front of the child, recall was probed in one of two ways. The experimenter pointed to one of the pictures and asked the child to tell her the identity of that picture; or, the name of one picture was repeated and the child was asked to point to its spatial location in the array. Therefore, accuracy of recall was measured without the need to say the full list. As can be seen in Figure 3.13, the results were straightforward: 7-year-olds showed effects of word length using this procedure; whereas 5-year-olds did not.

Henry (1991b) interpreted these results to mean that 5-year-olds did not use verbal rehearsal, so any evidence suggesting that they did was likely to reflect the demands of full verbal output producing a 'spurious' word length effect. Conversely, the results implied that 7-year-olds had begun to use either cumulative verbal rehearsal of the item list, or perhaps a simpler strategy of reciting the list through once, while they matched words to pictures at the recall phase. The main point, however, was that auditory presentation of items did not produce some form of 'compatible' verbal rehearsal in these young children (e.g. Halliday & Hitch, 1988); rather, it appeared that the requirement for full verbal output was responsible for word length effects.

Cowan et al. (1992) concluded, at much the same time, that verbal output was responsible for word length effects in adults. They used an innovative 'mixed lists' method. Memory was tested for lists containing short words first followed by long words, or long words first followed by short words. The reasoning was that if output delay was important, then saying long words first should allow more decay to take place than saying short words first.

The results supported Cowan et al.'s output delay hypothesis. The lists containing short words first were easier to recall than the lists containing long words first, because short words created less output delay. However, note that in this study Cowan et al. (1992) asked their participants to 'remember the words by rehearsing them silently' (p. 5), so the conclusions may be restricted

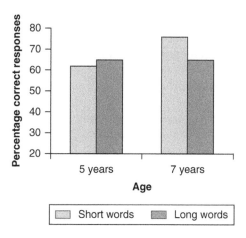

Figure 3.13   Mean proportion of correct responses on a probed memory span task for short and long words in children of 5 and 7 years

Source: data adapted from Henry (1991b)

to situations in which we know rehearsal is taking place. This may not always be the case for children, as we have already discussed. For further research on output delays in adults, see Avons, Wright & Pammer (1994); Baddeley, Chincotta, Stafford & Turk (2002); and Dosher & Ma (1998).

Sequential readout

An alternative proposal was put forward by Gathercole and Hitch (1993). They argued that verbal rehearsal in children developed gradually, perhaps starting with simple overt naming of each item as it was presented. Rehearsal may then develop into covert (i.e. subvocal) naming, and gradually the mature form of covert cumulative rehearsal for groups of items would emerge. Gathercole and Hitch (1993) suggested that rehearsal developed more rapidly with auditory presentation than visual presentation, because of the close and direct links between hearing and speaking. This could explain the differences in results between auditory and visual presentation.

Nevertheless, it was still necessary to explain how word length effects arose in young children, if they were not using mature rehearsal. Gathercole and Hitch (1993) suggested that word length effects arose as a consequence of the links between hearing and speaking. They speculated that a process of 'sequential readout' was necessary in order to recall an auditory list verbally. In this process, each sound representation in the phonological store had to be mapped onto the abstract articulatory commands required for spoken speech. In other words, the sound input had to be converted to speech commands. Gathercole and Hitch hypothesised that sequential readout would take longer for long words, because they contain more sound information. Hence, fewer long words from the phonological store could be converted into articulatory commands before the critical two-second time limit of the store was exceeded. With development, more sophisticated rehearsal strategies could be used in order to enhance recall, by refreshing the decaying phonological store.

Therefore, there are at least two possible explanations for the differences between auditory and visual presentation in relation to verbal rehearsal in young children. These accounts are not fundamentally different. Both assume that processes involved in the preparation for and/or execution of verbal output after a child has heard a list of memory items could be responsible for word length effects, rather than verbal rehearsal. Similarly, both accounts accept that full cumulative verbal rehearsal in its mature form is not used by young children.

Simple rehearsal strategies

Finally, we consider further evidence to support the notion that young children might use very simple forms of rehearsal and that these simple rehearsal strategies may produce word length effects in some circumstances.

For many years, it had been noted that young children sometimes label or name items as they are presented (e.g. Ferguson & Bray, 1976), and that this might affect recall. Certainly, effects on recall consistent with verbal encoding had been found using visual presentation of pictures (Hitch, Halliday, Schaafstal & Heffernan, 1991). But what about auditory presentation? After all, it was with auditory presentation that evidence for these apparently early rehearsal strategies had been found.

Yuzawa (2001) tested auditory memory span for unfamiliar short and long words in 34 Japanese children (3 to 6 years), using full verbal recall. The key manipulation concerned the rate at which words were presented. Note that in most memory span experiments, words are presented every one or two seconds. This might mean that children have time to repeat short words, but not long words. Therefore, Yuzawa made sure that, in one condition ('control'), there was enough time between words for each child to repeat every short word presented twice, but to repeat long words only once. This necessitated a presentation interval between each word of between 2.2 and 2.5 seconds. In a second condition ('experimental'), every child had enough time to repeat all words twice. The strength of this study was that these timings were separately measured for every participant, by assessing articulation times for all words (therefore, they were slightly different for each child and went up to around 3.5 seconds).

Yuzawa (2001) hypothesised that if word length effects arose from using very simple rehearsal strategies, they should disappear in the condition where children had time to repeat both long and short words twice, because the amount of simple rehearsal that could be done on both types of words would be the same. Word length effects should remain, however, in the condition where children had time to repeat short words twice, but long words only once, because the memory trace for long words should be weaker as a result of fewer rehearsals.

This is broadly what was found, as illustrated in Figure 3.14. The word length effect was much more marked in the condition where children had less time to repeat long words. When they had time to repeat long words twice, the word length effect was reduced. Yuzawa (2001) concluded that very young children use a rudimentary form of rehearsal, repeating each word they hear in the interval before the next word is presented.

Therefore, word length effects in very young children probably reflect rudimentary or simple verbal labelling strategies, whereby words are repeated individually after they are presented. In standard memory span tasks with short gaps between words, there is little time to repeat long words, so they receive fewer rehearsals and are, hence, not recalled so well.

Summary

According to a strong version of the working memory model, verbal rehearsal plays a pivotal role in the development of PSTM in typical children. However, there are a number of problems with this assumption. First, verbal rehearsal cannot be the sole factor accounting for developmental improvements in memory span, because age differences remain when rehearsal is prevented. Secondly, we have seen that verbal rehearsal develops gradually with age, and is not generally present in children under the age of seven, although it

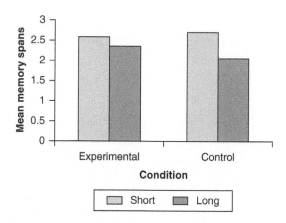

Figure 3.14   Mean memory spans for short and long words in the control condition (time to repeat short words twice and long words once) and in the experimental condition (time to repeat both short and long words twice)

Source: data adapted from Yuzawa (2001)

remains possible that very young children use primitive forms of rehearsal. Thirdly, word length effects, regarded as indicating the use of verbal rehearsal, seem only to be found with auditory presentation in younger children, and not with visual presentation. All of these problems posed questions in relation to the central role given to verbal rehearsal in the development of PSTM in typical children.

We have discussed research that has questioned the reliability of word length effects in reflecting the use of verbal rehearsal; as well as other possible explanations for why rehearsal may develop earlier with auditory as opposed to visual presentation. These alternative explanations (speech output delays, sequential readout) both assume that preparing speech output codes/plans for long words is more difficult and time-consuming than creating speech output codes/plans for short words, hence, word length effects arise through links between hearing and speaking. More recent research has acknowledged the fact that verbal rehearsal may take many forms, ranging from rudimentary to sophisticated, and that these strategies develop gradually in typical children. Simple rehearsal strategies may be responsible for evidence of word length effects in auditory PSTM tasks. However, we finish with a cautionary note about word length effects in the Debates and Issues box below.

Debates and Issues 3.1   Word length effects

Although we have concluded that rehearsal may develop *earlier* with auditory as opposed to visual presentation, this is in fact an area of debate. For example, Hulme, Silvester, Smith and Muir (1986) found clear evidence for word length effects using visual presentation in children between the ages of 4 and 10 years. For many years, I struggled to understand these results, but some of my own research has also found similar evidence: i.e. word length effects with visual presentation appearing in children as young as 4 years (Henry et al., 2000).

There is no easy way to understand these conflicting results, and this may be why intensive research in this area has waned in the past ten years. It has proved extremely complicated to understand exactly which types of processes word length effects reflect in young children; and the differing results with auditory and visual presentation are just one example of the difficulties in this area.

It is still possible that the assumptions we have made about the relationships between verbal rehearsal, speech output and naming are open to question. In fact, the next section examines some research that questions these assumptions, by taking an *even more critical* approach to the supposed link between word length effects and verbal rehearsal.

Issue 6: Does the word length effect even have an articulatory basis?

Several theorists have questioned whether word length effects have an articulatory basis at all. In fact, Brown and Hulme (1995) modelled the effects of word length on memory span without using a verbal rehearsal process, arguing that simple trace decay plus redintegration could account for word length effects quite straightforwardly. This section summarises several problems with accounts of word length effects based on rehearsal and/or articulatory processes. The research is necessarily with adults, as such work is not available for children.

One early difficulty with the working memory model's proposal that word length effects were based on articulatory rehearsal was the finding that individuals who have congenital or acquired difficulties with articulation (known as dysarthria or anarthria) still showed word length effects (Baddeley & Wilson, 1985; Bishop & Robson, 1989; Waters, Rochan & Caplan, 1992; although see Carlesimo, Galloni, Bonanni & Sabbadini, 2006). This should not have been possible for individuals who could not articulate words, although explanations at the time stressed that it might be possible for those with dysarthria to rehearse using internal speech planning mechanisms even if the actual speech output was impaired.

A second problem also emerged. Baddeley et al. (1975) had found evidence for word length effects even when phonological length (number of syllables and number of individual sounds, or phonemes) was matched, yet pronunciation durations differed. Box 3.2 gives examples of such materials; try saying these two-syllable words yourself, to see whether you find them to be 'longer' or 'shorter' in duration.

Box 3.2   Examples of materials matched on phonological length, but with different pronunciation durations (examples taken from Baddeley et al., 1975)

Short items: wicket, pectin, Bishop
Long items: coerce, harpoon, Friday

Unfortunately, although several authors replicated these 'word duration' effects using similar materials (Baddeley & Andrade, 1994; Cowan et al., 1992; Longoni, Richardson & Aiello, 1993), others did not when they used wider or different pools of words (Caplan, Rochon & Waters, 1992; Lovatt, Avons & Masterson, 2000, 2002). Even when exactly the same stimuli were used for the 'short' and 'long' conditions, with imposed variations in pronunciation duration, some found word length effects (Cowan, Nugent, Elliott & Geer, 2000: English words) and others did not (Service, 1998, 2000: Finnish words). This debate remains unresolved, but represents a potential difficulty for assumptions regarding an articulatory basis for word length effects.

A third argument against a role for articulatory rehearsal in explaining word length effects was presented by Romani, McAlpine, Olson, Tsouknida and Martin (2005). They found that removing the possibility for rehearsal did not always remove word length effects. They prevented rehearsal in adult students using articulatory suppression (participants must repeat an irrelevant sound throughout the memory span task to stop them using verbal rehearsal), then assessed memory span for words and nonwords varying in syllabic length. Under suppression, there was a reversal of the word length effect for real words; whereas the word length effect remained very strong for nonwords.

The working memory model would predict that word length effects should disappear for both words and nonwords, because once rehearsal is prevented, we should no longer see effects of word length. How can the results of Romani et al. (2005) be accounted for? The authors argued that long items have more phonological units to be remembered, which makes them more difficult than short words, because it is more likely that at least some information from the long words will be lost. Therefore, long words are simply more difficult to remember than short words due to their increased phonological complexity.

This provides a neat explanation for why suppression did not abolish word length effects for nonwords. However, why did word length effects disappear for real words under suppression and, in fact reverse? Romani et al. (2005) explained this unusual result with reference to redintegration. Real long words are easier to reconstruct at the point of recall, if the phonological information about them has partially decayed. This is because there is likely to be more remaining information left over in a long word with which to reconstruct it. Equally importantly, there will be fewer alternative responses for a partially decayed long word than for a partially decayed short word. Figure 3.15 illustrates one example of this.

When articulatory suppression is used, individuals are forced to rely more on redintegration to remember the items, so the usual word length effect is reversed. Obviously, for nonwords, the effect of redintegration is irrelevant or at least largely reduced, because nonwords do not have entries in the lexicon. Therefore, there is no compensatory redintegration advantage for long nonwords.

Campoy (2008) also argued that articulatory processes (either verbal rehearsal or output effects) are not necessary to produce word length effects. He used a matching span technique with fast presentation rates. The adult participants were presented with two lists of words and stated whether items in both lists were in the same order. The matching span method combined with a fast presentation rate ruled out the possibility of using rehearsal, and also ensured that no verbal output was required. In these circumstances, word length effects were still found. Campoy (2008) argued that word length

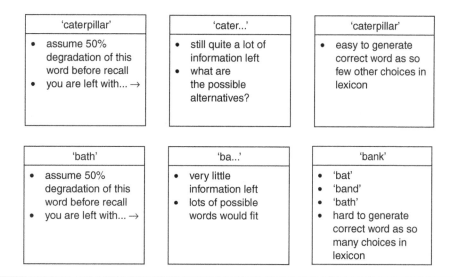

Figure 3.15   Illustration of how redintegration (reconstruction) at the point of recall is easier for long words than short words

effects were caused by the greater phonological complexity of long words leading to more interference as each new word was presented.

Finally, two further studies with adults have provided evidence against both the articulatory duration (i.e. working memory model) and the phonological complexity explanations of word length effects. Hulme and colleagues (Hulme, Surprenant, Bireta, Stuart & Neath, 2004; Hulme, Neath, Stuart, Shostak, Surprenant & Brown, 2006) now argue that the likelihood of recalling a particular item depends on its relative distinctiveness compared to other items in the list.

Overall, therefore, it is no longer appropriate to assume that word length effects always reflect articulatory processes (either verbal rehearsal or verbal output) as put forward by the working memory model. There remains no general agreement as to a single explanation for word length effects, and alternative accounts have difficulties in dealing with the full range of evidence. It may be possible that some combination of rehearsal, output delays, phonological complexity and item distinctiveness play a role in accounting for word length effects, but their individual contributions may differ depending on the precise requirements of the PSTM task being used.

Summary
Some authors question whether word length effects have any articulatory basis at all. Evidence suggests that word length effects can occur in tasks with no articulatory requirements, and such results present a challenge for the working memory account of PSTM. Caution should be used, therefore, in interpreting word length effects in studies of typical (and atypical) development.

Issue 7: Other relevant measures of speed

Dosher and Ma (1998) noted that, in adults, memory span corresponded to the number of items that could be recalled in about four to six seconds. This is considerably longer than the hypothesised length of the phonological store of up to two seconds, emphasising that the speed of spoken recall might be an important factor in the development of memory span. We have discussed articulation speed at some length, but generally assumed that this reflected the speed of verbal rehearsal. What processes might underlie the speed of spoken recall?

Cowan, Nugent, Elliott, Ponomarev and Saults (1999) hypothesised that at least two speed measures were relevant to the development of memory span. The first was speed of articulation, a measure we have already discussed. The second measure was speed of spoken recall. Cowan et al. (1999) proposed that these two measures were independent of each other, because there was no correlation between them. Together however, the two measures accounted for 87% of the developmental changes in digit span. Cowan et al. (1999) concluded that articulation speed reflected the efficiency of verbal rehearsal; whereas speed of recall reflected something rather different – the efficiency of lexical search processes. Both of these speed measures were argued to contribute to the development in memory span.

However, as we saw earlier, correlations between variables cannot be used as evidence that changes in one variable cause changes in the other. Although somewhat more complex than correlations, the statistical techniques used by Cowan et al. (1999) were related to correlations and hence, could not be used as causal evidence.

Consequently, Cowan, Elliott, Saults, Nugent, Bomb and Hismjatullina (2006) put forward the following argument. If speed of recall is an important factor in the development of memory span, increasing children's speed of recall should produce a corresponding increase in memory span. They carried out an experiment that was similar to the one discussed earlier by Hulme and Muir (1985). Hulme and Muir had attempted to increase articulation rate in children to test whether such increases (assumed to reflect verbal rehearsal rate) would increase memory span. Unfortunately, they were unable to increase articulation rate to any great degree. Cowan, Elliott et al. (2006) used exactly the same logic, but attempted to increase speed of recall.

Thirty-eight 8-year-olds were administered a number of digit span tests that required full verbal recall. In Phase 1, all children were asked to repeat the lists at whatever speed they liked. The key manipulation occurred in Phase 2, where half of the children were asked to speak their responses as quickly as they could without making errors. Phase 3 was a repetition of Phase 1. Figures 3.16a and 3.16b illustrate the results. There were clear increases in speed of recall for the children asked to recall lists quickly (3.16a). However, there were absolutely no increases in memory spans for these children (3.16b).

Therefore, Cowan, Elliott et al. (2006) queried their earlier hypothesis that developmental increases in speed of recall were one cause of the increase in memory span with age. They concluded that correlations between speed

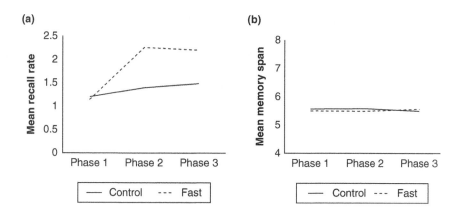

Figure 3.16(a) and 3.16(b)   Mean recall rates for 8-year-old children (a). The 'control' group were asked to recall digits at whatever speed they liked in Phases 1, 2 and 3: the 'fast' group were asked to recall the items as quickly as they could without making errors in Phase 2. Mean memory spans for these two groups are displayed (b)

and memory of any kind must be treated with extreme caution. This is a useful lesson for any area. Whilst correlations between factors can be used to develop hypotheses regarding potential causal relationships, experimental manipulations are required to substantiate these speculations.

Summary
Other interesting measures of speed that might be related to the development of PSTM have been proposed, including the speed of recalling a list. Whilst this seemed to be a plausible factor in explaining the development of PSTM in typical children, experimental evidence has failed to confirm its causal role.

Overall summary

The phonological loop component of the working memory model provided the springboard for an elegant and simple account of the development of phonological short-term memory (PSTM) in children that emerged in the early 1980s. The working memory account was as follows: developmental increases in articulation rates were responsible for developmental increases in PSTM.

PSTM had already received a great deal of attention in the child and adult literature at this time, given the importance of PSTM in respect of general intellectual development and academic progress. This meant that the understanding of PSTM and its characteristics was sophisticated, well-researched and hotly debated. The working memory account had a rapid impact on the field and generated a great deal of research.

However, several problems with the working memory/phonological loop account of PSTM development emerged quite rapidly. We have explored seven of these issues, which entailed delving into some thorny and rather difficult theoretical arguments. Updated or revised versions of the working memory model have been discussed, but many of the problematic issues in relation to articulation rates and word length effects are by no means resolved, and the updated models may still be regarded as inadequate in some important respects. Overall, articulation rates may be implicated in explaining the development of PSTM in typical children, but they are certainly not the only relevant factor. We also saw that important contributions are made by long-term knowledge; and that the interpretation of word length effects remains an area of considerable and ongoing debate.

Next, we will look at the development of the three other components of working memory (visuospatial sketchpad, central executive, episodic buffer). You will notice that the theoretical specification of the working memory account with regard to these components is not as detailed as it was for the phonological loop.

Further reading

Chapters and reviews

Cowan, N. (1997). The development of working memory. In N. Cowan (Ed.), *The development of memory in childhood*. Hove, East Sussex: Psychology Press. Still a great synthesis of the area.

Cowan, N. & Kail, R. (1996). Covert processes and their development in short-term memory. In S.E. Gathercole (Ed.), *Models of short-term memory*. Hove, East Sussex, UK: Psychology Press. Includes a strong focus on covert articulation/rehearsal.

Gathercole, S.E. & Hitch, G.J. (1993). Developmental changes in short-term memory: A revised working memory perspective. In A. Collins, S.E. Gathercole, M.A. Conway and P.E. Morris (Eds.), *Theories of memory* (pp. 189–209). Hove: Laurence Erlbaum Associates. A very helpful chapter outlining the working memory perspective.

Henry, L.A. & Millar, S. (1993). Why does memory span increase with age?: A review of the evidence for two current hypotheses. *European Journal of Cognitive Psychology, 5*, 241–287. A detailed review of item identification speed and articulation rate as explanations for the development of PSTM.

Research papers

These are listed in the order that they are mentioned in the chapter, rather than in alphabetical order.

Hulme, C., Thomson, N., Muir, C. & Lawrence, A. (1984). Speech rate and the development of short-term memory span. *Journal of Experimental Child Psychology, 38*, 241–253. A classic paper in support of the working memory account.

Ferguson, A.N., Bowey, J.A. & Tilley, A. (2002). The association between auditory memory span and speech rate in children from kindergarten to sixth grade. *Journal of Experimental Child Psychology, 81*, 141–156. A very thorough exploration of the impact of different methods of measuring articulation rate.

Kail, R. (1997). Phonological skill and articulation time independently contribute to the development of memory span. *Journal of Experimental Child Psychology, 67*, 57–68. Presents an adapted model incorporating articulation rate and phonological skills.

Ferguson, A.N. & Bowey, J.A. (2005). Global processing speed as a mediator of developmental changes in children's auditory memory span. *Journal of Experimental Child Psychology, 91*, 89–112. A demanding, detailed read, but summarises the articulation rate hypothesis and Kail's contributions very well; then goes on to test Kail's model.

Henry, L.A. & Millar, S. (1991). Memory span increase with age: A test of two hypotheses. *Journal of Experimental Child Psychology, 51*, 459–484. Compares the articulation rate hypothesis and the identification time hypothesis, also looks at word familiarity.

Hitch, G.J., Halliday, M.S., Dodd, A. & Littler, J.E. (1989). Development of rehearsal in short-term memory: Differences between pictorial and spoken stimuli. *British Journal of Developmental Psychology, 7*, 347–362. A classic paper comparing visual and auditory presentation in relation to word length effects.

Hitch, G.J., Halliday, M.S. & Littler, J.E. (1989). Item identification time and rehearsal rate as predictors of memory span in children. *Quarterly Journal of Experimental Psychology, 41A*, 321–337. Compares two key accounts of the development of PSTM and explores articulatory suppression.

Turner, J.E., Henry, L.A. & Smith, P.T. (2000). The development of the use of long-term knowledge to assist short-term recall. *Quarterly Journal of Experimental Psychology, 53A*, 457–478. Explores the use of redintegration in children.

Henry, L.A. (1991). The effects of word length and phonemic similarity in young children's short-term memory. *Quarterly Journal of Experimental Psychology, 43A*, 35–52. Explores verbal output as an explanation for word length effects in young children.

Yuzawa, M. (2001). Effects of word length on young children's memory performance. *Memory & Cognition, 29*(4), 557–564. Looks at simple, early developing rehearsal strategies.

Cowan, N., Elliott, E.M., Saults, J.S., Nugent, L.D., Bomb, P. & Hismjatullina, A. (2006). Rethinking speed theories of cognitive development: Increasing the rate of recall without affecting accuracy. *Psychological Science, 17*(1), 67–73. Attempting to increase memory span by increasing the rate of recalling lists.

Potential exam questions

1 Critically evaluate whether the phonological loop model provides a good account of the development of phonological short-term memory in typical children.

2 Are word length effects reliable indicators of verbal rehearsal in young children?

3 Do developmental increases in articulation rate cause corresponding developmental increases in memory span? Illustrate your answer using experimental research.

4

Working Memory and Typical Development: Part 2

Learning outcomes

At the end of this chapter, you should have a critical understanding of the development of visuospatial short-term memory, the central executive and the episodic buffer in typical children. You should also be able to discuss whether the working memory system as a whole is structured along similar lines in children and adults. Finally, you should have an insight into the roles of the knowledge base, memory strategies and metamemory in the development of memory and how these concepts might relate to working memory.

Introduction

Typically developing children do not have known developmental disorders (for example, autism, Down syndrome or dyslexia) and are developing at broadly the rate that we would expect (they have a 'typical' range of intellectual abilities, usually measured using a standardised IQ test, i.e. 80+). Therefore, these are children with no intellectual disabilities and no specific developmental disorders. We will be looking at different atypical populations in later chapters that vary in terms of whether they have intellectual disabilities and/or specific developmental disorders.

When the working memory model was originally used to explain memory development in typically developing children, the emphasis was on the phonological loop. We considered evidence concerning the development of the phonological loop in Chapter 3, and several key difficulties with the model were discussed in detail.

However, researchers taking a working memory perspective had less to say about typical development in relation to visuospatial short-term memory (VSSTM), the central executive and the episodic buffer. In this chapter, some of the research that has contributed to our understanding of development in each of these components will be examined. If you need a reminder about any of the components of the working memory model, refer to Chapters 1 and 2 or look at the 'aide memoire to the working memory model' at the end of Chapter 2 for a summary.

The visuospatial sketchpad

The visuospatial sketchpad is a temporary store for visual and spatial information that can be utilised during thinking, remembering and processing tasks (Logie, 1995). In this section, research relevant to the development of visuospatial short-term memory (VSSTM) in typical children will be considered.

There is no doubt that the amount of visuospatial information that children can recall in immediate memory tasks increases with age. For example, a common measure of spatial memory, Corsi span, increases up to an average of five and a half items by the age of 15 years (Issacs & Vargha-Khadem, 1989). Similarly, the ability to remember information contained in 'grid' patterns of black-and-white squares improves with age (Wilson, Scott & Power, 1987).

There is also good evidence that in children, as in adults, VSSTM is distinct from phonological short-term memory (PSTM). In other words, the two 'slave' subsystems, designed for storing visuospatial and phonological information respectively, are separate and independent of each other. Such evidence was provided by Pickering, Gathercole and Peaker (1998) in a study of 5- and 8-year-old children. The children were given memory span tasks that assessed PSTM (digit span and letter span) as well as VSSTM (Corsi or spatial span). On the whole, there were no significant associations between these two types of tests, suggesting that they measured different memory systems.

Much of the research on VSSTM in children has attempted to establish whether there are separable visual versus spatial components within this system, as has been found for adults (e.g. Darling et al., 2007, see Chapter 1). We will now consider some of this work.

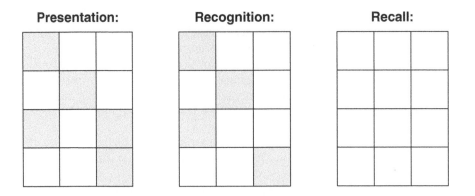

Figure 4.1   Example of matrices presented to children in the recognition and recall conditions of a visual remembering task

Source: adapted from Logie and Pearson (1997)

Logie and Pearson (1997) assessed the development of visual and spatial memory in 5-, 8-, and 11-year-old typically developing children (numbers of participants in each age group ranged from 40 to 62). Their rationale was that if visual and spatial memory developed at different rates, this would be evidence that there were two systems, one visual and one spatial, with separate developmental trajectories. Conversely, if visual and spatial memory developed together at the same rate, this would be evidence that there was one unified system.

The visual task used by Logie and Pearson (1997) was to remember which squares in a matrix had been coloured in, as illustrated in Figure 4.1. On some trials, children had to recognise one changed square in the matrix, and on other trials they had to recall the positions of all coloured squares. The spatial task was a standard Corsi span task (see Chapter 2), which involved the child attempting to remember sequences of blocks arranged randomly on a wooden board and pointed to sequentially by the Experimenter. The child had to recognise a missing item in a repeated sequence, or recall the full sequence in the correct order. Hence, the visual and spatial tasks both had recognition and recall conditions.

On measures of both recognition and recall, Logie and Pearson (1997) reported that developmental improvements were significantly more rapid for the visual task than the spatial task. These different rates of development supported their argument that different systems were involved in the short-term storage of visual as opposed to spatial information, within the visuospatial sketchpad.

Hamilton, Coates and Heffernan (2003) went on to look at this issue with children and young adults across a wider age range: 5–7; 8–10; 11–13; and 18–25 years. Hamilton et al. (2003) replicated the finding that the visual component of the visuospatial sketchpad developed quite quickly between

5 years and adulthood; whereas the spatial working memory component showed a slower, steadier developmental improvement. Again, this provided more evidence that these two systems were separate.

Finally, Pickering et al. (2001) examined memory for visual versus spatial information in a detailed investigation of children in three age bands: 5, 8 and 10 years (16 to 20 in each group). Pickering et al. (2001) wondered whether the difference between visual and spatial tasks could be better captured by contrasting what they referred to as 'static' memory for visual details (no movement information) versus 'dynamic' memory for movement sequences (similar visual details, but the addition of movement information). The static matrices task was exactly like the one used by Logie and Pearson (1997) in their full recall condition (see Figure 4.1 above). The dynamic matrices task was similar, except that each coloured square flashed black, one at a time, in sequence. The child had to point to the positions that had flashed on the matrix in the correct order. Therefore, this task resembled the Corsi or spatial span task. The advantage of these tasks is that they were perfectly matched on all characteristics except whether the information was presented all at once (static) or in sequence (dynamic).

Pickering et al. (2001) found that memory for static information was better than memory for dynamic information for children at all age levels. In addition, memory for static information showed steeper developmental increases than memory for dynamic information. These results were similar to those reported in previous studies: memory for visual information developed more rapidly than memory for spatial information.

Pickering et al. (2001) concluded, as had others, that there were two distinct mechanisms in the visuospatial sketchpad, one visual and one spatial. However, they also argued that the distinction between visual and spatial information may be better captured by considering whether the information to be remembered is static in nature (i.e. visual) or incorporates movement (i.e. spatial) (see also Cornoldi & Vecchi, 2003). Therefore current research supports the utility separating out visual and spatial short-term memory, even if there is some disagreement about the best terminology to use.

Cornoldi and Vecchi (2003) also considered a series of interesting papers showing that children who have low visuospatial intelligence (yet good verbal intelligence) show selective difficulties in VSSTM. This implies that the mechanisms responsible for visuospatial intelligence may be related to those responsible for VSSTM.

Summary

Visuospatial short-term memory (VSSTM) increases with age and appears to be quite distinct from phonological short-term memory. There is good evidence that VSSTM in typically developing children can be separated into two components: memory for spatial information and memory for visual information.

Do young children prefer to use visual codes?

This question received considerable attention from working memory researchers in the late 1980s. They noted that if we ask children to remember lists of pictures of familiar objects, they have the choice between remembering the pictures as images (i.e. visual coding in the visuospatial sketchpad) or naming the pictures and attempting to remember the verbal labels (i.e. verbal coding in the phonological loop). A series of studies by Graham Hitch and his colleagues provided evidence for a shift from visual to verbal coding during the early school years, using a clever set of picture stimuli that looked similar to each other, described as 'visually similar'. We will look at one of these studies to illustrate the findings.

Hitch, Halliday, Schaafstal and Schraagen (1988) asked 5- and 10-year-old children to remember a series of visually similar pictures. All were long, thin objects drawn at a 45° angle and presented as black and white line drawings (e.g. 'knife', 'pen', 'tie'). Items in a further 'long name' condition provided a comparison; these items were designed to be more difficult for children who adopted a strategy of naming the pictures and attempting to recall these names. Examples of these types of pictures are given in Box 4.1. Items in the 'control' condition were not visually similar, nor did they have long names.

The logic of this experiment was to assume that children who tried to remember pictures as visual images would show poorer performance in the visually similar condition, but would not be affected by longer names. By contrast, children who attempted to remember the pictures using their names would not be affected by visual similarity, but they would find pictures with longer names more difficult (see Chapters 1 and 3 for further details regarding 'word length effects').

Box 4.1

Pictures that look similar ('visually similar'):

Pictures with long names:

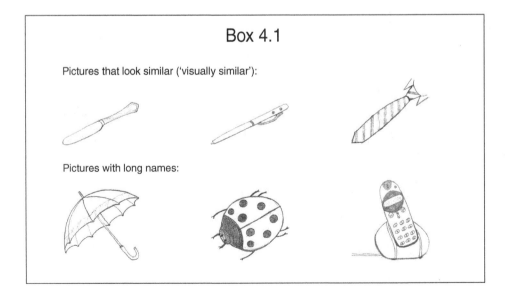

Hitch et al. (1988) found clear evidence for a switch from visual strategies at 5 years to verbal naming strategies at 10 years. Five-year-olds showed more difficulties in remembering visually similar items (a 'visual similarity effect'), whereas 10-year-olds showed more difficulties in remembering long-named items (a 'word length effect'). See also Hitch, Woodin & Baker, 1989; Hitch et al., 1991; Longoni & Scalisi, 1994 and Palmer, 2000a, for further evidence to support this view; although note that a few studies have failed to find visual similarity effects in young children (Henry, 2008; Hitch, Halliday, Dodd & Litter, 1989).

Summary

Several studies have suggested that 4 to 5-year-old children prefer to use visual codes to remember pictures, whereas older children are more likely to use verbal coding. This illustrates a developmental shift from visual to verbal coding. We will come back to visual and verbal coding later in the chapter when we discuss memory strategies.

The central executive

The development of 'central executive-loaded' higher order processing skills has received considerable attention in the literature, but not all of this work takes a 'working memory' perspective. At this point, it is useful to emphasise some differences in terminology that exist in the literature. Work that takes the Baddeley and Hitch working memory model as its theoretical basis will generally use the term 'working memory' to refer to the system as a whole, and make a clear distinction between tasks measuring different components of working memory. However, many authors, particularly those in North America, use the term 'working memory' to refer to a specific working memory skill: in our terminology, 'executive-loaded working memory'. This particular use of terminology arose out of the very influential work by Daneman and Carpenter (1980), which has had a significant impact on the field. Those with a more clinical or neuropsychological background might also use the term 'working memory' to refer to a range of skills, all of which are likely to require processing plus storage – key elements for any executive-loaded working memory measure. For a reminder of the types of tasks considered to measure executive-loaded working memory please refer back to Chapter 2.

The discussion that follows attempts to bring together relevant literature from different theoretical and clinical perspectives on working memory and executive functioning. Therefore, it is important when reading research papers and chapters to be alert to the fact that authors may use the term 'working memory' in somewhat different ways and from different theoretical perspectives. In the next section, the structure of central executive skills in adults and children will be discussed.

The structure of central executive processing in adults and children

Executive skills are a constellation of abilities required to deal with unfamiliar situations or novelty. These skills include being able to: plan ahead (planning); generate new solutions (fluency); switch attention from one thing to another as necessary (switching or set shifting); ignore readily available information that is not currently useful (inhibition); and remember important details relevant to the task (executive-loaded working memory). In short, these are higher level thinking and attentional skills for dealing with complex problem-solving and behavioural regulation, just the activities hypothesised to be performed by the central executive of working memory (refer to Chapters 1 and 2 for further information).

Many authors believe that executive skills should be subdivided into separate areas that are, nevertheless, loosely related. Another way of saying this is that executive abilities are at least partly 'fractionated' or divided (e.g. Lehto, 1996) into separate subcomponents. However, not all authors agree with fractionation; and some would maintain that executive functioning should be considered as a single skill or ability (see Duncan, Emslie, Williams, Johnson & Freer, 1996).

Nevertheless, there is probably more research supporting the fractionation position, in particular a classic paper by Miyake et al. (2000), so this is the approach taken in the current book. The next question to address is which sub-skills should be considered as making up the broader concept of executive functioning?

Several authors have emphasised or carried out research on three areas of executive functioning: switching/set shifting; working memory/updating; and inhibition (Fisk & Sharp, 2004; Huizinga et al., 2006; Lehto et al., 2003; Miyake et al., 2000; van der Sluis, de Jong & van der Leij, 2007). Therefore, all three of these areas will be included in discussions of research evidence presented in this book. However, based on an influential paper in this area by Pennington and Ozonoff (1996), two additional areas of executive skill will also be included: planning and fluency (see also Fisk & Sharp, 2004, who found evidence for a 'fluency' component of executive functioning); as well as dual task performance and random generation where relevant (see Chapter 2). Note that executive-loaded working memory and updating are often seen as measuring the same underlying skill (e.g. St Clair-Thompson & Gathercole, 2006) so will be considered together. Box 4.2 summarises the areas of executive skill that will be considered.

Box 4.2   Types of executive skills covered, where relevant, in this book

1   Working memory/updating – carrying out processing and storage concurrently
2   Set shifting/switching – moving fluently between different sets of instructions or tasks

---

3 Inhibition – preventing the execution of a behaviour that comes readily to mind
4 Planning – organising and planning a sequence of actions
5 Fluency – generating items according to a rule
6 Dual task performance – doing two things at once
7 Random generation – producing lists of 'random' numbers

If executive tasks in general measure particular types of important skills, we should find correlations (relationships) between different executive abilities. However, such correlations are often quite low and not always significant (Miyake et al., 2000). This could be for several reasons. First, executive functioning tasks often demonstrate rather low reliability. This means that if we give a task to a person one day and then retest them several days or weeks later, the relationship between the two scores is not always strong. Miyake et al. (2000) and others (e.g. Henry & Bettenay, 2010) have pointed out that we may have to accept low reliability in executive tasks, because they are designed to assess a person's response to novelty, and, therefore, retesting with the same task will obviously render it less able to capture responses to 'novelty'.

A second reason for low correlations between different executive tasks could be that many commonly used measures were developed as practical tools for assessing patients with frontal lobe damage rather than as experimental tasks to assess a particular theoretical model. Hence, executive tasks are often clinically useful, but highly complex in terms of demands, making them difficult to categorise and interpret at a theoretical level. Miyake et al. (2000) give the example of the Wisconsin Card Sorting Task (WCST, see Chapter 2), which is generally regarded as a measure of set shifting/switching. However, this test has also been described as assessing inhibition, problem-solving, working memory and categorisation (see also Fisk & Sharp, 2004).

It is beyond the scope of this book to do more than alert the reader to these difficulties with the concept and measurement of executive functioning. In this and later chapters, research evidence pertaining to executive functioning in typically developing children and those with developmental disorders will be reviewed, but it must always be kept in mind that many of the assumptions about the types of executive functions measured by commonly-used tasks can be questioned.

Next, we consider research evidence in relation to the structure of executive functioning. Please refer to Chapter 2 for details about the tasks discussed in the next sections.

Research evidence on the structure of executive functioning

Several rather complex papers have considered the structure of executive functioning in adults. For example, Miyake et al. (2000) examined three executive functions in a sample of 137 adult undergraduates (set shifting, working memory, inhibition). The authors tried to use the simplest and purest measures of each executive skill, and included three assessments of each (several more 'complex' measures of executive functioning were also included, but these were treated separately). Using a statistical technique, Miyake et al. (2000) extracted the common variance from the three tasks that measured each executive skill, producing what are known as 'latent variables'. These latent variables were argued to capture the essence of each executive skill. Miyake et al. (2000) found good evidence that set shifting, working memory and inhibition were clearly distinguishable executive skills. In addition, these areas of executive skill were modestly related to each other. Figure 4.2 illustrates their findings.

These findings suggested that executive abilities were fractionated, yet moderately related to each other. In other words, there was both 'unity and diversity of executive functions' (Miyake et al., 2000: 50).

Fisk and Sharp (2004) examined executive functioning in 95 adults with a broader age range (20 to 81 years), and included several 'complex' executive tasks commonly used in the literature (e.g. WCST, Stroop, executive-loaded span, word fluency). These authors used a technique known as factor analysis to look at which tasks were most related to each other. Fisk and Sharp (2004) found evidence for the same three areas of executive skills as Miyake et al. (2000), namely, working memory, inhibition and set shifting. However, they found additional evidence for a fourth factor reflecting word fluency, which they interpreted as the 'efficiency of access to long-term memory'. One of the

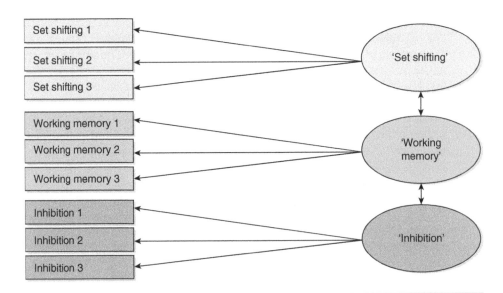

Figure 4.2 A three-factor model of executive functioning: three 'simple' tasks (on the left) measured each executive skill; and the best model for the nine tasks incorporated the three executive abilities (on the right), which were themselves moderately related

Source: adapted from Miyake et al. (2000)

key departures from the findings of Miyake et al. (2000), however, was that Fisk and Sharp (2004) found little evidence that different executive areas were related to each other. Therefore, there remains some debate regarding relations between different areas of executive skill in adults.

With respect to children, the results are somewhat less straightforward. Several studies have found evidence for differing executive skill areas, which makes interpretation tricky. For example, in one of the first studies of its type, Levin et al. (1991) assessed 52 typically developing children on a range of executive measures (e.g. Wisconsin Card Sorting Test, word fluency, design fluency, Tower of London, the Go-No Go task of inhibitory control). An exploratory principal components analysis (to see whether the executive skills could be reduced to a smaller number of related abilities) revealed three factors, which Levin et al. (1991) interpreted as 'freedom from perseveration' (could this mean 'inhibition' or 'switching'?), 'semantic association/concept formation' and 'planning'. These factors do not map directly on to those described in the earlier adult studies.

Similarly, Welsh, Pennington and Groisser (1991) looked at the performance of 100 children (3 to 12 years) on a range of executive measures (e.g. verbal fluency, Tower of Hanoi, Wisconsin Card Sorting Test, Matching Familiar Figures test). They also performed a principal components analysis, but only on the data for children 8 years and older. This revealed three factors, interpreted as 'speeded responding', 'set maintenance' (could this mean set shifting?) and 'planning'. Again, these factors are somewhat hard to interpret, with variations in terminology used adding to the difficulties. Finally, Klenberg, Korkman and Lahti-Nuuttila (2001) looked at 400 Finnish children and found evidence for four executive functioning factors in the 7–12 age range including 'fluency', 'visual attention', 'auditory attention' and 'inhibition'.

It is, however, important to note that many of the executive tasks in these studies were 'complex' (as opposed to 'simple' measures of executive skills) and could have involved more than one executive ability. This is likely to make interpretation of executive 'factors' more difficult.

More recently, studies have attempted to examine executive functioning in children with respect to the tripartite structure (working memory, inhibition, set shifting) put forward by Miyake et al. (2000).

For example, Lehto et al. (2003) examined executive functioning in 108 8- to 13-year-old children. A range of tasks were incorporated including the Trail Making Task, word fluency, mazes, spatial working memory and the Tower of London. Using factor analysis on a subset of eight key executive measures, Lehto et al. (2003) found evidence for three separate factors, which they interpreted (with some reservations) as reflecting working memory, inhibition and set shifting. It is important to note that some of these interpretations could be open to criticism as they were necessarily post-hoc and counterintuitive in some cases. For example, word fluency and the Trail Making Task were both interpreted as reflecting the executive skill of set shifting. This is not controversial in the case of the Trail Making Task, but it is in the case of word fluency. In addition, Lehto et al. (2003) noted that the tasks they used were 'complex' measures of executive functioning, rather than the more pure assessments used by Miyake et al. (2000). Therefore, caution must be used in comparing the two studies directly.

Nevertheless, the fact that Lehto et al. (2003) found broadly similar results in their sample of children as earlier work had found in adults supports the view that executive functioning may be similarly structured throughout development. Lehto et al. (2003) also assessed whether there were correlations between different types of executive measures, finding weak but significant relationships. This supported Miyake et al.'s (2000) contention that different types of executive functions are loosely related to each other.

Huizinga et al. (2006) used a method very similar to that of Miyake et al. (2000) with large samples of 7-, 11-, 15- and 21-year-olds (n = 384 in total). Three measures each of working memory, set shifting and inhibition were included so that the authors could use the 'latent variable' approach, which extracts the common variance shared between similar measures. An attempt was made to choose simple executive tasks that could be regarded as pure measures of the construct in question. Two 'complex' executive measures were also included (Wisconsin Card Sorting Test, Tower of London), but these were considered separately. Although Huizinga et al. (2006) found good evidence for latent variables corresponding to working memory and set shifting (and these two variables were modestly related to each other), this was not the case for inhibition. The three measures of inhibition were not well related to each other, despite the fact that all three tasks required the control of competing responses and, theoretically, would have been expected to measure the same underlying construct.

By contrast, St Clair-Thompson and Gathercole (2006), in a sample of 11- and 12-year-old children (n = 51), found evidence that inhibition and working memory were separate components of executive functioning, but that switching was not. This study included six different measures of verbal and visuospatial executive-loaded working memory (ELWM), some of which would be described as 'updating' and some of which would be described as 'complex memory span'. In fact, the complex span and updating measures clustered together, indicating that they measured common skills. St Clair-Thompson and Gathercole (2006) concluded that ELWM and inhibition were distinct domains of executive functioning. They also found evidence for additional components within ELWM reflecting modality-specific storage systems (i.e. verbal versus visuospatial).

Finally, van der Sluis et al. (2007) attempted to address the 'task complexity' problem by statistically removing the variance in each of their executive tasks that was associated with non-executive skills. This, they argued, would give a pure reflection of executive skills, uncontaminated by other cognitive influences (mainly processing speed). Measures of inhibition, shifting and updating were administered to 172 children of ages 9–12 years; and van der Sluis et al. (2007) found good evidence for factors corresponding to shifting and updating. They were not able, however, to identify a separate inhibition factor.

Overall, therefore, there remains some disagreement in the developmental literature regarding the key component skills that may be relevant to executive functioning. Possibly the most robust evidence for a distinct domain of executive functioning relates to ELWM. However, differences in the rates of development for certain executive skills and difficulties in comparing studies that have used 'pure' versus 'complex' measures of executive functioning make drawing definitive conclusions about core areas of executive functioning in typical children difficult.

Summary
There is support for the notion that executive functioning is structured similarly in children and adults. However, differences between studies on children and adults indicate that there may be important developmental changes. Further research is required before definitive conclusions in this area can be made.

The development of executive skills in childhood

The working memory model has rather little to say about the development of the central executive in children. Even in adults, this part of the model was relatively unexplored until quite recently.

However, there are some straightforward questions we can ask about executive skills. For example, are there developmental improvements or progressions in executive functioning throughout childhood? The answer to this is certainly yes. Executive functions develop rather slowly from infancy (e.g. Diamond & Golman-Rakic, 1989) through early childhood and adolescence, and may still improve into young adulthood (e.g. Anderson, 2002; Garon et al., 2008; Huizinga et al., 2006; Levin et al., 1991; Welsh et al., 1991). Therefore, the development of executive functioning is quite protracted. Evidence for this developmental progression will be looked at in more detail shortly.

A second question concerns the importance of executive skills. As we will see later in this chapter, executive skills are likely to be central in relation to the use of memory strategies and in relation to metamemory (knowledge about one's own memory). In addition, executive functioning is argued to be an absolutely essential cognitive skill, as it underpins successful goal-directed behaviour and is linked to educational skills such as reading, vocabulary development and mathematics attainment (we will not consider this research, but this is a good area for an extended/optional essay: see list of references and suggested questions at the end of the chapter).

We will come back to some of these issues later in the chapter, but for now will examine research evidence relevant to the question: 'What is the nature of developmental improvement in executive skills?'

Throughout this book discussions of executive skills are divided into two categories: (1) executive-loaded working memory (the type of 'working memory' that requires processing plus storage); and (2) other measures of executive functioning (including fluency, inhibition, set shifting and planning). The reason for this is to keep a clear distinction between executive skills that are very obviously related to the working memory framework (and which are often referred to in the literature as 'working memory' – see earlier discussion of terminology issues); and the broader conceptualisation of executive abilities beyond working memory.

Executive-loaded working memory

There is no doubt that executive-loaded working memory (ELWM) improves with age. There are many examples of studies that illustrate this; here we look at one classic study from the literature.

Siegel and Ryan (1989) examined the performance of typical children (7–8 years, 9–10 years, 11–13 years: sample sizes 40, 23 and 11 respectively) on two ELWM tasks. A listening span measure (sentence span) required children to supply the final word for a series of sentences (e.g. 'in summer it is a very ...'; 'with dinner we sometimes eat bread and ...'), then recall the sentence-final words in the correct order. The second ELWM task was counting span, originally developed by Case et al. (1982). Here, the child had to count yellow dots in a field of blue and yellow dots that were arranged in random irregular patterns. The answers from each count then had to be recalled in the correct serial order. Both of these tasks are regarded as 'executive-loaded', because they require concurrent processing and storage.

Figure 4.3 illustrates the mean scores on both of the ELWM measures for children in each age group. Clear improvements with age were seen on both tasks.

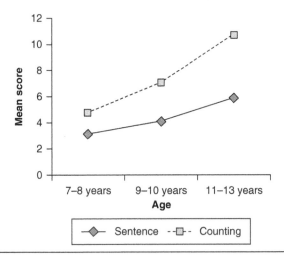

Figure 4.3 Mean scores on two measures of executive-loaded memory for typical children between the ages of 7 and 13 years: sentence span and counting span

Source: data adapted from Siegel and Ryan (1989)

Siegel and Ryan (1989) also included children who had specific learning difficulties, in particular those with reading and arithmetic problems, but we will return to this data when considering working memory skills in children with dyslexia (Chapter 6).

Why does ELWM improve with age? Case et al. (1982) argued that as children get better at the processing requirements of these tasks, this frees up more capacity for storage. This is known as a 'resource-sharing' model, because it assumes that there is one fixed amount of capacity and that this must be shared between processing and storage. With age, children are more able to devote their capacity to storage rather than processing, i.e. they use their capacity more efficiently to remember more items. The Debates and Issues box below explores more recent work on this resource-sharing model. See also Tam, Jarrold, Baddeley and Sabatos-DeVito (2010) for evidence that children use both verbal rehearsal and attentional refreshment strategies in ELWM tasks and that these might develop at different rates.

Debates and Issues 4.1   Resource-sharing?

The resource-sharing model has had an enormous impact on the literature and still represents an important way of conceptualising the development of executive-loaded working memory (ELWM) in children. However, a comprehensive series of studies by Towse and colleagues (Hitch et al., 2001; Towse & Hitch, 1995; Towse, Hitch & Hutton, 1998, 2002) suggest that resource-sharing is not the only relevant factor we need to consider.

Towse and colleagues agree that younger children take longer to carry out the processing part of ELWM tasks, but, in a series of cleverly designed studies, they have found evidence that longer processing times impose *longer delays* between storage and eventual recall. This means those with poorer processing abilities suffer an extra burden, because more stored information has *decayed* before the point at which it can be recalled. Hence, Towse and colleagues argue that low performance on ELWM tasks can reflect delays between processing and storage, not necessarily resource-sharing. To read more about this, see Towse and Hitch (2008).

This area has also developed even further more recently, with a new model of 'time-based resource-sharing' proposed by Barrouillet, Gavens, Vergauwe, Gaillard and Camos (2009).

Both of these papers are listed under Further reading at the end of this chapter.

Summary

Executive-loaded working memory (ELWM) increases gradually with age, possibly because children become more efficient at the processing part of the tasks, freeing up more capacity for storage. There are, however, alternative explanations for developmental changes in ELWM that emphasise the role of delays between storage and recall. Recent work has also emphasised that children may adopt different strategic approaches to improve recall.

Other measures of the central executive

Other executive skills also show clear evidence of developmental improvement. We will return to some of the papers mentioned earlier in order to assess age-related changes in fluency, inhibition, set shifting and planning.

For example, Levin et al. (1991) in their study of executive functioning in children between 7 and 15 years found developmental improvements in set shifting, fluency, planning, memory strategies and inhibition. Adult levels of performance were reached on set shifting (Wisconsin Card Sorting Test) and inhibition (Go-No Go task) by 12 years; whereas fluency (word and design), planning (Tower of London) and memory strategies (California Verbal Learning Test) continued to develop through adolescence.

Welsh et al. (1991) examined 3- to 12-year-olds and also found improvements with age on a range of executive tests assessing planning, inhibition, set shifting and fluency. Adult levels of performance were reached on set shifting (Wisconsin Card Sorting Test) and inhibition (Matching Familiar Figures Test) by 10 years. Verbal fluency and complex planning (Tower of Hanoi) were later to mature (after the age of 12). These results almost exactly replicated Levin et al. (1991) and supported the contention that there were clear developmental increases in EF skill, which varied somewhat depending on the executive ability. Similarly, Klenberg et al. (2001) assessed children aged 3 to 12 years on a wide range of executive tasks and found clear evidence for developmental improvements: inhibition matured first; followed by selective and sustained attention; and then fluency.

Finally, Huizinga et al. (2006) found further evidence for variations in developmental improvements in executive functioning. Performance on working memory measures improved between the ages of 7 and 15 years; the 'cost' set shifting declined from 7 to 15 years; and inhibition performance improved gradually between 7 and 15 years on two tasks, with further improvements into adulthood on a third measure (Stroop task). (See Davidson et al., 2006, for a detailed study of the relationships between working memory, inhibition and task switching).

However, Lehto et al. (2003) found rather less evidence for developmental improvements in executive functioning in the age range of 8 to 13 years. Although measures of working memory and set shifting matured with age, there was little evidence for developmental improvements in inhibition. This study did utilise a smaller age range, so this might explain why fewer developmental changes were found.

Summary
With few exceptions, most investigations of developmental change in executive functioning have produced robust evidence for improvements in performance with age. Different aspects of executive skill seem to mature at different rates.

In particular, adult levels of performance are reached earlier on measures of set shifting and inhibition, than on measures of planning, fluency (and ELWM). As pointed out by Lehto et al. (2003), however, some developmental differences may depend on the exact nature of the tasks that are used and, hence, vary between studies.

The episodic buffer

The episodic buffer is the component of working memory responsible for binding information from the other components together into a coherent episode. It also acts as a link to long-term knowledge, which can be used to enhance working memory performance.

The first issue that must be dealt with concerns whether there is such a thing as a separate 'episodic buffer' component in typically developing children. Alloway et al. (2004) argued that the recall of spoken sentences was one way of capturing how a child might integrate or 'bind' information from the phonological loop (the slave system designed to hold verbatim information about individual words and their order), with information, knowledge and analysis carried out on the sentences by the language processing system.

In fact, we know that it is easier to remember words embedded in sentences than unrelated words (Baddeley, 1986). This is because it is possible to use language knowledge, such as understanding of how sentences are put together, grammatical knowledge and typical word order – as well as semantic knowledge (factual knowledge about the world) about the content/meaning of the sentence – to support immediate recall. Box 4.3 gives an example of recalling ten connected words in a sentence, versus recalling ten similar words that are not presented in a sentence context.

Box 4.3   Remembering sentences versus unrelated words

Try remembering the following ten words in the correct order:

'Yesterday, my sister made a delicious chocolate and almond cake.'

Now, try remembering the following ten words in the correct order:

'brother, walnut, his, ate, cinnamon, horrible, tomorrow, plus, scone, the'

The words in both sets are matched for number of syllables, grammatical part of speech, and semantic category where appropriate.

Nevertheless, the first set is much easier to remember in order, because the words form a meaningful sentence.

Alloway et al. (2004) assessed a large sample of 4- and 5-year-old children (n = 633) on several working memory measures, including sentence recall. They found that performance on this measure was distinct from performance on measures that assessed the phonological loop and the central executive. In other words, Alloway et al. (2004) argued that sentence recall assessed a separate component of working memory, concluding that this was initial evidence that the episodic buffer can be distinguished from other components of working memory in young children.

The next question concerns whether there are developmental changes in the functioning of the episodic buffer. Sluzenski et al. (2006) examined the binding of visuospatial information in a relational memory task. Children looked at 16 sets of pictures, which all came in groups of three: (1) first the child saw an animal on its own, (2) next he/she saw a background on its own, and (3) then he/she saw the animal in a background ('you will see an animal, then a place where that animal likes to be – his favourite place, and then you will see that animal in his favourite place'). This was an incidental learning task, because none of the children were told they might have to remember this information.

Performance on the animals and backgrounds binding task was examined in samples of 4- and 6-year-olds, in a series of three studies. Sluzenski et al. (2006) were interested in how well the children would later recognise the separate pieces of information (i.e. the animals and the backgrounds), as opposed to how well they would recognise the combined information (i.e. the animals in their background). Recognising the combined information was a measure of binding. In fact, although both age groups performed similarly when recognising the separate pieces of information, 6-year-olds were better than 4-year-olds at remembering the combined information.

This was initial evidence that the ability to bind information about different aspects of a picture together, and remember it over short delays, improved with age. By contrast, adults carrying out the same tasks were no better than 6-year-olds, suggesting that this particular type of binding may be fully developed by 6 years. However, further research will be needed to confirm this finding of very early maturation of episodic binding abilities (e.g. see Lloyd et al., 2009).

Sluzenski et al. (2006) also included a second measure of *verbal* binding in their series of experiments: recalling a short story about a young girl making a cake. This type of naturalistic remembering task should require the integration of information from several sources: verbatim memory for words from the phonological store; information from long-term semantic memory (about similar stories one has heard before and other factual knowledge about the content of this story); and relevant knowledge about the structure of language, grammar and word order.

The results showed that 6-year-olds recalled more information about the story than 4-year-olds. This is not a surprising result, and there is plenty of other relevant literature showing clear developmental improvements across a wide age range in episodic remembering tasks, including the ability to remember stories, personally experienced events and witnessed events (e.g. Foley, Johnson & Raye, 1983; Piolino, Hisland, Ruffeveille, Matuszewski, Jambaqué & Eustache, 2007; Schneider & Pressley, 1997).

However, the new feature to the Sluzenski et al. (2006) study was that they looked at the relationship between their picture task and their story remembering task. They found modest correlations between the two binding tasks (.40), suggesting that both of these measures assessed something in common. This could be interpreted as evidence in favour of a general episodic buffer component which binds information from different sources together, regardless of exact content.

Returning to the issue of early maturation of binding abilities, there are two further studies that have examined age differences in feature binding.

First, Cowan, Naveh-Benjamin, Kilb and Saults (2006) looked at children of 8 and 10 years (over 40 participants in each group) and compared them with 53 younger (age 20 years) and 28 older (age 71 years) adults. Participants viewed several randomly placed coloured squares in an array. This array was then removed and replaced with a new array that could contain one change. The changes could be of two types: (1) the colour of one item was altered and replaced with a new colour; or (2) the colour of one item was altered and replaced with a colour that had already been present in the original array. Detecting this second type of change required the binding of visual object information (the coloured square) and spatial information (the location of the square) so that the participant noticed a change in the combined features. Cowan, Naveh-Benjamin et al. (2006) found that children were less likely to notice the binding change than young adults (although the poorest performance was shown by older adults). Therefore, binding appeared to improve with age through to adulthood, but it showed steep declines in older adults.

Secondly, Shing, Werkle-Bergner, Li and Lindenberger (2008) merged several important theoretical areas, which are relevant to the issue of binding. Shing et al. (2008) argued for a two-component model of episodic memory, including an associative component – very like the concept of binding that we have been discussing – and a strategic component. This is easier to grasp using an example of their task, which was to associate two words together such as 'apple-road'. Automatic associations between the words would reflect the associative component; whereas using particular strategies to enhance the link between the words, such as visualising a road made of apples or a single apple in the middle of a road, would reflect the strategic component.

The main point made by Shing et al.'s (2008) study of word association, was that the associative component seemed to develop earlier in children, of ages 8–10 and 13–15 years, than the strategic component. They argued that children possess a 'readily functional' (i.e. 'ready to go') associative ability that can be used extremely effectively. By contrast, strategic binding relies on executive skills, which are slower to develop, with continuing development during the teenage years into young adulthood.

Why might associative binding abilities mature earlier than strategic binding abilities? Shing et al. (2008) suggested that this was because the maturation of the key neuronal structure responsible for association, i.e. the hippocampus, develops and matures before the key neuronal structure responsible for strategic control, i.e. the pre-frontal cortex (regarded as fundamental to executive abilities). Although the authors note that this distinction may be somewhat simplistic, it does help to outline possible relationships between the episodic buffer and executive control. It also nicely complements Baddeley's (2007) supposition that binding operations in some circumstances may be relatively automatic, whereas in other circumstances they may require executive control.

Summary

Research evidence suggests that a separate episodic buffer component responsible for binding information from different sources together is present in typically developing children as well as adults. The development of automatic binding abilities appears to be relatively rapid, and may mature as early as 6 years. Binding that requires strategic control is likely to mature much later, because the use of strategies requires executive resources, which take considerably longer to reach full maturity.

Having discussed each component of working memory in relation to typical development, we now go on to examine whether the structure of working memory overall is the same in children as it is in adults.

Is the structure of working memory the same in children and adults?

There is evidence that the functional organisation of working memory corresponds to the major components of the working memory model (Baddeley, 2000, 2007; Baddeley & Hitch, 1974) from age 4–6 years in typically developing (TD) children (Alloway et al., 2004; Gathercole, Pickering, Ambridge & Wearing, 2004 – although with some reservations for 4–6-year-olds; Swanson, 2008). To illustrate these findings, one relevant study will be described in detail.

Gathercole, Pickering, Ambridge & Wearing (2004) pointed out that the working memory model was developed on the basis of evidence from adults, therefore, it was possible that the 'final state' or developed working memory system in adults may differ in important respects from the 'developing' system in children. For example, the division of working memory into separate components specialised for dealing with different types of information may not be characteristic of younger children. It is possible that children have a more undifferentiated or nonspecialised memory system.

To test this, Gathercole, Pickering, Ambridge & Wearing (2004) assessed over 700 children of ages 4 to 15 years on a range of working memory measures. These included three measures of the phonological loop (digit, word and nonword span); three measures of the visuospatial sketchpad (Corsi span, pattern span and maze recall); and three measures of the central executive (reverse digit, listening and counting span). Their basic question was as follows: did measures of each component of working memory relate more closely to each other than to measures of different components? If so, this would provide evidence that working memory is divided into three components corresponding to the phonological loop, the visuospatial sketchpad and the central executive in children across a range of ages.

First, Gathercole, Pickering, Ambridge & Wearing (2004) confirmed that all of the measures of working memory showed substantial increases with age, supporting a large amount of previous literature.

Next, Gathercole, Pickering, Ambridge & Wearing (2004) used confirmatory factor analysis to check whether the best account for all of their data would be the standard three-factor model of working memory corresponding to the phonological loop, the visuospatial sketchpad and the central executive. In short, the data did fit this three factor model, although it was not possible to draw strong conclusions for the 4- and 5-year-olds as they did not complete the full battery of tasks. Gathercole, Pickering, Ambridge & Wearing (2004) concluded that the structure of working memory was the same in children over the age of 6 years as it was in adults. Figure 4.4 illustrates the findings.

For further detailed discussion of the distinction between short-term working memory and ELWM in children, please see Swanson (2008).

Summary

Working memory in children and adults appears to have the same three-component structure corresponding to the phonological loop, the visuospatial sketchpad and the central executive. Other work also suggests that the episodic buffer forms a distinct component in children as it is hypothesised to do in adults (Alloway et al., 2004).

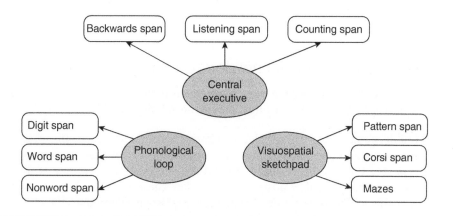

Figure 4.4 Diagram illustrating the relationship between measures of working memory in children

Source: adapted from Gathercole, Pickering, Ambridge & Wearing (2004)

What other factors are important for memory development?

In the traditional literature on memory development, many authors emphasise what might be called the 'big four' factors believed to be responsible for developmental improvements in memory. These are: knowledge base; memory strategies; metamemory; and capacity (Ceci, Fitneva & Williams, 2010).

In our discussion of working memory development so far, some of these factors have been dealt with in detail and others touched upon. For example, the issue of capacity has been central to the working memory account. In particular, we saw in Chapter 3 that developmental increases in articulation rate (possibly related to general improvements in processing speed) were argued to underlie developmental increases in memory span. The underlying assumption was that capacity could be more efficiently used with faster rates of verbal rehearsal.

The issue of knowledge base was also discussed in relation to work showing the contribution made by the familiarity of the items to be remembered; this issue was also relevant to the proposed role of the episodic buffer in providing links between the various working memory systems and stored knowledge. Memory strategies were also discussed, but this was confined to a consideration of verbal rehearsal; and several difficulties with the working memory model's assumptions about this strategy were outlined (Chapter 3). Metamemory, on the other hand, has not yet been discussed.

In the remaining sections of this chapter, we revisit or consider anew these four important factors, pointing out how each can contribute to our understanding of working memory development. These discussions are necessarily brief accounts of very large literatures in each case. The Further reading section at the end of this chapter gives several suggestions for those who are interested in finding out more.

The contribution of the knowledge base

> Children are better able to recall events if their semantic knowledge to interpret the event is strong. (Robertson & Köhler, 2007: p. 3180)

Children can have extremely detailed knowledge and understanding of particular areas and this helps them to recall information. For example, Chi (1978) reported that 10- to 11-year-old child chess experts were better at memorising legitimate chess positions than adult chess novices; despite the fact that the adults were better at remembering lists of digits than the children. These results suggested that the large differences in memory performance usually found between children and adults could be overcome if children had very rich domain-specific knowledge. Hence, it has long been acknowledged that the child's 'knowledge base' is strongly implicated in the development

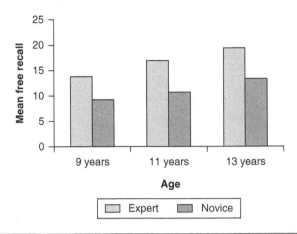

Figure 4.5   Mean free recall (units of information) of a soccer-related story for 'expert' and 'novice' children at three age levels

Source: data adapted from Schneider et al. (1989)

of memory (Kail, 1990; Murphy, McKone & Slee, 2003; Schneider & Pressley, 1997).

We will look at one further example of an experimental study to illustrate this point. Schneider, Körkel and Weinert (1989) asked large samples of 9-, 11- and 13-year-old children to remember a short story about a soccer game (n = 576 for Experiment 1, n = 185 for Experiment 2). The crucial manipulation was that all children were given a questionnaire on their soccer knowledge and the sample was divided into soccer 'experts' who scored highly on the questionnaire and soccer 'novices' who obtained lower scores.

There were various measures to assess how well the children remembered the soccer story across the two experiments including: free recall of the text; remembering details about the text; filling in missing words from the text; and recognising sentences from the text. Schneider et al. (1989) found that there were no expert/novice differences for the recognition of sentences measure, however, on every other measure the experts at each age level performed better than novices. Even when the authors subdivided the experts and novices into higher and lower aptitude children, this did not change the results. Aptitude level made no difference to performance, but expertise level did (accounting for more than 25% of the variation in performance on each measure). Figure 4.5 illustrates these results in relation to one measure, that of free recall.

These results suggested that rich domain-specific knowledge was even more important than a child's general ability for performance on a structured episodic remembering task (see also Brainerd, Reyna & Ceci, 2008). We can interpret these findings in relation to the episodic buffer, by assuming that individuals with a greater degree of relevant long-term knowledge were more able to use it to support their performance on an episodic remembering task.

Schneider et al. (1989) also pointed out an important educational implication of their findings. Lower ability children should be more likely to achieve academic success in school when interested, motivated and highly familiar with the topic or area of work.

Summary

A child's knowledge base has a marked impact on his or her ability to remember information. The richness and extensiveness of a child's understanding in particular areas of expertise can contribute to impressive memory performance and may also be a way of maximising academic success in lower ability children. The proposed episodic buffer of working memory can be regarded as a link to this repository of long-term knowledge and expertise.

Memory strategies

Memory strategies are deliberate and effortful methods used to enhance memory performance. They require a person to assess the remembering task, think of a suitable strategy to improve performance, utilise that strategy, monitor the success of the strategy, and change or adapt the strategy if necessary. The fact that memory strategies are deliberate, available to consciousness and goal-orientated suggests that they involve high-level skills. These skills sound very much like 'executive functioning', so it is likely that the use of memory strategies can be regarded as drawing on central executive resources, for planning, implementation and monitoring (see also later section on metamemory). It might also be suggested that the episodic buffer could be recruited to bind relevant information together, utilise long-term knowledge and perhaps offer extra storage capacity.

However, the working memory model account of typical development says very little about memory strategies, with the exception of verbal rehearsal. This is in contrast to the wider literature on memory development, which has placed great emphasis on the development of a range of memory strategies. Many authors consider that improvements and developments in the use of memory strategies play a central role in the development of memory in children (e.g. Flavell, 1985; Kail, 1990; Schneider & Pressley, 1997). In this section, the main types of memory strategies will be examined. In addition, possible links between memory strategy use and different components of the working memory model will be considered.

As already noted, memory strategies encompass anything a person might do in order to try to remember something more successfully. They are deliberate, in the sense that the person chooses to do something to improve their memory. Some examples of memory strategies are given in Box 4.4, roughly in order from least to most sophisticated.

Box 4.4   Examples of memory strategies

Verbal labelling/naming

A child says the name of a presented item; this strategy can be used for verbally presented items, but is probably most useful for items presented as 'nameable' pictures. Often, naming is regarded as a precursor to verbal rehearsal (see next example).

Verbal rehearsal

A child verbally recites the full list of memory items, possibly more than once, in order to keep them in mind. Cumulative verbal rehearsal involves adding each new item to the rehearsal list as it is presented. Verbal rehearsal can be overt (the item names are said out loud) or covert (the item names are whispered or said internally).

Chunking

The child recodes two or more stimulus items into one item or chunk. For example, if the words 'book' and 'shop' appeared in the same study list they could be recoded into one item 'bookshop'.

Grouping

The child imposes groups on the study input, for example dividing a six digit list into two groups of three digits. Grouping is useful for helping to remember telephone numbers; we can divide long numbers into area codes and personal numbers by pausing (spoken form) or leaving a space (written form).

Organisation

The child looks for links between study items and puts related items together. For example, animals could be grouped together, methods of transport could be grouped together, or household objects could be grouped together. This helps in recalling information by increasing the links between related items. Once one of the items from a linked group is retrieved it acts as a cue for retrieving the other items.

Flavell (1970; Flavell et al., 1966) did a great deal of work on memory strategies, drawing a distinction between children that did not and could not use a strategy even when instructed to; and children that could use a strategy, but chose not to. The former were said to be 'mediationally deficient' and the latter were said to be 'production deficient'.

This distinction remains useful, because many children are classifiable into a 'pre-strategies' stage, where they do not approach remembering tasks in a strategic manner. However, a significant number of slightly more advanced children may have particular strategies available to them, but not be able to use them in an appropriate context. Why might this be? The most common explanation is that a child requires a certain amount of processing resources in order to concurrently carry out the memory task whilst implementing and checking the effectiveness of a memory strategy. These types of processes require higher-level executive skills, which develop with age, as we have seen.

Familiarity with remembering tasks and practice with using strategies may reduce processing loads by 'routinising' some of the task demands. For example, in the first stages of learning how to use a strategy, executive demands may be too high for the child to use the strategy properly in the correct context. Alternatively, the child may select the wrong strategy for a particular context or carry out the strategy ineffectively. It is only with practice and adequate executive resources that the child can use a strategy appropriately in the correct context and monitor whether it increases their memory performance. Early use of deliberate memory strategies, therefore, may be 'faulty' and not actually aid recall (Baker-Ward, Ornstein & Holden, 1984).

Another way of looking at this is in terms of the 'mental effort' requirements of a task. Guttentag (1984) argued that more complex cumulative rehearsal strategies cannot be used by young children because they do not have the mental resources available to carry them out. The relationship between mental effort requirements and executive abilities is probably very close. There are many examples noted in the literature where children can use a strategy in certain circumstances, but only if task support is given; when this support is removed, the child can no longer use the strategy. There is also the evidence alluded to above that when children first start to use strategies they may not be effective at improving recall. All of this suggests that using memory strategies is taxing and requires a considerable amount of mental effort or central executive processing resources. The terminology may be different, but we are likely to be talking about the same thing.

Therefore, it is likely that the development of memory strategy use in both children and adults involves a complex interplay between strategy knowledge and experience, capacity limitations and the familiarity of the material to be remembered. All of these factors can be accounted for by the working memory model if we consider the interaction of several relevant components: the phonological loop/visuospatial sketchpad; the central executive; and links to long-term memory and additional storage capacity via the episodic buffer. Capacity limitations in working memory are likely to play a large role in the flexible development and use of a range of memory strategies; and in whether strategy use improves recall.

We finish this section with another debate in the current literature.

Debates and Issues 4.2   Utilisation deficiencies?

Recent work has focused on a 'new' phase of strategy development characterised by what are known as *utilisation deficiencies*: here, a child *uses* a particular strategy, but experiences no gain in terms of *improvement* memory performance (Miller & Seier, 1994). We have already suggested that this may often be the case for young children using very new strategies. However some researchers have applied this concept much more widely by suggesting that utilisation deficiencies are commonly seen throughout development when children develop new memory strategies. This point of view remains controversial, however, as some authors claim that utilisation deficiencies do not even exist!

Possibly the most convincing evidence in favour of utilisation deficiencies was reported in a study with *adults*, which required participants to carry out a very challenging memory task with highly unfamiliar materials. Gaultney, Kipp and Kirk (2005) trained adults to use an organisational strategy to improve their recall of nonwords. Although the adults used the strategy correctly, it did not immediately lead to benefits in relation to memory performance. Gaultney et al. (2005) concluded that the effortfullness of executing this organisational strategy with highly unfamiliar material led to utilisation deficiencies. If you would like to read more about this debate, see also Schwenck, Bjorklund and Schneider (2007).

Summary

Memory strategies are deliberate, planned and goal-orientated activities used to improve memory performance. The ability to use memory strategies increases markedly with age, possibly in line with the development of executive processing capacity. The use of memory strategies is demanding such that successful usage is likely to depend on the resources of the central executive and overall capacity in the working memory system.

A more detailed look at verbal rehearsal

This section takes a more detailed look at the strategy of verbal rehearsal. We examine how it develops with age in typical children in a way that is rather more complex and nuanced than the original working memory model had assumed.

When the working memory model was applied to children, there was a specific role for the strategy of verbal rehearsal within the phonological loop component of working memory (see Chapter 3). Improvements in the speed of verbal rehearsal were believed to be responsible for developmental improvements in memory span for verbal materials such as words and digits. In terms of the original working memory model, rehearsal was viewed as a strategy that all children used. We saw, however, that there were difficulties with this strong version of the model. Modifications to the working memory model resulted in a weakening of this position – younger children were viewed as using an automatic and/or simpler form of verbal rehearsal than older children (Gathercole & Hitch, 1993). Nevertheless, verbal rehearsal remained at the heart of the working memory model's account of the development of working memory in children.

The more general literature on the development of verbal rehearsal going back to the 1960s (see Kail, 1990; or Schneider & Pressley, 1997 for excellent reviews), however, takes a somewhat different view. We referred to this briefly in the previous chapter, but the essence of the argument is that verbal rehearsal develops gradually with age. Younger children are most unlikely to use the strategy at all and older children develop increasingly sophisticated rehearsal strategies that can be flexibly adapted to particular remembering tasks.

In short, even the modified version of the working memory model cannot capture the full developmental trajectory of verbal rehearsal in typical children. This section will consider some of the relevant research.

Verbal naming

We first consider the case of verbal naming, a strategy that has been regarded as a prerequisite for the development of verbal rehearsal. In the late 1960s and early 1970s, many studies looking at how well children could recall visually presented materials assessed verbal naming, or 'labelling' as it was often described. There was considerable argument over whether children of 4 or 5 years would label pictures or colours when asked to recall them. Equally, there was argument as to whether labelling, if carried out, actually improved recall (Bernbach, 1967; Bush & Cohen, 1970; Hagan & Kingsley, 1968; Keely, 1971; Kingsley & Hagan, 1969; McCarver & Ellis, 1972). The results were largely inconclusive, because no one could agree on exactly which types of items to present in order to assess the role and usage of labelling.

This all changed when Conrad (1971) came up with a better method of examining whether young children labelled items in order to try to remember them. Conrad (1971) was interested in the age at which children began to use verbal labels to 'mediate' recall. This can be regarded as a deliberate strategy if the items presented are visual. With visual items such as pictures, it is not mandatory to name them, particularly if the recall method does not require speech output. Pictures can be recalled simply as visual items. If there is evidence that children are naming pictures, we can conclude they are using a labelling strategy deliberately.

Conrad exploited a finding in the adult literature known as the 'phonological similarity effect' which refers to poorer recall of similar sounding words (Baddeley, 1966; Conrad & Hull, 1964 – see Chapter 1). Words that sound the same become confused when ordered recall is required if we use the *names* of the pictures to remember them. Conrad's reasoning was that only children using picture names to remember lists should find phonologically similar items difficult. See Box 4.5 for examples of pictures with similar sounding names (phonologically similar) as well as control pictures with dissimilar sounding names.

Box 4.5 Examples of pictures

Pictures with similar sounding names ('phonologically similar'):

Pictures with dissimilar sounding names ('control'):

Conrad (1971) gave children between the ages of 3 and 11 years lists of such pictures to recall. A series of pictures was displayed to the child, it was then concealed, and the child was given a full duplicate set of the pictures and asked to recreate the list in order. Conrad (1971) found that only children with a mental age of over 5 years showed the effect of phonological similarity; i.e. poorer performance on the pictures with similar sounding names. These findings suggested that there was a gradual development in the use of verbal names to aid recall after the age of 5 years.

So how are children of 5 years and younger remembering pictures if they are not using the verbal naming strategy? Work considered earlier in this chapter by Graham Hitch and his colleagues (Hitch et al., 1988, 1991; Hitch, Woodin & Baker, 1989) suggested that 4- to 5-year-old children preferred to remember lists of pictures using visual memory codes. Hitch and colleagues concluded that there was a developmental shift in the strategies adopted to recall lists of pictures. At the age of 5 years, visual strategies predominated, and there was no evidence for the use of a naming strategy. By the age of 10 years, however, children were consistently using the names of pictures to recall them.

Palmer (2000a) took this research even further. She tested children of 3 to 8 years on their ability to remember lists of pictures that were either visually or phonologically similar. She also tested the same children a year later to see the extent to which new strategies may have developed. Again, children were shown lists of pictured items and asked to recall them verbally.

Palmer (2000a) found that children of 3 to 4 years showed no evidence of either visual or phonological similarity and concluded that these children were in a pre-strategy phase. Five-year-old children showed visual similarity effects; and children aged 6 to 8 years showed both visual similarity and phonological similarity effects. These results were largely consistent when Palmer tested the children a year later. Therefore, taken together with the earlier research on 10-year-old children, there was evidence for a four-stage development in strategy use on visual picture memory span tasks, summarised in Box 4.6.

Box 4.6   The four-stage development of verbal and visual strategies in relation to picture memory span tasks (Palmer, 2000a)

1   Phase 1 children use no particular strategy.
2   Phase 2 children begin to use visual memory strategies.
3   Phase 3 marks the beginning of verbal strategy use, but children also retain visual strategies, hence, *dual* visual and verbal coding.
4   Phase 4 represents mature strategy use, where children use predominantly verbal memory strategies.

The latter two 'verbal' stages may be characterised by development from simple verbal naming strategies to cumulative verbal rehearsal, although both can be regarded as voluntary verbal strategies.

The research just described suggests that the gradual development of verbal naming strategies is a factor behind the increase in picture memory span with age. Performance on this task goes up from under two items below the age of 5 years when children are in their pre-strategic phase, to around four items by the age of 9 or 10 years when children have reached mature verbal strategy use (Henry, 2008). The correspondence between the emergence of verbal strategies and the increase in picture memory span suggests that the one causes the other. Of course, we cannot provide direct evidence that strategy development is the only factor behind picture span improvements, as the evidence required to answer this question would involve a careful tracking over time of the links between strategy development and span improvements.

Other research has illustrated another very important point. Just because older children and adults use verbal strategies in this particular picture memory span task, it does not mean that they have lost the ability to use visual strategies. When task demands are altered such that using verbal strategies is impossible, we see re-emerging evidence for the use of visual strategies (Logie, Della Sala, Wynn & Baddeley, 2000; Walker, Hitch & Duroe, 1993). This suggests that new strategies are gradually added to a child's repertoire and the child chooses the most effective strategy for the particular circumstances.

This is a good example of why utilising memory strategies could be thought of as an executive-loaded task. The child must appraise the memory requirements, choose an appropriate strategy, monitor the effectiveness of the strategy and change it when necessary. These are a demanding set of requirements, which is why we do not see mature use of the most effective verbal strategies in this task until children are around 9 to 10 years old. We will come back to this issue shortly when we discuss metamemory.

Summary

Verbal naming may be the first step a child takes towards using verbal rehearsal. It develops at around the age of 6 years according to research evidence in relation to the development of phonological similarity effects. Deliberate verbal naming strategies may coexist with earlier (less mature) visual strategies between the ages of 6 to 8 years. However, by the age of 10 years, most children appear to use predominantly verbal naming strategies in standard picture memory span tasks.

Verbal rehearsal

As we saw in Chapter 3, verbal rehearsal develops gradually from the age of about 7 years in typical children. Flavell et al. (1966), in a classic study, observed children performing picture remembering tasks and looked for evidence of lip movements or verbalisations, which might imply the use of verbal rehearsal. By the age of 10 years, most children showed at least some instances of verbalisations (85%); many children showed such evidence at 7 years (60%); whereas verbalisations were relatively rare in 5-year-olds (10%) as we would expect.

McGilly and Siegler (1989) used an even richer and more detailed approach to study the development of verbal rehearsal in large samples of 5/6-, 6/7- and 8/9-year-olds (around 30 per group). All children were asked to remember series of three or five digits, with a short delay before recall. The authors were particularly interested in what the children did during this delay so they video-recorded all participants to examine rehearsal-related actions. These included covert whispering, moving of lips, saying numbers out loud and repeated nodding of the head. In addition, at the end of each trial, each child was asked exactly what he/she had done to remember the numbers. Using both sources of information, McGilly and Siegler (1989) classified each child's behaviour on every trial into three categories: (1) repeated rehearsal which involved saying the list of numbers more than once (this was the most sophisticated rehearsal strategy); (2) single rehearsal which involved saying the list of numbers once only; and (3) no rehearsal.

It is worth looking at the results in some detail as they illustrate that although the use of rehearsal increased with age, children used a range of approaches. Table 4.1 illustrates these results. In the youngest group, repeated rehearsal was less often used than single rehearsal (24% of trials versus 56% of trials),

Table 4.1 Percentage of trials on which three strategies (repeated rehearsal, single rehearsal and no rehearsal) were used by children between the ages of 5 and 9 years

Age	Repeated rehearsal	Single rehearsal	No rehearsal
5–6 years	24	56	20
6–7 years	63	29	8
8–9 years	78	16	5

Source: data adapted from McGilly and Siegler (1989)

whereas for the oldest children repeated rehearsal was more often used than single rehearsal (78% versus 16%). Children frequently did different things on different trials and although there was a gradual shift with age towards more use of repeated rehearsal, even the oldest children did not always use this strategy.

It is important to note, however, that the children in this study were prompted to use some sort of strategy during the delay period. The experimenter said that they 'could say the numbers in their head' if they liked. Therefore, the rates of rehearsal may be slightly higher in this study than in others not employing such prompting. However, the authors accounted for their increased rates of rehearsal differently. They pointed out that looking at videotaped behaviours during the memory task as well as asking children what they had done on each trial led to more detection of rehearsal activities. McGilly and Siegler (1989) noted that if they had only used observable behaviours, rates of rehearsal would have been considerably lower.

Similar work confirms and extends these developmental trends using 'free recall' techniques. Free recall tasks in this context require children to remember 18 to 20 words presented at very slow rates (five seconds per item). Participants in several related studies (Cuvo, 1975; Ornstein, Naus & Liberty, 1975; Ornstein, Naus & Stone, 1977) were encouraged to speak out loud any verbal rehearsal that they carried out. The experimenters noted that young children tended to rehearse single words at a time, usually the word that had just been presented. By contrast, older children and adults were much more likely to rehearse larger groups of words, regarded as a more sophisticated implementation of the rehearsal strategy. Kunzinger (1985) replicated these results in a longitudinal study, finding that 7-year-olds had an average rehearsal set-size of 1.7 items and that this had increased two years later to an average set-size of 2.6 items.

Recent work using the free recall paradigm has contributed further to our understanding of how verbal rehearsal develops. Lehmann and Hasselhorn (2007) conducted a two-year longitudinal study with 76 children who were 8 years old at the beginning of the project, testing them on five separate occasions for their ability to remember lists of 12 familiar words. The items were presented very slowly, with one word every eight seconds (children heard the words and simultaneously saw a card containing a picture and the printed name of the item). Children were instructed to say out loud whatever they were thinking or doing whilst trying to memorise the items and all sessions were videotaped.

Lehmann and Hasselhorn (2007) classified the children's behaviours in great detail and the five categories they identified are outlined in Box 4.7, together with their change in percentage occurrence over the two years of the study (incorporating the five separate testing occasions – 'times 1 to 5').

Box 4.7   Free recall strategies in 8- to 10-year-olds and their percentage occurrence, Lehmann and Hasselhorn (2007)

1   Labelling: speaking aloud the name of one item once during the interstimulus interval. This declined with age from 41% at time 1 to 26% at time 5.
2   Single-word rehearsal: repeating the name of one item several times during the same interstimulus interval. This remained stable between times 1 and 5 at 11%.
3   Cumulative rehearsal: repeating a set of words containing at least two items. This increased with age from 17% at time 1 to 46% at time 5.
4   Association/elaboration: trying to link two or more items together (e.g. there is *rain* on the *lake*). This remained stable between times 1 and 5 at 8–9%.
5   No observable strategy: This reduced with age from 23% at time 1 to 8% at time 5.

Again, here was clear evidence that simple measures of verbal behaviour, such as labelling, declined with age, whereas the more sophisticated cumulative rehearsal strategies increased. However, the authors noted that cumulative rehearsal was very variable between different list positions as well as between different children. In fact, children were likely to use more than one strategy in trying to remember any particular list, most often labelling and cumulative rehearsal. As a general rule, labelling was more likely to occur at later list positions, whereas cumulative rehearsal was more likely to occur at earlier list positions. Lehmann and Hasselhorn (2007) concluded that 'children switch during the list learning process from cumulative rehearsal to labelling' (p. 1079).

Rehearsal set sizes also increased from just over 1 word at the age of 8 years to 2 words at the age of 10 years. This was probably related to their executive-loaded working memory (ELWM) capacity. Why? Children with higher scores on a measure of ELWM (reverse digit span) showed more evidence of using cumulative rehearsal and demonstrated larger rehearsal set sizes. Finally, children using more cumulative rehearsal remembered more words. This indicated that they were beyond the 'utilisation deficiency' stage and had the mental (or executive) resources required to perform a memory task and implement a sophisticated memory strategy at the same time. Nevertheless, Lehmann and Hasselhorn (2007) speculated that children may switch from cumulative rehearsal to labelling as they go deeper into a list, because the ELWM load of cumulative rehearsal becomes too great.

Summary

The development of verbal rehearsal is a complex and involved process. This is not a strategy that suddenly emerges in an 'all or nothing' fashion. Detailed investigations of the development of verbal rehearsal have indicated that although the strategy emerges gradually with age, several types of simple and complex rehearsal strategies can coexist at the same time for any particular child. In fact, children can even use both simple and complex strategies during the same trial in free recall tasks. Therefore, it is important to take the complexity of rehearsal development into account when theorising about how working memory improves with age.

Metamemory

Metamemory refers to 'knowledge about memory' (Schneider & Pressley, 1997). This includes things like understanding when 'active' memory is necessary and what sorts of things you have to do in order to remember things. Relevant knowledge about memory includes knowing about characteristics of the memory task or the materials that are to be remembered. For example, knowing that remembering larger sets of items will be more difficult than remembering smaller sets of items; and that familiar items are easier to remember than unfamiliar items. Knowledge of person characteristics may also be relevant, such as that adults might generally remember more than children; or that memory may vary for the same person when the situation changes. Similarly, knowledge about different memory strategies is part of our armoury of knowledge about memory.

So far, we have discussed knowledge about memory that could be stored in long-term memory: i.e. a repository of helpful information that might be brought to bear in remembering tasks. Another important facet of metamemory, however, is the notion that there is executive control of the memory system, which takes into account capacity limits and whether strategies are available or not. To achieve a memory goal, a person must have a realistic awareness of his or her own memory limitations as well as the flexibility to select and possibly change memory strategies to help achieve that goal (Kail, 1990). This executive control extends to monitoring how effective particular strategies are in achieving memory goals. Individuals with more advanced metamemory skills will be able to replace ineffective memory strategies with effective ones and be aware when goals are not being reached (e.g. Brown, 1975).

Therefore, metamemory as a concept seems to encompass: (1) long-term knowledge about memory-relevant issues (that might be accessed via the episodic buffer of working memory); and (2) executive control of remembering processes that might include strategy selection, monitoring of performance, strategy switching as appropriate and recognition of resource limitations (which is most likely controlled by the central executive). Ceci et al. (2010: 466) developed a similar distinction, referring to metamnemonic knowledge ('insights about tasks, strategies or internal cognitive abilities') and metamnemonic regulation ('two processes involved in the coordination of memory: monitoring and control'). Ceci et al. (2010) also suggested that the prefrontal cortex (linked to executive functioning) is likely to be closely linked to the second type of metamemory, namely monitoring and control.

How does metamemory develop in typical children? There is an enormous literature on this issue, but we will look at some key studies that give a flavour of the relevant issues.

Children develop in their sophistication and understanding about the types of factors relevant to remembering tasks. For example, Kreutzer, Leonard and Flavell (1975) conducted a detailed interview study of memory-relevant knowledge in 5-, 6-, 8- and 10-year-old children. These authors asked the children questions about how they remembered things, and which things were easier or harder to remember. All of the questions were about everyday memory tasks such as how they might remember to take their skates to school the next morning; or whether they should dial a telephone number immediately after hearing it or get a drink of water before dialling.

Although quite a reasonable range of knowledge was uncovered, even in the younger children, Kreutzer et al. (1975) found that 5- to 6-year-olds tended to come up with external memory strategies such as writing a note on leaving the skates in an obvious place; older children were somewhat more likely to mention internal strategies such as rehearsal or organisation. However, because this study relied on interviewing young children, it is possible that restricted vocabulary knowledge and language skills reduced the children's ability to describe their memory knowledge (Schneider & Pressley, 1997).

Wellman (1977) used a completely non-verbal technique to test metamemory in even younger children (ages 3, 4 and 5 years). Pairs of pictures illustrated certain memory-relevant factors. For example, a boy trying to remember 18 objects versus a boy trying to remember three objects; someone trying to remember in a noisy background versus a non-noisy background; and someone trying to remember with some help versus having no help. There were also three memory-irrelevant items such as children with red or black hair trying to remember things. For each pair of pictures, the child was asked to point to which child had the hardest task. The results showed that 74% of the children appeared to make valid memory judgements (i.e. they rated the harder tasks correctly, noted that memory-irrelevant variables made no difference and could justify their ratings with minimal verbal descriptions).

Studies such as these suggest that children's understanding about memory-relevant factors and how to succeed in memory tasks becomes more sophisticated and detailed with age. Further research revealed that children also become more realistic about their memory limitations as they grow older.

Flavell, Friedrichs and Hoyt (1970) asked children aged 5, 6, 7 and 9 years to remember series of pictures. They were given as much time as they wanted, but were asked to judge when they were ready to recall all of the pictures correctly. Flavell et al. (1970) found that preschool children were poor at judging when they were ready to recall the pictures, whereas older children were much more accurate. Another technique is to ask children how many items they think they can recall. Flavell et al. (1970) tested this with lists of up to ten pictures and found that preschool children were very inaccurate, with over 50% thinking that they could recall all ten items. In a similar study, Henry and Norman (1996) asked 80 4- and 5-year-old children to predict how many pictures out of ten they thought they could remember. Again, children were highly inaccurate, with estimated picture spans of eight items, despite the fact that their actual picture spans were around two items.

Similarly, Cunningham and Weaver (1989) asked 6 year olds to predict their ability to remember ten words, but did this in two ways. Following the earlier method, 58% of the children predicted that they could recall all ten items, in line with previous findings. However, in a slightly different condition, children were asked to turn off a tape recorder playing the words after as many words as they thought they could remember. In this condition, only 17% predicted that they could recall all ten words. Therefore, fairly young children can be more accurate in predicting memory performance if they have online experience with a task.

Finally, it is of interest whether children with better metamemory actually show better memory performance. Schneider and Pressley (1997) considered several meta-analyses of this question and concluded that the overall correlation between metamemory and memory was .41. This represents a moderate relationship between the two variables, suggesting that those with better metamemory do indeed show better memory performance as we might expect.

We finish this section by coming back to the 'big four' factors implicated in children's memory development: knowledge base; strategies; metamemory; and capacity. A recent theory developed by Ceci et al. (2010) suggests that developments in all of these areas 'catalyse each other' (p. 465). In other words, improvements in one area enrich and increase performance in the other areas. Ceci et al. (2010) suggest that even very young children can show surprisingly high levels of metamemory when their memory representations are extremely rich and highly developed. They argue that children are only able to successfully monitor their memory performance (i.e. at the executive level) when their representations are rich and flexible, probably because rich representations 'free up' more capacity for monitoring.

There is even recent evidence to suggest that developments in metamemory may stimulate developments in strategy use. A longitudinal study by Grammer, Purtell, Coffman and Ornstein (2011) tracked both metamemory and strategy use (in relation to semantic sorting strategies) in 107 6-year-old children over a period of one year, testing the children on both of these skills in four consecutive school terms. In each test session, training in a sorting strategy was given to see how developments in metamemory and strategy use proceeded over time. These authors assessed three possible hypotheses: (1) metamemory and strategy use developed in tandem i.e. at the same time; (2) growth in metamemory preceded developments in strategy use; and (3) developments in strategy use preceded growth in metamemorial understanding. The evidence favoured the second hypothesis that metamemorial understanding developed somewhat in advance of strategic sorting strategies. Grammer et al. (2011) concluded that metamemory was important for the subsequent development of memory strategies.

Summary
Metamemory refers to the knowledge a person has about their own memory. This knowledge develops gradually with age in typical children, in terms of how much they understand about their own memory processes, their recognition of memory limitations and the ability to choose relevant strategies. Metamemory is likely to be strongly related both to executive functioning and to level of stored memory knowledge. These two facets of metamemory may be linked to the central executive and the episodic buffer of working memory respectively.

Overall summary

In this chapter we have considered the visuospatial sketchpad, the central executive and the episodic buffer of working memory in relation to typical development. Unlike the previous chapter on the development of the phonological loop, the working memory model did not always provide a detailed set of predictions to guide our discussions. Why was this? Put simply, the working memory model's account of memory development focuses largely on the phonological loop. Relatively little detail has been put forward on the types of mechanisms that might be responsible for developmental improvements in the other systems of working memory.

Nevertheless, we did come to a number of conclusions. First, visuospatial short-term memory (VSSTM) was found to increase with age and form a distinct and separate system from phonological short-term memory. There was good evidence that VSSTM in typically developing children could be separated into at least two components: one dealing with spatial information and one dealing with visual information. There was also evidence for a developmental shift from visual to verbal coding, which could be explicitly linked to two working memory systems (the phonological loop and the visuospatial sketchpad).

Secondly, executive-loaded working memory (ELWM) and other executive skills were found to improve with age, but there was evidence that different aspects of executive functioning matured at different rates. Adult levels of performance were reached earlier on measures of set shifting and inhibition, than on measures of planning, ELWM and fluency.

Thirdly, working memory in children and adults appeared to have the same three-component structure corresponding to the phonological loop, the visuospatial sketchpad and the central executive. In addition, the episodic buffer seemed to represent a distinct component of working memory in children as it is hypothesised to do in adults (Alloway et al., 2004). Fourthly, developmental research on binding tasks relevant to the episodic buffer suggested that automatic binding abilities may develop rapidly, but that binding requiring strategic control may mature later, probably in line with developing executive capacity.

Finally, we discussed more traditional approaches to memory development in children; and outlined the 'big four' factors that have been identified to explain mechanisms underlying improvements in memory with age (knowledge base, memory strategies, metamemory, capacity limitations). In relation to this work, the working memory account of memory development has largely been concerned with capacity limitations and one particular memory strategy (verbal rehearsal), although recent revisions have explicitly considered the role of knowledge base.

It is striking, however, that the revised working memory model provides many new points of intersection between the various working memory components and these 'big four' factors. An exploration of these points of contact would be a powerful way of advancing the field. The considerable strengths of the working memory approach can be retained, largely the concise and unified way of looking at how important memory systems interact; yet the breadth and detail of more traditional work on memory development can be used to enhance and enrich our ways of thinking about this area.

Several suggestions as to how this might be done can be made. For example, a child's knowledge base can have a marked impact on the ability to remember information, so a more explicit consideration of how this information might be accessed via the episodic buffer would be a valuable approach to take. Similarly, the use and sophistication of memory strategies increases markedly with age, but the richness and complexity of these developments is not captured by the working memory model. Future research could look at how changes in strategic memory behaviour relate to working memory development and consider the role played by parallel developments in executive skills (which we have suggested underpin the child's ability to use strategies effectively). Finally, the concept of metamemory brings together both knowledge (the episodic buffer) and executive control (the central executive) and has obvious implications for memory development. At present, this is not an area that has been addressed by researchers taking a working memory perspective. An interesting question that recent work has begun to address, is whether knowledge about memory develops in parallel with changes in executive control and strategic behaviour.

To conclude, research in the area of memory development in typical children could be considerably enriched if the working memory perspective were integrated with traditional approaches to the study of memory development.

Further reading

Chapters/reviews

Gathercole, S.E. (1998). The development of memory. *Journal of Child Psychology and Psychiatry, 39*(1), 3–27. An excellent and thorough account of the whole area.

Towse, J.N. & Hitch, G.J. (2007). Variation in working memory due to normal development. In A.R.A. Conway, C. Jarrold, M.J. Kane, A. Miyake & J.N. Towse (Eds.), *Variation in working memory*. pp. 109–133. Oxford: Oxford University Press. A detailed and sophisticated account of executive-loaded working memory.

Reading relevant to the knowledge base, memory strategies and metamemory

Bjorklund, D.F. & Douglas, R.N. (1997). The development of memory strategies. In N. Cowan (Ed.), *The development of memory in childhood*. pp. 201–246. Hove, East Sussex: Psychology Press. A clearly written chapter covering strategies, knowledge base and metamemory with an excellent historical perspective.

Joyner, M.H. & Kurtz-Costes, B. (1997). Metamemory development. In N. Cowan (Ed.), *The development of memory in childhood*. pp. 275–300. Hove, East Sussex: Psychology Press. A clearly presented outline of metamemory development in children.

Kail, R. (1990). *The development of memory in children*, 3rd ed. New York: W. H. Freeman and Company. A classic book – very clear, thorough and readable.

Schneider, W. & Pressley, M. (1997). *Memory development between two and twenty*, 2nd ed. Mahwah, NJ: Lawrence Erlbaum Associates. A detailed tour de force that still stands as an exceptional account of the area, but somewhat more demanding.

Research papers

These are listed in the order that they are mentioned in the chapter, rather than in alphabetical order.

Logie, R.H. & Pearson, D.G. (1997). The inner eye and the inner scribe of visuo-spatial working memory: Evidence from developmental fractionation. *European Journal of Cognitive Psychology, 9*(3), 241–257. Examining visual and spatial working memory in typical children.

Hitch, G.J., Halliday, S., Schaafstal, A.M. & Schraagen, J.MC. (1988). Visual working memory in young children. *Memory & Cognition, 16*, 120–132. The switch from visual to verbal coding.

Palmer, S. (2000a). Working memory: A developmental study of phonological recoding. *Memory, 8*(3), 179–193. More detail on the switch from visual to verbal coding.

Miyake, A., Friedman, N.P., Emerson, M.J., Witzki, A.H., Howerter, A. & Wager, T.D. (2000). The unity and diversity of executive functions and their contributions to complex 'frontal lobe' tasks: A latent variable analysis. *Cognitive Psychology, 41*, 49–100. A demanding but classic paper on executive functioning in adults.

Lehto, J.E., Juujärvi, P., Kooistra, L. & Lulkkinen, L. (2003). Dimensions of executive functioning: Evidence from children. *British Journal of Developmental Psychology, 21*, 59–80. Executive functioning in children.

Siegel, L.S. & Ryan, E.B. (1989). The development of working memory in normally achieving and subtypes of learning disabled children. *Child Development, 60*, 973–980. Executive-loaded working memory in typical and atypical children – also useful for Chapter 6.

Barrouillet, P., Gavens, N., Vergauwe, E., Gaillard, V. & Camos, V. (2009). Working memory span development: A time-based resource-sharing model account. *Developmental Psychology, 45*, 477–490. A new perspective on ELWM.

Sluzenski, J., Newcombe, N.S. & Kovacs, S.L. (2006). Binding, relational memory, and recall of naturalistic events: a developmental perspective. *Journal of Experimental Psychology: Learning, Memory, and Cognition, 32*(1), 89–100. Relevant to the development of the episodic buffer.

Gathercole, S.E., Pickering, S.J., Ambridge, B. & Wearing, H. (2004). The structure of working memory from 4 to 15 years of age. *Developmental Psychology, 40*, 177–190. Exactly what it says in the title!

Schneider, W., Körkel, J. & Weinert, F.E. (1989). Domain-specific knowledge and memory performance: A comparison of high- and low-aptitude children. *Journal of Educational Psychology, 81*, 306–312. The effects of the knowledge base on memory performance.

McGilly, K. & Siegler, R.S. (1989). How children choose among serial recall strategies. *Child Development, 60*, 172–182. A detailed look at verbal rehearsal in children.

Wellman, H.M. (1977). Preschoolers' understanding of memory-relevant variables. *Child Development, 48*, 1720–1723. A classic paper on metamemory – very short and easy to read.

Optional or extended essay topic for a piece of coursework

Option 1: 'What are the relationships between working memory, executive functioning and educational achievement in typically developing children?'

Use the current chapter for background understanding and setting the scene. Then look at the following papers in order to get an idea of the research evidence linking educational achievement, working memory and executive functioning. You should also search for more recent papers using your library's psychology databases.

Baddeley, A.D., Gathercole, S.E. and Papagno, C. (1998). The phonological loop as a language learning device. *Psychological Review, 105*, 158–173.

Bayliss, D.M., Jarrold, C., Gunn, D.M. & Baddeley, A.D. (2003). The complexities of complex span: Explaining individual differences in working memory in children and adults. *Journal of Experimental Psychology: General, 132*(1), 71–92.

Bull, R. & Scerif, G. (2001). Executive function as a predictor of children's mathematics ability: Inhibition, switching and working memory. *Developmental Neuropsychology, 19*, 273–293.

Bull, R., Espy, K.A. & Wiebe, S.A. (2008). Short-term memory, working memory, and executive functioning in preschoolers: Longitudinal predictors of mathematical achievement at age 7 years. *Developmental Neuropsychology, 33*, 205–228.

Gathercole, S.E., Pickering, S.J., Knight, C. & Stegman, Z. (2004). Working memory skills and educational attainment: Evidence from National Curriculum assessments at 7 and 14 years of age. *Applied Cognitive Psychology, 18*, 1–16.

Grimley, M. & Banner, G. (2008). Working memory, cognitive style, and behavioural predictors of GCSE exam success. *Educational Psychology, 28*(3), 341–351.

Leather, C. & Henry, L.A. (1994). Working memory span and phonological awareness tasks as predictors of early reading ability. *Journal of Experimental Child Psychology, 58*, 88–111.

St Clair-Thompson, H.L. & Gathercole, S.E. (2006). Executive functions and achievements in school: Shifting, updating, inhibition, and working memory. *Quarterly Journal of Experimental Psychology, 59*, 745–759.

Swanson, H.L. (2008). Working memory and intelligence in children: What develops? *Journal of Educational Psychology, 100*(3), 581–602.

van der Sluis, S., de Jong, P.F. & van der Leij, A. (2007). Executive functioning in children, and its relations with reasoning, reading, and arithmetic. *Intelligence, 35*, 427–449.

Option 2: 'How can professionals in educational settings best cater for children with working memory difficulties?'

Use the current chapter for background understanding and setting the scene. Then look at the following papers/books in order to get an idea of the research evidence linking educational practice and working memory limitations. You should also search for more recent papers using your library's psychology databases.

Elliott, J. G., Gathercole, S. E., Alloway, T. P., Holmes, J. & Kirkwood, H. (2010). An evaluation of a classroom-based intervention to help overcome working memory difficulties and improve long-term academic achievement. *Journal of Cognitive Education and Psychology, 9*(3), 227–250. Adapting classroom practice for children with working memory limitations has limited effects.

Gathercole, S.E. & Alloway, T.P. (2008). *Working memory and learning: A practical guide for teachers*. London: SAGE Publications Ltd. A very clear book covering the working memory model, how working memory is related to academic achievement and interventions for children with poor working memory.

Gathercole, S.E., Lamont, E. & Alloway, T.P. (2006). Working memory in the classroom. In S.J. Pickering (Ed.), *Working memory and education* (pp. 241–271). London: Elsevier, Academic Press. How to adapt teaching styles for children with weak working memory.

Holmes, J., Gathercole, S.E. & Dunning, D.L. (2009). Adaptive training leads to sustained enhancement of poor working memory in children. *Developmental Science, 12*, F1–F7. A promising intervention to improve working memory.

Minear, M. & Shah, P. (2006). Sources of working memory deficits in children and possibilities for remediation. In S.J. Pickering (Ed.), *Working memory and education* (pp. 273–307). London: Elsevier, Academic Press. A discussion of methods that have been used to improve working memory in children with a range of developmental disorders.

Pickering, S.J. (2006). *Working memory and education*. London: Elsevier, Academic Press. An excellent collection of chapters on working memory in a range of developmental disorders.

Potential exam questions

1 What do we know about the development of the 'central executive' component of working memory in typically developing children?

2 Can traditional research on children's memory development contribute to our understanding of working memory?

5

Working Memory in Children with Intellectual Disabilities

Learning outcomes

At the end of this chapter, you should have a good understanding of how to define, assess and classify intellectual disabilities (ID). You should also have an appreciation of why the choice of appropriate comparison groups is crucial for research in this area. You should be able to take a 'critical' view of the research evidence concerning whether children with intellectual disabilities show difficulties with one or more of the four components of working memory according to Baddeley's revised model (Baddeley, 2007). Finally, you should have some insight into two further issues: the impact of the severity of ID on working memory; and whether the structure of working memory is similar in those with ID and typically developing individuals.

Introduction

Children with general (or non-specific) intellectual disabilities do not have known specific developmental disorders (for example, autism, Down syndrome), but have generally slower rates of development than 'typical' children. They would be expected to have IQ scores in the lower range (i.e. standardised scores below 70/75) and difficulties with everyday living. We will look at other populations of children with atypical development who have specific syndromes or disorders in later chapters.

Intellectual disabilities (ID) represent 'the most common developmental disorder and the most handicapping of the disorders beginning in childhood' (Harris, 2006: p. 79). Many regard ID as the disorder that limits participation in society more than any other (Harris, 2006), yet recent research in this area has been relatively limited and restricted to a small pool of researchers (Hodapp & Dykens, 2009). Nevertheless, there is a reasonably large literature on memory development in children with ID, generally reporting memory deficits that include: poor short- and long-term memory; difficulties with encoding; poor use of retrieval cues; and inefficiency in the use of memory strategies such as rehearsal (for reviews see Borkowski, Peck & Damberg, 1991; Detterman, 1979; Ellis, 1978; Weiss, Weisz & Bromfield, 1986).

Much of this literature has not taken a 'working memory' perspective, so in this chapter we will use the working memory framework to structure the discussion of memory skills in children with ID. Bear in mind that this model is a theory, and one important question is whether this theory is successful in accounting for both typical and atypical development. In fact, we have already seen some limitations to the working memory model in the discussion of evidence for memory development in typically developing children. Given that all theories of cognitive development should have a degree of universality (e.g. Pennington, Moon, Edgin, Stedron & Nadel, 2003), they should be able to account for both typical and atypical development. This is one of the key issues that can be addressed when looking at a range of children who have different types of development.

In this chapter, we will present background information on ID, discuss how to define and assess ID, and then look at working memory skills in this population.

Intellectual disabilities

Definitional issues

Before we start describing what intellectual disabilities (ID) are, it is important to briefly discuss what they have been called in different settings and in different continents. Historically in the US, the term 'mental retardation' was used, although this has recently been replaced with the term 'intellectual disabilities'. Similar movements have taken place in Europe towards the term 'intellectual disabilities' such that most major academic journals throughout the world now use this term.

In the UK, this term 'learning difficulties/disabilities' is more prevalent, particularly in educational and clinical settings. Since the late 1970s, special schools catering for children and young people with ID have been known as 'schools for children with moderate or severe learning difficulties', depending on the level of severity of the ID. Hence, children and young people with mild to moderate intellectual disabilities are often referred to as having 'MLD' (moderate learning difficulties) and children and young people with severe intellectual disabilities are referred to as having 'SLD' (severe learning difficulties).

One further area of confusion is that in the US, the term 'learning difficulty' refers to a specific difficulty with learning such as dyslexia or dyscalculia, rather than the broad difficulties with learning that are referred to in the UK with the same term. Therefore, in this book, we will use the term 'intellectual disabilities' throughout, because this term is less open to confusion.

This chapter reviews the evidence for working memory difficulties in individuals with 'non-specific aetiology', or general ID; in other words, individuals for whom no specific disorder (e.g. Down syndrome) has been identified. However, we first look at how to define and assess ID.

What are intellectual disabilities?

Intellectual disabilities (ID) refer to cognitive and adaptive difficulties that have their onset early in life. The simplest definition of ID is based around a low level of cognitive functioning, or IQ (intelligence quotient). Those with an IQ of less than 70 would fall into the intellectually disabled range. However, most definitions also require that there is some impairment in social adaptation (e.g. daily living skills, communication, socialisation, motor skills).

According to Volkmar and Dykens (2002), if we take the 'IQ of less than 70' definition, rates of ID are between 2% and 3% of the population. If we also require a degree of social impairment (e.g. sufficient to require services), rates of ID are somewhat lower at around 1% of the population (Volkmar & Dykens, 2002). Many with milder forms of ID in the preschool years will not yet have come to the attention of services; equally many will acquire better adaptive skills as they grow up and achieve independence by adulthood. In other words, rates of ID may be lower in preschoolers and adults than in school-age children. ID is associated with psychosocial adversity (e.g. disadvantaged families) and is somewhat more common in males (a ratio of 1.5:1).

Rates of ID may be higher or lower, depending on the type of IQ measure used and whether or not full populations or registers of individuals known to services are examined. For example, Simonoff et al. (2006) argued that the prevalence of ID is much higher when researchers examine whole populations (for example, an entire borough) as opposed to registers. They also argued that generational increases in IQ (the 'Flynn effect'; Flynn, 1987) may lead to underestimates of the prevalence of ID if older IQ tests are used (because everybody does better).

Levels of ID can range from borderline through to profound. These levels are generally assessed using measures of intellectual ability (IQ tests), combined with indices of the person's ability to carry out daily living skills and/or live independently.

Box 5.1 gives an approximate indication of the IQ levels and estimated ability to live independently associated with different classifications of ID. Some variations occur in precise IQ ranges used to describe different levels of impairment. Importantly, IQ tests are only estimates of ability and clinical judgment is often a key factor for diagnosis. Both the *ICD-10* (World Health Organisation, 1992) and the *DSM-IV, DSM-IVTR* (American Psychiatric Association, 1994, 2000) classification systems use these broad descriptive levels (Volkmar & Dykens, 2002). A cut-off point of around 39–40 to differentiate between moderate and severe ID is most practical for research purposes, because available tests of intellectual functioning across the full range of abilities do not generally provide standardised scores below 39 or 40 (e.g. Henry, 2001; Henry & Gudjonsson, 2003).

Box 5.1   Levels of intellectual disabilities

- *Borderline*   IQ of about 70 to 79. A mild form of impairment, a very good chance of living independently.
- *Mild*   IQ of 50–55 to around 70. A reasonable chance of living independently or semi-independently.
- *Moderate*   IQ of 35–40 to 50–55. Likely to require at least some level of support in daily living skills.
- *Severe*   IQ of 20–25 to 35–40. A high level of support and supervision required throughout life.
- *Profound*   IQ less than 20–25. May have very limited ability to carry out any self-care tasks.

Most of those with ID fall into the mild range (around 17 out of 20). A smaller proportion have moderate ID (around 2 in 20). The remaining individuals are either severely or profoundly impaired (1 in 20). There are some clearly understood causes of ID that can happen prenatally (before birth), including: chromosome abnormalities (Down syndrome); inborn errors of metabolism (phenylketonuria); genetic conditions (fragile X, tuberous sclerosis); toxins (foetal alcohol syndrome); maternal illness (diabetes, pre-eclampsia); seizures; and cerebral palsy. There are also causes that can occur during birth, just after birth or during childhood, including: foetal distress/hypoxia; complications caused by prematurity; endocrine disorders (hypothyroidism); trauma (central nervous system damage); toxins (lead poisoning); and infections (meningitis). Therefore, ID includes a heterogeneous range of conditions and disorders, and treatment needs to be determined on an individual basis to reflect this variety (Harris, 2006). Up to half of those with ID (and more often those with mild ID) have no clear biological or organic cause for their ID, although, with advances in diagnosis and detection of disorders, some of these individuals may receive diagnoses in the future.

Those with ID are often divided into two groups, one demonstrating a clear biological or organic cause for their difficulties; and the other demonstrating no such organic cause. For this second group, researchers often assume that the causes of their difficulties are to do with the environment – described in earlier literature as 'sociocultural familial' (e.g. Zigler, 1969). The difficulty with this approach can be that advances in molecular genetics mean that we are likely to find new causes for ID, possibly changing the sociocultural familial group. In fact, although this distinction remains useful, it can be difficult to differentiate between these two groups (Volkmar & Dykens, 2002).

Given these perspectives, there are two approaches to research on children with ID. The first approach involves looking at children with ID who have specific disorders where we know the exact cause (e.g. Down syndrome or Williams syndrome). This is the approach taken in Chapter 7. The second approach involves looking at children with non-specific ID, where we do not know the precise cause. This is the approach taken in the current chapter.

Research with non-specific ID groups is valuable, because it allows us to isolate the effects of ID on development, quite apart from the effects of having a particular syndrome or disorder. As already noted, we will consider working memory among those with specific developmental disorders/syndromes in later chapters.

How do we measure intellectual disabilities?

ID can be measured using assessments of cognitive level, better known as IQ tests, as well as assessments of daily living skills and the ability to manage an independent lifestyle. IQ scores are calculated to have a mean level of 100, and a standard deviation of 15, so scores below 70 would be classified as in the ID range.

Often, the concept of 'mental age' is useful. Mental age is another way of describing the developmental level of a person with ID and can be calculated using a standard assessment of intellectual ability. We look at the child's achievement level on an IQ test and work backwards to ascertain the age at which most typically developing children would reach this level. This is the mental age; and most IQ tests provide tables to perform this calculation quickly. The concept of mental age may be easier to understand using a concrete example, so this is provided in Box 5.2.

Box 5.2   Interpreting IQ and mental age

IQ tests are standardised so that the mean is always 100 and one standard deviation always equals 15 IQ points. In other words, 67% of all children will fall between IQ 85 and 115; 95% of children will fall between IQ 70 and 130. Scores above and below these levels are exceptional.

(Continued)

What do IQ scores mean? Take, for example, two children with chronological ages of 12 years and 4 months. One child may have an IQ of 100 which will tell us that she is progressing just as would be expected compared to her peers. In other words, this child has an average ability. The second child may have an IQ of 50 which will tell us she is substantially behind her peers in terms of cognitive or intellectual development – in other words, she has a moderate ID and her rate of attaining cognitive milestones is delayed.

Another way of describing these two children is to use their mental ages. This means the equivalent age at which they are performing on a measure of intellectual ability (some current examples are: Wechsler Intelligence Scale for Children IV, British Ability Scales III, Raven's Progressive Coloured Matrices, Stanford-Binet Intelligence Scale 5).

Our child with an IQ of 100 will have a mental age of 12 years 4 months – exactly the same as her chronological age.

Our child with an IQ of 50 will have a mental age of 6 years 2 months – considerably below her chronological age. The larger the discrepancy between chronological age and mental age, the lower the IQ.

As discussed, mental age can be derived from standardised intelligence tests and used as an approximate measure of the child's current developmental level. Some authors question whether mental age is adequate to reflect developmental level (Sternberg & Spear, 1985), but others have defended it as a broad and multifaceted measure (Zigler, 1969). In practice, virtually all researchers in this area use mental age as a measure of cognitive functioning.

The importance of comparison groups

Research on cognitive development among those with ID can only be interpreted sensibly with reference to appropriate comparison groups. In other words, those with atypical development must be compared to some other reference group or groups, to see how they differ. The conclusions drawn about whether difficulties are present or not must always be qualified by the comparison groups that have been employed in any particular research study.

The first and most straightforward contrast would be children with ID and typically developing children of the same chronological age. This is known as a 'CA' (chronological age) comparison/match. Participants can be individually matched in pairs (every child with ID is matched for chronological age to a typically developing child); or researchers can ensure that the overall mean age and range of ages in each group is equivalent.

A second useful contrast is the mental age comparison/match ('MA'). For this comparison, typically developing children who are younger in chronological age than those with ID are selected. They are selected based on their mental ages, such that they match the children with ID. Again, children with ID can be individually matched for mental age to typically developing children; or the researcher can ensure that the overall group means and ranges for mental age are equivalent.

When the group of interest has both a specific developmental disorder/syndrome and ID, researchers often use an additional comparison group of individuals who have just ID. For a group of individuals with Down syndrome plus ID, for example, one would include individuals who just have ID of the same severity (and have the same chronological age). This 'ID only' comparison group allows researchers to examine three possible hypotheses: 1) whether any impairments found in the group of interest might be related to having the specific syndrome; 2) whether impairments might be related to having ID; or 3) whether having both a specific syndrome and ID might result in a 'double' or additional impairment compared to children with typical development.

However, group matching is actually a very complex issue in the study of intellectual and developmental diabilities. For example, there are many difficulties associated with matching individuals who have very uneven performance profiles on the types of ability tests that are generally used for matching. We also risk obtaining unrepresentative samples if many children are excluded from research studies, because of difficulties with matching participants across groups. You can read more about this in Jarrold and Brock (2004), listed under Further reading at the end of the chapter. Some of these issues will be discussed further in later chapters when we look at syndromes that are associated with ID such as Down and Williams syndrome (Chapter 7).

For now, however, we will focus on the most commonly used comparison groups, summarised in Box 5.3.

Box 5.3   Comparison groups used in research on developmental disorders and intellectual disabilities (ID)

Chronological age comparison/match (CA)
Typically developing children of the same age as the group of interest

Mental age comparison/match (MA)
Typically developing children of the same mental age as the group of interest

Comparisons with ID only (ID)
Children who have intellectual disabilities (ID), but do not have an associated developmental disorder are useful comparison groups when the group of interest has both ID *and* a developmental disorder. The 'ID only' children should have chronological and mental ages that are comparable to the group of interest to ensure that the levels of disability are equated.

Models of intellectual disabilities

The following sections outline three models of cognitive development in individuals with ID that can be helpful for understanding memory perform- ance and putting it into developmental context. To test each model, particular types of comparison groups are required, and these are also discussed.

Developmental model

The developmental model (Zigler, 1969; Zigler & Balla, 1982) assumes that cognitive development proceeds through stages, although it does not commit itself to any particular stage model. There are two key concepts to this model. First, children with ID go through the same sequence of cognitive stages as typically developing children, only more slowly (this is known as the 'similar sequence hypothesis'). Note that children with ID may not necessarily reach the highest stages of development. The second key concept is that children with ID are assumed to have the same cognitive structures as typically developing children (this is known as the 'similar structure hypothesis'). This means they carry out cognitive tasks in the same way as typically developing children.

Zigler (1969) stated that at any particular point, the child with ID will be behind typically developing children of the same chronological age, but should obtain levels of performance largely in line with their mental age level. Hence, children with ID show slower development, but go through the 'typ- ical' stages at the points we would expect them to, and carry out cognitive tasks as we would expect them to. The developmental model was intended to explain ID of the socio-cultural/familial type, i.e. that which encompasses individuals who do not have known brain damage or specific syndromes. Mental age comparison groups are essential in evaluating this model, as the fixed reference point for this model is mental age level. In order to find evi- dence in support of this model, we must evaluate whether individuals with ID are performing cognitive/memory tasks at a level commensurate with their current mental age.

Difference model

A second model of cognitive development in children with ID, put forward by Milgram (1973) and Ellis (1969; Ellis & Cavalier, 1982), is the 'difference model'. The main premise is that cognitive functioning in children with ID is different from that of typically developing children. Usually, authors sug- gest that there is a structural deficit in the cognitive architecture (e.g. a weak stimulus trace, Ellis, 1963) or a process deficit (e.g. absence of verbal rehearsal, Belmont, 1978; Ellis, 1970). According to the difference model, children with ID do not go through the same cognitive stages as typically develop- ing children, because their cognitive architecture is not the same. They carry out cognitive tasks differently to typically developing children, as they have impairments in some or all of the components required to carry out cognitive tasks. Milgram (1973) suggested that the difficulty amongst those with ID was particularly to do with verbal aspects of encoding, output and organisation.

According to the difference model, we should expect to see performance that is worse than mental age level (Milgram, 1973) and/or worse than chronological age level (Ellis, 1969). Individuals with ID are assumed to rarely use optimal cognitive mechanisms or strategies to carry out tasks, because key components/strategies are missing or impaired. Some authors have put forward a 'positive' difference model (see Kohlberg, 1968). Here, it is argued that performance will sometimes be better than mental age level, because individuals with ID may have greater experience and knowledge than the younger typically developing comparisons and this can produce a performance advantage.

Whichever version of the difference model is tested, it is vital to include a comparison group matched for mental age, as this is the level that performance is compared to. Some versions of the model rest on chronological age comparisons (Ellis, 1969), which require the inclusion of a chronological age comparison group.

For further information about developmental and difference models, please see Bennett-Gates and Zigler (1998), listed under Further reading.

Optimal performance

On some occasions, the memory performance of individuals with ID can be extremely good and reach chronological age-appropriate levels (e.g. on tests of incidental memory, where a memory test is unexpected – see Burack & Zigler, 1990; or review by Weiss et al., 1986). Authors sometimes refer to age-appropriate levels of performance among individuals with ID as reflecting their 'optimal performance' (Burack & Zigler, 1990).

Hence, an optimal performance approach to cognitive functioning in individuals with ID makes the following argument. Memory performance in individuals with ID varies according to remembering demands. In naturalistic, everyday situations, individuals with ID would be expected to perform well. However, on laboratory measures of memory performance, explicitly described as 'tests' (perhaps where we might expect individuals to utilise particular memory strategies), performance of those with ID is expected to be much poorer. There is evidence to support optimal performance for children with ID when they are tested using naturalistic remembering tasks (e.g. remembering a witnessed event) as opposed to when they are given formal memory tests (Burack & Zigler, 1990; Henry & Gudjonsson, 1999; Weiss et al., 1986); although children with mild ID maybe more likely to reach this level than children with moderate ID (Henry & Gudjonsson, 2003).

To assess 'optimal performance', we must include a chronological age matched comparison group of typically developing individuals. This is the group against which we can evaluate the 'best potential' of individuals with ID.

Box 5.4 summarises the three models of cognitive development in children with ID.

Box 5.4   Three approaches to cognitive development in children with ID

The developmental model   Children with ID show slower development, but go through the same developmental stages as typically developing children. Performance is expected to be largely in line with mental age for all cognitive tasks that are affected by developmental factors.

The difference model   Children with ID do not go through the same stages as typically developing children. They carry out cognitive tasks differently, because they have impairments in some or all of the components required to carry out cognitive tasks. Performance is often expected to be worse than mental age for cognitive tasks.

Optimal performance   Children with ID perform at their best on naturalistic, everyday memory tasks. Poorer performance will be seen on more artificial tasks – e.g. laboratory tests of memory, where children with ID will not tend to use a range of appropriate memory strategies to increase performance. There are no expectations that children with ID will perform at the same level across all cognitive tasks, but performance may reach the level of chronological age under 'ideal' circumstances.

We will now consider working memory in individuals with ID. As noted at the beginning of this chapter, researchers looking at memory processes in children and adults with ID have concluded that such individuals have a wide range of memory difficulties (for reviews see Hale & Borkowski, 1991; Weiss et al., 1986). Explanations for these memory difficulties include the following: (1) memory traces decay more rapidly in individuals with ID (Ellis, 1963); (2) those with ID do not employ relevant memory strategies such as verbal rehearsal (Belmont & Butterfield, 1971); and (3) individuals with ID have difficulties with tasks requiring 'logic, strategy, and foresight' (Byrnes & Spitz, 1977: 567).

We will restrict our consideration to research evidence relevant to whether children and young people with ID have difficulties with working memory, but will consider some of these explanations in later sections. Each of the four components of working memory will be considered separately, starting with the phonological loop. If you need a reminder about any of the components of the working memory model, refer to Chapters 1 and 2 or look at the 'aide memoire to the working memory model' at the end of Chapter 2 for a summary.

Summary
We have defined intellectual disabilities (ID), discussed how to assess ID, and noted the importance of comparison groups in experimental studies investigating cognitive performance in those with ID. We have also considered three broad theoretical approaches to understanding cognitive performance differences between those with ID and those with typical development. The presence (or not) of working memory impairments in individuals with ID is of particular importance, given at least 50 years of research suggesting that memory limitations are one of the key difficulties they face.

The phonological loop

There is probably more evidence for impairments in phonological short-term memory (PSTM – reflecting the operation of the strictly limited speech-based phonological loop) in those with intellectual disabilities (ID), than there is for any other component of working memory. Even before the working memory model was developed, Milgram (1973) reviewed a large number of studies and concluded that children with ID showed a developmental lag in terms of verbal processes.

One point is worth mentioning before we review the evidence. We will consider comparisons between individuals with ID and mental age matched typical children to test the developmental versus differences models. However, many studies also include chronological age matched typical children to test whether optimal performance may be reached. However, in virtually all studies described below, those with ID performed at a lower level than chronological age comparisons (e.g. Henry, 2001; Schuchardt, Gebhardt & Mähler, 2010). Therefore, the emphasis will be on the mental age comparison group in the following discussions.

Early experimental evidence

Many studies of phonological short-term memory (PSTM) in individuals with ID predate the development of the working memory model, but can nevertheless be interpreted within the theoretical framework of the phonological loop. For example, Fagan (1968) compared digit recall in 13 11- and 12-year-old children with ID (mean IQ 74), comparing them with 13 mental age matched typically developing 8-year-olds. Children with ID obtained lower digit recall scores than the comparison children. On the other hand, Brown (1974) investigated digit span in children with ID (mean IQ 74/78), comparing them to typically developing children of the same mental age, and found no differences between the groups (although the sample size of ten children in each group was small). One thing to point out with both of these studies is that the children with ID were probably more accurately described as having 'borderline' ID, given their mean IQs.

Marinosson (1974) included a wider range of ability levels in his study of PSTM (auditory sequential memory), comparing children with mild ID (mean IQ 61), moderate/severe ID (mean IQ 41) and typically developing children matched for mental age (5½ years). Sample sizes of 30 children per group gave this study more power to detect group differences. Indeed, Marinosson (1974) found that children with mild and moderate/severe ID obtained scores that were significantly lower than the typically developing comparisons.

So, are there real impairments in PSTM in children with ID, compared to mental age matched comparison groups? One difficulty with early work is that children and young people were often drawn from institutionalised settings, and this may have affected their motivation and the expectations of those around them for success on memory and learning tasks. It is important, therefore, to re-evaluate these results with new samples of individuals who have not experienced long-term institutional care.

Recent work using the working memory framework

More recent work has used the working memory model explicitly as a theoretical framework. Additionally, broad changes in provision for individuals with ID in Western Europe and the United States have dramatically reduced the numbers of children in institutionalised care, hopefully reducing potential confounding effects of reduced motivation and low expectations.

A series of studies by Hulme and Mackenzie (1992) looked at measures of PSTM in children with Down syndrome and severe ID. For the moment, we will focus on the group of individuals with severe ID and come back to the individuals with Down syndrome in Chapter 7.

Hulme and Mackenzie (1992) included 55 young people and adults with non-specific aetiology severe ID, as well as 55 typically developing 6-year-olds. The groups were matched for mental age, using a measure of verbal intelligence called the English Picture Vocabulary Test (EPVT). This test assesses a person's ability to point to a named item from a choice of four pictures. The typically developing comparison group allows us to establish whether individuals with ID achieved working memory performance levels in line with their mental age.

The results were very straightforward. Individuals with severe ID obtained mean digit spans of three items, whereas typically developing children obtained significantly higher spans of four items. These results indicated that the presence of severe ID was related to impairments in PSTM. Importantly, this was in comparison to mental age level, supporting the 'difference' model – suggesting that those with ID process, store and retrieve phonological information differently from those without ID.

Hulme and Mackenzie (1992) replicated this result using measures of word span. They also demonstrated that young people with severe ID did not show word length effects (refer to Chapters 1, 2 and 3 for further information about word length effects and their relationship with verbal rehearsal). This absence of word length effects suggested that young people with ID did not use verbal rehearsal, although note that we must be cautious about making assumptions about what word length effects mean (see Chapter 3). Hulme and Mackenzie (1992) argued that the phonological store itself was not impaired in individuals with ID, but that the verbal rehearsal processes backing up this store were not used efficiently. This points to a deficiency in the strategic control of the phonological loop (the 'articulatory rehearsal mechanism', see Chapter 1) among individuals with ID, rather than any inherent structural deficit in phonological storage (the 'phonological store').

A key point to make about the Hulme and Mackenzie (1992) study is that they included participants with severe ID. It is possible that deficits in phonological loop functioning may be confined to individuals with more severe levels of ID, and this needs evaluating.

Therefore, Henry and MacLean (2002) investigated working memory skills in children with mild to moderate ID, including two assessments of PSTM (word and digit span). There were 53 children with ID, with a mean IQ of 57 (age 11–12 years). Comparison groups included a chronological age (CA) group of 45 typical children (mean IQ 104, age 11–12 years) and a mental age (MA) group of 41 children (mean IQ 101, age 7–8 years). All children were given a typical comprehensive assessment of cognitive functioning, using verbal and non-verbal reasoning tasks from the British Ability Scales (BAS II, Elliott et al., 1996).

Henry and MacLean (2002) found that children with ID obtained significantly lower scores on digit and word span compared to the chronological age comparison group. This was not a surprising finding, as it simply showed that individuals with ID did not keep pace with their chronological age peers on measures of PSTM. In comparison with the mental age group, children with ID were not impaired on digit span, but they did obtain significantly lower scores on word span. This suggested that digit span kept pace with mental age among those with ID (developmental model), whereas word span fell behind mental age (difference model). Figure 5.1 illustrates this data.

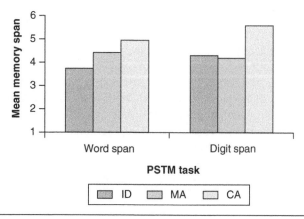

Figure 5.1   Mean digit and word spans for children with ID and comparison groups matched for mental and chronological age

Source: data adapted from Henry and MacLean (2002)

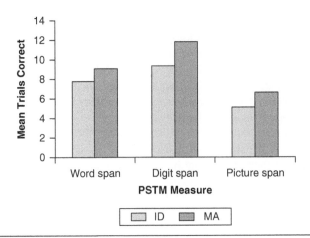

Figure 5.2 Mean trials correct on three measures of phonological short-term memory for children with ID and mental age matched comparisons

Source: data adapted from Henry and Winfield (2010)

The differences between word and digit span were difficult to explain, so a further study investigated a similar range of working memory measures in a new sample of children with ID (Henry & Winfield, 2010). Thirty-five children with mild to moderate non-specific ID (mean IQ 57) were compared to 32 typically developing 6- to 8-year-old children of similar mental ages (mean IQ 101). Three assessments of PSTM (word span, digit span, picture span) all showed the same results. Children with ID obtained significantly lower scores than typical children (see Figure 5.2).

These findings add to the conclusion that PSTM is impaired in children with non-specific ID. Some form of impairment in PSTM in individuals with ID has also been reported in several other studies (Bayliss, Jarrold, Baddeley & Leigh, 2005; Numminen, Service & Ruoppila, 2002; Russell et al., 1996; Schuchardt et al., 2010; Van der Molen, Van Luit, Jongmans & Van der Molen, 2007, 2009) and endorsed in a meta-analysis (Kavale & Forness, 1992; see Hasselhorn & Mähler, 2007, for a discussion). However, there are a few reports of no differences between children with ID and those matched for mental age on measures of PSTM (Connors, Carr & Willis, 1998; Hasselhorn & Mähler, 2007; Jarrold & Baddeley, 1997; Jarrold, Baddeley & Hewes, 1999).

The fact that so many studies have found at least some evidence for impairments in PSTM in children with ID compared to mental age matched comparisons suggests that there is some level of impairment in the phonological loop component of working memory, although it may not always be detected due to differences in sampling. If correct, such a conclusion would support the difference model in respect of PSTM, implying that there are either structural or strategic weaknesses in children with ID that impact on PSTM.

Could it be possible that impaired PSTM is a defining characteristic of intellectual disability? In fact, Ellis (1963) suggested something similar nearly 50 years ago, but his comments concerned short-term memory in general. Ellis (1963) argued that the quality of the 'stimulus trace' for any perceptual event was 'impoverished' in terms of its amplitude and duration in individuals with ID. Subsequent work did not support this broad suggestion (e.g. Fagan, 1968; Henry & Gudjonsson, 2004; see also Kail, 1990 for a similar conclusion), although a modified version of this theory cannot be ruled out. For example, Spitz (1966) argued that individuals with ID had weaker automatic encoding processes and Ellis and Meador (1985) argued that weaker automatic encoding processes interacted with reduced strategy use.

There is also evidence that speed of information processing and scanning is slower in children with ID (e.g. Anderson, 2001; Henry & Gudjonsson, 2007; Kail, 1992b). In fact, general speed of information processing has often been associated with some form of general intelligence factor known as g (Jensen, 1998; Nettlebeck, 1987). Kail (1992b) argued that slow speeds of information processing represent a key factor in explanations for the causes of ID; similarly, Anderson (2001) claimed that 'a low IQ represents a pervasive and enduring condition caused by slow speed of processing' (p. 296). Therefore, when we evaluate working memory performance in individuals with ID, it may be important to take account of speed of information processing in any theoretical explanations that are proposed.

One advantage of taking a working memory perspective is that working memory is not regarded as a unitary system; in other words, we may have different abilities to retain phonological, visual, spatial (perhaps kinaesthetic and other sensory) information. This means that there may be many sub-types of short-term memory storage, not all of which are necessarily weaker in individuals with ID. Slower speeds of information processing may have smaller or greater effects on these different sub-types of memory storage.

Although many authors have proposed that PSTM is impaired in individuals with ID, the question of *why* this might be the case remains to be answered. Interestingly, since the 1970s, authors have kept returning to an absence of verbal strategies (e.g. Bray & Turner, 1986). However, consideration of possible strategic difficulties among individuals with ID must be made in the context of potential effects of slower speeds of information processing on the one hand, and greater knowledge and life experience on the other. It is by no means the case that these issues have been resolved. At present, our theoretical understanding of ID remains speculative. In this book, we will confine the majority of our discussion to working memory, but try to take account of other key issues. Therefore, in the next section we will discuss the issue of strategic impairment in relation to verbal rehearsal among children with ID.

Verbal rehearsal in children with ID

Early work by Belmont and Butterfield (1969, 1971) suggested that young people with ID did not use verbal rehearsal. For example, Belmont and Butterfield (1971) looked at how teenagers with and without ID tried to learn six-item lists of visually presented letters. The experimenters allowed participants to choose the pace of presentation of the letters, and performed a detailed analysis of the pause times between items. The assumption was that participants using verbal rehearsal would pause longer between items, the deeper they went into the list; this was because an ever increasing number of items would take progressively longer to rehearse before the next item was added.

In fact, Belmont and Butterfield (1971) found that individuals with ID did not show increasingly longer pauses as they proceeded through the list; whereas typical teenagers did. Figure 5.3 illustrates this data.

Many subsequent researchers looked at this and related issues, concluding that short-term memory difficulties among those with ID could be accounted for with respect to 'missing' memory strategies (e.g. Ellis, 1978).

However, there were a number of methodological limitations to the Belmont and Butterfield (1971) study. There were no reports of IQ levels or precise ages in the ID or comparison groups, so it is hard to evaluate whether this was an exact chronological age comparison. As discussed earlier in this chapter, the nature of the comparison group is crucial in terms of the conclusions we can draw, and a mental age comparison group would also be valuable. In addition, all participants received six-item lists of letters, which may

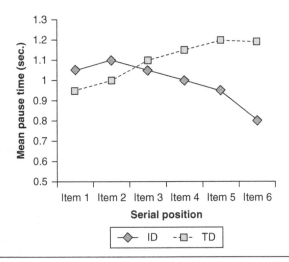

Figure 5.3 Mean pause times on lists of six letters for teenagers with ID compared to typically developing (TD) teenagers

Source: data adapted from Belmont and Butterfield (1971)

have meant that the task was considerably more difficult for those with ID, if they had lower levels of PSTM.

Hulme and Mackenzie (1992), in a series of studies we have already considered, adopted the working memory framework to examine verbal rehearsal by examining word length effects in individuals with ID. We have already touched on this, but it is worth emphasising again. Remember from Chapters 1 and 3, that word length effects are often used to indicate whether participants are using verbal rehearsal. In general, the presence of word length effects may indicate the use of verbal rehearsal, although this interpretation has been increasingly contested (see Chapter 3). Nevertheless, Hulme and Mackenzie (1992) found that individuals with ID did not show word length effects and interpreted these findings to indicate that individuals with ID were not employing verbal rehearsal.

There are several further studies that have examined verbal rehearsal in individuals with ID, but the results are not in complete agreement as we shall see.

Russell et al. (1996) were primarily interested in rehearsal processes among children with autism (we will return to this study in Chapter 8), but they included a comparison of 10-year-old children with mild/moderate ID and typically developing 6-year-olds matched for mental age (n = 33 in each group). Russell et al. (1996) used several measures of word span (PSTM), employing words of different lengths to test for the presence of verbal rehearsal. Both samples had a mean verbal mental age of 6 years, tested using a receptive measure of vocabulary (British Picture Vocabulary Scale – see earlier for a brief description).

The important feature of this study was the response methods that were used. Hulme and Mackenzie (1992) had used verbal recall only, whereas Russell et al. (1996) used either a verbal recall method, or a non-verbal recall method (pointing to pictures of the items on a response board), to control for any potential effects of speech output. This is an important methodological detail, because verbal output of the list can produce word length effects in itself, without the participants using verbal rehearsal (e.g. Cowan et al., 1992; Henry, 1991b).

The results indicated that children with ID had significantly lower word span scores (mean 2.9 words) than typically developing children (mean 3.6 words), providing more evidence for a deficit in PSTM among children with ID. Word length effects were found for both groups of children; these were small in the condition that did not require verbal output and somewhat larger in the verbal output condition.

These results could suggest that children in both groups were using verbal rehearsal. However, there are two reasons to doubt this. The first concerns correlations between articulation rate and memory span. When children use verbal rehearsal, we expect to see a correlation between memory span and articulation rate (see Chapter 3 – children who can rehearse faster are supposed to be able to remember more words). This correlation was found for the typically developing children, but not for the children with ID. Secondly, the effects of word length could have been the result of a less sophisticated verbal naming strategy (simply naming some of the words once only), which cannot be regarded as full verbal rehearsal. In summary, Russell et al. (1996) concluded that individuals with ID were not using verbal rehearsal (see Jarrold et al., 2000, for similar results).

Hasselhorn and Mähler (2007) looked at word length effects and articulation rates in 10-year-old German children with mild/borderline ID (mean IQ 79). Their comparison groups included mental and chronological age matched typically developing children (sample sizes = 22). As can be seen in Figure 5.4, both typically developing groups showed effects of word length, but the children with ID did not. This, again, suggested that children with ID did not use verbal rehearsal.

Hasselhorn and Mähler (2007) went on to investigate the relationship between articulation rate and memory span in each of their three samples. There were significant correlations between articulation rate and memory span in both comparison groups, but not in children with ID. Again, these results supported their conclusion that children with ID did not use verbal rehearsal strategies.

Therefore, there is no clear agreement as to whether or not word length effects are found in children with ID. Nevertheless, many authors have come to the same conclusion that children with ID do not use verbal rehearsal. There are some differences between the samples, as Hulme and Mackenzie included teenagers with severe ID, Russell et al. assessed children with mild/moderate ID and Hasselhorn and Mähler used slightly more able children with mild/borderline ID. It is possible, therefore, that differences in sampling could account for the fact that some studies found word length effects and others did not. Equally, small methodological variations such as the method of recall or the method of

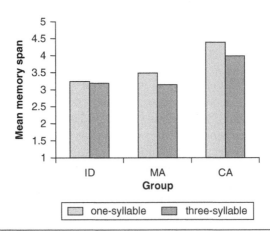

Figure 5.4 Mean memory spans for one- and three-syllable words for 10-year-old children with mild to borderline ID. Comparison groups include children matched for mental age (MA) and chronological age (CA)

Source: data adapted from Hasselhorn and Mähler (2007)

presenting the words could play a part. For example, Hasselhorn and Mähler equated the length of time to present lists of short and long words to reduce differences in output delay, which the other studies did not do.

Nonetheless, the similarities in *conclusions* across these studies, that children with ID do not use verbal rehearsal, are noteworthy. Given the difficulties in interpreting word length effects discussed in Chapter 3, this technique is perhaps not the most reliable way of assessing verbal rehearsal processes. Ideally, future research will use a range of methods (perhaps including observational techniques) to examine verbal rehearsal in individuals with ID.

Summary

Perhaps the most consistent finding in the literature on working memory in children with ID is that there are impairments in phonological short-term memory (PSTM). These findings support the 'negative difference' model, suggesting that children and young people with ID do not remember phonological information over short periods of time as well as typically developing children of the same mental age. It is less clear why there may be difficulties with PSTM. Although most authors agree that individuals with ID are unlikely to use verbal rehearsal, we cannot say whether other structural impairments, in the phonological store, for example, or in processing speed might be implicated.

Debates and Issues 5.1   Training phonological short-term memory in children with intellectual disabilities

If children with ID have difficulties with PSTM and do not seem to use verbal rehearsal, perhaps training them to use verbal rehearsal strategies might solve their memory problems?

Although we will not review the relevant evidence in detail, many studies in the 1970s and 1980s employed *rehearsal training interventions* to try to ameliorate short-term memory difficulties in those with ID. To summarise the findings, children and young people with ID could be trained to use verbal rehearsal, and these effects could last for several months if training had been thorough (Brown, Campione & Murphy, 1974).

However, rehearsal training interventions did not usually generalise to other remembering tasks *beyond* the precise task used in training unless specific extra tuition was given on exactly why the strategy had worked. This made the benefits of the training much more difficult to apply to everyday life.

Another difficulty was that PSTM memory differences between those with ID and CA comparisons did not entirely disappear after training, despite the fact that such

(Continued)

differences were often reduced (see Kail, 1990, for a discussion). This meant that researchers were still left pondering the reasons for fundamental differences in PSTM between children with ID and typical development.

This type of research fell out of fashion for many years, but recent developments have seen a resurgence of interest in working memory interventions of a slightly different kind – please see Debates and Issues 5.2 on page 173 for further details.

The visuospatial sketchpad

Early experimental evidence

Visuospatial short-term memory (VSSTM) is supported by the limited capacity visuospatial sketchpad, and concerns short-term recall of visual, spatial and possibly kinaesthetic information. In a study already mentioned by Marinosson (1974), a measure of visual sequential memory (recalling abstract figures) was included, which assessed the visual component of the visuospatial sketchpad. Marinosson (1974) found that children with mild and moderate/severe ID obtained lower visual memory scores than typically developing children. However, more recent work has found contradictory results in relation to VSSTM difficulties in children with ID, as is discussed below.

Recent work using the working memory framework

Returning to a study mentioned earlier, using the working memory model as a theoretical framework, we can assess both visual and spatial aspects of the visuospatial sketchpad. Henry and MacLean (2002) included measures of spatial (Corsi) span and pattern span. Recall that children with mild and moderate ID were compared to typical children of comparable mental age and chronological age (see earlier for details). Henry and MacLean (2002) found, for both spatial and pattern span, that children with ID obtained significantly *higher* scores than children matched for mental age; although they were still significantly below the chronological age comparison group. These results were intriguing as they suggested that VSSTM was better than mental age level in children with ID. Figure 5.5 illustrates these results.

Here was some evidence for a 'positive' difference model, whereby the increased age and experience of the children with ID may contribute to better memory performance in certain areas. Henry and MacLean (2002) noted that it was not possible to use verbal strategies on either of these tasks, so the absence of verbal naming and/or rehearsal may be what distinguishes children with ID from typical comparisons.

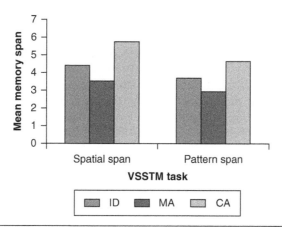

Figure 5.5 Mean spatial span and pattern span scores for children with intellectual disabilities and comparison groups matched for mental and chronological age (MA and CA respectively)

Source: data adapted from Henry and MacLean (2002)

Rosenquist, Conners and Roskos-Ewoldsen (2003) also found that children with ID performed better on a visual complexity task than mental age matched peers. Similar findings have been reported for adults with ID by Martin, West, Cull and Adams (2000). They compared performance on the verbal and visual memory subtests from the Rivermead Behavioural Memory Test, finding 'best' performance on the visual subtests (and poorest performance on the verbal subtests – in line with our conclusion from the previous section).

However, not all authors have found this positive difference result. At least four papers have found *equivalent* scores on measures of VSSTM between those with ID and mental age matched comparisons. For example, Jarrold et al. (1999) compared 13-year-olds with severe ID to 5-year-old typically developing children (n = 16 in each group, matched for mental age) and found no significant differences in performance on either a Corsi span task (spatial span) or a pattern span task. Henry and Winfield (2010), in a study discussed in the previous section, included measures of spatial span and pattern span, finding no significant differences between 11–12-year-old children with ID and typically developing 7-year-olds, with similar mental ages. Jarrold and Baddeley (1997) reported the same findings in relation to Corsi span in a sample of 8-year-olds with moderate ID. Finally, using three measures of VSSTM, Schuchardt et al. (2010) found mental age-appropriate performance in 15-year-olds with mild/moderate and borderline ID.

Confusingly, there is also some evidence for a *deficit* in VSSTM in those with ID. Bayliss et al. (2005) investigated a large sample of teenagers with mild to severe ID (n = 50, mean IQ = 55), comparing them to typical children of the same mental age (7 years) on a range of measures. They found that the adolescents with ID obtained lower Corsi span scores than younger children matched for mental age. Similarly, Van der Molen et al. (2009) reported poorer performance on Corsi span, but not pattern span, in a sample of 49 adolescents with mild ID (compared to 29 typical children matched for mental age). Finally, Numminen et al. (2002) examined this issue in adults with severe ID (n = 26), reporting that they obtained lower scores on Corsi span than typically developing 5-year-olds (n = 26) matched for mental age.

Summary
It is difficult to draw firm conclusions about the performance of individuals with ID on measures of visuospatial short-term memory (VSSTM). Results are so mixed that we are unable to ascertain whether performance in those with ID keeps pace with mental age, falls behind mental age or exceeds mental age. It may be that methodological variations between studies account for some of the differences in results (developmental level of the individuals concerned, severity of the intellectual disability, method of assessing intellectual ability, nature of the span measures), but a full explanation is not available at present.

The central executive

The central executive is responsible for higher order cognitive processing, and the following discussion will be split into two sections: (1) tasks that measure executive-loaded working memory (ELWM); and (2) tasks that measure other aspects of executive control, broadening our consideration of the central executive into other aspects of relevance for cognitive functioning.

Executive-loaded working memory

Many of the studies already discussed included measures of executive-loaded working memory (ELWM), the ability to process and store information concurrently, therefore we will revisit some of them here.

We briefly mentioned a study by Conners et al. (1998) in the previous section. Of relevance here is that they included a measure of reverse digit span in their study of 11-year-old children with mild to moderate ID. Reverse digit span is argued to require ELWM, as we saw in Chapter 2. Connors et al. (1998) found that children with ID performed at the same level on reverse digit span as a group of 7-year-old typically developing children matched for verbal mental age; although both of these groups obtained lower scores than children in a chronological age comparison group. This study included a good sample size of around 30 participants per group and all were thoroughly tested for IQ using a short form of the Wechsler Intelligence Scale for Children (WISC-R).

Brown (1974), in his study of 10/11-year-old children with borderline ID, also found no significant differences on reverse digit span between children with ID and typically developing mental age matched children, although note that this study employed a small sample size (ten in each group). Similarly, in their study of adults with ID, Numminen et al. (2002) found no differences between adults with severe ID and children matched for mental age (n = 26 in each group), on reverse digit span.

It would, however, be desirable to replicate these findings using a broader range of ELWM tasks. Henry and MacLean (2002) (see earlier for details) included three measures of ELWM (reverse digit span, listening span and odd one out span), finding that 11/12-year-old children with mild to moderate ID performed at their mental age level on odd one out span and reverse digit span, and slightly above mental age level on listening span. Therefore, there was no evidence for deficits in children with ID in comparison to mental age matched typical peers. The usual impairment, in relation to chronological age peers, however, was found (see also Alloway (2010) for similar chronological age comparisons). Figure 5.6 illustrates these results.

Bayliss et al. (2005), in their thorough investigation of ELWM in 50 young people with ID, used carefully controlled tasks in the verbal and visuospatial domains. Care was taken to examine the processing element

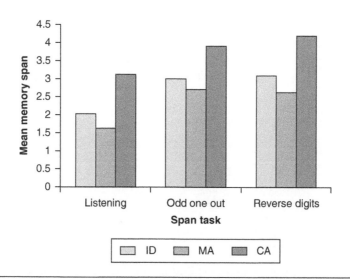

Figure 5.6 Mean span scores on three measures of executive-loaded working memory by children with ID, typically developing children of the same mental age (MA) and chronological age (CA) comparison samples

Source: data adapted from Henry and MacLean (2002)

of each ELWM task, as well as simple storage capacity in each domain, as well as combined processing plus storage performance. Interestingly, Bayliss et al. (2005) found that the teenagers with ID were not as good on the storage capacity measures as peers matched for mental age (weaker digit span and Corsi span as we have mentioned in earlier sections), but they were quicker on the processing measures. In terms of processing plus storage, i.e. the ELWM measures, there were no significant differences between the groups. Figure 5.7 illustrates these results. The authors concluded that young people with ID utilise processing and storage resources somewhat differently to typically developing children, obtaining the same scores in a different manner.

Similarly, Henry and Winfield (2010) in their study comparing 11–12-year-old children with ID to 7-year-old typically developing children (mental age comparison), found no differences between the groups on measures of listening span and odd one out span (see also Schuchardt et al., 2010 for a replication using backwards digit and counting span).

Overall, these results suggest that there are no marked MA-relative impairments in ELWM in children with ID, either for verbal or visuospatial measures. However, it may be that there are subtle differences in how these tasks are carried out, or in the relative strength of the components skills (Bayliss et al., 2005). Further research in this area will be needed to confirm these speculations.

However, it must be noted that other work has found ELWM difficulties in individuals with ID, in comparison to typical children matched for mental age.

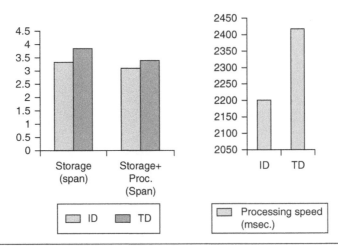

Figure 5.7   Mean performance on storage only tasks; processing plus storage tasks; and processing only tasks, for teenagers with ID and typically developing comparisons matched for mental age. Note that processing tasks are illustrated separately as the data refer to milliseconds as opposed to span scores

Source: data adapted from Bayliss et al. (2005)

For example, Russell et al. (1996) (see earlier phonological loop section for details) found ELWM difficulties in 11-year-old children with mild to moderate ID, compared to mental age matched typical children, using three separate measures (counting span, odd man out span, sums span). Van der Molen et al. (2009) reported similar findings using listening span and reverse digit span in a sample of adolescents with mild ID. Finally, Carretti, Belacchi and Cornoldi (2010), looking at adults with mild to moderate ID (n = 28), found impairments in relation to typical children matched for non-verbal mental age (6 years) on two very demanding measures of ELWM (dual task word span, updating word span); but not on a less demanding measure (reverse word span).

Therefore, the results in the area of ELWM are mixed, such that it is difficult to conclude whether or not individuals with ID show impairments in relation to their mental age level. Carretti et al. (2010) made the interesting argument that as ELWM tasks become more demanding (requiring more 'active' executive control), differences between adults with ID and typical comparison groups matched for mental age become larger. This general idea could explain the conflicting results in relation to children with ID, if we assume that studies finding group differences used somewhat more demanding tasks. However, post hoc comparisons across experiments are not ideal. Further research will be required to test this proposition rigorously, using carefully matched samples of children with ID and a range of tasks with varying levels of executive demands.

We finish this section with a brief description of a promising new intervention to improve ELWM in young people with ID in the 'Debates and Issues 5.2' box.

Debates and Issues 5.2   Training executive-loaded working memory in adolescents with intellectual disabilities

Van der Molen et al. (2010) resurrected interest in the issue of memory training interventions for children with ID. Their goal was ambitious – to try to improve *working memory and academic skills* in teenagers with mild and borderline ID (IQ 55–85). Van der Molen et al. (2010) developed an intervention involving five weeks of practice on one executive-loaded working memory (ELWM) measure, the odd one out task, whereby the participant chooses the 'odd' item from an array of three (processing) and must remember its spatial location (storage). For five weeks, each student practised three times a week for six minutes at a time with this 'odd yellow' training intervention. Some individuals were allocated to a 'control' condition in which only the odd one out choice (processing) was practised, and not the location memory (storage).

(Continued)

This easily implemented intervention had immediate beneficial effects on phonological short-term memory (PSTM) after the training period. Interestingly, when the authors went back ten weeks after the intervention had finished, even more improvements were seen. Visuospatial short-term memory (VSSTM) scores had improved and the children were doing better on an arithmetic test.

These results suggested that training interventions based on ELWM tasks were much more effective in improving working memory and academic achievement in young people with ID than earlier interventions based on PSTM had been. This is a promising new area for development with enormous potential to benefit children and young people with ID.

Summary

Many studies have reported no differences between children with ID and typical children matched for mental age on measures of executive-loaded working memory (ELWM). However, the literature is not consistent in this area, with several reports of impairments in relation to mental age. It is possible that ELWM tasks that require high levels of executive control are particularly difficult for individuals with ID. Promising interventions that may improve working memory and academic skills in children with ID are currently being developed.

Other measures of the central executive

A programme of research was undertaken by Spitz and colleagues in the late 1970s and early 1980s, looking at what they described as tasks requiring 'logic, strategy, and foresight'. These included several problem-solving tasks, most notably the Tower of Hanoi (Borys, Spitz & Dorans, 1982; Byrnes & Spitz, 1977; Spitz, Webster & Borys, 1982). Of course, recent terminology would refer to this task as a measure of *executive planning and problem solving*, (See Chapter 2 for details of the Tower of Hanoi test).

In the studies by Spitz and colleagues, samples of institutionalised young adults with ID were compared to typical children of the same mental age. The general finding was that the performance of those with ID in solving the Tower of Hanoi problem was below mental age level, by around three years (Borys et al., 1982; Byrnes & Spitz, 1977; Spitz et al., 1982). Those with ID were more likely to ignore the rules of the game to reach a goal and use inferior strategies that were not sufficiently geared towards planning ahead (Borys et al., 1982).

Similarly, Vakil, Shelef-Reshef and Levy-Shiff (1997) found that young adults with ID (mean IQ 60, range 54–75) required more moves to complete the Tower of Hanoi task (and took longer over each move) than 9- to 12-year-old children matched for mental age. These authors also included the Porteus mazes task in their study (regarded as a measure of planning, see Chapter 2), finding that the young adults with ID also completed fewer mazes correctly (see also Spitz & DeRisi, 1978).

These results implied that there were executive difficulties among young adults with ID in relation to tasks that required planning and problem solving, compared to children matched for mental age. Such findings, if verified, would support the difference model.

However, a more recent study failed to replicate these differences. Numminen, Lehto and Ruoppila (2001) examined adults with ID (IQ 35–70, n = 24), living in the community. These authors found that adults with ID obtained equivalent overall scores compared to typically developing children matched for mental age (5½ years on the Raven's Coloured Matrices Test, n = 24) on the Tower of Hanoi test. There were, however, some subtle differences between the groups: adults with ID needed slightly more trials to succeed on the task; and violated rules more often. Note, however, that the performance of older adults with ID (n = 46) on the Tower of Hanoi task was found to be unimpaired by Danielsson, Henry, Rönnberg and Nilsson (2010), using a closely matched comparison group of CA peers with the same levels of education (n = 92). These latter findings suggest that difficulties with planning and problem-solving may not be characteristic of adults with ID, but it would be valuable to repeat this research with children.

There is also some evidence in relation to the executive skill of *fluency* for individuals with ID. Returning to the study by Conners et al. (1998) (described earlier), we can examine the results for a measure of letter fluency. Here, no differences in the ability to generate new exemplars were reported between children with ID and mental age matched typical children. Henry (2010) replicated these findings using a similar 'category generation' fluency task, with groups of 11/12-year-old children with ID (mental age 7 years, mean IQ = 55, n = 39), as well as chronological age and mental age matched typical comparisons (n = 25 in each). Although she found no mental age-relative difficulties with fluency, performance was poorer compared to chronological age level (see also Alloway, 2010, Glidden & Mar, 1978, and Danielsson et al., 2010, for similar findings in relation to chronological age comparison groups). Therefore, recent research on the executive skills of planning/problem-solving and fluency indicates that there are relatively few difficulties in these areas for individuals with ID, at least in relation to mental age level. However, it would be useful to look at a wider range of executive tasks.

Van der Molen et al. (2007) carried out probably the most comprehensive assessment of executive skills in children with ID to date. They included several measures of executive functioning (category fluency, letter fluency, dual task performance, mazes and random number generation). Fifty adolescents with mild ID (mean age 15 years) were compared to 25 typically developing adolescents of the same chronological age, as well as 25 younger children of comparable mental age (10 to 11 years). Note, however, that the mean non-verbal IQ level of the teenagers with ID, based on Ravens Standard Progressive Matrices (a measure of fluid intelligence), was 70, so these individuals encompassed those with a range of abilities, some of whom may not be classified as having ID in the strict sense.

Figure 5.8 illustrates the results for each of the tasks. In no case did children with ID perform any differently from children in the mental age comparison group. With the exception of the dual task measure, those with ID obtained significantly lower scores than children in the chronological age comparison group, as would be expected. Overall, therefore, children with ID did not differ from their mental age matched peers on a range of executive measures (fluency, dual task performance, planning and random number generation), supporting the developmental model.

Therefore, a series of early studies found deficits in executive performance in adults with ID compared to mental age level, whereas, newer research has shown far fewer such executive difficulties. How can we account for the contrast in findings? One of the key features of at least some of the older studies was that the individuals with ID were living in institutions. It is possible

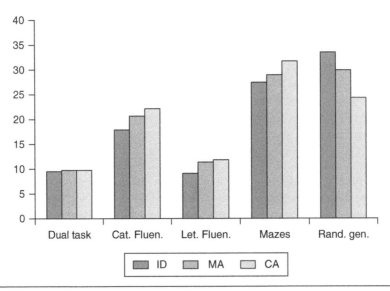

Figure 5.8 Mean performance for children with mild ID, mental age matched comparisons and chronological age matched comparison[5] on five measures of executive functioning (dual task, category fluency, letter fluency, mazes, random number generation: higher scores = less randomness i.e. poorer performance). Note that the original scores on dual task performance are divided by ten for ease of illustration

Source: data adapted from Van der Molen et al. (2007)

that evidence for the 'difference' position emerges when institutionalised participants with ID are assessed; whereas evidence for the 'developmental' position is found for those living in the community.

Why would this be? Adults with ID living in institutions may have relatively limited opportunities to engage in thinking, planning, reasoning and problem-solving tasks that might develop or challenge their executive abilities. On the other hand, adults living in the community should naturally meet day-to-day challenges that require forward planning, thinking and reasoning skills. Therefore, generational changes in the provision for adults with ID, moving towards community care with targeted support, may have led to a relative increase in executive skills. This type of conclusion would tie in with find-ings showing that children with Down syndrome show stronger academic achievements when placed in mainstream schools (Laws, Byrne & Buckley, 2000), possibly because these settings are more challenging and staff have higher expectations of the children.

Summary
There is relatively little work examining executive functioning more broadly in children and young people with ID. Recent evidence suggests that executive functioning in individuals with ID is largely at a level that would be expected on the basis of their mental age, supporting the developmental model.

The episodic buffer

The episodic buffer is responsible for providing a link between working memory and long-term knowledge, as well as acting to bind information from different modalities into a coherent episode. This component is particularly interesting with regard to individuals with ID, because life experience, seman-tic knowledge and general knowledge are all likely to favour individuals with ID in any comparisons that we draw with children matched for mental age (who are by definition, younger). For example, Numminen et al. (2002) found evidence that the 'knowledge base' of individuals with ID was more extensive than that of typically developing mental age matched comparisons. They hypothesised that individuals with ID might depend more on long-term memory support whilst carrying out working memory tasks, although they did not directly investigate this.

Note that assessments of episodic buffer functioning are not designed to evaluate directly how good long-term memory is, i.e. can an individual store and retain material over long time periods. If you would like to read more about long-term memory in individuals with ID see Turnure (1991) who argues that LTM capacity is largely intact among those with ID. Rather, we are attempt-ing to understand how individuals with ID use their long-term memory to support working memory and produce coherent memory representations by binding together relevant information. The question is whether these processes are broadly in line with mental age or chronological age. We will now consider some relevant evidence on episodic buffer functioning in individuals with ID.

A study by Lukose (1987) examined the relationship between knowledge and memory performance in teenagers with ID. She compared 20 15-year-olds with ID (mean mental age of 9.8 years) to mental and chronological age-matched comparison groups: these included 20 typically developing 9-year-olds; and 20 typically developing 15-year-olds. Participants were shown picture cards of common objects and there were six slightly different picture remembering tasks. In some tasks, the pictures could be put into related groups, in others the pictures were unrelated, and in others the pictures were presented in the context of a story. For half of these tasks, the young people in the chronological age comparison group obtained the highest scores, as might be expected. However, for the remaining picture recall tasks, there were no significant differences between the ID and CA groups and in no case did the young people with ID obtain lower scores than children in the mental age matched comparison group. In fact, scores were significantly higher than mental age level in the ID group on two out of the six measures; these were the conditions that allowed long-term knowledge to be used to support recall.

These results suggested that individuals with ID could potentially benefit from their greater experience with and knowledge about memory items in episodic remembering tasks. Lukose (1987) argued that the best performance among the young people with ID was obtained for memory tasks that imposed some degree of organisation on the items, for example, presenting items within a story context or presenting related items that could potentially be clustered together. There are a number of other episodic remembering tasks that may also assess the binding information from long-term memory with information in other working memory systems, and these are outlined below (see also Chapter 2).

- *Story recall.* Recalling short stories (e.g. paragraphs) coherently is much easier if supported by our understanding of the structure of language, the vocabulary, the content of the passage and the structure of typical narratives. This information needs to be integrated with memory traces from the phonological loop, and 'modality free' representations held in the episodic buffer. Storage in the phonological loop alone is insufficient to support story recall. The episodic buffer is hypothesised to create a 'novel episode', by combining activated representations from long-term memory with information in the phonological loop, drawing on executive resources to maintain this new representation (Baddeley & Wilson, 2002).
- *Paired associate learning.* Participants learn pairs of pictures, words or other items over several trials. Once learning has taken place (e.g. hair–road; stove–cook; cake–boat), the participant is presented with the first item of each pair and asked to recall the second item. In some versions of this test, some items are already associated (stove–cook), so long-term knowledge is likely to aid learning. Performance on this task can be hypothesised to reflect

the capacity of the phonological store, activated long-term knowledge about the meanings of words and potential associations between them, the quality of the integrated 'novel episodes' created by the episodic buffer, and the efficiency the relevant executive processes recruited to maintain these representations.

We will now look at studies that have examined these episodic remembering tasks in children with ID, in order to gain some insight into the binding of long-term knowledge with information from other working memory systems in those with ID.

There is a long history of studies examining paired associate learning in children with ID. For example, Winters, Attlee and Harvey (1974) assessed 32 institutionalised 13-year-olds with ID (mean IQ 60), 32 non-institutionalised 12½-year-olds with ID (mean IQ 64), and 32 typically developing children. All three groups had the same mental age (7 years). The task was to learn eight pairs of drawings (e.g. onion–shoe, train–cat, nose–milk) to a criterion of one perfect recall (or 30 trials, whichever was the sooner). Winters et al. (1974) found no significant differences between non-institutionalised teen-agers with ID and the mental age comparison group. These results suggested that non-institutionalised teenagers with ID were as able to use long-term knowledge in a paired associate learning task as typically developing children of the same mental age, supporting the developmental model (see also Cantor & Ryan, 1962).

However, the institutionalised children in Winters et al.'s (1974) study took longer to learn the picture pairs than the mental age matched comparison group, suggesting that they were less able to use long-term knowledge to support episodic learning. Similar results were found by Iscoe and Semler (1964), when they looked at children with ID in residential schools. Their 48 children with ID were less able to learn six pairs of items (presented as related pairs such as banana–orange or unrelated pairs such as banana–shoe) over 12 trials, than mental age matched typically developing children (n = 48). Again, these results emphasise the point that using institutionalised groups of individuals with ID may underestimate potential performance.

In a more recent study, Henry (2010) looked at children with mild and moderate ID (mean IQ 55) in non-residential settings, comparing them with typical children matched for mental and chronological age (see previous section for details). Included in the study were two remembering tasks from a standardised memory battery (Test of Memory and Learning, TOMAL): (1) recalling three short stories read out by the examiner ('memory for stories'); and (2) learning to link pairs of words together over several trials ('paired associate learning'). Responses were scored for the number of units of information correctly recalled, largely corresponding to short phrases of meaningful information (memory for stories); or number of words correctly recalled throughout the learning and test phases (paired associate learning). Performance on both tasks in children with ID was at mental age level, although lower than chronological age (see Figure 5.9).

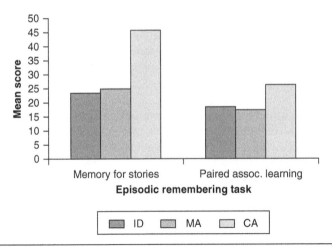

Figure 5.9 Mean scores on story recall and paired associate learning for children with ID, and mental age (MA) and chronological age (CA) matched typical children

Source: data adapted from Henry (2010)

These results suggested that children with ID performed at their mental age level on verbal episodic remembering tasks, giving a preliminary indication that the binding together of relevant long-term knowledge and information in active working memory in the episodic buffer may be developmentally appropriate in terms of mental age (supporting the developmental model).

However, Carlesimo, Marotta and Vicari (1997) presented a somewhat more complex set of findings. They compared the performance of teenagers with non-specific ID (n = 15) to that of typical 9-year-old children matched for mental age on a range of tasks, some of which are relevant to our discussion. On a measure of prose recall, the teenagers with ID obtained lower scores than the typical children (although very few details were given about this test, and scores were only out of eight, so the story must have been very short). This finding contrasted with that reported by Henry (2010) whereby story recall was at a mental age-appropriate level in children with ID.

Nevertheless, Carlesimo et al. (1997) found an interesting result on another measure, which involved recalling a list of 12 words over five separate learning/recall trials. The crucial manipulation was that many of the words were related to each other. Although the teenagers with ID recalled slightly fewer words on each trial (seven) than the typical children (eight), those with ID showed more evidence of clustering the related items together (e.g. animals, fruits, body parts). This suggested that these individuals were using stored long-term knowledge about semantic relatedness to a greater extent than the typical children. Not only was this evidence that individuals with ID may use long-term knowledge to support recall *more effectively* than their mental age level would suggest, it was also somewhat surprising evidence for the use of a relatively sophisticated memory strategy (semantic organisation) in individuals that are generally regarded as non-strategic.

Therefore, binding together relevant long-term knowledge and active information from working memory in verbal remembering tasks may be at or above developmentally appropriate (mental age) levels for children with ID in at least some cases. However, this conclusion must be regarded as tentative, as this is not a well developed area of research and the findings remain somewhat inconsistent.

Turning to non-verbal binding tasks, a limited number of studies have revealed difficulties in individuals with ID. Non-verbal paired associate learning tasks, may, for example, require the participant to learn sets of colours paired with nonsense shapes. In two studies, differences between adults with ID and children matched for mental age on such tasks have been reported, regardless of whether individuals were living in institutions or not (Blue, 1970; Vakil et al., 1997).

Jarrold, Phillips and Baddeley (2007) looked at non-verbal binding on a task which required participants to integrate item and location information. Performance was impaired in 10-year-old children with moderate ID, in comparison with typical 5-year-olds matched for non-verbal mental age. Danielsson, Rönnberg, Leven, Andersson, Andersson & Lyxell (2006) also reported that adults with ID showed more conjunction errors than typical adults on a face recognition binding task, utilising combinations of inner and outer details from unfamiliar images of faces.

Non-verbal materials may, therefore, present fewer opportunities than familiar verbal materials for integrating long-term knowledge with active information in working memory, but further research will be necessary to test this speculation in more detail.

Summary
On at least some verbal binding tasks, non-institutionalised children with ID have been shown to achieve levels of performance that are at least as good as their mental age level. However, the limited evidence in relation to non-verbal binding tasks points to below mental age performance. These findings are preliminary at present, as there is relatively little data available; it would be useful to compare verbal and non-verbal tasks of equivalent difficulty in future research.

Final comments

Severity of intellectual disabilities

It may be that the severity of ID is a key factor to take into account when evaluating potential working memory difficulties. A few studies have included individuals with different levels of ID, which allows investigation of this issue.

For example, Henry (2001) examined a range of working memory skills among 11- to 12-year-old children with borderline (n = 10), mild (n = 21) and moderate ID (n = 22), comparing them to typically developing children of the same chronological age (n = 25). All participants were assessed using two scales from an established IQ battery (British Ability Scales II, Elliott et al., 1996); and differences in working memory performance as a function of severity of ID were examined.

All groups with ID showed significantly weaker PSTM than *chronological age* comparisons, although this was marginal for children with borderline ID. This implied that there was a general deficit in PSTM in relation to chronological age, regardless of ID severity, but that this was greater for those with mild and moderate ID. For VSSTM, children with borderline ID showed no impairments in comparison to chronological age; but children with mild and moderate ID were impaired. For ELWM, children with borderline ID were not impaired in comparison to chronological age; whereas children with mild and moderate ID were. In summary, children with mild and moderate ID showed working memory difficulties in all three components, compared to chronological age level, but those with borderline ID only showed PSTM difficulties. However, the sample size for children with borderline ID was rather small, which means that power to detect working memory impairments may have been compromised.

Therefore, Schuchardt et al. (2010) revisited this issue, including 15-year-olds with mild ID (n = 22), borderline ID (n = 19) and typical development (n = 25). These authors found that those with mild ID showed greater difficulties with working memory in all three areas tested (PSTM, VSSTM, ELWM) than those with borderline ID. However, both groups were impaired relative to chronological age. These results suggested that even borderline ID was associated with across the board working memory impairments compared to chronological age level (see Alloway, 2010, for similar findings in relation to borderline ID).

Therefore, ID appears to be associated with working memory impairments in relation to chronological age as would be expected, but *greater levels* of ID may be associated with *greater levels* of difficulty. Henry (2001) noted that children with moderate ID could only deal with 1.5 items in ELWM, which would be expected to impact negatively on typical classroom learning (i.e. when the child hears instructions and must keep them in mind while listening to something else or beginning an activity). Therefore, low working memory scores among those with ID have serious implications for school learning and academic achievement (see Alloway & Temple, 2007; Bayliss et al., 2005; and Henry & Winfield, 2010 for data relating to this issue).

Summary
Working memory difficulties are more pronounced in children who have more severe levels of ID. However, even those with borderline ID can show chronological age related impairments.

Is the structure of working memory in children with ID the same as that in typically developing children?

We saw in Chapter 4 that the structure of working memory in typically developing children conforms broadly to a three-component model of working memory from the age of 4 to 6 years (Alloway et al., 2004; Gathercole, Pickering, Ambridge et al., 2004). Similarly, ELWM is constrained by the same factors in children and adults, namely processing speed, storage ability and a hypothesised 'executive ability' (Bayliss et al., 2003). The current section assesses whether the functional organisation of working memory and the mechanisms underlying ELWM in individuals with ID are the same as those in typically developing children.

The data from Henry (2001 – see earlier for details) suggested that the functional organisation of working memory was very similar in children with ID and typical children. The strongest and most robust correlations were between measures assessing the same component. For example, measures of PSTM (digit span, word span); VSSTM (pattern span, spatial span); and ELWM (listening span, odd one out span) were most strongly related to each other. These patterns were very similar to those found in the typical children, implying that the structure of working memory was not different in those with ID. Similar findings were reported by Henry and Winfield (2010), supporting the general conclusion that the functional organisation of working memory does not differ in children with ID.

However, there are limitations to the conclusions that can be drawn by looking at correlations between measures. A more convincing approach is to use 'principal components analysis' to explore which working memory variables 'load' together on the same components. Van der Molen (2010) carried out such a study with large samples of 10- and 15-year olds with mild to borderline ID (around 100 participants in each age group, IQ range 55–85). She reported that working memory was organised more with respect to domain of functioning (i.e. verbal versus visuospatial tasks) in these young people with ID, than in terms of the tripartite system of the original working memory model. In particular, Van der Molen (2010) found that measures of PSTM and verbal ELWM loaded together on the same 'verbal' component; whereas measures of VSSTM and visuospatial ELWM loaded together on what could be interpreted as a 'visuospatial' component (note that the 'low' loadings have been excluded in this interpretation). However, a weakness of this study was that no typical comparison group was included.

Slightly different results have been reported with adults. Numminen et al. (2000) assessed 46 adults with ID (mean age 49 years, mean mental age 6 years, estimated verbal IQ 63) on an extensive battery of working memory tests, academic skills (reading, writing, mathematics) and vocabulary. They found good evidence that the measures of PSTM were related to each other. However, the VSSTM measures and the ELWM measures all seemed to be interrelated. Numminen et al. (2000) concluded that there were two key components to working memory in adults with ID: one reflected PSTM and the other reflected more general working memory resources (a combination of VSSTM and ELWM).

Numminen, Lehto and Ruoppila (2001) went on to look at the relationship between these two working memory components and performance on the Tower of Hanoi puzzle (a measure of executive functioning) in the same sample. Tower of Hanoi scores were related to the general working memory component but not the PSTM component. These results imply that we are right to consider ELWM and executive functioning as related constructs, even if they do assess slightly different subcomponents of a 'fractionated' set of executive abilities.

Summary

In terms of the functional organisation of working memory, there is some agreement that a phonological short-term memory (PSTM) component can be distinguished in both children and adults with ID. However, the findings are not in complete agreement with respect to whether working memory is divided in terms of 'domain' of functioning (verbal versus visuospatial) or in terms of more separate PSTM, VSSTM (visuospatial short-term memory) and ELWM (executive-loaded working memory) components. Further research using large samples of individuals with a wide range of ages and abilities would contribute to our understanding of whether working memory is organised similarly in all individuals with ID, regardless of age or ability.

Debates and Issues 5.3   Delving deeper into the *mechanisms* underlying executive-loaded working memory (ELWM)

Bayliss et al. (2005) examined the *mechanisms underlying* ELWM, wondering whether the *processing* and *storage* aspects of ELWM tasks would be equally efficient and important for those with ID.

Bayliss et al. (2005) assessed ELWM in a sample of 50 teenagers with ID (estimated verbal IQ 55, mental age 7 years), comparing them with 50 typical children matched for mental age. The authors assessed ELWM, but were careful to measure the processing and storage aspects separately.

- For children with ID, *storage* ability was related to ELWM performance, but *processing* efficiency was not. This contrasted with the findings for typically developing children; for them, both storage ability and processing efficiency were related to ELWM.
- In addition, Bayliss et al. (2005) noted that children with ID achieved the same scores on ELWM measures as typical children, but using a *different combination* of working memory resources. Children with ID were better at *processing*, but weaker on *storage*.

Hence, children with ID may be more dependent on the efficiency of processing and executive resources than typical children when carrying out ELWM tasks, because they have storage difficulties. These findings raise all sorts of interesting questions about whether *improving* processing efficiency in those with ID might make up for storage limitations in a range of everyday learning tasks, i.e. can we apply these findings to tasks beyond the 'theory-driven' ELWM measures?

Overall summary

This chapter began with a discussion of intellectual disabilities (ID), and then moved on to consider the somewhat contradictory research evidence relating to working memory performance in this population. Several conclusions were reached based on comparing individuals with ID to mental age comparison groups, which is the most theoretically interesting contrast. Such comparisons assess whether working memory performance in individuals with ID is developmentally appropriate, i.e. at the level that would be expected based on mental age (developmental model); or falls behind what might be expected on the basis of mental age ('negative' difference model).

The first conclusion was that children and young people with ID seemed to have impairments in phonological short-term memory (PSTM), supporting the difference model. Although there was some degree of debate around this issue, difficulties in PSTM represented the most commonly reported impairment in the literature in relation to individuals with ID. We touched upon possible reasons for this difficulty, including one of the most popular explanations (and one that has been around for some time) that individuals with ID fail to boost their memory capacities by using appropriate memory strategies.

Drawing firm conclusions about visuospatial short-term memory (VSSTM) in individuals with ID was virtually impossible, because the evidence was so mixed. Some authors found impairments in children and young people with ID in comparison to those matched for mental age, others found no differences between the groups, and still others found that individuals with ID had better VSSTM than comparisons matched for mental age. This represented a bewildering array of contradictory findings, which will require further research to disentangle.

With respect to executive-loaded working memory (ELWM), the research findings were also somewhat inconsistent. We noted, however, that some authors have suggested ELWM tasks requiring high levels of executive control may be particularly difficult for individuals with ID (leading to poorer performance), whereas performance on less demanding tasks may be developmentally appropriate. This is an interesting avenue to explore in future research and promises to enrich our understanding of the nature of cognitive limitations in those with ID.

In relation to other areas of executive functioning, recent evidence has tended to suggest that there are no difficulties relative to mental age, supporting the developmental model. However, we should remain cautious about such findings as the literature in this area is only just developing and remains limited in scope. Finally, another small but developing literature suggests that the binding of verbal information in the episodic buffer of working memory may be relatively unimpaired in individuals with ID. However, caution is again warranted, because of the limited range of research evidence in this area. In addition, reports of difficulties on non-verbal binding tasks have emerged, which need further evaluation.

Overall, individuals with ID are severely under-researched in the general literature on intellectual and developmental disorders, given the sheer numbers of individuals who have these difficulties. As noted by Hodapp and Dykens (2009), this currently 'unfashionable' area would benefit enormously from an influx of new research interest.

Further reading

Chapters, books and reviews

Bennett-Gates, D. & Zigler, E. (1998). Resolving the developmental–different debate: An evaluation of the triarchic and systems theory models. In J.A. Burack, R.M. Hodapp & E. Zigler (Eds.), *Handbook of mental retardation and development* (pp. 115–131). Cambridge: Cambridge University Press. More on the developmental–difference debate.

Harris, J.C. (2006). *Intellectual disability: Understanding its development, causes, classification, evaluation and treatment.* New York: Oxford University Press. A very detailed consideration of intellectual disabilities.

Hulme, C. & Mackenzie, S. (1992). *Working memory and severe learning difficulties.* Hove: Lawrence Erlbaum Associates. A thorough set of studies with clear explanations of the working memory model.

Kail, R. (1990). *The development of memory in children*, 3rd edn. New York: W.H. Freeman and Company. See Chapter 7 for a review of early evidence on memory development in children with ID.

Rutter, M., Bishop, D., Pine, D., Scott, S., Stevenson, J., Taylor, E. & Thapar, A. (2008). *Rutter's child and adolescent psychiatry*, 5th edn. (Chapter 49). Oxford: Blackwell Publishing Ltd. A very good overview of intellectual disabilities.

Volkmar, F. & Dykens, E. (2002). Mental retardation. In M. Rutter & E. Taylor, *Child and adolescent psychiatry*, 4th edn. (pp. 697–710). Oxford: Blackwell Science. An equally good overview of intellectual disabilities.

Research papers

These are listed in the order that they are mentioned in the chapter, rather than in alphabetical order.

Jarrold, C. & Brock, J. (2004). To match or not to match? Methodological issues in autism-related research. *Journal of Autism and Developmental Disorders, 34*, 81–86. An excellent discussion of the difficulties associated with matched comparison groups in the study of developmental disorders.

Henry, L.A. & MacLean, M. (2002). Working memory performance in children with and without intellectual disabilities. *American Journal on Mental Retardation, 107*, 421–432. Assesses three of the four components of the working memory model, including chronological and mental age comparison groups.

Bayliss, D.M., Jarrold, C., Baddeley, A.D. & Leigh, E. (2005). Differential constraints on the working memory and reading abilities of individuals with learning difficulties and typically developing children. *Journal of Experimental Child Psychology, 92*, 76–99. A large-scale study covering three of the four components of working memory; particularly strong on executive-loaded working memory. Also includes relationships between reading and working memory.

Van der Molen, M.J., Van Luit, J.E.H., Jongmans, M.J. & Van der Molan, M.W. (2007). Verbal working memory in children with mild intellectual disabilities. *Journal of Intellectual Disability Research, 51*(2), 162–169. A thorough study of verbal executive processes in teenagers with ID.

Russell, J., Jarrold, C. & Henry, L. (1996). Working memory in children with autism and with moderate learning difficulties. *Journal of Child Psychology and Psychiatry, 37*, 673–686. A detailed examination of phonological short-term memory and executive-loaded working memory in children with ID. Also relevant to Chapter 8 on autism spectrum disorders.

Carretti, B., Belacchi, C. & Cornoldi, C. (2010). Difficulties in working memory updating in individuals with intellectual disability. *Journal of Intellectual Disability Research, 54*(5), 337–345. A comparison of executive-loaded working memory measures that vary in their levels of executive demands.

Henry, L.A. (2010). The episodic buffer in children with intellectual disabilities: An exploratory study. *Research in Developmental Disabilities, 31*, 1609–1614. Presents some exploratory findings in relation to the episodic buffer in children with ID.

Henry, L.A. & Winfield, J. (2010). Working memory and educational achievement in children with intellectual disabilities. *Journal of Intellectual Disability Research, 54*(4), 354–365. Clear results pertaining to three of the four components of working memory, using mental age comparisons; also looks at how these measures relate to reading, spelling and mathematics.

Optional or extended essay topic for a piece of coursework

'Critically evaluate whether there are relationships between working memory and academic achievement in children and young people with intellectual disabilities.'

Use the current chapter for background understanding and setting the scene. Then, read the following papers (some of which are repeated from the previous reference section) to get more detail with respect to the research evidence. You should also search for more recent papers using your library's Psychology databases.

Alloway, T.P. & Temple, K.J. (2007). A comparison of working memory skills and learning in children with developmental coordination disorder and moderate learning difficulties. *Applied Cognitive Psychology, 21*, 473–487.

Bayliss, D.M., Jarrold, C., Baddeley, A.D. & Leigh, E. (2005). Differential constraints on the working memory and reading abilities of individuals with learning difficulties and typically developing children. *Journal of Experimental Child Psychology, 92*, 76–99.

Conners, F.A., Atwell, J.A., Rosenquist, C.J. & Sligh, A.C. (2001). Abilities underlying decoding differences in children with intellectual disability. *Journal of Intellectual Disability Research, 45*, 292–299.

Henry, L.A. & MacLean, M. (2003). Relationships between working memory, expressive vocabulary and arithmetical reasoning in children with and without intellectual disabilities. *Educational and Child Psychology, 20*, 51–64.

Henry, L.A. & Winfield, J. (2010). Working memory and educational achievement in children with intellectual disabilities. *Journal of Intellectual Disability Research, 54*(4), 354–365.

Numminen, H., Service, E., Ahonen, T., Korhonen, T., Tolcanen, A., Patja, K. & Ruoppila, I. (2000). Working memory structure and intellectual disability. *Journal of Intellectual Disability Research, 44*(5), 579–590.

Potential exam questions

1 Do children with intellectual disabilities show working memory difficulties? Illustrate your answer with research evidence relating to all four components of Baddeley's revised working memory model.

2 What are the key features of a methodologically sound experiment looking at working memory in children with intellectual disabilities?

3 Critically evaluate whether working memory impairments in individuals with intellectual disabilities reflect delays in development or differences in development.

6

Working Memory, Dyslexia and Specific Language Impairment

Learning outcomes

At the end of this chapter, you should have a good understanding of two disorders that most researchers agree are somewhat overlapping: dyslexia and specific language impairment. You should be able to describe the types of working memory difficulties that are characteristic of both disorders, along with key evidence to support these conclusions. Although working memory difficulties in dyslexia and specific language impairment appear to involve verbal memory problems, you should also be able to identify a number of debates and unresolved issues which require further research and investigation.

Note that children with dyslexia and specific language impairment have a known developmental disorder, but they do not have general intellectual disabilities. On the whole, they are developing at broadly the rate we would expect in areas outside their specific disability (i.e. they have a 'typical' range of non-verbal intellectual abilities, usually measured using an IQ test, i.e. standardised scores of 80+). Therefore, these are children with a specific developmental disorder, but not a general intellectual disability. We look at different atypical populations that vary in terms of whether they have intellectual disabilities and/or developmental disorders in other chapters.

Introduction to dyslexia

Dyslexia is an example of a specific learning disability, because it affects one domain, whilst leaving other skills intact. This chapter will focus on children who have difficulties with reading accuracy rather than reading comprehension; in other words, they find it difficult to read accurately and fluently. Dyslexia is probably one of the most studied and well understood cognitive difficulties (Hulme & Snowling, 2009), and there are many excellent sources of information about the disorder. Here, we briefly review the disorder, before moving on to consider relevant research on working memory. If you would like to read more about the development of reading skills and dyslexia, please refer to Snowling and Hulme (2008) or Hulme and Snowling (2009), listed in Further reading at the end of the chapter.

What do we know about dyslexia? Reading difficulties affect between 4 and 8% of schoolchildren in English-speaking countries (Snowling & Hulme, 2008), with a slight preponderance of boys (ratios of 1.5:1 to 3:1 have been reported). There is good evidence for a moderately important genetic influence on dyslexia (e.g. Pennington & Olson, 2005); and studies of the molecular basis of dyslexia suggest a linkage on a site on chromosome 6 (Snowling & Hulme, 2008). Environmental factors such as the mother's education, quality of schooling and exposure to print in the home are also important (e.g. Hulme & Snowling, 2009). Research using brain imaging has shown that there may be abnormalities in the functioning of language areas in the left hemisphere and this work offers promising new avenues to explore (Hulme & Snowling, 2009).

Precise descriptions of dyslexia are somewhat difficult as definitions of the disorder vary. Nevertheless, the key feature of dyslexia seems to be difficulties in the ability to decode, or read, words. Many researchers would also state that these difficulties stem from weaknesses in the phonological component of language (e.g. Hulme & Snowling, 2009); and that the reading difficulties should be unexpected, given the person's age/developmental level, intelligence (although this can be somewhat controversial) and other cognitive (e.g. language) and academic abilities. There may also be variable difficulties with writing and spelling in many individuals with dyslexia.

Often, there is an expectation that an individual with dyslexia will have intellectual functioning that is in the average range (i.e. an IQ of 85 or greater) and demonstrate poor literacy skills, despite the fact that they have had adequate opportunities to learn, normal or near normal hearing and no other developmental disorder that might interfere with learning (Bishop & Snowling, 2004; Pickering, 2006b). Many authors, however, simply define 'poor reading' as a score below a certain percentile (e.g. 25th) on a standardised reading test. Whether or not to use IQ scores in defining dyslexia is under debate. One view is that although IQ is moderately related to reading accuracy, it makes little difference in terms of teaching interventions whether children have high or low IQs. Similarly, many theories that attempt to explain the causes of dyslexia do not differ for children with different IQ levels (Hulme & Snowling, 2009). Nevertheless, most research studies do use some kind of definition that considers the role of IQ, as we shall see.

Possible causes of dyslexia have received considerable attention. Most often, weaknesses in phonological processing are regarded as critical (phonological processing refers to speech processing skills, particularly those skills that are involved in remembering or naming speech-related material; the perception of speech seems less affected). Many theorists view these problems as the 'core' explanation for dyslexia (Hulme & Snowling, 2009; Stanovich & Siegel, 1994; Vellutino, Fletcher, Snowling & Scanlon, 2004). However, this is not the only plausible explanation for the disorder. For example, difficulties with processing auditory information rapidly (Tallal, 1980), or automatising complex skills may also be implicated (Nicholson & Fawcett, 1990). For further discussion of these theories, please see Vellutino et al. (2004), listed under Further reading.

There are other interesting features to dyslexia, outlined by Snowling and Hulme (2008). First, dyslexia may be more common in some languages than others: e.g. for children learning English versus children learning a language such as German (although making such comparisons is notoriously difficult). Why might this be? German is a 'regular' language, such that speech sounds are mapped directly onto written forms. It is always possible to decode a German word by converting each letter into its appropriate sound (note that the key feature of dyslexia for native speakers of regular languages such as German may be a lack of *fluency* in reading). By contrast, English is more 'irregular', with many oddities in terms of mapping speech sounds onto written form. A good example is the word 'yacht'. Unless you recognise this word visually, it would be impossible to pronounce by converting letters into sounds. Such irregularities present children with considerable challenges when learning to read English.

A second interesting point to note about dyslexia is that the most obvious characteristics/symptoms of dyslexia may vary with age (Snowling & Hulme, 2008). At the early stages of reading, difficulties with decoding individual words may be predominant; yet later in development, comprehension and fluency problems may be more obvious, as reading demands during school-based tasks are increased. Adults with persistent literacy problems may have enduring difficulties with spelling or written expression, even if they have developed reasonably fluent reading (Maughan et al., 2009; Rutter, Kim-Cohen & Maughan, 2006).

Dyslexia is associated with many other developmental disorders, such as attention deficit hyperactivity disorder, specific language impairment and developmental coordination disorder. Therefore, it is most important when considering research in this area to ensure that samples are carefully ascertained. If individuals have dyslexia plus another developmental disorder, such as attention deficit hyperactivity disorder, it makes drawing conclusions about 'pure' dyslexia very difficult (Pickering, 2006). There are also a number of other specific learning difficulties, including problems with numeracy, that need to be carefully distinguished from dyslexia, as these difficulties can often co-occur.

Box 6.1 takes a look at yet another disorder, which is closely related to dyslexia: children with this particular disorder are known as 'poor comprehenders'. We will not be covering this disorder, but you can read about it in Nation (2005) or Hulme and Snowling's (2009) chapter on poor comprehenders (see reference list at the end of the book).

Box 6.1   Poor comprehenders

Poor comprehenders are able to decode words effectively, which means that they do not have difficulty with the process of reading. Their reading out loud is accurate and competent, so teachers often do not notice that they have any problems.

However, these children have difficulties in understanding what they read. Fluent reading is combined with a lack of understanding of the content of the text, hence the description 'poor comprehenders'.

See Nation (2005) or Hulme and Snowling (2009) for further details.

Before looking at working memory difficulties in individuals with dyslexia, it is important to note that there are many similarities between dyslexia and specific language impairment (SLI – see later in this chapter). It is also possible that the overlap between dyslexia and SLI may be as high as 50% (McArthur, Hogben, Edwards, Heath & Mengler, 2000). These issues have led some authors to argue that both disorders might be caused by the same underlying problems.

However, in this book, we will take the view that, in dyslexia, the problems are relatively restricted to literacy; whereas, in SLI, the difficulties are much broader and encompass the production and comprehension of spoken language as well (following Bishop & Snowling, 2004). One way of thinking about this is that individuals with SLI are more likely to have difficulties with both phonological skills and language skills; whereas individuals with dyslexia are more likely to only have difficulty with phonological skills (Bishop & Snowling, 2004). We will return to this at the end of the chapter.

In the following sections, research evidence concerning the working memory strengths and weaknesses of individuals with dyslexia will be outlined for each of the components of the working memory model. We will be considering what is often known as 'developmental dyslexia'. This is distinguished from 'acquired dyslexia', which refers to reading difficulties that have arisen due to brain injury or insult. If you need a refresher on any of the components of the working memory model, refer to Chapters 1 and 2 or look at the 'aide memoire to the working memory model' at the end of Chapter 2 for a brief reminder.

The phonological loop

Introduction

The phonological loop is the component of working memory responsible for phonological short-term memory (PSTM) performance; and we have already noted that one of the key impairments in those with dyslexia is in phonological processing. Such tasks include phonological awareness, phonological coding in working memory and rapid access to phonological information in long-term memory (Torgesen & Burgess, 1998). Therefore, it seems likely, from the outset, that PSTM might be problematic in children with dyslexia. This is, in fact, the case and relevant research evidence will be presented in the next sections. In addition, we will also look at phonological coding in children with dyslexia, as this skill is highly relevant to the phonological loop component of working memory.

There are many studies on this topic and some of the results can be quite confusing and apparently contradictory. This is partly because many studies have been concerned not only with whether there is a deficit in PSTM among children with dyslexia, but whether phonological coding strategies are somehow 'deficient' in these individuals. As we will see, the results seem to be slightly different for beginning readers as opposed to those who have made some progress with literacy. Therefore, it is most important to consider the stage of reading children are at when they take part in experimental studies.

It is also crucial to consider the precise way that 'materials to be remembered' are presented when assessing the phonological loop in children with dyslexia. Recall from Chapter 1 that one of the key features of the phonological store is that it is based on holding in mind sound or speech information. This means that similar sounding items become confused and are harder to recall if phonological storage has taken place. Importantly, with auditory presentation of materials, access to the phonological store is 'obligatory', so that we should expect all children, regardless of disability, to show phonological similarity effects with auditory presentation unless there are serious difficulties with the operation of the phonological store. With visual presentation of nameable items, such as letters or words, the situation is different. Access to the phonological store is 'optional' and relies on the person translating the visual items into a phonological code (i.e. naming the items – this is usually called verbal or phonological recoding/coding) and, then entering them into the phonological store. This is a strategic decision on the part of the learner and reflects the 'optional' operation of the articulatory rehearsal mechanism.

Therefore, in considering the phonological loop in individuals with dyslexia, we will make careful distinctions between whether auditory or visual presentation of items has been used. Auditory presentation allows us to assess the operation of the phonological store, and gives an indication of a basic ability to remember and utilise phonological information. Visual presentation, on the other hand, allows us to assess the strategic use of phonological coding in short-term memory. Either or both of these skills may differ in individuals with dyslexia. We will dip into this extensive research literature to consider several key studies that illustrate the main findings. Finally, the role of verbal rehearsal for children with dyslexia will be assessed.

Auditory presentation

This section will consider auditory presentation of speech items. According to the working memory account of the phonological loop, auditory presentation should ensure obligatory access of the memory materials to the phonological store. In this way, we can assess how well the phonological store operates for children with reading difficulties or dyslexia.

In a classic and often quoted study, Shankweiler, Liberman, Mark, Fowler and Fischer (1979) looked at the recall of rhyming versus non-rhyming strings of letters in 7- to 8-year-old children. The children were divided into three groups (samples of 13 to 17 in each) that were matched for verbal IQ. Those with 'poor' reading were around a year behind on a standardised test of reading; those with 'marginal' reading were about half a year behind; and those with 'superior' reading were nearly two years in advance of their age. All children heard five-item strings of letters (e.g. 'B, P, G, V, D'; vs 'H, S, L, R, Y') and were asked to write down the letters in correct serial order immediately after presentation. Figure 6.1 illustrates the results from this experiment in terms of mean errors (excluding the marginal reading group as they did not differ from the poor reading group).

There were two key findings. First, superior readers made fewer errors in remembering the lists, suggesting that they had better PSTM than poor readers. Secondly, although both groups were less able to recall similar as opposed to dissimilar letters (indicating a phonological similarity effect), this effect was much larger in the superior readers, suggesting that the utilisation of speech

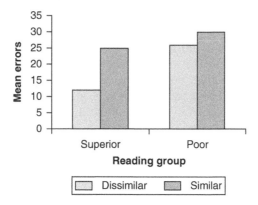

Figure 6.1 Mean number of errors on lists of auditorily presented phonologically similar and dissimilar letters, by children with poor or superior reading

Source: data adapted from Shankweiler et al. (1979)

coding in PSTM was weaker in poor readers. Similar findings with rhyming sentences and word strings were reported by Mann et al. (1980) – please see references at the end of the book if you would like to read about this work.

Shankweiler et al. (1979) concluded that children with poor reading had difficulties with phonological encoding. At the time, their findings were not discussed in terms of the current version of the working memory model, however, they do imply that difficulties occurred at the stage of obligatory phonological representation in the phonological store. Shankweiler et al. (1979) speculated that difficulties with phonological encoding in children with poor reading could be caused by difficulties in establishing phonological representations, or from difficulties in accessing them (the issue of redintegration that we covered in Chapter 3 may be relevant here). Surprisingly, over 30 years later, we are still unable to answer this question definitively.

Johnston (1982) examined the same issues with a wider age range, including groups of children and young people with dyslexia in three age bands (9, 12 and 14 year olds). Comparison groups of individuals matched for chronological and reading age were also included (each sample included about ten children). However, the matching of verbal IQ between the groups was not entirely successful. Although the comparison groups had verbal IQs of around 100 in each case, the groups with dyslexia had verbal IQs of 95, 84 and 96 respectively.

Nevertheless, Johnston's argument was extremely pertinent: she proposed that phonological coding difficulties may change with age and development in children with dyslexia. In order to test this, she used the same method as Shankweiler et al. (1979), asking children and young people to recall auditorily presented strings of letters that were either phonologically similar or dissimilar.

Two key results were noteworthy. First, Johnston (1982) replicated the finding that individuals with dyslexia made more errors than typically developing children; and this was true at all three age levels. Hence, here was more evidence for difficulties with PSTM in those with dyslexia (although remember that the verbal IQs were not matched). Secondly, the phonological similarity effect was present and equally strong in all groups, unlike the findings of Shankweiler et al. (1979) with younger poor readers. The results are illustrated in Figure 6.2.

Johnston (1982) suggested that at earlier stages of reading, there may be phonological encoding difficulties in children with dyslexia. However as reading progresses, those with dyslexia show equivalent effects of phonological similarity in comparison with typical children matched for chronological age. These results imply that phonological encoding is slightly delayed (up to 7–8 years) in children with dyslexia; but, thereafter (age 9 years and beyond), it operates without major difficulty and 'normal' effects of phonological similarity emerge. However, there remain other factors that reduce the capacity of PSTM in children with dyslexia.

In response to these findings and various other contradictory reports in the literature, Siegel and Linder (1984) tested Johnston's hypothesis directly,

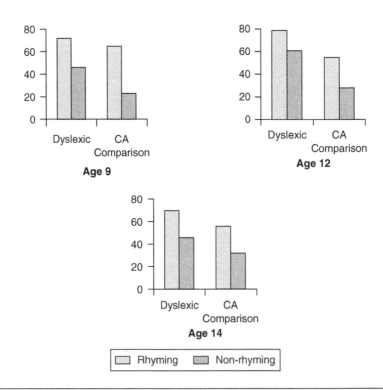

Figure 6.2   Mean percentage of errors on lists of auditorily presented phonologically similar and dissimilar letters, by children with poor or average reading

Source: data adapted from Johnston (1982)

by including both younger and older dyslexic readers in their study. Children between 7 and 13 years were assessed (7–8; 9–10; 11–13 years). Samples included 9–21 children in each group with reading disabilities, and 22–33 children in each comparison group. Again, children were asked to recall strings of rhyming or non-rhyming letters that were presented in the auditory modality.

Firstly, Siegel and Linder (1984) replicated the finding that most studies agree on: the ability to recall strings of letters was weaker in children with dyslexia than in typical development. Therefore, this supported the view that there is a clear impairment in PSTM for those with dyslexia (see also review by Jorm, 1983).

Secondly, Siegel and Linder (1984) found that all groups of children showed a significant phonological similarity effect except one: the youngest reading disabled group. Therefore, this provided converging evidence that in the early stages of reading development, children with reading difficulties show reduced sensitivity to phonological similarity, implying there is a developmental delay in relation to obligatory phonological encoding. However, by 9 or 10 years of age, even children with reading difficulties show robust phonological similarity effects.

Overall, these studies provide evidence that the phonological store operates as we would expect in children with dyslexia, but only after they have begun to make some progress with reading. Poor readers take longer to reach a stage of reading proficiency such that they show 'typical' phonological similarity effects with auditorily presented materials. However, despite this evidence of 'typical' performance, there are still weaknesses in the capacity of the phonological store, which are currently unexplained.

There is also considerable evidence for weak PSTM among children with dyslexia using another task – nonword repetition (refer back to Chapter 2 for a description of this auditory PSTM task). We will look at one study as an example.

Roodenrys and Stokes (2001) compared nonword repetition in three groups of 16 children: 8-year-olds with specific reading disability; 8-year-olds without reading difficulties matched for chronological age and IQ; and 6-year-olds matched to the reading disability group on reading age. The children with reading disabilities were at least 21 months behind their chronological age on standardised measures of reading ability. Roodenrys and Stokes (2001) found that children with specific reading disabilities and those in the reading age comparison group obtained significantly lower scores on the Children's Test of Nonword Repetition (Gathercole, Willis, Baddeley & Emslie, 1994) than those in the chronological age comparison group. Therefore, there were deficits in PSTM in children with dyslexia using the nonword repetition task, but these difficulties did not exceed reading age (see also Catts, Adlof, Hogan & Ellis Weismer, 2005).

One potential problem with concluding that PSTM (as measured by nonword repetition) is a core deficit in those with dyslexia, pointed out by Bishop and Snowling (2004), is that this skill is somewhat influenced by literacy. For example, Castro-Caldas, Petersson, Reis, Stone-Elander & Ingvar (1998) found that illiterate adults were weaker on this task than comparisons who could read. This suggested that the process of learning to read was improving performance on nonword repetition. However, although it may be that learning to read improves nonword repetition skills to some extent, most authors agree that there is, nevertheless, a real weakness in nonword repetition among those with dyslexia that cannot be explained fully by weak reading skills.

Summary

Children with dyslexia show impairments in PSTM. They also show delays in the use of phonological coding, even when memory items are presented auditorily, although once reading has developed to a certain level, phonological coding proceeds in a typical manner.

Visual presentation

As we have seen, young readers with dyslexia showed evidence for phonological encoding difficulties with auditory presentation, whereas older readers with dyslexia did not. It might be expected that visual presentation of the memory items would present even greater difficulties for children with dyslexia, because to use phonological coding with visual items, they must first be named: i.e. translated to a verbal code prior to entry into the phonological store. This additional step of 'phonological coding' is not required with auditory presentation (refer to Chapter 1 for details).

In two of the studies already mentioned, the authors compared auditory and visual presentation, so we will consider their findings now. Shankweiler et al. (1979) and Siegel and Linder (1984) both found that it made absolutely no difference whether auditory or visual presentation was used. In other words, all but the youngest reading disabled children showed 'typical' phonological similarity effects with both visual and auditory presentation.

This leads to the conclusion that, regardless of input modality, the use of phonological coding develops more slowly in children with dyslexia, but it does develop. Although we might expect input modality to have a considerable impact on the ease with which phonological coding can be used, surprisingly, this seems to make no difference.

One further study is worth mentioning in this context. It is of considerable methodological importance that task difficulty is equivalent when we compare phonological similarity effects in children with dyslexia and chronological age comparisons. Most of the studies already discussed gave all children lists of the same length – usually five or six items long. These lists may have been considerably more difficult for children with dyslexia, given we have established they have lower scores on measures of PSTM.

Consequently, Johnston, Rugg and Scott (1987) developed a revised method of assessing the phonological similarity effect in good and poor readers. Their innovation was first to measure the memory spans for all children to establish a baseline span. Then, they compared recall for rhyming and non-rhyming letters in the usual way, but presented lists for each child that were at span level. This meant that the task was of equal difficulty for all participants and, consequently, a fairer test.

Johnston, Rugg and Scott (1987) examined 8- and 11-year-old poor readers, defined as having reading ages at least 12 months behind their actual age, but IQs of at least 90. They were compared to chronological and reading age-matched comparisons, with approximately 20 children in each group. The findings were very clear. First, the usual PSTM deficit was confirmed: the chronological age comparison group had higher memory spans than either the poor readers or the reading age comparison group. These two latter groups did not differ, suggesting that PSTM was at a level commensurate with reading age for the poor readers. Secondly, the size of the phonological similarity effect was identical in the 8- and 11-year-olds, regardless of which reading group they fell into. In fact, there was absolutely no relationship between the size of the phonological similarity effect and reading ability (see also Macaruso, Locke, Smith & Powers, 1996 for a similar finding).

Therefore, these results agreed with previous conclusions: (1) children with dyslexia have a PSTM impairment (see also meta-analysis reported in Swanson, 2006); and (2) once reading has begun to develop in poor readers, phonological coding proceeds in the same way as it does for typical readers. Note that the study by Johnston, Rugg and Scott (1987) did not include beginning readers, so they were not able to comment on the proposal that phonological similarity effects are weaker in younger poor readers.

Johnston, Rugg and Scott (1987) speculated on why poor readers may have PSTM difficulties. They pointed out that poor readers are slower and less accurate when they name pictures, objects and letters; and that this may cause weak PSTM for visual materials, as well as making reading slower and more error prone. They also made a very interesting suggestion that poor readers may be more reliant on visual strategies than other children. Some evidence exists to support these suggestions. Palmer (2000b) used a memory span for pictures task (refer to Chapter 4 for details) and found that the ability to access phonological codes in PSTM (i.e. use phonological coding with visually presented materials) was related to reading development in a sample of typically developing children. This was even after the effects of age, intelligence and general working memory capacity had been statistically controlled. Further, the ability to inhibit less mature visual coding strategies (after the age of 7 years) was also linked to reading success. Although this work was not with poor readers *per se*, it did suggest that accessing phonological codes and inhibiting visual codes were both related to reading development.

McNeil and Johnston (2004) went on to address these issues directly in a sample of 18 12-year-old poor readers, all of whom were a minimum of two years behind their chronological age on reading performance. The poor readers were compared to 19 typically developing 7-year-olds with no reading difficulties; and the groups were matched for reading age (8 years) and IQ

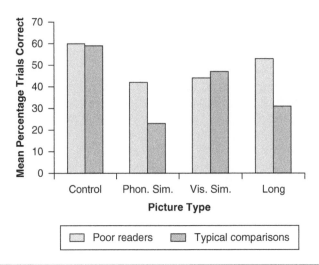

Figure 6.3 Mean percentage of correct trials on picture memory span including pictures with phonologically similar names, visually similar appearance or long names

Source: data adapted from McNeil and Johnston (2004)

(109 versus 106). The picture memory span task employed pictures that were phonologically similar, visually similar or long-named (to assess word length effects, which may indicate the use of verbal rehearsal). (See Chapter 4 for picture memory span tasks.)

Figure 6.3 illustrates the results. The first thing to note was that there were no overall group differences in picture span, suggesting that the children with reading difficulties had picture memory spans that were consistent with their reading age.

However, the more interesting results related to the types of similarity effects shown in each group, as these gave an indication of the types of memory coding strategies that were used. Although both groups showed a phonological similarity effect, this was significantly smaller in the poor readers. This suggested that poor readers had a reduced sensitivity to phonological similarity, in comparison to reading age matched younger children. In addition, the typically developing children showed a word length effect, whereas the poor readers did not. This suggested that verbal rehearsal was not used by poor readers, but that the typical 7-year-olds had begun to use this strategy (consistent with the research reviewed in Chapter 3). Finally, poor readers showed a small but significant visual similarity effect, which implied that they were still using a less mature visual strategy. However, there was a tendency for the typical 7-year-olds to also show a visual similarity effect, but this was not significant. Therefore, drawing conclusions about potential differences in visual coding between these two groups is probably not warranted based on these findings.

McNeil and Johnston (2004) repeated their experiment on the same samples using auditory presentation. Note that, in this case, it was not necessary for the children to convert the pictures to sounds via internal naming, as the stimuli were already in a verbal form. With this presentation method, poor readers showed the usual effects of phonological similarity (in fact, slightly larger effects than the reading age comparison group) and of word length. This suggested that poor readers were perfectly able to use verbal codes (and even verbal rehearsal), but decided to 'opt out' of verbal coding to some extent when stimuli were presented as pictures. There was some evidence of visual coding in the poor readers (a significant visual similarity effect) and the authors suggested that poor readers may have used 'mental images' of pictures (perhaps facilitated from the earlier experiment using pictures) to aid their recall.

Palmer (2000c) also presented evidence that teenagers with dyslexia show visual similarity effects alongside phonological similarity effects, implying that visual coding may be a preferred strategy for those with dyslexia. Note also that many of the processes involved in naming pictures are relevant to reading. Producing verbal labels for printed words or pictures are both symbol conversion tasks, whereby visual information is converted to a phonological code. It is, therefore, not surprising that these two skills are strongly related in typical development (Palmer, 2000b) and may be slightly delayed in poor readers.

Summary

Children with dyslexia show impairments on visually presented PSTM tasks. Phonological coding of visually presented items develops slightly late in poor readers, although once it has developed, it proceeds in a similar way as it does in typically developing children. There is some evidence that phonological coding may not always be the coding method of choice for children with dyslexia, if visual strategies can be used.

Verbal rehearsal

Difficulties with phonological coding in children with dyslexia may also be related to verbal rehearsal. Recall from Chapter 3 that there are many debates concerning the relationship between verbal rehearsal, articulation rate and the development of memory span. However, what is not in question is that verbal rehearsal is a strategy that develops gradually with age in typically developing children (usually from around the age of 7 – Gathercole & Hitch, 1993; Henry & Millar, 1993). Is it delayed in children with dyslexia?

There is some fairly convincing evidence that children with dyslexia are less likely to use verbal rehearsal. For example, Spring and Capps (1974) found that dyslexic boys were much less likely to carry out cumulative verbal rehearsal than children with typical development.

Similarly, Macaruso et al. (1996) found that young people (10–19 years, mean IQ 108) with poor reading (at least two years behind age level) did not show word length effects on a picture memory span task, compared to a typical comparison group of the same chronological age (n = 26 in each group). This suggested that poor readers were not utilising verbal rehearsal. The usual effect of phonological similarity was found, in line with the results reviewed earlier, indicating that poor readers do use phonological coding once they reach a certain stage of development in reading. Macaruso et al. (1996) went on to suggest that children and young people with dyslexia have less precise phonological codes and lower speeds of articulation, which both contribute to the breakdown of verbal rehearsal. This seems plausible, as rehearsing items that may become confused due to imprecise phonological codes will be challenging.

Macaruso et al. (1996) provided detailed analyses of serial position curves to support their arguments, looking at levels of recall at the beginning, middle and ends of lists. Poor readers were able to use phonological codes at the beginning of the list, but this broke down for later serial positions, suggesting that increasing confusion had a negative impact on the use of phonological coding and verbal rehearsal. Findings such as these imply that children and young people with dyslexia struggle with the consistent utilisation of cumulative verbal rehearsal strategies.

However, the study by McNeil and Johnston (2004) described in the previous section alerts us to a possible important caveat to this conclusion. Children with dyslexia, in their study, showed no evidence of word length effects in a picture memory span task (see Figure 6.3). This replicated the Macaruso et al. (1996) findings. However, in the case of word length effects with auditory presentation, remember that the poor readers in the McNeil and Johnston study did show word length effects.

Hence, children with dyslexia may be less likely to use verbal rehearsal with visually presented materials such as pictures, than with verbally presented materials. However, great caution must be used in interpreting these findings. In Chapter 3, a detailed explanation was given as to why word length effects are difficult to interpret with auditory presentation. We will not repeat this here, but suffice to say that word length effects with auditory presentation are not necessarily an indication of verbal rehearsal. Therefore, it is probably safer to examine the use of verbal rehearsal with reference to visually presented memory span tasks, as the interpretation of word length effects in such tasks is less controversial.

Finally, it is worth pointing out that PSTM deficits in children with dyslexia have been explained by some authors with reference to slow articulation rates. This type of explanation is based on the assumption that those with slower articulation rates are less able to recall items in memory span tasks, because they adopt much slower rates of verbal rehearsal. (See Chapter 3 for further information about this issue in relation to typically developing children.) McDougall, Hulme, Ellis and Monk (1994) suggested that differences in memory span between children who vary in reading ability are entirely accounted for by differences in articulation rate. In other words, when you control for the slower articulation rates of children with dyslexia, they no longer differ from comparison groups in terms of memory span (i.e. the PSTM deficit disappears).

Unfortunately, two subsequent studies have not replicated this finding. Avons and Hanna (1995) and Roodenrys and Stokes (2001) found that controlling for articulation rate did not eliminate differences in memory span between children with and without reading difficulties. These latter results suggest that differences in articulation rate and verbal rehearsal cannot account fully for the PSTM difficulties found in those with dyslexia.

Summary

Children and young people with dyslexia show reduced evidence of verbal rehearsal in memory span tasks that involve visually presented materials. This suggests that the verbal rehearsal strategy may be difficult or particularly effortful for individuals with dyslexia. However, it does not appear that differences in articulation rate between those with and without dyslexia can account fully for their PSTM difficulties.

Overall summary

Children with dyslexia have weak PSTM, whether assessed using visual or auditory materials. Children with dyslexia at the beginning stages of reading also have difficulties in using phonological codes, suggesting that the operation of the phonological loop may be delayed. The difficulties faced by children with dyslexia in terms of PSTM could stem from problems with both the phonological store and the articulatory rehearsal mechanism, i.e. both components of the phonological loop, but conclusions in this area remain tentative.

We finish this section with a brief description of an ongoing debate in this area.

Debates and Issues 6.1   PSTM and dyslexia

Theoretically, there are two opposing views about how PSTM difficulties could relate to the *causes* of dyslexia.

1 Some authors argue that dyslexia is caused by general problems with phonological processing, and that weak PSTM is one of the 'side-effects' of this broader problem. In this view, PSTM is not seen as the main cause of the problems associated with dyslexia.

2 However, an alternative view is that weak PSTM *in itself* does cause at least some of the difficulties found in dyslexia. In this view, weak PSTM is given a much more prominent role in terms of causing the difficulties seen in dyslexia.

(Continued)

It is beyond the scope of this book to discuss the complex interplay between these two positions, but if you are interested in reading more about it, please see Hulme and Snowling (2009) for an excellent discussion.

What is not in doubt, however, is that PSTM problems are characteristic of many children and young people who have dyslexia, regardless of whether they actually cause the disorder in the first place.

The visuospatial sketchpad

Next, we will look at whether visual and spatial short-term memory is impaired in children with dyslexia. Many theorists over the years have considered visual difficulties to be common in children with dyslexia. In fact, prior to the 1970s, dyslexia was often viewed as a perceptual disorder, in which letter and word learning was disrupted by weak visuospatial abilities (for example, reversing or inverting words and/or letters). However, during the 1970s and 1980s, a consistent body of evidence emerged to suggest that visuospatial abilities, and in particular visuospatial short-term memory (VSSTM), were not impaired in children with dyslexia. We will look at some classic studies to illustrate the findings.

Vellutino and colleagues were among the first to challenge the 'perceptual deficit' view of dyslexia (e.g. Vellutino, Pruzek, Steger & Meshoulam, 1973; Vellutino, Steger, DeSetto & Phillips, 1975). In an initial study, Vellutino et al. (1973) assessed samples of poor and average readers (21 in each group) who were 10 to 13 years old. All participants had verbal or performance IQs of 90 or above; and the poor readers were at least two years behind their chronological age level on assessments of reading. Although IQ differed between the samples (96 versus 109), the analyses took this into account statistically. The task was to recall Hebrew words, 3–5 letters long, written in the Hebrew alphabet (unfamiliar to these participants). Therefore, this was a visual recall task involving ordered recall of between three and five visually unfamiliar symbols. Box 6.2 gives some examples of Hebrew letters.

Box 6.2   Examples of some Hebrew letters

כ ג נ ד ת

Vellutino et al. (1973) found that poor and average readers showed no differences in the proportion of Hebrew letters they could remember, implying that VSSTM was not impaired in children with dyslexia. Vellutino et al. (1975) went on to replicate this finding on a wider age range of children (7 to 14 years), using a recognition procedure.

It could be argued, however, that the Hebrew letters employed in these studies may be given names such as 'backwards c'; 'the kicking one', or 'the seven'. Therefore, it is important to repeat these findings with stimuli that are not easily nameable. Swanson (1978) did this by asking 9-year-old children to recall lists of black-on-white nonsense shapes. The methodological innovation was to compare recall in groups of children who were not taught names for the nonsense shapes, with recall in children who were taught names for the nonsense shapes. The samples included children who had reading difficulties and those with typical development; and the groups were carefully matched in terms of mean IQ and chronological age (there were 15 participants in each of the four groups). The nonsense shapes were random and had no particular association with real objects.

Swanson (1978) found no differences in recall between the two groups who had not been taught names for the shapes, suggesting that VSSTM was not impaired in children with dyslexia. However, in the groups that had been taught names for the nonsense shapes, the results were entirely different. Here, poor readers showed clear recall deficits compared to the comparison group. In other words, changing this visuospatial STM task into a verbal STM task revealed a deficit in those who had reading problems. This ties in well with research reviewed earlier, that there are PSTM difficulties in children with dyslexia.

In another very significant study, Liberman, Mann, Shankweiler and Werfelman (1982) used a recognition memory test for several different types of stimuli: nonsense designs; photographs of unfamiliar faces; and three-letter nonsense syllables. Only the nonsense syllables could be 'named'. For each stimulus type, children were shown a baseline set of ten items, followed by 70 further items that had to be classified as 'old' or 'new', based on whether they were seen in the baseline set. The children were 7- and 8-year-olds selected from school classes based on their performance on standardised reading tests (there were 18 good readers and 18 poor readers). IQ did not differ significantly between the groups, although the good readers did have slightly higher scores (114 versus 108).

Liberman et al. (1982) found that there were no significant group differences in the percentage of correct responses for nonsense designs or faces; but poor readers were weaker than good readers when attempting to remember the nonsense syllables. This provided more evidence for memory difficulties in relation to 'linguistic' items, in contrast to unimpaired performance in relation to purely 'visuospatial' stimuli.

Katz, Shankweiler and Liberman (1981) argued that it was important to test whether the same results would be found using a more traditional span task that required serial order memory. In this experiment, memory for nonsense designs was contrasted with memory for nameable pictures (e.g. 'kite, horse, fish, sheep, tree'). On each trial, children attempted to reproduce the order of an array of five stimuli. Each array was shown for four seconds, after which the child was given five cards, each illustrating one of the stimuli, and asked to put them in the correct order. The participants were 21 good readers and 21 poor readers, selected from classes of 7- to 8-year-olds based on their reading scores on a standardised test. The groups were matched for age, but the IQ of the good readers was somewhat higher (115) than that of the poor readers (107).

Katz et al. (1981) found that the two reading groups did not differ in their ability to put nonsense drawings in the correct order (mean scores of 5.6 versus 6.7), but that good readers were significantly better at performing the task with nameable pictures (mean scores of 11.1 versus 14.1). This finding remained significant when the IQ differences were controlled statistically.

Therefore, a range of evidence suggests that VSSTM is not impaired in children with dyslexia. Nevertheless, many of these studies have considered materials that are more visual in nature, rather than explicitly assessing spatial short-term memory. Gould and Glencross (1990) remedied this gap in the literature, using age and IQ-matched samples, finding that performance on the Corsi blocks task (refer to Chapter 2 for details) was no different in poor readers (score = 6.11) as compared to typical children (score = 6.16).

Overall, there is quite a substantial literature suggesting that VSSTM is not generally impaired in children with dyslexia (see also meta-analysis by Swanson, 2006). This finding is important, because it suggests an area of strength for these individuals. It also suggests that 'general factors such as inattention and lack of motivation cannot account for their lower performance with verbal material' (Macaruso et al., 1996: 135). However, some authors (e.g. Pickering, 2006b) have noted a handful of studies showing that some children with dyslexia may have rather specific difficulties with VSSTM, so such problems should not be ruled out in individual cases (for further information see Howes, Bigler, Lawson & Burlingame, 1999).

Summary.
There is consistent evidence that children with dyslexia do not have difficulties with visuospatial short-term memory (VSSTM). This appears to be an area of relative strength for most individuals with dyslexia, although difficulties cannot be ruled out in all individual cases.

The central executive

Several authors, such as Swanson (2006) have argued that there are two separate working memory difficulties in those with reading disabilities: (1) impairments in PSTM; and (2) impairments in executive-loaded working memory (ELWM). We have already considered impairments in PSTM in relation to children with reading difficulties. The following sections review research on ELWM and other areas of executive skill in children with dyslexia.

Executive-loaded working memory

There is a considerable amount of evidence that children with dyslexia have difficulties with the concurrent processing and storage demands of executive-loaded working memory (ELWM) tasks. As it turns out, both verbal and non-verbal measures of ELWM seem to be affected. We will base the following discussion on Swanson's (2006) recent review of this literature and his meta-analysis of studies in the area (see also Jerman & Swanson, 2005).

Swanson (2006) found 28 studies suitable for inclusion in a meta-analysis on ELWM and reading disabilities. Meta-analysis is a method of pooling data from many similar studies to determine whether reliable effects are found, and, if so, how large they are (see Box 6.3 for a brief explanation). Swanson (2006) was careful to consider only those studies that reported IQ and reading scores; and presented data in such a form that effect sizes could be calculated. All of the studies assessed groups of children with reading difficulties using comparison groups matched for chronological age and intelligence. The age range covered by the articles extended from 5 years to adulthood and the measures of ELWM included both verbal and visuospatial assessments.

Box 6.3   Meta-analysis

Meta-analysis is a way of pooling the results from a large number of studies. This gives us greater *power* to detect differences between groups and is particularly useful if individual studies have small sample sizes. We can also look at whether certain factors ('*moderators*') affect the differences, e.g. whether group differences are there for children with dyslexia at all ages tested.

The results of each individual study are expressed as an *effect size* – in other words, the mean difference between children with dyslexia and typical comparisons on a particular executive task, divided by the pooled standard deviations. Effect sizes (*d*) allow the authors to compare different studies using the same scale.

An *effect size of 1* means that there is a one standard deviation difference between the means of the groups with and without dyslexia. Effect sizes, by convention, are regarded as either small ($d = .20$), medium ($d = .50$) or large ($d = .80$) (Cohen, 1988).

Swanson (2006) reported that the average effect size, reflecting the overall mean differences in performance between the poor readers and the chronological age comparison groups, was .81. This implies that the differences between poor and average readers on measures of ELWM were 'large' in size;

approaching one standard deviation of the mean. The findings were the same for children of all ages and did not appear to be related to IQ. Most importantly, Swanson (2006) argued that these impairments were equally true for visuospatial and verbal ELWM tasks, suggesting that poor readers had difficulties with the domain general system responsible for ELWM, rather than specific difficulties with verbal tasks.

In order to illustrate these results, we will look at a paper by de Jong (1998) (see also Siegel & Ryan, 1989, for a similar study). De Jong (1998) included some impressive controls for factors other than executive skills that might account for differences between reading groups. In this study, 18 10-year-olds with reading difficulties (IQ 80+; reading at least two years behind) were compared to separate comparison groups matched for reading age and chronological age (n = 18 in each case) on a range of ELWM tasks. These tasks included reading span, counting span and computation span (please refer to Chapter 2 for details).

Figure 6.4 illustrates the results of this study. De Jong (1998) found that children with reading disabilities were significantly weaker on both reading and counting span than those in the chronological age comparison group, but that there were no differences on computation span. The significant group differences remained even when group differences in speed of information processing and simple word/digit span were controlled statistically. De Jong (1998) concluded that children with reading disabilities have a general deficit in ELWM capacity in tasks assessing both language and numerical skills. This deficit was above and beyond their weaknesses in PSTM and slower speeds of information processing. There were no differences, however, between the

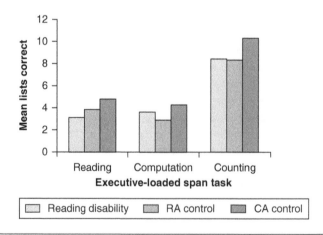

Figure 6.4 Mean performance of children with reading disabilities, as well as comparison groups matched for reading age (RA) and chronological age (CA) on three tasks assessing executive-loaded working memory

Source: data adapted from de Jong (1998)

reading disability and the reading age comparison groups, indicating that the impairments did not exceed reading level.

One limitation with this study is that it did not specifically examine purely visuospatial ELWM, as both computation and counting span are reliant to some extent on verbal skills. Therefore, Swanson (2003) included a purer measure of visuospatial ELWM in a subsequent study (as well as two verbal measures). Large samples of skilled readers (n = 126) and learning-disabled readers (n = 100), between the ages of 6 and 30 years, were compared. All poor readers had full-scale IQs of at least 85 and standardised reading scores below the 25th percentile.

Swanson (2003) found that the poor readers showed weaker performance on all ELWM measures, regardless of whether they were verbal or visuospatial. These results supported Swanson's view that ELWM is impaired in individuals with reading disabilities, regardless of the domain of processing (verbal or visuospatial). One potential weakness with this study was that the poor readers also had rather low mathematics scores, therefore, Swanson (2003) statistically controlled for both reading and maths skills in a second analysis. The reading group differences were still present, suggesting that even when we take into account weak maths and reading, poor readers still have ELWM impairments.

Finally, Smith-Spark and Fisk (2007) confirmed these findings in a sample of young adults with dyslexia (n = 22), comparing them to an IQ- and age-matched comparison group (n = 22). On three measures of ELWM (reading, computation and spatial working memory spans) the adults with dyslexia obtained significantly lower scores. Therefore, difficulties were again found on both verbal and visuospatial measures. Smith-Spark and Fisk (2007) further reported that when the relevant simple short-term memory measure was statistically controlled (word and digit span for verbal ELWM; and Corsi span for visuospatial ELWM), reading group differences remained. These results supported the view that there are basic difficulties with ELWM in individuals with reading disabilities, even when other relevant factors such as baseline PSTM or VSSTM are statistically controlled.

Summary
Children (and adults) with reading disabilities have clear deficits in executive-loaded working memory (ELWM), whether or not these skills are assessed in the verbal or visuospatial domain. These difficulties cannot be accounted for by weak component skills (e.g. weak PSTM). This suggests a domain general difficulty with ELWM rather than a specific difficulty with verbal tasks.

Other measures of the central executive

Findings are somewhat more conflicting in the broader area of executive functioning. One difficulty with research in this area is that few studies have looked at a range of executive skills. We will look at one exception to this, a study by Reiter, Tucha and Lange (2004).

Reiter et al. (2004) assessed a sample of 42 children with dyslexia (IQ 90+; below 16th percentile on standardised reading tests), comparing them with typical chronological age-matched children who had good to average grades at school (although IQ was not measured). A range of executive measures encompassed tasks that evaluated ELWM, inhibition, planning and fluency.

The results were somewhat mixed. Executive-loaded working memory was impaired in the children with dyslexia for both verbal (backward digit span) and visual tasks, confirming the findings reviewed in the previous section. Fluency was also impaired, and these results were consistent across several different assessments (letter, category and design fluency). However there were group differences on some measures of inhibition, but not on others, which made interpreting the results difficult. Similarly, on the planning and problem-solving test (Tower of London), there were significant group differences for planning time, but not in terms of the number of correct solutions. Finally, there was no evidence for group differences on switching (Modified Wisconsin Card Sorting Test, Trail Making Test Part B – please refer to Chapter 2 for a reminder about these tests). Therefore, the authors argued that certain executive functions were impaired (working memory, fluency), but others showed partial or no impairments (inhibition, planning, switching).

Other studies (e.g. Everatt, Weeks & Brooks, 2008; van der Sluis, de Jong & van der Leij, 2004) have failed to find executive difficulties in children with reading disabilities in the areas of inhibition and switching. For example, van der Sluis et al. (2004) included 21 children with reading disabilities (age 10 years, reading at least 1.5 school years behind) and 19 chronological age comparison children matched for verbal reasoning (two other study groups are not discussed here). On various measures of inhibition and switching (including the Trail Making Test), children with reading disabilities showed no impairments compared to the chronological age comparison group.

There is also some relevant evidence in relation to dual task performance. Swanson (1993) found that skilled readers were better able to carry out a dual task procedure than those without reading difficulties. Participants (n = 14, age 12–13 years, two years behind in reading) had to remember strings of digits whilst at the same time sorting cards (that varied in terms of verbal or visuospatial characteristics) into categories. When the strings of digits were relatively short (three digits), those with reading difficulties were as good as a chronological age comparison group (n = 14) without reading difficulties. However when longer lists of digits (six digits) were presented, the performance of individuals with reading difficulties dropped and was significantly lower than that of the comparison group. These results suggested there were impairments in dual task performance in young people with reading difficulties when the processing demands were high. However, the secondary task (remembering digits) was in itself an area of difficulty for individuals with dyslexia (PSTM), so reduced performance may have reflected this PSTM impairment.

Finally, a recent meta-analysis looked at 48 studies into executive functioning in children with reading difficulties. Meta-analysis allows authors to look at the results from a range of different studies together (refer back to Box 6.3 for a brief explanation). Booth, Boyle and Kelly (2010) found that children with reading difficulties were impaired on measures of executive functioning when compared to typically developing children. The overall effect size was .57, which is 'medium'. However, these findings reflected a combination of many types of executive measures, therefore, they cannot address whether particular areas of executive functioning may or may not be impaired. Booth et al. (2010) did emphasise, however, that distinguishing between verbal and non-verbal tasks should be priority for future research.

Summary
Executive-loaded working memory (ELWM) is impaired in children with dyslexia, regardless of whether it is assessed in the verbal or non-verbal domain. The findings in relation to other executive skills are less clear. From the limited research available, fluency may be impaired, but there are fewer reports of difficulties in the executive areas of inhibition, planning and switching. However, further research in children with dyslexia is required to assess executive skills in verbal versus non-verbal domains.

The episodic buffer

There has been some research looking at the role of long-term memory in supporting PSTM performance in children with dyslexia. Such research is relevant to the proposed episodic buffer, via its role in binding long-term knowledge with information from other working memory systems (in this case, the phonological loop).

We will re-examine the study by Roodenrys and Stokes (2001) in order to address this issue. These authors included comparisons of memory span for three types of one-syllable materials: familiar words (bath, cake, leaf); short nonwords that were highly 'word-like' (bip, veet, gub); and short nonwords that were not so 'word-like' (tuss, tarl, chig). Recall that Roodenrys and Stokes (2001) included three groups of children: those with specific reading disabilities, chronological and reading age matched comparison groups. The key question was whether the effects of familiarity of the materials (i.e. potential long-term memory contributions) would vary between groups.

Figure 6.5 illustrates the results of this study. As you can see, the children with specific reading disability had lower scores than the chronological age comparison group, but were virtually identical to the reading age control group. This replicates research we reviewed earlier, that children with dyslexia have PSTM difficulties, which do not exceed reading age level. However, the extent of the lexical advantage for remembering highly familiar words as opposed to nonwords was exactly the same in all three groups.

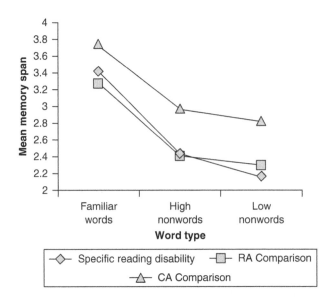

Figure 6.5 Mean memory spans for familiar words, high 'word-like' nonwords and low 'word-like' nonwords in children with specific reading disability, chronological age (CA) and reading age (RA) comparison groups

Source: data adapted from Roodenrys and Stokes (2001)

These results suggested that the binding of long-term knowledge with information held in the phonological loop via the proposed episodic buffer did not differ in those with and without reading difficulties.

Summary
This brief consideration of binding in the proposed episodic buffer implies that there are no fundamental weaknesses in binding information from long-term memory with verbal material stored in the phonological loop for children with dyslexia. However, as research is limited in this area, further work including measures of non-verbal binding is required.

Summary: Dyslexia

Children with dyslexia have difficulties with reading words accurately and fluently. These reading difficulties are unexpected, given the child's age, intelligence and other cognitive abilities. One of the most popular explanations of dyslexia focuses on weaknesses in the phonological component of language processing.

This chapter has outlined evidence that children with dyslexia have weak PSTM for serially ordered verbal materials, whether assessed using visual or auditory presentation. The difficulties faced by children with dyslexia in terms of PSTM may lie in both the phonological store and the articulatory rehearsal mechanism (the two components of the phonological loop). By contrast, children with dyslexia do not seem to have difficulties with VSSTM, suggesting that the operation of the visuospatial sketchpad is intact.

With respect to the central executive, some areas appear to be impaired in children with dyslexia, including executive-loaded working memory (ELWM) and fluency. There is currently little evidence for difficulties in the areas of inhibition, planning and switching. Almost no evidence is available concerning the episodic buffer in children with dyslexia, but no fundamental weaknesses in the verbal binding of information from the phonological loop with long-term knowledge were reported in one relevant study.

Next, we turn to a related developmental disorder, specific language impairment.

Introduction to specific language impairment

Specific language impairment (SLI) refers to delayed or disordered language development in the absence of any obvious cause. It does not include children who have language difficulties caused by mental or physical disability, hearing loss, emotional problems or severe environmental deprivation. In addition, individuals with SLI should have non-verbal abilities in the average range (although this can change over time). Hence, SLI does not include children who have difficulties with all aspects of learning, including language (intellectual disabilities).

SLI is known as a specific learning disability, because it affects some aspects of cognitive functioning but not others. On the whole, the disability is selective to language, although this is open to debate, as we will see later in this chapter. Sometimes SLI is referred to as 'developmental language disorder'.

Diagnosis of SLI generally rests on three key features:

1 Language skills are not in line with other aspects of intellectual development. For example, abilities outside the area of language, such as non-verbal skills, are at the level we would expect for a typically developing child. In practice, this usually means that a child's non-verbal IQ is over 80.
2 The language difficulty has an impact on the child's social or academic functioning.
3 The child does not meet criteria for pervasive developmental disorder (PDD – these are disorders along the autism spectrum that often have associated language difficulties).

SLI is relatively common, with an estimated prevalence of between 3% and 6% of the population (Hulme & Snowling, 2009). There are several risk factors for SLI: males are more commonly affected than females (3 or 4:1); being a later born child in a large family is also a risk factor; and twin studies have shown that SLI is highly heritable (Bishop, 2002a). There may be abnormalities in brain anatomy and structure in children with SLI (Ullman & Pierpont, 2005). Additionally, SLI often co-occurs with dyslexia, ADHD, developmental coordination disorder and autism, and the overlap in diagnostic categories (co-morbidity) often complicates conclusions about each individual disorder (Hulme & Snowling, 2009).

Although one form of SLI may have a relatively straightforward genetic origin on chromosome 7 (a particular mutation was found on this chromosome in several members of one UK family, many of whom had speech and language impairments, Lai et al., 2001), recent evidence suggests that the genetic aetiology of SLI in most cases is complex and likely to arise from multiple deficits. These deficits (possibly on chromosome 16) are likely to interact both with each other and with relevant environmental factors (Hulme & Snowling, 2009). Hence, many authors (e.g. Bishop, 2006) refer to these complex interactions in terms of 'additive risk factors' (p. 1164); acknowledging that the more difficulties faced by an individual, the greater the likelihood of a language disorder.

Language develops late in children with SLI and is characterised by a slow rate of continuing development (Hulme & Snowling, 2009). Weaknesses generally occur in all areas of language including: phonology (the sounds of language that convey different meanings); vocabulary; and grammar. However this varies some areas may be more affected than others. Many individuals with SLI have difficulties with grammatical morphemes or inflectional morphology; and using word order to signal meaning. For example, they may have trouble with modifying the forms of words to fit their roles in sentences: adding inflectional endings such as 'ed' and 'ing'; creating plurals; using articles such as 'a', 'an' or 'the' in the appropriate context; and using auxiliary verbs e.g. 'is running'. Children with SLI can also have varying difficulties with expressive language (producing language for others to hear) and receptive language (understanding the language spoken by others). Box 6.4 gives some examples of the types of tasks children with SLI might find difficult.

Box 6.4   Examples of language tasks that a child with SLI may find difficult

- Q: 'Here the boy is raking the leaves. What has he just done?'
- A: '**Raked** the leaves'

Pinker (1994) quotes the 'wug' test.

- A child is shown a picture of a birdlike creature and told it is a 'wug'. Then a picture of two of these creatures is shown and the child is told 'Now there are two of them; there are two _____'.
- Answer: 'wugs'

Language difficulties can lead to peer relationship problems, fewer friends and poorer social skills. SLI often persists into later childhood, adolescence and adulthood (50–90% of cases, Hulme & Snowling, 2009); and children with lower IQs are more likely to show persistent language difficulties (Bishop & Edmundson, 1987). There is also evidence that non-verbal IQ actually declines with age in children with SLI (e.g. Botting, 2005), so the difficulties of those with SLI may become worse as they grow older. Individuals with SLI often have significant problems with reading (Bishop & Snowling, 2004) and these literacy difficulties appear to have a strong genetic influence (Bishop, 2001). Unfortunately, the educational, psychosocial and mental health outcomes for young adults with SLI are relatively poor (e.g. Clegg, Hollis, Mawhood & Rutter, 2005; Young et al., 2002).

Theories put forward to account for SLI often focus on a particular aspect of language that is weak, such as grammar or auditory processing (these are known as domain specific positions, see Gopnick & Crago, 1991; Rice & Wexler, 1996; van der Lely, 2005). Other theories focus on some general difficulty with broader cognitive processes (known as domain general positions). General difficulties might occur in working memory and/or processing speed (Leonard, Ellis Weismer, Miller, Francis, Tomblin & Kail, 2007) or in procedural memory (Ullman & Pierpont, 2005: 'Procedural Deficit Hypothesis'). We will mention some theories in our discussions of working memory and executive functioning in children and young people with SLI. However, theories of SLI will not be the focus of this chapter. If you would like to read more about this area, please refer to an excellent chapter by Hulme and Snowling (2009); details are provided under Further reading at the end of this chapter.

We will now examine working memory skills in children with SLI, taking each component of the working memory model in term. As in other chapters, the first area discussed will be the phonological loop, a component of working memory that has received a great deal of attention in children with SLI.

The phonological loop

Introduction

We have already seen that children with dyslexia have difficulties with the phonological loop component of working memory. Children with SLI also seem to have difficulties with phonological short-term memory (PSTM). These difficulties are so serious, that many researchers have suggested that impairments in PSTM are the root cause of SLI in the first place; and can be viewed as a 'marker' for the disorder (e.g. Bishop, North & Donlan, 1996; Montgomery, 2002). Other theories have suggested that difficulties with perceiving speech or carrying out complex tasks might cause SLI. Brief explanations of these positions are given below (see Box 6.5).

Box 6.5   Examples of theories explaining the deficits in SLI

Poor phonological short-term memory capacity (e.g. Gathercole & Baddeley, 1990; Montgomery, 2002)

- Weak ability to recall verbal information in immediate memory. We will consider this theory in the current section.

Poor phonological sensitivity (e.g. Kamhi & Catts, 1986; Metsala, 1999)

- Difficulties in perceiving speech distinctions and poor representations of speech sounds. We will not consider this theory directly.

Poor processing capacity (e.g. Ellis Weismer et al., 2000; Marton & Schwartz, 2003)

- Problems in carrying out complex tasks such as executive-loaded working memory tasks. We will consider this theory in the section on the central executive

---

Why might difficulties with PSTM cause SLI? The hypothesis is that children with SLI have a limited ability to create and store accurate phonological (sound) representations. This means that when they hear a new word, they find it difficult to remember its precise sound characteristics. For example, if you try to repeat a word in an unfamiliar language, this will be much easier if you can remember exactly what it sounded like. Children with SLI, it is argued, do not retain precise representations of new words, so find repeating unfamiliar words very difficult. This also means that they do not easily form stable long-term representations for new words, hence must hear new words many more times in order to retain them. As such, children with SLI take much longer to learn vocabulary.

Additionally, poor PSTM may make it hard for children with SLI to note and remember key grammatical information about words. For example, noting the difference between 'hibernated' and 'hibernates'. Grammatical information contained in words is often subtle, compared to information about meaning. Weak PSTM could lead to the child focusing on the basic information (meaning) at the expense of more subtle details. Also, one must often keep in mind an entire sentence or clause in order to make sure that grammatical information is consistent. This may be particularly challenging for children with SLI if their PSTM is limited.

Over time, all of these difficulties stemming from poor PSTM may restrict and delay the acquisition of new vocabulary and grammatical knowledge in children with SLI. Having set the scene for why we might expect weak PSTM to be related to language difficulties, the next section considers experimental evidence concerning PSTM in children with SLI.

Experimental evidence for weak PSTM

In order to assess phonological short-term memory (PSTM) difficulties in SLI, many researchers have used the nonword repetition task rather than memory span measures. The argument in favour of using nonword repetition is that test items are nonwords and, therefore, not in the child's current vocabulary. Hence, resultant scores may be 'purer' measures of PSTM than measures employing familiar words. Performance on memory span measures using familiar words can be supported by long-term memory (see Chapter 3; Chapter 2 also provides a review of methods to measure PSTM).

Many studies have also demonstrated correlations or causal links between performance on nonword repetition tasks and the development of vocabulary knowledge in toddlers (Stokes & Klee, 2009) and school-age children (e.g. Gathercole, 2006; Gathercole & Baddeley, 1989; Michas & Henry, 1994). Nonword repetition, therefore, appears to be linked with vocabulary development in typical children (see also Baddeley et al., 1998).

We will now look at some experimental studies that have investigated PSTM in children with SLI. A study exploring such abilities in detail was carried out by Gathercole and Baddeley (1990) and generated a great deal of interest in the area.

Gathercole and Baddeley (1990) assessed six children with SLI (8-year-olds) in great detail, using a range of cognitive, language and PSTM tests. The children with SLI were individually matched to children in two separate comparison groups: one matched for language ability (these were younger children, because those with SLI had low language scores); and one matched for non-verbal intellectual ability (these children were the same chronological age as the children with SLI: remember that non-verbal abilities in those with SLI are largely age-appropriate). These comparison groups allow us to determine whether children with SLI have memory impairments compared to children of the same age (and non-verbal ability); but also whether these deficits might be particularly severe and occur in relation to much younger children who have the same language age. If the evidence supports this latter conclusion, we know that the PSTM deficits are worse than the language deficits, a very powerful finding. Children were also screened for hearing difficulties (hearing problems would affect the ability to carry out PSTM tasks and obscure the results).

The children with SLI were 20 months behind their chronological ages on vocabulary and reading, and 18 months behind on comprehension. However, their non-verbal ability scores were about right for their ages, as expected. Therefore, the typical SLI pattern of relatively average non-verbal abilities, together with a selective impairment in language skills was shown.

In terms of PSTM performance, Gathercole and Baddeley (1990) found that children with SLI were poorer than both comparison groups on standard measures of memory span. (The authors used word span for familiar words with a picture pointing recall method, just in case the children with SLI might have had speech output problems.) Children with SLI also obtained significantly poorer scores on the nonword repetition test in relation to both comparison groups. In fact, their nonword repetition scores were, on average, four years behind chronological age level. Children with SLI had particular difficulty with three- and four-syllable nonwords, suggesting that the greatest problems occurred when the capacity of the phonological store was stretched. Overall, this evidence for PSTM impairments was powerful, indicating that the weaknesses went beyond language age level.

Although the sample size was very small (in some analyses as low as five children with SLI), Gathercole and Baddeley (1990) did include a range of very effective control conditions to rule out other explanations for poor PSTM performance in children with SLI. First, they checked that those with SLI were not impaired in their perceptual discrimination of speech sounds. To do this, they presented pairs of nonwords or words to each child and asked them to judge whether they were the same or not (all were Consonant Vowel Consonant [CVC] words in pairs such as 'CAT/HAT' or 'ROG/ROG', and half were different, half the same). Children with SLI showed no deficits on this task, suggesting that they could detect the difference between similar sounding words. Note that although other studies have replicated this finding (Edwards & Lahey, 1998; Marton & Schwartz, 2003), there are occasional reports of subtle difficulties with perceptual discrimination (Montgomery, 1995).

A second control used by Gathercole and Baddeley (1990) was to check that the articulation rates did not differ between groups (according to the working memory account, articulation rate is an important determinant of how good a person's PSTM is – see Chapters 1 and 3 for more details). There were no deficits here either. In fact, subsequent authors have agreed that there are no articulation rate differences between children with SLI and typical comparisons (e.g. Montgomery, 1995).

Therefore, children with SLI showed an impairment in PSTM and these results could not be explained in terms of poor speech perception or slow articulation rates. The authors concluded … 'phonological storage skills play an important role in the development of a range of complex higher level linguistic abilities such as reading, vocabulary, and comprehension' (p. 357). They speculated that PSTM deficits could be responsible for the underlying language problems of children with SLI. This was a strong conclusion, and Box 6.6 summarises the strengths and weaknesses of this study that you should take into account in evaluating their findings.

Box 6.6   Strengths and weaknesses of Gathercole and Baddeley's (1990) study

Good points

- Strong comparison groups (verbal and non-verbal ability matched)
- Several PSTM tasks (various word and picture span measures and nonword repetition)

- Ruled out other explanations for group differences (poor speech discrimination and speech output problems)

Weak points

- The sample size was very small. This means that the effects, being significant, must have been very large, but we should be cautious about generalising these results to the larger population of children with SLI

In fact, van der Lely and Howard (1993) came up with a further criticism of Gathercole and Baddeley's results. They argued that children with SLI perform below chronological age level on practically any task involving language skills. Perhaps poor performance on nonword repetition and other measures of PSTM was a consequence of the SLI? Deciding which impairment comes first is often a tricky issue in studies of developmental disorders.

Van der Lely and Howard (1993) suggested that one can only evaluate this issue properly using comparisons between children with SLI and younger children matched for language ability. If there is a PSTM deficit for those with SLI, even compared to language-age matched children, this would suggest that the PSTM deficit came first. Looking at the data of Gathercole and Baddeley (1990) very carefully, van der Lely and Howard (1993) claimed that the language-age matched children were not as impaired as had at first been thought. They also failed to replicate this language-age impairment in their own, very similar study.

So is there really a PSTM impairment in SLI? Overall, the answer has to be yes. There are many subsequent studies that have shown clear PSTM deficits in SLI using nonword repetition tasks. For example, Dollaghan & Campbell (1998); Edwards & Lahey (1998); Ellis Weismer, Tomblin, Zhang, Buckwalter, Chynoweth & Jones (2000); Laws & Bishop (2003); Marton & Schwartz (2003); and Pickering & Gathercole (2004).

We will look in detail at just one of these studies, that by Bishop et al. (1996), because it provided a replication and extension of the Gathercole and Baddeley (1990) findings. They also tried to address the 'causality' issue, raised by van der Lely and Howard (1993).

Bishop et al. (1996) re-tested the proposal that children with SLI have an impairment in PSTM. In their words: 'Children who are poor at retaining a short-term representation of a sequence of speech sounds will have difficulty forming long-term representations of new words, and in identifying syntactic structures' (p. 392). Their study investigated the performance of children with SLI (drawn from a twin study) on the nonword repetition task, utilising a much larger sample. Box 6.7 describes the participant groups.

Box 6.7   Participant groups in Bishop et al.'s (1996) study

- All children were 7- to 9-years old and had nonverbal IQ's in the normal range
- There were three groups:

    1. Children with *persistent* SLI (n = 39)
       Had SLI at the time of testing
    2. Children with *resolved* SLI (n = 13)
       Had SLI in the past, with regular speech and language therapy for at least one
       year, but were now recovered
    3. Comparisons matched for non-verbal IQ
       No language difficulties (n = 79)

The rationale for including a 'resolved' SLI group was that if these children still showed a PSTM deficit, even when their SLI had been successfully treated, this would be good evidence that the underlying deficit in SLI was still in PSTM. This experimental design cleverly countered the van der Lely and Howard (1993) criticism that deficits in verbal memory may have been a consequence of SLI. All of the children were tested on nonword repetition, and the SLI children were given extensive tests of language function to ensure that they had language difficulties, together with non-verbal IQs in the average range (IQ 80+).

Bishop et al. (1996) found that those with persistent SLI obtained significantly lower scores overall on the nonword repetition test than those in the typical comparison group. As had been found in the Gathercole and Baddeley (1990) study, children with SLI had particular difficulties with longer nonwords: they were near ceiling for 2-syllable nonwords, but significantly worse than the typical children when repeating 3-, 4-, and 5-syllable nonwords. However, the most interesting result was that even children with resolved SLI (normal current scores on language tests) showed significantly lower overall scores on nonword repetition. In fact, they did not differ from the persistent SLI group, suggesting that they still had a deficit in PSTM. Figure 6.6 illustrates these results.

Therefore, Bishop et al. (1996) replicated Gathercole and Baddeley's (1990) finding that children with SLI showed PSTM deficits. The authors argued that children in the 'resolved' SLI group still showed PSTM impairments, but that they had learned to compensate for their difficulties. Therefore, the PSTM deficit was not a consequence of poor language, because the children with resolved SLI no longer had poor language, but they still had the 'original' deficit in PSTM. In addition, Bishop et al. (1996) found evidence that weaknesses in nonword repetition performance were

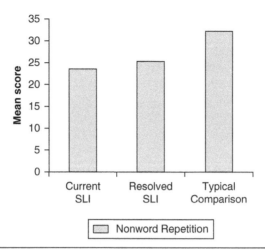

Figure 6.6 Mean nonword repetition scores for children with current SLI, resolved SLI and typical children

Source: data adapted from Bishop et al. (1996)

'heritable', i.e. that the nonword repetition test could be a genetic 'marker' for SLI.

Finally, Estes, Evans and Else-Quest (2007) conducted a meta-analysis of all of the studies that had looked at nonword repetition performance in children with SLI (refer back to Box 6.3 for brief details about meta-analysis). Estes et al. (2007) found that the overall difference between children with SLI and age-matched comparisons in 23 separate studies was large (an overall effect size of 1.27). This finding added to the convincing case for PSTM impairments in children with SLI.

As so many studies have found deficits in nonword repetition in children with SLI, the nonword repetition task has been suggested as a useful clinical tool for screening children for SLI (e.g. Archibald & Gathercole, 2006a; Bishop et al., 1996; Montgomery, 2002).

However, some authors have wondered whether nonword repetition deficits really reflect PSTM difficulties. Some believe that several other non-memory skills are involved in nonword repetition (e.g. Snowling, Chiat & Hulme, 1991) and that these other skills may be the root problem in SLI rather than PSTM. Similarly, Estes et al. (2007) noted that: 'A child's ability to repeat a nonword may be affected by any of the component skills involved in the process of hearing, encoding, and producing a word form' (p. 178)

Archibald and Gathercole (2006a) addressed the issue of 'other' component skills involved in nonword repetition in their chapter (see Further reading section at the end of this chapter) and described them as the following:

1   Vocabulary. Having a larger vocabulary may help in repeating nonwords, because of increased knowledge of the language (e.g. rules about how words are made).
2   Phonological sensitivity/awareness. Having better phonological awareness may mean that children are better at breaking up novel word forms before repeating them.
3   Speech output skills. Having better speech output skills makes the nonword repetition task easier, as the task requires verbal output.

Note that children with SLI, broadly speaking, are unlikely to have large vocabularies, good phonological sensitivity or well-developed speech output skills. Therefore, one cannot easily dismiss the argument that nonword repetition tasks may detect a range of difficulties in addition to PSTM. If nonword repetition tasks do detect a broad range of difficulties, it is very likely that children with SLI might have several problems in carrying them out. Nevertheless, Archibald and Gathercole (2006a) argued that even if these other component skills are impaired in SLI, there still remains a substantial additional PSTM impairment.

Therefore, the conclusion that children with SLI do badly on nonword repetition tasks is not in question. However, the interpretation of this finding, i.e. whether this represents a PSTM impairment, is still under debate.

What about other measures of PSTM such as word span or digit span? There is plenty of evidence, from a range of studies, that word and digit span are impaired in children with SLI. For example, Hick, Botting and Conti-Ramsden (2005) compared 4-year-old children with SLI, to typically developing children matched for chronological age and non-verbal ability (there was also a group of children with Down syndrome and we will come back to them in Chapter 7). Hick et al. (2005) used measures of digit and word span and one particularly strong feature of this study was that all children were assessed at three separate time points over 12 months. The results indicated that children with SLI obtained significantly lower scores than the typical children on digit and word span at all three time points.

The weakness with this study was the rather small sample sizes, with only nine children in the SLI group and 12 children in the typical group. However, similar findings were obtained in a comparable study with much larger sample sizes, although using only one assessment period. Henry, Messer and Nash (in prep) looked at 40 children with SLI (mean age 11½, range 10 to 14 years), comparing them with 40 typical children matched for chronological age. There was also a comparison group of 40 typical children matched for language age (6–10 years with a mean language age of 7½). All participants were given a large battery of language and cognitive tests, including several measures of working memory from the Working Memory Test Battery for Children (Pickering & Gathercole, 2001); Performance on a non-verbal reasoning task was in the average range for all participants.

Henry et al. (in prep) found that, on a measure of word span, the children with SLI obtained levels of performance that were lower than the typical children matched for chronological age. However, on a measure of nonword span, the children with SLI obtained levels of performance that were lower than typical children matched for language age. These results suggested that children with SLI have difficulties with PSTM, compared to peers of the same age; but that these difficulties were even more marked for nonwords. The implication of this result was that remembering familiar words was somewhat easier for children with SLI, than remembering nonwords. Perhaps this was because they could use long-term knowledge to support memory performance when the items were already known. When words were novel 'nonword' items, far less long-term knowledge was available to support recall (i.e. via the episodic buffer).

Before we finish this section it is worth briefly considering whether children with SLI have difficulties with phonological coding and/or verbal rehearsal. Although some evidence for rehearsal difficulties has been reported (Kirchner & Klatzky, 1985), several of the studies we have already considered did not find differences in the sensitivity of children with SLI to phonological similarity, word length, semantic similarity or lexicality (Gathercole & Baddeley, 1990; van der Lely & Howard, 1993). These findings suggested that children with SLI process, store and recall phonological items in the same way as typical children in memory span tasks, but may have a reduced 'capacity' phonological store.

Further evidence that children with SLI do not differ from typical children in terms of verbal rehearsal was found in a study by Balthazar (2003). She looked at word length effects in a sample of 11 children with SLI (7-year-olds), comparing them to children matched for chronological age and language age (these were younger 4-year-olds). Word length effects were examined using full verbal recall of the list or probed recall for just one list item. All three groups of children showed word length effects in the full recall condition, but word length effects did not emerge for any group in the probed recall condition. These findings suggested that children with SLI did not show *differences* in terms of their use of verbal rehearsal compared to typical children. It was likely that none of the groups were using verbal rehearsal, but that full verbal output may have produced word length effects in the absence of rehearsal (for further details about such 'output effects' please refer to Chapter 3). Ideally, however, we would investigate the development of verbal rehearsal and phonological coding in children with SLI throughout the period in which these processes are believed to develop, namely from 4 years through to 10 years.

Summary

Children with SLI have marked difficulties with phonological short-term memory (PSTM), particularly when assessed using nonword repetition and nonword span tasks. On these nonword measures, performance can be even lower than language age level. The impairment in PSTM has been argued by some to be the root cause of SLI. The logic is that poor PSTM prevents children with SLI from: (1) learning words effectively and rapidly; and (2) noting and remembering the parts of words that denote tense and other grammatical information.

The visuospatial sketchpad

From the characteristics of SLI that we have already identified, many researchers would predict that no difficulties with visuospatial short-term memory (VSSTM) should be found. However, there is evidence emerging for subtle difficulties in those with SLI on some non-linguistic tasks such as mental rotation, number skills and motor skills (Bishop, 2002b; Cowan, Donlan, Newton & Lloyd, 2005; Johnston & Ellis Weismer, 1983). For this reason, it becomes less straightforward to predict whether or not we might expect VSSTM impairments. At present, the research findings are somewhat mixed as we shall see below.

Archibald and Gathercole (2006b) found no evidence for VSSTM difficulties in children with SLI. Their participants included three groups of children with non-verbal abilities above 85: 15 children with SLI (9 years); 15 age matched peers (9 years); and 15 language matched peers (6 years). This three-group design was a strength of the study. The test of VSSTM was the 'dot matrix task'. Children saw a grid containing 20 empty squares, and a series of red dots appeared, one at a time, in several of these squares. After the final red dot had left the screen, the child was asked to point to the spatial positions that each dot had appeared in (in the correct serial order). This was a simple measure of VSSTM, which was likely to be more an assessment of spatial than visual VSSTM, because it required memory for spatial locations rather than visual detail.

Figure 6.7 illustrates the results for the dot matrix task (and several other executive-loaded visuospatial measures that will be discussed in the next section). In short, Archibald and Gathercole (2006b) found no significant differences between children with SLI and age matched comparisons on the dot matrix tasks, hence, no evidence for a deficit in VSSTM. In fact, it was the younger language age matched comparison children who obtained significantly lower scores, reflecting developmental differences.

Henry et al. (in prep), in a study mentioned earlier, also assessed 'spatial' short-term storage, employing 'Block Recall' (a measure of spatial span from the Working Memory Test Battery for Children, Pickering & Gathercole, 2001). As we have seen, they included large samples of children and young people with SLI and chronological and language age comparison groups. Those with SLI showed no significant impairments in Block Recall compared to the chronological age comparison group. They did better than the language age comparison group, mirroring the findings of Archibald and Gathercole

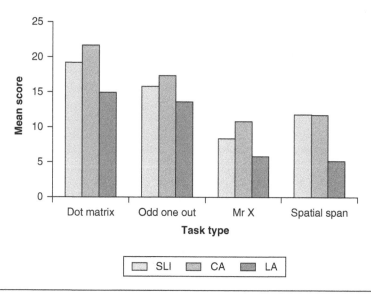

Figure 6.7 Mean scores on a range of visuospatial measures for children with SLI; typical comparisons matched for chronological age (CA) and language age (LA)

Source: data adapted from Archibald and Gathercole (2006b)

(2006b). Hence, two studies have found no impairments in the spatial element of VSSTM in children with SLI.

By contrast, some studies have reported difficulties with VSSTM. Hoffman and Gillam (2004) required children to remember the locations of a sequence of Xs that appeared, one at a time, on a 6 x 6 square grid. It was very like the dot matrix task used by Archibald and Gathercole (2006b). Participants included 24 children with SLI (9 years) and 24 children with the same level of non-verbal IQ, matched for chronological age (9 years). Whilst children with SLI could remember around three Xs in the correct order, the comparison children could remember an average of four Xs and this difference was significant.

Hick et al. (2005) also found some evidence for difficulties with VSSTM in a sample of nine very young children with SLI (4 years). As we saw earlier, these children were compared to 12 typically developing children of the same chronological age over a period of 12 months. On a measure of 'pattern recall', which required children to remember the spatial location of pictures of sharks presented on paper 'grids' coloured to represent the sea, Hick et al. (2005) reported that some of the children with SLI showed distinct difficulties with this task, and that their performance did not improve over the three testing sessions. However, overall group differences between children with SLI and typical comparisons were not significant. Hick et al. (2005) speculated that, because there was a great deal of variation in performance levels on this task for children with SLI, further investigation would be valuable.

Therefore, it is possible that there are real, but relatively variable, impairments in VSSTM among children with SLI. However, it is important to note that several studies have not found overall group differences, even using large sample sizes. If there is wide variability in scores on VSSTM tasks among children with SLI, it may be worth looking at subgroups of those who show impaired versus unimpaired performance in future studies.

Summary

Evidence is mixed as to whether there are impairments in VSSTM in children with SLI. Even if there are impairments, they are likely to be smaller and more variable than the large and consistent deficits we have seen in PSTM. Further research is required in order to thoroughly test VSSTM in children with SLI, including measures of both the visual and spatial components. This work is important, because if VSSTM is a relative strength for many children with SLI, treatments could be designed to take advantage of it.

The central executive

The discussion of the central executive component of working memory will begin with a consideration of central executive-loaded working memory (ELWM). Following this, other areas of executive functioning will be considered. Identifying executive weaknesses in individuals with SLI is particularly important, as difficulties with such skills are related to educational achievement in those with SLI (Young et al., 2002).

Executive-loaded working memory

Executive-loaded working memory (ELWM) skills in those with SLI have become an area of great interest, building on the work looking into PSTM. Theoretically, ELWM has been regarded as pivotal to the ability to produce and comprehend language, because these skills require the active maintenance and integration of verbal material in the working memory system (Ellis Weismer, Evans & Hesketh, 1999). Therefore, we will consider some of the evidence on ELWM in children with SLI, making a clear distinction between verbal and visuospatial tasks, because it is possible that performance levels on these two types of task differ.

Verbal tasks

Ellis Weismer et al. (1999), in an already classic study, carried out an assessment of ELWM in children with SLI. They looked at how well children with SLI performed on a listening span task, which is a verbal measure (the child must say if sentences are true or false, then remember the final word from

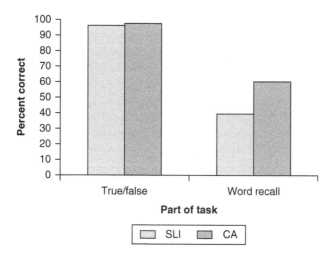

Figure 6.8   Mean performance on the true/false and word recall components of the listening span task by children with SLI and chronological age-matched (CA) typical comparisons

Source: data adapted from Ellis Weismer et al. (1999)

each sentence – refer to Chapter 2 for details). The 20 children with SLI had a mean age of 7 years, non-verbal abilities in the average range and normal hearing. They were compared to 20 typically developing children matched for chronological age and maternal educational level, although those with SLI had slightly lower non-verbal IQs.

Ellis Weismer et al. (1999) found that both groups were equally good at the true/false component of the task (i.e. the processing), but children with SLI were significantly worse at recalling the words (i.e. the storage). Hence, once storage and processing were combined, the hallmark of 'executive load', those with SLI had difficulties. Even when the small differences in non-verbal abilities between the groups were statistically controlled, there was still a group difference in verbal ELWM. Figure 6.8 illustrates these results.

Similarly, Marton and Schwartz (2003) reported that 7- to 10-year-old children with SLI obtained much lower scores on a listening span task than children matched for chronological age. The size of the difference between the two groups was reported as 'large'. Archibald and Gathercole (2006a) reported that, on a combined measure of ELWM (listening, counting and reverse digit span), 9-year-old children with SLI were substantially below normative performance. We can get some indication of the level of deficit of the children with SLI by considering the average standardised score for their 15 participants. It was 74.4 (s.d. 7.07), which is nearly 26 points below the mean (100) and well outside the typical range. However, this study did not include any 'dedicated' matched comparison groups.

Finally, Henry, Messer and Nash (2011) compared 41 children with SLI (with a relevant diagnosis, low scores on several aspects of language and average non-verbal abilities) to 88 typically developing comparison children on a measure of verbal ELWM. Rather than limiting the comparison group to those matched for chronological or language age, these authors statistically controlled for group differences in age, verbal IQ and non-verbal IQ. This had the advantage of retaining as much natural variation as possible in the comparison group, so as not to skew the results by selecting only participants who matched the children with SLI in respect of chronological or language age. On the test of verbal ELWM (listening recall), children with SLI obtained lower scores than typical comparisons, despite the stringent controls for age, verbal and non-verbal IQ. This suggested that young people with SLI showed significant difficulties with verbal ELWM over and above their age and general ability.

Summary
There is convincing evidence from a number of different studies for a verbal executive-loaded working memory (ELWM) impairment in children and young people with SLI.

Visuospatial tasks

Turning to visuospatial ELWM, the predictions are less clear. There may be a verbal executive deficit in children with SLI, because of the well-established PSTM impairment and general verbal/language difficulties. This would tie in with theories of SLI that emphasise language specific deficits (e.g. Gopnick & Crago, 1991). However, it would be premature to make assumptions about visuospatial ELWM tasks, given the somewhat mixed evidence concerning simple measures of VSSTM reviewed in the previous section. In addition, there are theories of SLI that point to general processing difficulties that are not restricted to language areas (e.g. Leonard et al., 2007; Ullman & Pierpont, 2005). See also a number of studies suggesting difficulties with non-verbal skills in children with SLI (Bishop, 2002b; Cowan et al., 2005; Johnston & Ellis Weismer, 1983), which may impact on VSSTM.

Archibald and Gathercole (2006b), in a study mentioned earlier, included three measures of visuospatial ELWM, requiring concurrent processing and storage in the visuospatial domain. These included: odd-one-out span (see Chapter 2); Mr X (two figures appear, each with one outstretched hand to the left or the right carrying a ball; one figure can be rotated to eight possible positions i.e. appears sideways, upside down etc., and the child must judge whether both figures carry the ball in the same hand); and spatial span (children judge whether shapes are mirror images of each other).

Archibald and Gathercole (2006b) found that children with SLI were not significantly worse than comparison groups (peers matched for chronological and language age) on any of the ELWM tasks, although, in some cases, the language-age matched comparisons were poorer (they were, after all, younger children). Please refer back to Figure 6.7 in the previous section on VSSTM for an illustration of the results. Therefore, this study provided no evidence for impairments in visuospatial ELWM in children with SLI.

However, there is emerging evidence that there are in fact deficits in visuospatial ELWM in children with SLI. Marton (2008, Experiment 1) examined this issue in some detail, comparing 40 children with SLI and 40 typically developing children of the same age. All of the children were 5 and 6 years of age, and the typically developing children were matched to the children with SLI on a simple VSSTM test. The purpose of this matching was to control for basic VSSTM, before examining executive-loaded visuospatial abilities. However, group differences did remain for non-verbal IQ (SLI = 98; typical children = 111).

There were three visuospatial tasks that varied in their executive demands. In 'space visualisation', participants chose one of two wooden blocks that would fit into a particular shaped hole, using mental rotation. This task demanded working memory as well as other executive skills such as planning, behaviour monitoring and inhibition. For 'position in space', participants matched one set of four abstract stimuli to another identical set presented amongst three 'foils'. For half of the trials, the initial stimulus set was left in view, but for the remainder of the trials the working memory demands were increased by removing the initial stimulus set from view. 'Design copying' required participants to copy lines and abstract figures – this test of visuospatial storage, monitoring and planning, had low executive demands.

Figure 6.9 illustrates Marton's (2008) results. Children with SLI obtained significantly lower scores on all three tasks than the typical children. However, we have already noted that the two groups differed in terms of non-verbal IQ, so the authors repeated their analyses using a statistical technique to control for these differences. Group differences remained for space visualisation and position in space, but were no longer significant for design copying. Therefore, children with SLI showed difficulties with demanding executive tasks in the visuospatial domain. On the less demanding design copying measure, group differences were accounted for by differences in non-verbal IQ.

Im-Bolter et al. (2006) also investigated ELWM in a large sample of 10-year-old children with varying degrees of SLI (n = 45), comparing them with typical children. The samples were well matched for age, non-verbal ability and gender (although there was a tendency for non-verbal abilities to be slightly higher in the typical group). The ELWM task was a 'visual N-back task' (see Chapter 2), a test of updating, because the child must keep in mind the details of several stimuli at once in order to compare them with the current item. Im-Bolter et al. (2006) found that children with SLI were less able to identify targets in the N-back task, providing evidence for a visual ELWM impairment in children with SLI.

More evidence for visuospatial ELWM difficulties was found in the study by Henry et al. (2011) mentioned earlier. They included a measure of

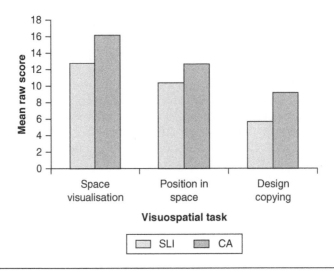

Figure 8.9 Mean raw scores on three executive-loaded visuospatial tasks for 5–6-year-old children with SLI and typical comparisons matched for chronological age (CA)

Source: data adapted from Marton (2008: Experiment 1)

visuospatial ELWM (odd one out span), finding that children with SLI obtained significantly lower levels of performance on this task than typical comparisons. These differences remained even after age, verbal IQ and non-verbal IQ had been statistically controlled, suggesting that problems with visuospatial ELWM were characteristic of individuals with SLI.

Therefore, at least three studies using large sample sizes and controlling for or matching on non-verbal IQ (and sometimes even verbal IQ), have found that children with SLI have difficulties with visuospatial ELWM. The age ranges covered by the three studies extend from 5 to 14 years, and present a fairly convincing case for difficulties in this area.

Summary
There is emerging evidence that visuospatial executive-loaded working memory (ELWM) is impaired in children and young people with SLI in comparison to typically developing peers.

Other measures of the central executive

A handful of studies have begun to look at executive functioning more broadly in children and young people with SLI. We will consider relevant studies that have included adequate comparison groups in the following areas: inhibition; fluency; switching; dual task performance; and planning. Please refer to

Chapters 1 and 2 for further details about executive functioning and the types of tasks used to measure these skills in the studies described below.

Bishop and Norbury (2005a, b) examined two aspects of executive functioning in children with SLI. First, the ability to generate novel ideas, which they referred to as 'generativity', but we have been describing as fluency (Bishop & Norbury assessed 'ideational' fluency). The second was the ability to inhibit a 'pre-potent' response (a response that the child is primed and ready to give), in other words, inhibition. Bishop and Norbury (2005a, b) published two separate papers on these tasks although the participants were the same. Therefore, we will consider the two studies together.

There were 17 children with SLI (between 6 and 10 years of age) and 18 typical children, broadly matched on chronological age and non-verbal ability. The specific ideational fluency tasks were as follows: a 'use of objects' task in which children were asked to think of as many uses for each object as possible (objects such as a brick, a mug and a pencil); and a 'pattern meanings task' whereby they were asked to ascribe possible meanings to a set of 'nonsense' line drawings. The two inhibition tasks were taken from the Test of Everyday Attention in Children (TEA-Ch, Manly et al., 1999), a standardised measure of attention and executive functioning: the 'Opposite Worlds' test required children to inhibit a naming response; and the 'Walk Don't Walk' test required the inhibition of a non-verbal response (see Chapter 2 for details).

The results showed that children with SLI did not differ from the comparison group on the two fluency tasks, but they obtained significantly lower scores on both inhibition measures. These results implied that children with SLI had difficulties with inhibition, but not with ideational fluency.

Further evidence concerning the executive abilities of switching and planning was presented by Marton (2008, Experiment 2). Switching was assessed using a shortened version of the Wisconsin Card Sorting Test (WCST), and planning was assessed using the Tower of London test. The 9-year-old children with SLI (n = 25) were compared with typical children of the same age (n = 25), although note that there was a difference in non-verbal IQ between the two samples (SLI = 108; typical = 117).

Marton (2008) found significant group differences on the WCST for a number of measures, including perseverative errors. This implied that children with SLI were less flexible in changing strategy (i.e. switching) from one sorting principle to another in response to negative feedback, tending to stay with their current strategy, despite feedback that it was no longer appropriate. Differences between the groups were also apparent on some measures (see also Young et al., 2002) from the Tower of London. Children with SLI showed more evidence of impulsivity, because their initiation times to make moves were shorter; they also made more rule violation errors, suggesting that they were less able to keep task-relevant information in mind while carrying out the task. However, the overall moves and the time taken for solving problems did not differ between the groups.

Therefore, children with SLI had some difficulties with switching and planning. Unfortunately, Marton (2008) did not report her results using statistical analyses that controlled for the nine-point difference in non-verbal IQ between the SLI and typically developing groups. It is possible, therefore, that some of the group differences might be explained by higher non-verbal IQs in the comparison sample. An earlier study using very similar measures (Weyandt & Willis, 1994) failed to find SLI deficits on switching (WCST), contrary to the results of Marton (2008), but did find difficulties on the Tower of Hanoi test (which is similar to the Tower of London and also assesses planning/problem-solving).

Im-Bolter et al. (2006) evaluated inhibition and switching in addition to visuospatial ELWM, which we considered earlier. The measure of inhibition was the antisaccade task, which involved training children not to look at a target stimulus, in order that a second stimulus in a different spatial location could be seen very rapidly. Therefore, this task required inhibition of eye movements. The two measures of switching included a children's version of the Trail Making Task and a set shifting measure, based on switching between two different tasks.

Im-Bolter et al. (2006) found that children with SLI were no worse at switching than comparisons matched for chronological age (they were slightly slower on both tasks, but the 'cost' of switching between sets/tasks was no greater). By contrast, children with SLI were weaker at inhibiting automatic eye movements. Therefore, these results indicated that switching was not impaired in children with SLI, but there were difficulties with inhibition (see also Dibbets, Bakker & Jolles, 2006).

Finally, Henry et al. (2011) evaluated a range of executive skills in children and young people with SLI (see earlier for details regarding samples). Executive functioning measures included both verbal and non-verbal tasks in the following areas: fluency; inhibition; switching; planning; and executive-loaded working memory (which we have already discussed). After controlling for age, non-verbal IQ and verbal IQ, children with SLI showed weaker performance than typical children on measures of verbal fluency, non-verbal inhibition non-verbal planning, and both verbal and non-verbal ELWM. No difficulties were found on measures of switching.

Therefore, Henry et al. (2011) found evidence for executive functioning impairments in children and young people with SLI in several areas: ELWM, inhibition, planning and fluency; but not in switching. As these executive difficulties were not confined to verbal measures, it could be argued that they were not a consequence of weak language skills. However, further research is required to support such a strong conclusion, particularly as some have argued that verbal skills ('inner speech' for monitoring and aiding problem-solving) might be involved in carrying out both verbal and non-verbal executive tasks (Russell, Jarrold & Hood, 1999, see Chapter 8 for a more detailed discussion in relation to autism spectrum disorders). Nevertheless, several types of executive difficulties did appear to be characteristic of children with SLI.

Summary

Children and young people with SLI show difficulties with executive-loaded working memory (ELWM), inhibition and planning. They may also show difficulties with fluency, but there is less consistent evidence for difficulties with switching. These findings suggest that 'executive' difficulties with higher order thinking skills are characteristic of children with SLI.

Finally, we close this section by mentioning some other areas of debate in the literature on SLI that may be relevant for future research.

Debates and Issues 6.2   Speed of information processing in children with SLI and the 'specificity' of specific language impairment

Speed of information processing

Some authors have proposed that, alongside working memory difficulties, children with SLI have very slow speeds of information processing. In other words, they have difficulty in processing information crucial for language learning quickly enough.

For example, Miller, Kail, Leonard and Tomblin (2001) found that children with SLI were slow to respond on a range of speeded tasks, whether they involved language or not. Leonard, Ellis Weismer, Miller, Francis, Tomblin and Kail (2007) went on to show that working memory and information processing speed could be regarded as separate cognitive components, each contributing independently to language skill.

Therefore, children with SLI may have *two* deficits, one in speed of information processing and one in working memory, and these may both contribute to their language problems.

The 'specificity' of specific language impairment

Leonard et al. (2007) also found evidence for separate verbal and non-verbal processing factors in teenagers with SLI. Interestingly, they argued that there are *non-verbal weaknesses* in individuals with SLI, which adds to the growing evidence that SLI is not simply a disorder specific to language. Other evidence for non-linguistic difficulties in children with SLI includes reports of weaknesses in mental rotation, number skills and motor skills.

If you think about the evidence we have just reviewed in relation to executive functioning, this also suggests that the difficulties faced by individuals with SLI are not purely in the verbal domain. There was a significant degree of evidence for executive impairments in *non-verbal* tasks as well as verbal tasks (see also Henry, Messer and Nash, 2011).

The episodic buffer

There does not appear to be any work that explicitly examines the episodic buffer of working memory in children with SLI. However, there is some research that may be relevant. For example, Alt (2010) has addressed whether children with SLI have difficulties in using long-term memory to support new word learning. We will consider this paper as it gives some insight as to how children with SLI may utilise long-term memory information via the episodic buffer in a real-life word learning context.

Alt (2010) was interested in how well children with SLI can learn novel words in a 'fast mapping' paradigm. Hence, the children were asked to learn new words with fewer than three exposures to each item. Alt (2010) tested two alternative explanations for why children with SLI may find this task difficult: (1) they have capacity limitations in phonological short-term memory (PSTM); or (2) they are unable to efficiently use relevant information from long-term memory to support their learning.

Twenty 7- to 8-year-old children with diagnosed SLI (standard scores of less than 85 on a comprehensive language battery together with non-verbal intelligence scores of greater than 75) were compared to the same number of typically developing chronological age-matched children. The task was a game in which children helped a palaeontologist track 'never before seen' dinosaurs. During the game, each novel dinosaur was labelled twice by the Experimenter; and all dinosaur names were carefully controlled nonwords. The manipulations of interest in relation to the 'nonword dinosaur names' were: (1) nonword length, which was either short (two syllables) or long (four syllables); and (2) nonword phonotactic probability, which was either high (i.e. the adjoining sounds in the nonword were commonly found in English) or low (i.e. the adjoining sounds in the nonwords were not commonly found in English).

The logic of this study was as follows. If children with SLI have capacity limitations in PSTM, they should find long nonword names more difficult to learn than short nonword names – but crucially, this difference between long and short names should be much more marked than that shown by the typical children. By contrast, if children with SLI have difficulties in using information from long-term memory efficiently, they should find learning names with low phonotactic probability more difficult than learning names with high phonotactic probability – again, relative differences should be greater than those found in typical peers.

Alt (2010) assessed fast mapping performance by asking children to recognise and also produce the names of the dinosaurs. Her results supported the capacity limitations in PSTM hypothesis. Children with SLI were just as able to produce short dinosaur names as typical children, but showed greater difficulties in producing long dinosaur names. There were no relative differences between the groups for performance in respect of phonotactic probability. Although children with SLI obtained lower scores on both types of nonwords than typical peers, they did not show a relatively greater deficit on names that had low phonotactic probabilities.

Therefore, Alt (2010) found no evidence that the ability of children with SLI to use stored long-term knowledge about which sounds are most commonly found together in the English language was impaired. There was, however, evidence that PSTM capacity was reduced in children with SLI, in line with the work we reviewed earlier.

Summary

The use of long-term knowledge to support current learning may operate efficiently in children with SLI, but as yet we have very limited evidence in this area. It would certainly be worth examining a range of measures of 'binding' of information from different modalities and working memory systems in children with SLI in future research.

Summary: Specific language impairment

SLI is a developmental disorder that is associated with marked language difficulties, but not with overall intellectual disability or global delay. We have considered whether there are working memory impairments in individuals who have SLI.

Several conclusions were reached. Firstly, there was good, robust evidence for phonological short-term memory impairments (PSTM) in children with SLI; many even suggest that such difficulties should be a 'marker' or 'screening test' for the disorder. Secondly, the evidence in relation to visuospatial short-term memory (VSSTM) was mixed, so that strong conclusions could not be reached at present. Thirdly, with respect to central executive-loaded working memory (ELWM) and other aspects of executive functioning, it was noted that evidence is emerging for a range of difficulties among children with SLI. Areas of difficulty included ELWM, inhibition, planning and possibly fluency. These difficulties were not confined to verbal measures but extended to visuospatial tasks, suggesting that general executive difficulties may be characteristic of children with SLI. There did not, however, appear to be as much evidence for difficulties with set shifting/switching.

Finally, there was very limited evidence in relation to the functioning of the episodic buffer in children with SLI, but one relevant study found no difficulties in the accessing of relevant long-term memory information.

Overall summary/thoughts

We have seen that there are working memory difficulties of various types in individuals with SLI and dyslexia, but that there are still areas of debate and uncertainty in relation to both disorders. It is worth briefly considering the potential overlap between dyslexia and SLI in relation to current theorising on this issue, as new developments are likely to involve thinking about commonalities and differences between these disorders.

An important distinction between dyslexia and SLI was outlined by Bishop and Snowling (2004). They suggested that individuals with SLI have a 'double deficit'. They have weak phonological skills, reflected in their weak phonological short-term memory (PSTM), but they also have weak language skills incorporating grammar, syntax and semantics/vocabulary. By contrast, individuals with dyslexia have only a 'single deficit', in phonological skills, which is reflected in their weak PSTM. Therefore, these authors argued that the two disorders are not simply at different points on a continuum of severity, but that they reflect core deficits in either one area (dyslexia) or two (SLI). Much of the evidence that we have reviewed, particularly in relation to PSTM, is consistent with this point of view (i.e. it was concluded that children with both disorders showed PSTM impairments).

However, Catts et al. (2005) have taken a different position, that dyslexia and SLI are separate disorders. They have argued that children with SLI have one set of cognitive deficits, whereas children with dyslexia have another (phonological processing difficulties). Catts et al. (2005) found evidence that most affected children have either dyslexia or SLI, with the degree of overlap between the two disorders being limited to about 15 or 20%. Their findings contrasted with those of some other researchers who have found a much larger degree of overlap between dyslexia and SLI (e.g. McArthur et al., 2000, found an overlap of 50%).

It is not easy to resolve the differences between these findings, but such work does raise important issues in terms of the precise definitions used in collecting samples of children with these two disorders. For example, Catts et al. (2005) have suggested that many studies examining children with SLI may have inadvertently included children with dyslexia in their samples, skewing the results in this area. They found that the PSTM difficulties in children who had been carefully screened to have just SLI and not dyslexia were relatively mild, compared to the difficulties experienced by children who had dyslexia. Clearly, this result seems contrary to the literature reviewed earlier; however, it raises an important issue that should be addressed in future research.

Another perspective comes from Bishop (2006). She argues that it would be useful to look at different developmental disorders in terms of discrete deficits in underlying processes ('endophenotypes'), rather than in terms of overall clinical diagnoses. Having multiple cognitive difficulties (e.g. in PSTM, grammar, naming speed, auditory perception), which could all arise from different genetic or environmental causes, may increase the likelihood of having significant problems with reading and/or language. In other words, it might be possible to compensate for one difficulty using alternative skills, but when two or more coincide, they could produce an 'additive' degree of risk for overall impairment.

Therefore, future research on working memory in children with SLI and dyslexia should draw precise theoretical and descriptive distinctions between the two disorders. A focus on discrete underlying difficulties (including problems with working memory) might also reveal how multiple and additive risk factors contribute to language and reading disorders.

Further reading

Dyslexia: Chapters and reviews

Hulme, C. & Snowling, M.J. (2009). *Developmental disorders of language learning and cognition*. Chichester, West Sussex: Wiley-Blackwell. Read Chapter 2 (pp. 37–89) for a detailed and thorough account of reading disorders and phonological deficits.

Pickering, S. (2006b). Working memory in dyslexia. In T.P. Alloway & S.E. Gathercole (Eds.), *Working memory and neurodevelopmental disorders* (pp. 7–40). Hove: Psychology Press. A very helpful chapter that has as its focus working memory difficulties in dyslexia.

Snowling, M.J. & Hulme, C. (2008). Reading and other specific learning difficulties. In M. Rutter, D. Bishop, D. Pine, S. Scott, J. Stevenson, E. Taylor & A. Thapar (Eds.), *Rutter's Child and Adolescent Psychiatry*, 5th ed. (pp. 802–819). Oxford: Blackwell Science. An excellent overview of the area, which provides plenty of background information.

Vellutino, F.R., Fletcher, J.M., Snowling, M.J. & Scanlon, D.M. (2004). Specific reading disability (dyslexia): What have we learned in the past four decades? *Journal of Child Psychology and Psychiatry, 45*(1), 2–40. A good overview of the theoretical advances over the past 40 years.

Dyslexia: Experimental papers

These are listed in the order that they are mentioned in the chapter, rather than in alphabetical order.

Siegel, L.S. & Linder, B.A. (1984). Short-term memory processes in children with reading and arithmetic learning disabilities. *Developmental Psychology, 20*(2), 200–207. A good summary of the area on phonological short-term memory.

Roodenrys, S. & Stokes, J. (2001). Serial recall and nonword repetition in reading disabled children. *Reading and Writing: An Interdisciplinary Journal, 14*, 379–394. Useful for phonological short-term memory and an insight into the episodic buffer.

McNeil, A.M. & Johnston, R.S. (2004). Word length, phonemic, and visual similarity effect in poor and normal readers. *Memory & Cognition, 32*(5), 687–695. A useful update to the previous paper.

Katz, R.B., Shankweiler, D. & Liberman, I.Y. (1981). Memory for item order and phonetic recoding in the beginning reader. *Journal of Experimental Child Psychology, 32*, 474–484. The classic paper on visuospatial short-term memory in children with dyslexia.

De Jong, P.F. (1998). Working memory deficits of reading disabled children. *Journal of Experimental Child Psychology, 70*, 75–96. An excellent study of executive-loaded working memory.

Smith-Spark, J.H. & Fisk, J.E. (2007). Working memory functioning in developmental dyslexia. *Memory, 15*(1), 34–56. Another excellent study of executive-loaded working memory.

Reiter, A., Tucha, O. and Lange, K.W. (2004). Executive functions in children with dyslexia. *Dyslexia, 11*, 116–131. Covers a range of executive skills, which is unusual in this literature.

SLI: Chapters and reviews

Archibald, L.M.D. & Gathercole, S.E. (2006a). Short-term memory and working memory in specific language impairment. In T.P. Alloway & S.E. Gathercole (Eds.), *Working Memory and Neurodevelopmental Disorders* (pp. 139–160). Hove: Psychology Press. A very useful and thorough research-oriented book chapter.

Bishop, D.V.M. & Norbury, C.F. (2008). Speech and language disorders. In M. Rutter, D. Bishop, D. Pine, S. Scott, J. Stevenson, E. Taylor & A. Thapar (Eds.), *Rutter's Child and Adolescent Psychiatry*, 5th ed. (pp. 782–801). Oxford: Blackwell Science. An excellent overview of the area, which provides plenty of background information. Note that the relevant chapter in the previous edition of this book is also good.

Hulme, C. & Snowling, M.J. (2009). *Developmental disorders of language learning and cognition.* Chichester, West Sussex: Wiley-Blackwell. Read Chapter 4 (pp. 129–171) for a thorough introduction to SLI and theories about its causes.

Montgomery, J.W., Magimairaj, B.M. & Finney, M.C. (2010). Working memory and specific language impairment: An update on the relation and perspectives on assessment and treatment. *American Journal of Speech-Language Pathology, 19,* 78–94. An excellent overview of the evidence regarding working memory deficits and other related issues in children with SLI. Montgomery's (2002) earlier review is also excellent (see full references at end of book).

SLI: Experimental papers

These are listed in the order that they are mentioned in the chapter, rather than in alphabetical order.

Bishop, D.V.M., North, T. & Donlan, C. (1996). Nonword repetition as a behavioural marker for inherited language impairment: Evidence from a twin study. *Journal of Child Psychology and Psychiatry, 37*(4), 391–403. This is an excellent experimental study written in a clear and accessible style.

Gathercole, S.E. & Baddeley, A.D. (1990). Phonological memory deficits in language disordered children: Is there a causal connection? *Journal of Memory and Language, 29,* 336–360. This classic paper reports the original experiments outlining phonological short-term memory impairments in SLI.

Archibald, L.M.D. & Gathercole, S.E. (2006b). Visuospatial immediate memory in specific language impairment. *Journal of Speech, Language, and Hearing Research, 49,* 265–277. Evidence against visuospatial deficits in SLI.

Ellis Weismer, S., Evans, J. & Hesketh, L.J. (1999). An examination of verbal working memory capacity in children with specific language impairment. *Journal of Speech, Language and Hearing Research, 42,* 1249–1260. The first paper to look at executive-loaded working memory in children with SLI; clear design and results.

Henry, L.A., Messer, D.J. & Nash, G. (2011). Executive functioning in children with specific language impairment. *Journal of Child Psychology and Psychiatry doi: 10.1111/j.1469-7610.2011.02430.x.* Describes a range of executive difficulties in a large sample of children with SLI.

Marton, K. (2008). Visuo-spatial processing and executive functions in children with specific language impairment. *International Journal of Language and Communication Disorders, 43*(2), 181–200. A thorough experimental approach to SLI impairments in executive-loaded working memory in the visuospatial domain.

Bishop, D.M.V. & Norbury, C.F. (2005a). Executive functions in children with communication impairments, in relation to autistic symptomatology. 1: Generativity. *Autism, 9*, 7–27.

Bishop, D.M.V. & Norbury, C.F. (2005b). Executive functions in children with communication impairments, in relation to autistic symptomatology. 2: Response inhibition. *Autism, 9*, 29–43. These two papers both present evidence on the wider issue of executive functioning in children with SLI (and children with autism for comparison purposes).

Potential exam questions

1. Do children with SLI show specific impairments in phonological short-term memory, or do they have wider working memory problems?

2. Critically evaluate whether children with dyslexia have difficulties with working memory. Illustrate your answer with research evidence relating to all four components of Baddeley's working memory model.

3. Is it possible to distinguish between dyslexia and SLI in terms of their working memory strengths and weaknesses?

7

Working Memory in Children with Down Syndrome and Williams Syndrome

Learning outcomes

At the end of this chapter, you should have an understanding of the major characteristics of two developmental disorders, Down syndrome and Williams syndrome. You should also have a critical understanding of the types of working memory difficulties that are often characteristic of these disorders. You should be able to describe and evaluate research evidence pertaining to these working memory difficulties in respect of the four major components of the revised 'working memory model' (Baddeley, 2000).

Children with Down syndrome and Williams syndrome have a known developmental disorder and usually an intellectual disability (i.e. scores on a standardised IQ test in the lower ranges below 70/75). Therefore, any working memory difficulties they have could reflect the developmental disorder, the intellectual disability, or the combination of both. Down and Williams syndromes are covered together in this chapter, because they are often regarded as having opposite profiles of working memory strengths and weaknesses.

Introduction

Many, but not all, individuals with developmental disorders also have intellectual disabilities (ID), and this chapter will focus on individuals with two developmental disorders that are almost always associated with ID: Down syndrome and Williams syndrome. For this reason, if you have not read the chapter on working memory and ID (Chapter 5), you may wish to review the first part of it, which describes ID more generally.

It is important to bear in mind that investigating the potential causes of working memory difficulties in individuals who have developmental disorders associated with ID is a complex task. Researchers must consider whether any impairments in working memory might be a result of the ID, the developmental disorder itself or possibly both of these aspects. This will be a recurring theme in the present chapter.

We will now turn to discussing working memory in children with Down syndrome, introducing the disorder first, and then outlining research evidence in relation to each of the four components of working memory.

Down syndrome

Down syndrome is the most common cause of intellectual disability (ID) that can be easily identified. The prevalence is estimated at one in every 700–1000 live births (Kittler, Krinsky-McHale & Devenny, 2008). Potential reductions in prevalence rates after screening programmes were introduced in developed countries are believed to have been largely offset by maternal age factors: Down syndrome is more likely to occur in the infants of older mothers, and the age at which women have children has risen in recent years.

The physical features of Down syndrome include a shortening of all body parts, a wide flat face with a small nose, poor muscle tone, hearing difficulties (40% or more cases), speech-motor difficulties, associations with congenital heart disease and an increased risk for specific leukaemias and immunological deficiencies. Most individuals with Down syndrome (94%) have trisomy 21, an extra copy of chromosome 21 (Pennington et al., 2003). This occurs through a process known as nondisjunction, whereby one from the pair of chromosomes does not separate during meiosis. The number of genes on chromosome 21 is quite small, representing only 1–1.5% of the human genome; and this may explain why it is one of the only viable human auto-somal trisomies (Hattori et al., 2000). Work is ongoing to identify candidate genes that may lead to the neurological and neurobehavioural phenotype of Down syndrome, but progress to date has been hampered by the enormous complexity of the systems involved and the large number of potential candidate genes (Skuse & Seigal, 2008).

Brain development in those with Down syndrome does not follow the same path as typically developing children. Research studies have not currently identified differences at birth between the brains of individuals with and without Down syndrome, but such differences begin early and emerge throughout development into childhood, adolescence and middle age (e.g. delayed myelination, a reduction in the number of cortical granular neurons, narrowing of the superior temporal gyrus, diminished size of the brainstem and cerebellum, overall smaller brain size in general and in other specific areas such as the frontal lobes and hippocampus; see Nadel, 1999; and atrophy of the corpus callosum and hippocampus with age, Skuse & Seigal, 2008).

There are a number of behavioural and cognitive features that are often typical of those with Down syndrome (Chapman & Hesketh, 2000; Skuse & Seigal, 2008). Perhaps the most common cognitive feature is the presence of ID (Chapman & Hesketh, 2000). IQs are often between 25 to 70, with many individuals falling into the severe ID range (see Chapter 5 for details), and few reaching mental age levels beyond 7 to 8 years. However, despite this, there is considerable variability in intellectual ability among those with Down syndrome. Recent advances in educational provision and higher expectations have meant that many children with Down syndrome are educated in mainstream settings and there is evidence that this improves aspects of language and memory development (Laws et al., 2000).

Another commonly mentioned difficulty among those with Down syndrome relates to speech and language (Chapman & Hesketh, 2000). Several areas are generally impaired, including expressive language, articulation, phonology, vocal imitation and mean length of utterance. Difficulties are often more marked in expressive language than in language comprehension; in other words, the ability to produce language is less advanced than the ability to understand language. In comparison with verbal ability, non-verbal ability is less impaired. This contrast will be particularly important later in the chapter, because the working memory abilities of those with Down syndrome appear to mirror this pattern.

However, it is always important to stress that one should not necessarily expect uniform effects in any particular developmental disorder, and there is great variability in the expression of even what are regarded as 'characteristic' features of Down syndrome.

Finally, there are a few points to consider when evaluating research studies conducted with those who have Down syndrome. Hearing problems are common (Roizen, Wolters, Nicol & Blondis, 1993) and should always be carefully controlled for in experimental studies. Cognitive decline can occur early (40s) in Down syndrome due to an increased incidence of neuropathology and, hence, risk of Alzheimer's disease (Wisniewski & Silverman, 1998), so it is worth looking carefully at the ages of the samples included. Up to half of individuals with Down syndrome over the age of 50 can show evidence of symptoms related to the emergence of dementia (Chapman & Hesketh, 2000).

We will now consider working memory in individuals with Down syndrome, taking each component of working memory in turn. If you need a refresher on any of the components of the working memory model, please refer to Chapters 1 and 2 or look at the 'aide memoire to the working memory model' at the end of Chapter 2 for a brief reminder.

The phonological loop

Many authors have been interested in phonological short-term memory (PSTM) in individuals with Down syndrome, largely because of speculation that the language and memory difficulties of these individuals could be linked. Recall that the phonological loop is specialised for holding speech-based information. This led researchers to wonder whether this may represent an area of weakness for individuals with Down syndrome, who have speech and language difficulties.

There have been a number of studies carried out to examine PSTM in individuals with Down syndrome. One of the most detailed sets of experiments was carried out by Hulme and Mackenzie (1992). Their book is given in the list of Further Reading at the end of the chapter, and is a very readable account of a series of detailed studies.

Hulme and Mackenzie (1992) first set out to establish whether individuals with Down syndrome might have lower PSTM scores than comparison groups. They examined digit span in a large group (n = 55) of individuals with Down syndrome who had a mean chronological age of 16 years and a mean mental age of 6 years, hence they had severe ID. It is important to consider the comparison groups used by Hulme and Mackenzie (1992), as research in this area can only be interpreted correctly with this in mind.

The first comparison group included young people with 'non-specific' severe ID (i.e. ID with no identified developmental disorder) who were of a similar chronological age (19 years) and mental age (6 years) to the Down syndrome group. This group allows us to address the important question of whether it is just the presence of an ID that might lead to an impairment in PSTM, or whether the additional presence of Down syndrome is particularly relevant. The second comparison group included typically developing children with chronological and mental ages of 6 years. This group allows us to establish whether the individuals in the ID groups were achieving PSTM performance as expected, based on current intellectual level. Groups were matched on approximate verbal mental age using the English Picture Vocabulary Test (EPVT), which assesses the individual's ability to point to a named verbal item from a choice of four, all presented in picture format (receptive vocabulary).

The results were very straightforward. Individuals with Down syndrome and individuals with severe ID both obtained mean digit spans of three items. By contrast, the typically developing children obtained spans of four items. These results indicated that the presence of severe ID appeared to cause an impairment in PSTM. There was no evidence that having Down syndrome led to a greater impairment than having severe ID on its own.

However, Hulme and Mackenzie (1992) went on to carry out a detailed and comprehensive five-year longitudinal study of the working memory abilities of a subset of the younger individuals with Down syndrome. These included ten young people with Down syndrome who had a chronological age of 11 years and a mental age of 5 years at the beginning of the study; and eight young people with severe ID of a similar chronological (11 years) and mental age (5 years). The final group included 28 typically developing children who had both chronological and mental ages of 5 years.

Hulme and Mackenzie (1992) tested all participants three times on a digit span task, over a period of five years. Figure 7.1 illustrates the fact that digit span increased relatively little for children with Down syndrome, increased slightly for those with severe ID and increased markedly for typically developing children. Hulme and Mackenzie (1992) checked that their results could not be accounted for by slower articulation rates among those with Down syndrome (they could not), and went on to suggest that children with Down syndrome showed weaker PSTM, because they did not use verbal rehearsal.

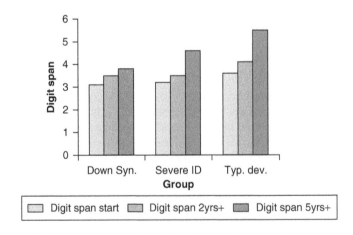

Figure 7.1   Mean digit spans over five years for individuals with Down syndrome, severe intellectual disabilities and typically developing children

Source: data adapted from Hulme and Mackenzie (1992)

These findings offered some support for the notion that digit span may be slightly more impaired in children with Down syndrome than children with severe ID, because the span levels and rates of improvement over five years were lowest for those with Down syndrome. The lack of improvement over five years in PSTM in those with Down syndrome has also been replicated by Laws and Gunn (2004) in a much larger sample of 30 adolescents and young adults.

Jarrold and Baddeley (1997) also looked at PSTM in children with Down syndrome, in order to investigate potential impairments in more detail. They compared children with Down syndrome (13-year-olds with severe ID) to 8-year-old children with moderate ID (n = 15 in each group). A second comparison group included 15 4- to 5-year-old typically developing children. All young people with Down syndrome were given a hearing test and the authors carefully ruled out possible hearing problems as an explanation for their results. The chronological ages differed between these three groups, so they were not quite ideal in terms of the criteria outlined in Chapter 5. However, the groups were matched for verbal mental age (4 years) using the British Picture Vocabulary Scale.

Jarrold and Baddeley (1997) found that there were significant differences between the groups on a measure of digit span: those with Down syndrome obtained poorer scores than those in the other two groups (typically developing, moderate ID). The results, therefore, supported the position that children with Down syndrome might have a specific impairment in PSTM, even when compared to children with ID.

There were two potential problems with this conclusion, however. First, the results were significant when digit span was scored without requiring the items to be recalled in correct serial order, but they missed significance when serial order was required. Typically, one would expect a digit span task to require serial order (see Chapter 2), so it would have been more convincing to have found significant findings with both scoring methods. A second issue was that Jarrold and Baddeley (1997) employed a comparison group with moderate ID, whereas their individuals with Down syndrome had severe ID. This means that the children with Down syndrome had more severe levels of ID than the children with moderate ID. Ideally, we would match the two groups on the severity of ID: i.e. both groups should have the same mental and chronological age. Otherwise, we cannot be sure that the differing severity of ID between the groups accounted for the group differences in terms of digit span.

An earlier study had looked at this issue using such groups, although the participants were somewhat older. Marcel and Weeks (1988) compared young people with Down syndrome (age 16) to young people of the same chronological age who had non-specific ID. The final typically developing comparison group included 5 year olds matched for verbal mental age to the other two groups (using a picture vocabulary scale; mean mental age 4–5 years). The important point about this design was that both of the ID groups were matched for severity of ID, because their chronological and mental ages were the same.

Measures of word span were used to assess PSTM. These tasks required non-verbal pointing recall, to remove the necessity for participants to recite the lists verbally, which may be difficult for individuals with Down syndrome (they often have articulation problems). The results showed that individuals with Down syndrome had the lowest span levels; individuals with severe ID obtained slightly higher scores; and both groups performed more poorly than the typically developing comparisons. A second experiment using digit span produced virtually identical results (see Figure 7.2).

These results suggested that there was a deficit in PSTM for those with severe ID, but that there was a larger deficit for those with Down syndrome. There are many subsequent studies that have found PSTM difficulties in children and adolescents with Down syndrome, in comparison to similar ability children with ID and/or in comparison to typically developing children of the same mental age (e.g. Bower & Hayes, 1994; Hick et al., 2005; Kanno & Ikeda, 2002; Lanfranchi, Cornoldi & Vianello, 2004; Laws, 2002; Pennington et al., 2003; Purser & Jarrold, 2005; Seung & Chapman, 2000; Vicari, Marotta & Carlesimo, 2004). There are very few exceptions to this finding (e.g. Vicari, Carlesimo & Caltagirone, 1995 in a study of teenagers with Down syndrome).

This evidence strongly suggests that weak PSTM is characteristic of those with Down syndrome, to a greater extent than it is characteristic of those with severe ID.

We have so far confined our discussion to studies with children and adolescents, but a study by Numminen, Service, Ahonen and Ruoppila (2001) found the same pattern of results in middle-aged adults with Down syndrome.

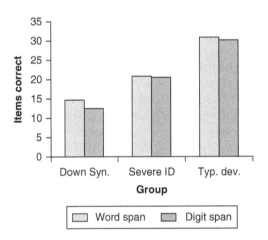

Figure 7.2 Mean performance on word and digit span tasks for individuals with Down syndrome, individuals with severe ID and typically developing comparison children

Source: data adapted from Marcel and Weeks (1988)

Numminen et al. (2001) used a range of PSTM tasks, including nonword span, nonword repetition and digit span, which was a methodological strength of the study. All participants were tested using a non-verbal measure of ability (Raven's Coloured Matrices) and the adults with Down syndrome were compared to adults with non-specific ID (n = 15 per group). Both groups had IQs in the mild to moderate ID range (35–70), and were matched for mental age (5 years).

Deficits were found on all three PSTM tasks for the adults with Down syndrome, as compared to the adults with ID (see Figure 7.3).

These results do seem reliable, as they have been largely replicated (using word and digit span tasks) in similar groups of 'older' adults with Down syndrome and comparison groups with non-specific ID (Kittler, Krinksy-McHale & Devenny, 2004, 2008); and in somewhat younger adults (Rowe, Lavender & Turk, 2006). Overall, therefore, adults with Down syndrome also appear to have a deficit in PSTM compared to matched comparison groups of adults with ID.

However, keep in mind that one potential difficulty with the 'older' adult studies is that although none of the participants had reported/demonstrated declines in cognitive functioning, it is possible that some individuals with Down syndrome may have shown subtle evidence of neuropathology (e.g. Adams & Oliver, 2010), given their mean ages were around 40 years. (Recall that there is an increased incidence of neuropathology associated with Alzheimer's disease in individuals with Down syndrome over 40 years.)

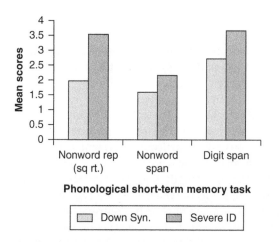

Figure 7.3   Mean performance on three phonological short-term memory tasks for adults with Down syndrome and adults with intellectual disabilities (note that scores for nonword repetition are square roots of the mean so that all three tasks can be represented in a similar scale on the same graph)

Source: data adapted from Numminen et al. (2001)

Summary
The results reviewed in this section support the conclusion that there is a deficit in PSTM in children, adolescents and adults with Down syndrome that is larger than the PSTM deficit found in comparable individuals with severe ID. This provides strong evidence that marked PSTM impairments are characteristic of individuals with Down syndrome. We will look at the research on visual and spatial short-term memory shortly, but before that, possible causes for the impairment in PSTM will be examined.

Why is phonological short-term memory impaired in those with Down syndrome?

There are a number of extraneous factors, not to do with memory, that might account for the deficit in PSTM in those with Down syndrome. It is important to rule out alternative explanations to be sure that any PSTM impairments are genuine.

For example, Brock and Jarrold (2005) carefully controlled for several such factors including visual/spatial span levels, speed of identifying digits, receptive vocabulary skill and non-verbal ability, concluding that impairments in digit span for those with Down syndrome were not accounted for by any of these factors. Jarrold, Purser and Brock (2006) went on to argue that the PSTM impairment in Down syndrome was not caused by problems with hearing, speech or deficient linguistic knowledge.

If there really is a deficit in PSTM for individuals with Down syndrome, what is causing the problem? Recall that the 'phonological loop' (Baddeley, 1986, 2007) consists of two parts: a phonological store and an articulatory rehearsal mechanism that is used for verbal coding and verbal rehearsal (see Chapter 1 for further details). Difficulties for those with Down syndrome could occur in either of these components.

Jarrold et al. (2000) examined whether children with Down syndrome might fail to utilise verbal rehearsal. The known difficulties that individuals with Down syndrome have with articulation may make verbal rehearsal difficult for them. Jarrold et al. (2000) asked participants to recall lists of words spoken by a computer in a 'game' format, that were either one syllable in length (short words) or three to four syllables in length (long words). This design allowed the authors to look for word length effects, which are often regarded as a marker for the use of verbal rehearsal (although this can be controversial – see Chapter 3).

Jarrold et al. (2000) compared 14 young people with Down syndrome (13 years), to 14 children with moderate ID (9 years) and 14 typically developing children (4 years). Although 'the two disability groups were not matched for chronological age or severity of ID, all groups were matched (4 years 7 months) for receptive vocabulary age (using the British Picture Vocabulary Scale).

The results were very straightforward. Jarrold et al. (2000) found that the groups did not differ in terms of whether or not they demonstrated word length effects. When full verbal recall of the lists was required, all groups showed word length effects; but when probed recall was required (just one word recalled from each list), no groups showed word length effects. These results are entirely consistent with discussions in Chapter 3 that full verbal recall of lists can cause 'spurious' word length effects (Henry, 1991b). Jarrold et al. (2000) interpreted their results to mean that none of their groups were using verbal rehearsal, so such deficits could not explain the weaker PSTM seen in those with Down syndrome. Similarly, articulation rates did not differ between the groups; and articulation rates were not correlated with PSTM performance, again supporting their conclusions (see Chapter 3 for further information on interpreting word length effects and the role of articulation rate).

Similar findings have been reported by Vicari et al. (2004) and Kanno and Ikeda (2002). Although there were differences in terms of whether word length effects were found in these two studies, in neither case did the authors report that word length effects varied between groups of individuals with Down syndrome and typically developing comparison children matched for mental age. Additionally, even if individuals with Down syndrome might show some deficits in the type of speeded articulation required for rehearsal, Jarrold, Cowan, Hewes and Riby (2004) have argued that this still cannot account for the PSTM deficit. In other words, individuals with Down syndrome probably do not use verbal rehearsal, and even if they do, slowed articulation rates are not enough to account for the size of their deficit in PSTM.

Jarrold et al. (2000) concluded that the PSTM impairment in Down syndrome must be located in the phonological store rather than in the articulatory rehearsal mechanism. They speculated that items in the phonological store might decay more rapidly, or that the capacity of this store might be reduced, in individuals with Down syndrome. However, Jarrold et al. (2000) did not find any evidence to suggest that the phonological store operated differently in those with Down syndrome compared to comparisons – this evidence is described in Box 7.1.

Box 7.1   Phonological similarity effects
in teenagers with Down syndrome

The phonological store is specialised for holding speech sounds for a brief period of time. We have already seen that if we ask people to recall lists of words that rhyme they find them more difficult than lists of words that do not rhyme (Chapter 1).

This is also true for teenagers with Down syndrome. Jarrold et al. (2000) compared performance on lists of words such as 'clock, fish, girl' versus lists such as 'bag, bat, cat'.

There were clear differences. On non-rhyming lists, the teenagers remembered 66% of the words, whereas on rhyming lists, they only remembered 47% of the words. Teenagers with Down syndrome showed a phonological similarity effect just like everybody else.

Currently, there is no evidence in favour of the decay hypothesis. Purser and Jarrold (2005) assessed this by including slow and fast presentation rates in a PSTM test. The logic was that performance should be better with fast presentation rates, because there was less time for decay. The task was to remember one named picture from a list of four presented on a computer screen in a random order. Teenagers and young adults with Down syndrome showed just as much reduction in recall with a slow presentation rate as a comparison group of typical children (matched for non-verbal mental age). Therefore, rates of decay in PSTM appeared to be the same in those with Down syndrome as they were in typical children.

This means that our current best hypothesis is that individuals with Down syndrome might have a restricted *capacity* phonological store.

Summary

Possible explanations for the deficit in phonological short-term memory (PSTM) in individuals with Down syndrome have been considered, but none have accounted for the difficulties. In particular, there do not appear to be differences in how the phonological store operates; nor can verbal rehearsal differences explain the findings. The most plausible explanation for the impairment of PSTM in individuals with Down syndrome is that they have a restricted *capacity* phonological store.

Finally, Box 7.2 discusses whether we can improve PSTM by training children with Down syndrome to use verbal rehearsal.

Box 7.2　Can we improve PSTM in children with Down syndrome?

A handful of studies have attempted to train children with Down syndrome in verbal rehearsal in order to improve their auditory verbal memory span. For example Conners, Rosenquist, Arnett, Moore and Hume (2008) found that a parent-implemented memory training intervention over one or two 3-month periods led to small gains in auditory verbal memory span and an increase in the use of phonological codes for a sample of 16 children with Down syndrome. The authors noted that even small improvements are important for individuals with severely restricted auditory verbal memory span.

Similarly, Broadley, MacDonald and Buckley (1994) found that training children with Down syndrome over two separate 6-week time periods on verbal rehearsal and using chunking and organisation in memory was successful. It not only improved immediate memory performance in a sample of 25 children with Down syndrome; but these improvements were still apparent 2 and 8 months after the end of the intervention.

Section summary
There is clear and consistent evidence that children, adolescents and adults with Down syndrome show an impairment in phonological short-term memory (PSTM). These difficulties have been found in relation to typically developing comparison groups of children matched for mental age, but also in relation to young people who have non-specific intellectual disabilities (ID). The overall conclusion from a range of studies is that having an ID is associated with some impairment in PSTM, but having Down syndrome is associated with a larger impairment. Hence, particularly weak PSTM is characteristic of those with Down syndrome. The current best guess for explaining this impairment is that individuals with Down syndrome have a restricted capacity phonological store.

The visuospatial sketchpad

Given the relatively strong evidence for an impairment in phonological short-term memory (PSTM) in those with Down syndrome, it is of interest to examine the other 'slave' system of working memory, the visuospatial sketchpad. This is an area where weaknesses in those with Down syndrome have not been documented, so researchers began with the hypothesis that individuals with Down syndrome would not show impairment in visuospatial short-term memory (VSSTM). We will revisit some of the studies discussed in the previous section on PSTM to examine this issue.

Jarrold and Baddeley (1997) included a measure of spatial memory, the Corsi span task, in their study (see previous section for details of participants). In terms of performance on Corsi span, the individuals with Down syndrome obtained scores that were no different from either comparison group – those with ID or typically developing children. This implied that there was no impairment in the spatial working memory component of the visuospatial sketchpad in young people with Down syndrome. Very similar results have been found by many other researchers, so they can be regarded as reliable. See Brock and Jarrold (2005), Jarrold et al. (1999), Kittler et al. (2008), Laws (2002), Pennington et al. (2003), Rowe, Lavender & Turk (2006); Visu-Petra, Benga, Ţincaş and Miclea (2007), and Wang and Bellugi (1994).

One point to emphasise about these studies is that they assessed the spatial component of the visuospatial sketchpad. Most authors believe that there is a separate, or at least linked, component of visual storage in the visuospatial sketchpad, so it is important to include measures of visual as well as spatial short-term memory. Otherwise, we do not obtain a full picture of the functioning of the visuospatial sketchpad in those with Down syndrome.

Laws (2002) investigated short-term memory for colours, to assess whether children and adolescents with Down syndrome might show an advantage for this type of visual information. The participants with Down syndrome (n = 16) were 7 to 17 years old (mean 11 years) and were matched individually to a comparison group of typically developing children who had a mean age of 4 years (range 2 to 6 years). Children were shown a series of coloured tiles (from a set of eight) in an array, which was then covered. Next, they had to reproduce the array with an identical set of tiles. The important manipulation, however, was that the colours were chosen to be difficult to name, making this a memory test for visual information rather than a memory test for colour names. Remember – if a child recodes the colours into 'names of colours', this becomes a test of PSTM.

Laws (2002) found that the performance of children with Down syndrome did not differ from that of the typically developing group. Note, however, that when she repeated the task using colour tiles that were easy to name, the typically developing group obtained higher scores, probably because they were using the colour names to remember the arrays. Therefore, these findings supported the notion that there were no deficits in visual short-term memory in children with Down syndrome, provided items were not easy to name.

The study by Numminen et al. (2001), described earlier, also included a visual memory task. As we saw, they compared adults with Down syndrome to adults with non-specific ID (see earlier for details) and the visual task was to remember matrices with some squares filled in and other squares left white. The results indicated that there were no differences between adults with Down syndrome and adults with ID.

Finally, Hick et al. (2005) also found no differences in performance between individuals with Down syndrome (n = 12, chronological age 9 years, mental age 4 years) and typically developing 3- and 4-year-olds on a 'pattern span' task, requiring children to remember the location of sharks on grids painted to look like the sea. In three separate testing sessions over a period of 12 months, no group differences emerged.

Overall, therefore, there is consistent evidence that visual and spatial VSSTM is not impaired in children, adolescents and adults with Down syndrome relative to typical children with the same mental age and individuals with non-specific ID. We will discuss one further relevant study by Lanfranchi et al. (2004) that confirms these findings in our next section on executive-loaded working memory.

Summary

There is no current evidence that individuals with Down syndrome show impairments in either the visual or spatial components of the visuospatial sketchpad. Compared to typically developing children of the same mental age, they obtain largely equivalent scores (and sometimes higher on Corsi span). Similarly, compared to individuals with non-specific ID, they show no disadvantage in performance. In short, visuospatial short-term memory (VSSTM) would appear to be a relative strength in individuals with Down syndrome.

However, we finish this section by noting that some evidence that suggests that this conclusion may be slightly simplistic – see the Debates and Issues box below.

Debates and Issues 7.1   Spatial short-term memory and Down Syndrome

Although we have concluded that visuospatial short-term memory in individuals with Down syndrome is not impaired relative to mental age, there is some evidence that suggests that there may be *subtle* difficulties in this area.

Lanfranchi, Carretti, Spanò and Cornoldi (2009) investigated *spatial* short-term memory tasks that involved movement, versus *spatial* short-term memory tasks that did not involve movement. One task involved remembering the path that a frog moved through on a small chessboard: this was described as the 'spatial sequential' task (the spatial task with movement). The other task involved learning the positions of some green squares on a small chessboard: this was described as the 'spatial simultaneous' task (the task without movement).

Thirty-four children and adolescents with Down syndrome were matched to equal numbers of typically developing children using a measure of verbal IQ. Lanfranchi et al. (2009) found that although there were no group differences on the spatial sequential task, the participants with Down syndrome obtained somewhat lower scores on the spatial simultaneous task.

These findings suggested that individuals with Down syndrome may have difficulty with spatial memory tasks that *do not involve movement sequences.* However, further research is required in this area, because the measures of 'visual' short-term memory that we have been discussing throughout this book are often based on the recall of 'matrices', rather like the ones used in this study for the spatial *simultaneous* task. Careful consideration must be given to exactly what makes a *visual* short-term memory task versus a *spatial* short-term memory task and the precise role of movement sequences.

Lanfranchi et al. (2009) argued that spatial short-term memory could be subdivided into sequential versus simultaneous components. This may be a good way of conceptualising VSSTM, provided that clear definitions for appropriate visual versus spatial tasks are agreed upon.

The central executive

The discussion of higher order processing skills carried out by the central executive will be split into two sections: (1) tasks that measure executive-loaded working memory (ELWM); and (2) tasks that measure other aspects of executive functioning.

Executive-loaded working memory

An increasing body of work has begun to address executive-loaded working memory (ELWM), i.e. the ability to process and store information concurrently, in individuals with Down syndrome. For example, Numminen et al. (2001) included two measures of ELWM in their battery of working memory measures (listening span and reverse digit span). Although the scores of adults with Down syndrome and adults with non-specific ID were both very low, there were no differences between them on either of these measures. This study offered no support for the notion of a deficit in ELWM among adults with Down syndrome.

A similar result was found for teenagers with Down syndrome (Pennington et al., 2003). These authors compared 28 individually matched pairs of participants: young people with Down syndrome (age 14 years) and typically developing comparison children (age 3 to 6 years). The pairs of participants were matched for mental age using a very full and comprehensive IQ measure (Differential Abilities Scale) and had an average mental age of 4½ years. They were also matched for parental education, gender and ethnicity. Amongst a thorough battery of episodic memory and central executive/working memory tasks, Pennington et al. (2003) included two measures of ELWM (spatial ELWM – a task requiring the participant to recall spatial positions over trials – and counting span – refer back to Chapter 2).

The results were clear: no evidence was found for group differences on either measure. Figure 7.4 illustrates these results, although note that the two ELWM measures are not to the same scale (scores on spatial working memory have been divided by 20).

Although these two studies have presented a consistent picture so far, unfortunately, there is new evidence that contradicts their findings.

For example, a very thorough investigation of ELWM in children with Down syndrome was carried out by Lanfranchi et al. (2004). In their first experiment on verbal ELWM, 18 children/adolescents with Down syndrome (7–16 years, mental age 5½ years) were compared to 18 typically developing children matched for mental age. The measures included simple word span, backwards word span, remembering the first words from multiple lists (multiple word span) and a dual task condition. The last three measures can all be regarded as executive-loaded, but Lanfranchi et al. (2004) argued that they were *increasingly* demanding on executive resources. This is difficult to verify, although the multiple word list and dual task conditions seem objectively more demanding, because they required participants to do or listen to two things at once and make decisions about what to do with the information.

Figure 7.5 illustrates the results. There were significant group differences on all four verbal measures, confirming the PSTM deficit in children with Down syndrome (word span), but also indicating that verbal ELWM was impaired. Differences in performance between children with Down syndrome and typically developing children were greatest for the most difficult dual task conditions.

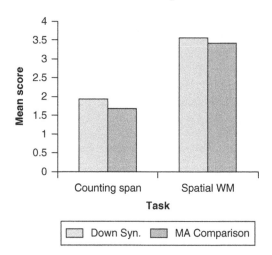

Figure 7.4   Mean counting span and spatial working memory scores for individuals with Down syndrome and mental age-matched typically developing children (note that scores on spatial working memory have been divided by 20)

Source: data adapted from Pennington et al. (2003)

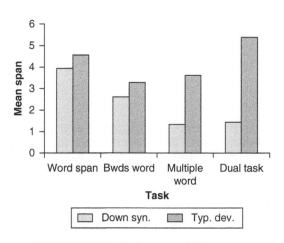

Figure 7.5   Mean verbal working memory scores for individuals with Down syndrome and mental age-matched typically developing comparisons

Source: data adapted from Lanfranchi et al. (2004)

Lanfranchi et al. (2004) went on to examine five visuospatial tasks that varied in executive demands in a second experiment. This time they included 22 children/adolescents with Down syndrome (11–18 years, mental age 4½) and 22 typically developing children matched for mental age. Note that compared to the first study, those with Down syndrome were more cognitively impaired, as they had higher chronological ages and lower mental ages. This means that caution should be exercised in comparing the results from the two experiments directly.

The visuospatial tests included memory for matrices (visual recall), memory for spatial positions (spatial span), reverse spatial span, remembering the starting positions of multiple spatial span trials (multiple spatial span), and a dual task condition. The first two measures can be regarded as simple tests of visuospatial memory; but the final three tasks can all be regarded as executive-loaded.

Lanfranchi et al. (2004) found that the two tasks with the highest executive loads were significantly more difficult for the individuals with Down syndrome (the multiple spatial span measure and the dual task condition). No group differences emerged on the two simple span measures, which confirms the findings we reviewed earlier on VSSTM. The numerical difference on the reverse spatial span measure was not significant. Figure 7.6 illustrates these results.

Lanfranchi et al.'s (2004) results, therefore, suggested children with Down syndrome had difficulties with ELWM on both verbal and visuospatial measures, compared to mental age-matched typically developing children.

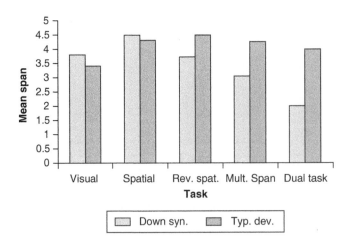

Figure 7.6   Mean visuospatial working memory scores for individuals with Down syndrome and mental age-matched typically developing children

Source: data adapted from Lanfranchi et al. (2004)

However, it is important to note that these findings would have been even more illuminating if a second comparison group of children with severe ID had been included. This would have allowed us to examine whether ELWM difficulties might be associated with severe ID, as opposed to Down syndrome in particular.

Are there really ELWM difficulties, given the inconsistent findings? The answer is probably yes. There are some further studies that support this conclusion. Vicari et al. (1995) found that backward Corsi span and backward digit span were impaired in teenagers with Down syndrome. Visu-Petra et al. (2007) found marginally significant differences between adolescents with Down syndrome and mental age-matched typically developing children on a spatial working memory test. Finally, at least two other studies have found deficits in ELWM in individuals with Down syndrome (Lanfranchi, Jerman, Dal Pont, Alberti & Vianello, 2010; Vicari, Verucci & Carlesimo, 2007).

Summary

There appears to be more evidence in favour of individuals with Down syndrome having difficulties with ELWM than against, although the findings remain somewhat inconsistent. It is very important to bear in mind, however, that we cannot at present draw conclusions about whether potential difficulties in ELWM might be caused by having a severe intellectual disability (ID). Most of the studies we have reviewed did not include comparison groups with non-specific severe ID, and such comparison groups are required in order to assess whether ELWM deficits may be characteristic of Down syndrome in particular as opposed to being linked with having severe ID.

Other measures of the central executive

If we broaden our focus beyond executive loaded working memory (ELWM), there is also emerging evidence for other executive deficits in individuals with Down syndrome. For example, Kittler et al. (2008) were interested in whether adults with Down syndrome would find carrying out two tasks at the same time particularly difficult. This 'dual task' processing is regarded by Baddeley as assessing central executive resources (see Chapters 1 and 2).

Kittler et al. (2008) compared 53 older adults with Down syndrome (mean IQ 53) to ten individuals with Williams syndrome (we will discuss this sample in the second half of this Chapter) and 39 individuals with mild to moderate non-specific ID (mean IQ 56). Participants were asked to place pegs in a peg board and at the same time repeat digits between zero and nine. There were no group differences in carrying out these tasks on their own, but the 'cost' of doing these two tasks concurrently was significantly greater for individuals with Down syndrome than for those with ID.

This result implies that there may be a central executive impairment in adults with Down syndrome. However, we do not know if the results would generalise to children with Down syndrome. This is a particularly relevant issue, as early onset dementia of the Alzheimer's type may start to hamper performance in older adults with Down syndrome. Kittler et al. (2008) were careful to exclude participants with any evidence of cognitive decline, but it is currently unclear whether impaired executive performance in older adults with Down syndrome might reflect early signs of dementia (Ball, Holland, Treppner, Watson & Huppert, 2010; Ball, Holland, Watson & Huppert, 2008). Another point concerns comparison groups. Ideally, it would be useful to include a typically developing mental-aged matched comparison group as well as a group of comparable individuals with ID. Finally, it would be useful to replicate these findings using a range of other executive tasks.

Lanfranchi et al. (2010) addressed some of these issues by examining the performance of 15 adolescents with Down syndrome (mental age 5 years) on a comprehensive range of executive tasks. The comparison group included 15 typically developing 5-year-old children, individually matched for mental age. Tasks assessed ELWM (using dual tasks and self-ordered pointing), inhibition (day/night task), switching (using a reduced version of the Wisconsin Card Sorting Test), planning (Tower of London), and fluency (using letters and semantic categories). (See Chapter 2 for details of tasks.)

Lanfranchi et al. (2010) found that adolescents with Down syndrome demonstrated significant difficulties with inhibition, switching, planning and ELWM, but they did not show difficulties with fluency.

Rowe, Lavender & Turk (2006) also assessed a range of executive skills in a sample of 26 younger adults with Down syndrome (ages 23–40 years), using a comparison group of equal numbers of adults with non-specific ID, matched for age and verbal IQ. They found small degrees of impairment on measures of verbal fluency, switching and planning. However, the most significant group difference occurred on their measure of switching (the Weigl Colour-Form Sort Test – see Chapter 2). Again, therefore, there was evidence for at least some difficulty with executive functioning in individuals with Down syndrome, this time in relation to a comparison group with non-specific ID.

Therefore, current research findings have shown impaired executive functioning in a range of areas for individuals with Down syndrome, in relation to typically developing children matched for mental age; and in comparison to comparable individuals with non-specific ID.

Summary
Evidence in relation to a range of measures of central executive functioning in adults and children with Down syndrome suggests at least some degree of difficulty, in relation to typical children matched for mental age and comparable individuals with non-specific intellectual disabilities (ID). However, research in this area is not extensive and further work on children and adolescents would be helpful, incorporating mental age matched

typically developing children, as well as comparable individuals with the same level of non-specific ID.

The episodic buffer

We will examine the operation of the proposed episodic buffer of working memory by looking at episodic memory tasks that require the binding of current information in working memory with relevant long-term knowledge. Such processes create unified, coherent memories for events, information or episodes.

The study discussed earlier by Pennington et al. (2003) included several measures of episodic memory that might involve binding information from different working memory systems with long-term memory. These included: supraspan word learning (learning a list of 15 words over five recall trials); learning where targets were placed in a virtual maze task; recognising patterns that had already been seen from a selection; and learning associations between abstract visual patterns and their locations ('paired associate learning').

The participants with Down syndrome obtained significantly or marginally lower scores than mental age-matched typical children on all four episodic memory tasks. These results suggested there might be weaknesses in the use of the episodic buffer in those with Down syndrome, whether as a result of the operation of the component itself, or as a result of weak long-term memory. Importantly, difficulties were found on tasks that would draw on visuospatial sketchpad resources (recognising patterns) as well as phonological loop resources (learning lists of words), so it would be difficult to account for the results solely in terms of the PSTM impairment we have already described. Indeed, Jarrold, Phillips and Baddeley (2007) have similarly argued that there is no link between PSTM difficulties and long-term memory for verbal materials in individuals with Down syndrome.

Visu-Petra et al. (2007) replicated the above deficit on paired associate learning in 25 children/adults with Down syndrome using exactly the same task (from the CANTAB), so this appears to be a reliable finding.

Carlesimo et al. (1997) also examined episodic memory in 15 adolescents with Down syndrome. They included two comparison groups: 15 adolescents with non-specific severe ID and 30 typically developing children matched for mental age. Therefore, this study could assess whether having severe ID on its own might cause difficulties with episodic memory. Mental age was evaluated using a comprehensive intelligence scale (Wechsler Scales) and all participants had a mean mental age of 9 years. The measures of episodic memory included word-list learning, prose recall (remembering a short story) and the ability to reproduce a complex visual figure from memory (Rey's figure) – tasks that should reflect verbal and visuospatial binding abilities respectively.

Results indicated that adolescents with Down syndrome obtained the lowest scores on word-list learning and prose recall. Participants with severe ID performed significantly better, and typically developing children obtained the highest scores (see Figure 7.7). For the Rey figure, those with Down syndrome obtained significantly poorer scores than those in both comparison groups, which did not differ.

Therefore, Carlesimo et al. (1997) demonstrated that having severe ID did lead to poorer performance on episodic memory tasks, compared to mental age level. However, having Down syndrome plus severe ID led to an even greater impairment. These results suggested that deficits in episodic memory may be characteristic of Down syndrome. Although the participants in this study had high mental ages (9 years), the findings were replicated, at least in relation to a typical comparison group, in a similar study of young adults with Down syndrome (mental age 6½ years) (Vicari, Bellucci & Carlesimo, 2000).

Another relevant study found that memory for sentences in adolescents and young adults with Down syndrome (n = 35, mental age 5 years) was poorer than that of typically developing children matched for mental age (Seung & Chapman, 2004). The participants were carefully screened for hearing difficulties and the results could not be accounted for by slower articulation rates in the Down syndrome group.

The sentence memory task could be regarded as measuring ELWM (with a contribution from PSTM), although it may also assess episodic buffer functioning (Baddeley, 2007). This is because participants can recall more words within grammatically correct sentences than they can in unrelated word lists by 'chunking' together phrases and using long-term knowledge of language and sentence structure to support recall. For example, Seung and Chapman

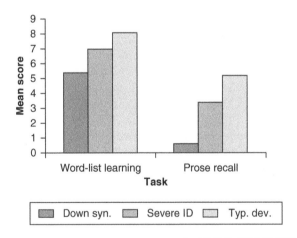

Figure 7.7 Mean performance of adolescents with Down syndrome, severe ID and mental age-matched typically developing children on word-list learning and prose recall

Source: data adapted from Carlesimo et al. (1997)

(2004) noted that digit span for individuals with Down syndrome was four syllables, whereas sentence span was six syllables. These differences were even more marked for typical children (five versus ten syllables). If sentence memory span measures executive functioning, PSTM and episodic buffer processing, these results suggest that some or all of these areas could be problematic for individuals with Down syndrome.

One possible reason for potential deficits in episodic buffer functioning among individuals with Down syndrome is that they have slow long-term memory access for lexical information. Some evidence to support this position has been put forward (Varnhagen, Das & Varnhagen, 1987). Yet other authors have argued that, in some cases, individuals with Down syndrome are more likely to use semantic information in short-term memory tasks than those with non-specific ID (Kittler, Krinsky-McHale & Devenny, 2004). Therefore, further research is required to explore possible explanations in more depth. Potential differences between verbal and visuospatial binding tasks would also be a promising avenue for future research, paying particular attention to PSTM weakness, given the profile of short-term memory abilities in individuals with Down syndrome.

Summary

Evidence suggests that adolescents with Down syndrome may have difficulty with binding information in verbal and visuospatial episodic remembering tasks. These difficulties have been found in relation to typically developing children matched for mental age, and in relation to comparable individuals with non-specific ID. Hence, the operation of the episodic buffer in binding relevant long-term memory information with current processing in working memory may be specifically impaired in Down syndrome. However, further research using a wider age range of individuals (including adults and children) and testing alternative explanations for these difficulties (e.g. weak PSTM) is required before definitive conclusions can be reached.

Summary: Down syndrome

Down syndrome is caused by an extra copy of chromosome 21 and is the most common cause of intellectual disability (ID) that can be easily identified. Although individuals vary, moderate to severe ID and marked speech and language difficulties are very common in those with Down syndrome. This chapter has reviewed working memory in children with Down syndrome in relation to comparison groups with non-specific ID and typical development (in both cases matched for mental age), and the findings are summarised below.

Individuals with Down syndrome showed particular difficulties with phonological short-term memory (PSTM) in relation to their mental age, and in relation to individuals with non-specific ID. Therefore, PSTM weaknesses appeared to be more marked in individuals with Down syndrome than they were in individuals with severe ID. By contrast, those with Down synsrome did not show similar relative impairments in visuospatial short-term memory (VSSTM). There was disagreement as to whether there were difficulties with executive-loaded working memory (ELWM) in those with Down syndrome, but recent research suggested that there were (in relation to mental age level). A growing literature on broader measures of executive functioning suggested that those with Down syndrome also have difficulties in these areas. Therefore, the central executive component of working memory may be impaired in individuals with Down syndrome. Future research is required to confirm this conclusion and specify the exact nature of such difficulties, particularly in relation to those with non-specific ID. Finally, evidence suggested that measures of episodic memory (that may assess binding within the episodic buffer) could be specifically impaired in individuals with Down syndrome.

We will now move on to discuss working memory in children with Williams syndrome.

Williams syndrome

Williams syndrome is a much rarer developmental disorder than Down syndrome, with an estimated prevalence of between 1 in 7500 and 1 in 20,000 (Stromme, Bjornstad & Ramstad, 2002). Williams syndrome was first described in the 1960s and the genetic basis for the syndrome was discovered in 1993. It is caused by gene deletions on chromosome 7 (Peoples et al., 2000); and the fluorescent in situ hybridisation (FISH) test can be used to identify approximately 96% of individuals with the disorder who have one copy of the elastin gene deleted. Hence, recent studies have been able to assess individuals with confirmed deletions rather than relying on clinical diagnoses which are likely to be less reliable.

Individuals with Williams syndrome tend to have facial dysmorphia (a distinctive facial appearance often described as 'elfin-like' with a wide mouth, short upturned nose and broad brow), growth deficiency, connective tissue abnormalities, cardiac/kidney problems, abnormal metabolism of calcium, hypersensitivity to sound, eating and sleeping difficulties, social disinhibition, high levels of anxiety, overactivity, impulsivity, and often ADHD (Howlin, Davies & Udwin, 1998). The personality of those with Williams syndrome has been described as gregarious, overfriendly, high in empathy, oversensitive, stubborn and anxious (Rowe & Mervis, 2006). Individuals with Williams syndrome also report quite high levels of specific fears and phobias (Dykens, 2003). There are no marked social deficits, as in autism/ASD, although peer problems and social isolation are often noted (Udwin, Yule & Martin, 1987). Children with Williams syndrome are often disinhibited – e.g. they may relate indiscriminately to unfamiliar children and adults and prefer adults to peers.

Williams syndrome has attracted attention because of its unusual pattern of relative strengths and weaknesses in cognitive tasks. It is characterised by relative deficits in non-verbal abilities, number/spatial cognition, and visuospatial construction (Martens, Wilson & Reutens, 2008); together with strengths in verbal abilities (e.g. Howlin et al., 1998; Udwin et al., 1987). For example, individuals with Williams syndrome may find drawing, copying (e.g. Vicari et al., 2007) and pattern construction very difficult. Although face processing in individuals with Williams syndrome has been regarded as a relative strength, recent evidence suggests there are developmental delays and differences in this skill (Karmiloff-Smith et al., 2004). Individuals with Williams syndrome may also show heightened responsiveness to and interest in music (Martens et al., 2008).

Most individuals with Williams syndrome have an intellectual disability (ID), with IQ in the mild to moderate ID range (Howlin et al., 1998; Udwin et al., 1987). A recent critical review of 47 studies concluded that the average full-scale IQ of individuals with Williams syndrome was 55 (range 26–82) (Martens et al., 2008). When IQ is clearly and reliably measurable, higher verbal than non-verbal scores may be expected, although this remains an area of debate (Martens et al., 2008). Jarrold, Baddeley and Hewes (1998) suggested that verbal abilities develop faster than non-verbal abilities in individuals with Williams syndrome, which means that differences between verbal and non-verbal abilities may become more apparent in older individuals.

In terms of brain structure and function, a recent review concluded that individuals with Williams syndrome have atypical brain morphology: there is reduced cerebral volume (in relation to white matter) but preserved cerebellar volume (Martens et al., 2008). There are also other abnormalities, which may be linked with specific behavioural and cognitive characteristics of individuals with Williams syndrome, but a lack of research using comparison groups other than typical children limits conclusions (Martens et al., 2008).

The linguistic abilities of individuals with Williams syndrome tend to be strong compared to their overall ability levels, with good use of language, vocabulary knowledge and use of grammar. Udwin et al. (1987) noted that children with Williams syndrome obtained 'encouraging' levels of reading and spelling. Wickes-Nelson and Israel (2006) similarly noted that:

> The communication style of children with the [Williams] syndrome has been described as coherent, fluent and 'pseudo-mature'.

Although language is a relative strength among individuals with Williams syndrome, it is, in fact, delayed compared to chronological age (Martens et al., 2008). There is evidence that language development proceeds in a typical manner in some areas of language development including word fluency, expressive vocabulary, complex syntax and mean length of utterance; yet is atypical in other areas including grammatical comprehension, reciprocal conversation and gender agreement (Martens et al., 2008). Some have suggested that both verbal and non-verbal abilities are delayed in Williams syndrome, but that the differential between the two becomes more exaggerated with development (Jarrold et al., 1998). Others have suggested that apparently good use of complex grammar could reflect the 'rote memorisation of phrases rather than the productive application of grammatical rules' (Robinson, Mervis & Robinson, 2003: 16).

A number of investigators have suggested that the relative strength of individuals with Williams syndrome in the verbal domain also applies to working memory. In particular, that individuals with Williams syndrome have strong phonological short-term memory (PSTM), but weak visuospatial short-term memory (VSSTM). We will consider this evidence in the following sections.

The phonological loop

It has been suggested that individuals with Williams syndrome have relatively strong phonological short-term memory (PSTM). Some authors have further suggested that strong PSTM could be responsible for the language strengths also seen in this disorder. We will consider whether individuals with Williams syndrome do have strong PSTM, paying particular attention to the groups to which they have been compared.

Klein and Mervis (1999) provided some evidence that PSTM might be a relative area of strength in children with Williams syndrome. These authors carefully matched pairs of children (9–10 years) with Williams syndrome and Down syndrome. There were 13 pairs who all had the same overall scores on a battery of tests of general cognitive abilities (mean age equivalent 4 years and 11 months). Next, Klein and Mervis (1999) looked at the pattern of scores on each sub-measure from the ability test, finding that children with Williams syndrome obtained higher scores on tests of verbal memory and numerical memory, which they interpreted as indicating a strength in phonological short-term memory (PSTM). By contrast, children with Down syndrome obtained higher scores on tests of block building and on a draw-a-child test, which they interpreted as indicating a strength in visuospatial construction. On other measures, there were no differences between the groups (measures that did not involve verbal memory such as word knowledge, verbal fluency and receptive vocabulary).

These results supported the view that there were different strengths and weaknesses in working memory among children with Down and Williams syndrome: with PSTM being a relative strength for individuals with Williams syndrome.

Wang and Bellugi (1994) also investigated this issue using more direct measures of PSTM (and VSSTM), namely, digit and spatial span. They examined ten 15-year-olds with Williams syndrome and nine 15-year-olds with Down syndrome, matched for IQ. Wang and Bellugi (1994) found that digit span scores were significantly higher in the Williams syndrome group, whereas spatial span scores were significantly higher in the Down syndrome group. Again, these results suggested a relative strength in PSTM for the adolescents with Williams syndrome, although the samples were small.

Yet the absence of additional experimental groups limits conclusions to simple comparisons between the two disorders. A difficulty with both of the above studies is that we do not know whether those with Williams syndrome might have shown difficulties in PSTM compared with individuals with non-specific ID. An ideal additional comparison group would be children with non-specific ID, matched for age and IQ (Rowe & Mervis, 2006).

This extra comparison group was included by Jarrold et al. (1999). They compared 12-year-old children with Down syndrome, 16-year-old adolescents with Williams syndrome and 12-year-old children with moderate ID. Although the chronological ages were not matched between all of the groups, the authors did take great care to assess both verbal and non-verbal mental age. They were not able to match on both of these measures across all three groups, so they used statistical techniques to control for the differences.

Jarrold et al. (1999) assessed the participants on measures of digit span (PSTM) and Corsi span (the spatial component of VSSTM – we will come back to these results in the next section). Figure 7.8 illustrates the findings. Adolescents with Williams syndrome did not show a deficit on PSTM (although those with Down syndrome did), therefore, they had no particular difficulties with PSTM compared to children with moderate ID and Down syndrome.

There are some limitations in relation to this evidence, however. As already noted, ideally, we would match on chronological age as well as controlling for verbal and non-verbal IQ, to ensure that the level of intellectual disability is broadly the same across all three groups. Otherwise, we are not comparing

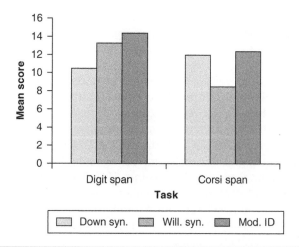

Figure 7.8 Mean scores on measures of digit span and Corsi span for young people with Down syndrome, Williams syndrome and moderate intellectual disabilities

Source: data adapted from Jarrold et al. (1999: Experiment 1)

like with like in terms of the severity of the ID. The results would also be strengthened by including an additional comparison group of typically developing children matched for mental age. This comparison group would allow the assessment of whether individuals with Williams syndrome have PSTM skills at the level we would expect given their mental age.

Several studies have, in fact, included typical comparison groups. For example, Laing, Hulme, Grant and Karmiloff-Smith (2001) compared 15 children and adults with Williams syndrome (average age 15 years, mean IQ 44) to 15 typically developing children (mean age 6 years) matched for verbal mental age and reading age. Although the main focus of this study was on reading skills, the authors included three measures of PSTM: digit span, word span and nonword repetition. Laing et al. (2001) found no differences between the groups on word span and nonword repetition, but the typical children obtained significantly higher scores on digit span (see also Menghini, Addona, Costanzo & Vicari 2010 for a 'marginally significant' group difference on digit span).

Robinson et al. (2003) tested a larger sample of 39 children with Williams syndrome (average age 10 years, mean IQ 68), comparing them with 32 typically developing 6-year-olds matched for level of receptive grammar. On two measures of PSTM (digit span, nonword repetition), there were no group differences in performance. Robinson et al. (2003) argued that grammatical skills in those with Williams syndrome were closely related to their performance on the PSTM measures, providing support for a link between PSTM and language.

These studies generally support the view that PSTM is broadly appropriate to mental age level in children with Williams syndrome. However, the issue of how to match individuals with Williams syndrome to typically developing comparison groups is very complicated. Individuals with Williams syndrome tend to obtain higher scores on measures of vocabulary, as this is an area of strength. Therefore, matching groups on vocabulary tests to achieve equivalent verbal mental ages requires slightly older samples of typically developing children. By contrast, matching groups on non-verbal ability (e.g. Raven's Coloured Progressive Matrices), which individuals with Williams syndrome are not so good at, requires slightly younger groups of typical children. Hence, the performance levels of typical comparison groups are likely to be higher for verbal mental age matched groups, and lower for non-verbal mental age matched groups. This can affect results, as illustrated by Grant et al. (1997). Here, individuals with Williams syndrome obtained equal scores on nonword repetition compared to a typical group matched for non-verbal mental age; but were slightly worse compared to a typical group matched for verbal mental age.

Jarrold et al. (2004) argued that the most stringent way to ascertain whether there are PSTM difficulties in individuals with Williams syndrome, was to compare them with individuals matched for verbal mental age. Jarrold et al. (2004) further argued that some differences between groups on PSTM tasks have emerged, because individuals with Williams syndrome might have slower articulation rates. Therefore, Jarrold et al. (2004) measured both word span and articulation rates in order to test their hypothesis. Their participants included 16 children, teenagers and young adults (ages 6 to 28 years) with Williams syndrome, and a comparison group of 16 typically developing children matched for overall verbal mental age (8-year-olds).

Jarrold et al. (2004) found that individuals with Williams syndrome had lower word spans than typically developing children. However, they were also slower to articulate words and reactivate items during pauses between words (see Chapter 3 for further details). Once these speech timing differences had been taken into account statistically, differences in PSTM between those with Williams syndrome and typical children disappeared. Jarrold et al. (2004) concluded that individuals with Williams syndrome do not show fundamentally weak PSTM, they simply show slower articulation rates, which can lead to lower performance.

Therefore, despite arguments over how best to choose comparison groups of typically developing children in studies of individuals with Williams syndrome, most of the research evidence is broadly consistent. Individuals with Williams syndrome do not show deficits on PSTM tasks, even compared to typically developing comparison groups matched for verbal mental age, once potential differences in articulation rates have been controlled.

On final point is discussed in Box 7.3: Laing, Grant, Thomas, Parmigiani, Ewing and Karmiloff-Smith (2005) did not find any evidence to suggest that the phonological store operated differently in those with Williams syndrome compared to typical children.

Box 7.3   Phonological similarity effects in children and adults with Williams syndrome

The phonological store is specialised for holding speech sounds for a brief period of time. We have already seen that if we ask people to recall lists of words that rhyme they find them more difficult than lists of words that do not rhyme (Chapter 1).

This is also true for adults/children with Williams syndrome. Laing et al. (2005) compared performance on lists of words such as 'coat, leg, thief' versus lists such as 'bag, hat, rat'. (see also Vicari, Carlesino, Brizzolara & Pezzini, 1996).

There were clear differences. Memory span for similar sounding words was lower for children/adults with Williams syndrome than for comparison groups of typical children matched for memory performance and verbal mental age. Individuals with Williams syndrome showed a 'phonological similarity effect' just like typical comparisons.

Summary

Individuals with Williams syndrome generally do not show deficits in phonological short-term memory (PSTM) compared to comparison groups of typical children matched for mental age. Nor do they show difficulties compared to comparable individuals with non-specific ID, although there is less research using such comparisons. PSTM appears to be an area of relative strength for individuals with Williams syndrome and it may be related to their good performance on some measures of language.

The visuospatial sketchpad

Several studies mentioned at the beginning of the previous section reported results suggesting that individuals with Williams syndrome have difficulties with visuospatial short-term memory (VSSTM). Jarrold et al.'s (1999) results (refer back to Figure 7.8) illustrate these findings and provide a useful starting point for this section. Participants with Williams syndrome obtained significantly lower scores on a measure of spatial short-term memory (Corsi span) than individuals in two comparison groups (those with Down syndrome and moderate ID).

Thus, there is evidence that spatial short-term memory may be impaired in those with Willliams syndrome. However, the visuospatial sketchpad is regarded as handling both visual and spatial information, so it is important to investigate both of these components of VSSTM in individuals with Williams syndrome.

Therefore, in a second experiment, Jarrold et al. (1999) included a visual task, 'pattern span' (recalling matrices in which some of the squares were filled by frogs on lily pads). Participants were 17-year-old adolescents with Williams syndrome, plus two separate comparison groups: those with moderate ID (13 years); and typically developing children. All groups were matched for non-verbal mental age (5½ years). Although the children with moderate ID were younger than the participants with Williams syndrome, the authors matched the 16 Williams participants to those in each comparison group individually, so this was methodologically rigorous. Jarrold et al. (1999) used a statistical technique to adjust for small remaining group differences on verbal mental age.

The results are illustrated in Figure 7.9. Adolescents with Williams syndrome obtained significantly poorer scores on Corsi (spatial) span than those in both comparison groups, confirming the spatial short-term memory deficit. The results for pattern span were not quite so clear. Adolescents with Williams syndrome obtained significantly poorer scores than comparisons with moderate ID, but their scores were not significantly different from those in the typically developing group. The unusual part of this finding was the relatively good visual short-term memory performance of children with ID (see also Henry & MacLean, 2002).

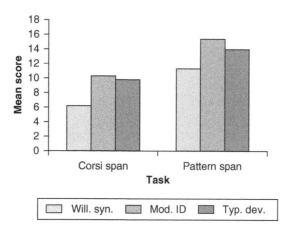

Figure 7.9   Mean scores on Corsi span and pattern span for adolescents with Williams syndrome, comparisons with moderate intellectual disabilities and typically developing children

Source: data adapted from Jarrold et al. (1999: Experiment 2)

Hence, adolescents with Williams syndrome may have more marked spatial than visual VSSTM impairments. Vicari, Bellucci and Carlesimo (2003) provided further support for this suggestion. They assessed 13 young adults with Williams syndrome (mean age 18 years, mean mental age 7 years), comparing them to 26 typically developing children with the same mental age. Similar to the previous study, two tasks measuring VSSTM were used: a spatial span task (memory for the spatial location of a series of items) and a visual span task (memory for the specific visual details and order of a series of red/green geometric shapes). Vicari et al. (2003) found that young adults with Williams syndrome showed an impairment in spatial span compared to the typical children, but they did not show a deficit on visual span. Figure 7.10 illustrates these results.

Vicari et al. (2006) replicated this result with a different sample of 19-year-olds with Williams syndrome, comparing them to typically developing comparison children matched for mental age (6-year-olds) (see also Vicari et al., 2007).

Therefore, it appeared that individuals with Williams syndrome did not show an impairment on visual short-term memory tasks, although they found spatial tasks more difficult. However, a further study by Jarrold, Phillips and Baddeley (2007) failed to find either visual or spatial VSSTM difficulties; and evidence has also emerged that both of these components may be impaired. We will look at one such study to finish this section.

Rhodes, Riby, Park, Fraser and Campbell (2010) assessed 19 children and adults with Williams syndrome (11–29 years, mean age 18), comparing them with: (1) typically developing children/adults matched for chronological age;

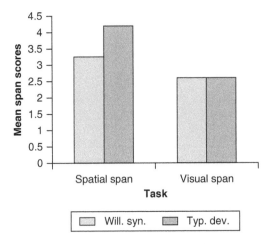

Figure 7.10   Mean scores on spatial and visual short-term working memory tasks for young adults with Williams syndrome and typically developing children of similar mental age

Source: data adapted from Vicari et al. (2003)

and (2) typically developing children matched for verbal mental age using a receptive vocabulary measure (British Picture Vocabulary Scale). These authors made the interesting point that measures of receptive vocabulary are best for matching mental age comparison groups, to avoid confounding executive skills with intellectual abilities. They argued that non-verbal tests such as Ravens may assess executive skills. This study was also methodologically rigorous, as participants were excluded if they had significant behavioural difficulties.

Rhodes et al. (2010) used a visual measure called 'delayed matching to sample', requiring participants to remember the visual features of a complex target and then choose that target from four later presented items. They also used a more standard measure of spatial (Corsi) span. The authors found that individuals with Williams syndrome were impaired on both of these tasks and in relation to both comparison groups (see also O'Hearn, Courtney, Street & Landau, 2009, for similar evidence).

Therefore, a range of evidence supports the conclusion that there are difficulties with VSSTM in individuals with Williams syndrome. The literature is quite consistent in relation to spatial difficulties (see also Menghini et al., 2010), but somewhat less consistent in relation to visual difficulties. Jarrold et al. (2007) pointed out that differences in results may depend on the age and developmental level of the participants with Williams syndrome and future research could look at developmental trajectories, i.e. how skills develop with cognitive maturity, in order to assess this directly. This approach has certainly yielded positive results in other areas of controversy (Karmiloff-Smith et al., 2004).

Another issue to bear in mind is that most studies of VSSTM in those with Williams syndrome have used typically developing comparison groups matched for mental age. In order to conclude that impairments in VSSTM are characteristic of Williams syndrome, rather than being related to having an intellectual disability, it would be highly desirable to have more research including comparison groups of similar ability individuals with non-specific ID. Future research must also consider 'best practice' in relation to matching comparison groups: currently, this seems to be using vocabulary measures to estimate verbal ability.

Summary

Individuals with Williams syndrome show impairments in visuospatial short-term memory (VSSTM) in relation to typically developing comparison children of the same mental age; and, where evidence is available, in relation to comparable individuals with non-specific ID. These difficulties may occur particularly on tasks assessing the spatial component as opposed to the visual component of VSSTM, but this evidence is not entirely consistent.

We finish this section with an exploration of drawing abilities in individuals with Williams syndrome and how this might be related to VSSTM (see Debates and Issues 7.2 box below).

Debates and Issues 7.2   Visuospatial short-term memory and drawing ability in Williams syndrome

Drawing and copying abilities in individuals with Williams syndrome have often been noted to be weak. However, one question that arises is whether this is because some of the *component skills* involved in drawing and copying might be impaired.

Nagai, Inui and Iwata (2011) have suggested that visuospatial short-term memory (VSSTM) is a fundamental component skill involved in drawing and copying. They argued that even if individuals with Williams syndrome can *trace* figures correctly, they may be unable to *copy* them or *draw* them from memory. Perhaps weak drawing and copying skills reflect, at least in part, VSSTM difficulties?

Nagai et al. (2011) devised an ingenious task which involved asking individuals with Williams syndrome to trace simple figures on a PC display screen. There were three conditions: (1) the figure appeared and immediately faded: this tested copying from memory; (2) the figure appeared and faded slowly: this was an intermediate condition where some support for VSSTM was provided; (3) the figure appeared and remained on the screen long enough for copying: this condition tested simple tracing ability.

(Continued)

Compared to typical children matched for drawing ability, adults with Williams syndrome found tracing and copying 'closed' figures (square, rhombus, pentagon, hexagon, concave polygon) more difficult overall, regardless of condition. In addition, whilst typical children benefited from the intermediate condition where some support for VSSTM was provided, this made no difference for the adults with Williams syndrome. Adults with Williams syndrome only showed a benefit to performance when the figure appeared and remained on screen long enough for copying in full to take place.

These results suggested that weak VSSTM does have an impact on copying abilities in individuals with Williams syndrome, although their tracing and copying abilities were still impaired even in the simple 'tracing' condition. Therefore, although VSSTM seems to be implicated in drawing difficulties among individuals with Williams syndrome, there are clearly other relevant factors too.

The central executive

Executive-loaded working memory

There is a growing body of work looking at executive-loaded working memory (ELWM) in individuals with Williams syndrome. One study mentioned earlier by Wang and Bellugi (1994) included reverse digit span, generally regarded as a measure of ELWM. They compared 15-year-olds with Williams syndrome and Down syndrome, finding no differences between the groups. Conclusions from these results, however, are limited, due to the absence of comparison groups. Those with both disorders might show impairments in ELWM compared to typically developing children of the same mental age and/or comparable individuals with non-specific ID.

Robinson et al. (2003) included one of these comparison groups, typical children matched for grammatical ability, in their study of children with Williams syndrome (see section on PSTM for details). These authors reported no group differences on reverse digit span. Devenny, Krinksy-McHale, Kittler, Flory, Jenkins & Brown (2004) included the other comparison group, individuals with non-specific ID (n = 33), in their study of 15 middle-aged adults with Williams syndrome. The samples were matched for age (50 years) and IQ (62/63). Again, there were no differences between the groups on reverse digit span. Therefore, compared to individuals with non-specific ID and typically developing children, individuals with Williams syndrome did not seem to show impairments in ELWM.

However, the studies just described used only one (verbal) task to assess ELWM. It is important to investigate visuospatial measures of ELWM, as we have already seen that at least some aspects of VSSTM are impaired in individuals with Williams syndrome.

Menghini et al. (2010) did just that, including measures of reverse digit and reverse Corsi (spatial) span. Participants included 15 children/adults with Williams syndrome (10–35 years, IQ 53, range 36–71), who had a mean mental age of 6 years. Their comparison group included 15 typically developing children matched for mental age on a non-verbal assessment of IQ. In contrast to the previous findings, Menghini et al. (2010) reported that individuals with Williams syndrome obtained significantly lower scores on both of the ELWM tasks. These results are illustrated in Figure 7.11.

Rhodes et al. (2010) replicated these findings in relation to spatial ELWM in a similar study (see section on VSSTM for details). However, it is important to note that these latter two studies only included comparison groups of typically developing children, so it is not clear whether individuals with Williams syndrome might have ELWM difficulties due to having intellectual disabilities (ID) or due to having Williams syndrome. Further research including comparison groups of similar ability individuals with non-specific ID is required to address this question.

Summary

The results are inconsistent in relation to whether individuals with Williams syndrome show difficulties with executive working memory (ELWM). In addition, a lack of evidence in relation to different types of comparison groups limits conclusions that can be reached in this area. Therefore, it would be highly desirable for future research to compare several verbal and visuospatial measures of ELWM and include two types of comparison groups (typically developing

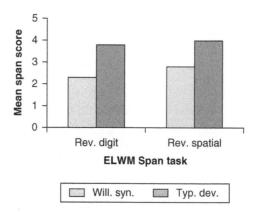

Figure 7.11 Mean scores on verbal and spatial executive-loaded working memory measures for individuals with Williams syndrome and typically developing comparison children matched from mental age

Source: data adapted from Menghini et al. (2010)

children matched for verbal mental age and comparable ability individuals with non-specific intellectual disabilities).

Other measures of the central executive

Looking more broadly at other measures of executive processing, we can revisit a paper mentioned earlier by Kittler et al. (2008). They had investigated how well middle-aged adults with Down syndrome, Williams syndrome and non-specific ID could carry out two tasks at the same time (refer to earlier section under 'Down syndrome' for details). Kittler et al. (2008) found that individuals with Williams syndrome had no more difficulty with dual processing than individuals in the ID group, offering no support for a specific impairment in this aspect of executive functioning.

However, there are some reports in the literature of difficulties with certain executive tasks. For example, Atkinson, Braddick, Anker, Curran, Andrew & Wattam-Bell (2003) found some evidence for difficulties with inhibition in a sample of children with Williams syndrome; but performance was compared to normative typical development rather than to a matched comparison group (see Porter, Coltheart and Langdon (2007) for similar results, with a comparison group of individuals with Down syndrome). Similarly, Vicari, Belluci and Carlesimo (2001) found that teenagers with Williams syndrome (n = 12, mental age 6 years) obtained lower scores on a test of planning (Tower of London) than typically developing mental age matched children.

Comprehensive studies of executive functioning in individuals with Williams syndrome are needed, however, in order to establish whether there might be a particular profile of executive difficulties across a range of tasks. We will discuss two recent experiments that provide such data (see Chapter 2 for details of executive tasks).

Menghini et al. (2010) looked at a wide range of executive skills including planning, switching, fluency and inhibition (and ELWM – see previous section). These authors compared adolescents with Williams syndrome to typically developing children matched for non-verbal mental age (see earlier for details). Adolescents with Williams syndrome showed significantly poorer performance on a number of executive measures: planning (Tower of London); switching (Weigl sorting, Trail Making Test); and inhibition (Opposite Worlds); but did not show difficulties with verbal (category) fluency.

Similarly, Rhodes et al. (2010), investigated a range of executive skills in a sample of children and adults with Williams syndrome. They employed two typical comparison groups, one matched for chronological age and one matched for verbal mental age (see earlier section on VSSTM for details).

Rhodes et al. (2010) found that performance on measures of switching (the ID/ED task), spatial working memory (a self-ordered searching task), and planning (Stockings of Cambridge) was poorer in individuals with Williams syndrome than in both comparison groups.

Therefore, recent evidence does suggest that individuals with Williams syndrome have difficulties in several areas of executive functioning: switching, planning and inhibition. However, there is almost no research comparing individuals with Williams syndrome to individuals of comparable ability but with non-specific ID. As such, we are not able to state with any certainty whether executive difficulties in those with Williams syndrome might be due to having an ID, or whether they are characteristic of the developmental disorder itself.

Summary

Emerging evidence suggests that there is some degree of executive impairment in individuals with Williams syndrome. Difficulties have been reported for planning, switching and inhibition; but not for fluency. As we saw in the previous section, the results in relation to executive-loaded working memory are inconsistent. Therefore, our tentative conclusion is that executive impairments are present in Williams syndrome. However, more detailed research with additional comparison groups of individuals with non-specific intellectual disabilities (ID) is required to pinpoint their exact nature and determine whether they are characteristic of Williams syndrome or related to having ID.

The episodic buffer

We will again look at episodic memory tasks that are hypothesised to involve binding of information from different working memory systems and long-term memory. Some studies referred to below have already been mentioned.

For example the study by Devenny et al. (2004), mentioned earlier, included one relevant measure of 'free recall'. The task was to learn a set of 12 items in four categories (e.g. fruit, animals). The items were presented as line drawings and were shown to participants over several learning trials, with the task being to try to learn the items in batches of four. The final test required participants to recall as many of the 12 items as they could. This task may assess binding of verbal information held in PSTM with long-term knowledge about the category membership of the items.

Devenny et al. (2004) found that middle-aged adults with Williams syndrome were less able to recall the items than a comparison group of adults with ID. However, this study must be interpreted in the context of potentially steep age-related declines in episodic memory performance among adults with Williams syndrome. The authors made just such an argument, claiming that the younger adult participants in their sample performed well on the test. Therefore, this study cannot comment on whether, prior to any age-related declines, individuals with Williams syndrome had levels of episodic memory in line with their general cognitive abilities.

The best way of looking at this is to examine episodic remembering in children and adolescents with Williams syndrome. Vicari et al. (2001) compared

12 teenagers with Williams syndrome (mental age 6 years) to 12 typically developing comparison children matched for mental age using the Stanford-Binet Intelligence Scale. The groups were matched for overall mental age, rather than for verbal or non-verbal abilities. Each participant was asked to recall a list of 12 words in any order. This task was repeated over five consecutive trials, together with a delayed condition 15 minutes after the last immediate recall trial. Although there were some numerical differences in immediate recall scores between the groups, these were not significant. Similarly, there were no differences on delayed recall, with both groups recalling approximately eight words.

Brock, Brown and Boucher (2006) addressed the same question in even more detail in a sample of 11 children/adolescents with Williams syndrome (mean age 13 years) and a typically developing comparison group (mean age 6 years). Groups were matched for verbal memory performance and non-verbal mental age (using Raven's matrices). Brock et al. (2006) again used a free recall task with 12 words, and repeated the task five times (sometimes using the same words each time and sometimes using different words).

Results overall showed that children with Williams syndrome recalled exactly the same number of words over five trials as the typically developing children. This was true regardless of whether new words were presented on each of the five trials, or whether the same words were repeated (either in the same or different orders). Figure 7.12 illustrates these results.

These two studies on free recall suggested that children and adolescents with Williams syndrome were as able to learn new information as well as typically developing children of the same mental age. On this basis, we could conclude that children with Williams syndrome have no particular difficulties

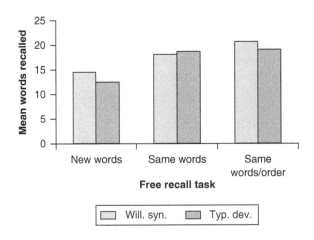

Figure 7.12 Mean free recall scores for children with Williams syndrome and typically developing children of a similar mental age

Source: data adapted from Brock et al. (2006)

with binding information from PSTM and long-term memory in free recall remembering tasks.

One issue to bear in mind with Brock et al.'s findings, however, is that having matched the two groups on verbal memory (the first trial of each free recall test), the authors found that the typically developing children had receptive vocabulary scores that were three years lower than those of the Williams syndrome children (although Ravens scores were matched). Again, we come back to controversies surrounding the basis upon which to match individuals with Williams syndrome to comparison groups. Brock et al. (2006) argued that it was most important to match on initial free recall ability, as otherwise the results for episodic learning over trials would be difficult to interpret, and this is absolutely right. However, children with Williams syndrome still showed levels of performance on the initial episodic remembering task that were lower than would be expected based on their verbal mental age.

Therefore, it may be that individuals with Williams syndrome have some difficulties with the amount they can recall in episodic remembering tasks in relation to verbal mental age, but their learning over trials seems to be exactly what it should be based on initial memory ability (although see Vicari et al., 1996, for a somewhat different viewpoint).

We have looked at verbal episodic remembering tasks that are assumed to involve binding, but it is also possible to assess non-verbal binding tasks. Jarrold, Phillips and Baddeley (2007) looked at this in a sample of 16 children and young adults with Williams syndrome (mean age 18 years). The comparison groups included typical children (n = 16) and children with moderate ID (n = 16), individually matched for non-verbal mental age on the Raven's Coloured Progressive Matrices (mean mental age 6 years for all groups).

The task was to remember whether a particular visual item had appeared in a specific location or not. Simple line drawings of stylised human figures that varied in terms of visual details (pattern, colour and whether the figure was the right way up or upside down) were presented in matrices (e.g. 1 x 2 or 2 x 2 grids etc.). After seeing each item displayed for three seconds, one item was re-presented in the matrix and the participant had to say whether the item had appeared in the spatial position illustrated. This required the binding of visual information about the stimulus together with spatial information about where that stimulus had been located.

Jarrold, Philips et al. (2007) found that the participants with Williams syndrome did not do as well on this task as the typical comparison group. However, the children with moderate ID also performed more poorly than the typical children. As individuals with Williams syndrome and individuals with moderate ID had difficulties with binding visual and spatial information, this would not appear to be a difficulty specific to Williams syndrome.

Summary
Individuals with Williams syndrome do not show difficulties with verbal binding in episodic remembering tasks compared to mental age matched

typical children. They may have difficulties with binding visual and spatial information, although these difficulties do not appear to be specific to Williams syndrome, as they also occur for those with non-specific ID. These conclusions are extremely tentative, however, as research in the area is not extensive and the restricted range of relevant tasks and comparison groups considerably limits conclusions.

Summary: Williams syndrome

Williams syndrome is a relatively rare genetic disorder characterised by mild to moderate intellectual disabilities, relative deficits in non-verbal abilities and relative strengths in verbal abilities. With respect to working memory, individuals with Williams syndrome did not show deficits in phonological short-term memory (PSTM), but they did show significant difficulties with visuospatial short-term memory (VSSTM), particularly spatial tasks. These findings have been reported in relation to typically developing children matched for mental age; and in relation to comparable individuals with non-specific ID, so these strengths/difficulties can be regarded as characteristic of Williams syndrome.

There appear to be some impairments in central executive processing among children with Williams syndrome, notably in planning, switching and inhibition. There are also reports of executive-loaded working memory (ELWM) difficulties, but findings in this area remain inconsistent. Nevertheless, much of the research in this area has only used mental age-matched comparison children so we cannot say whether executive difficulties are characteristic of Williams syndrome. Episodic buffer functioning may be intact in terms of binding verbal information in episodic memory tasks, but difficulties with binding visual and spatial information have been reported in those with Williams syndrome and non-specific intellectual disabilities (ID). Conclusions in this area remain tentative, however, as there is very little relevant research.

Overall summary

Individuals with Down syndrome have a specific impairment in phonological short-term memory (PSTM), whereas individuals with Williams syndrome show significant difficulties with visuospatial short-term memory (VSSTM), particularly on spatial tasks. This contrasting pattern of short-term working memory performance mirrors the general cognitive ability profile for each disorder and represents one of the clearest and most agreed-upon findings from the literature in this area.

With respect to the central executive and the episodic buffer, the research findings remain mixed in relation to both disorders. For example, some research studies on executive-loaded working memory (ELWM) have reported deficits in those with Down and Williams syndrome, whereas others have found no such difficulties. A growing literature on broader measures of executive functioning suggests that there are difficulties in individuals with both disorders, but much of this research has only been carried out in relation to mental age-matched typical children, so we cannot say whether such difficulties are characteristic of each disorder. Comparison groups with non-specific ID would help to clarify this issue.

It is important to point out, however, that research on executive functioning in individuals with Down and Williams syndrome remains relatively sparse; and there are several further debates and uncertainties in this area. One question concerns whether there might be differences between visuospatial and verbal tasks in the executive domain, an interesting issue given the domain-specific findings in relation to the phonological loop and the visuospatial sketchpad. Although executive resources are often believed to be 'domain-general' in typically developing individuals, we cannot necessarily make such assumptions in relation to those with atypical development. At present, there are very few studies that directly test this hypothesis in individuals with Down and Williams syndrome, but this is a promising avenue for future research.

Finally, binding within the episodic buffer appears to be impaired in individuals with Down syndrome, but such difficulties have also been reported in those with Williams syndrome. Again, more research using verbal and visuospatial binding tasks and comparison groups of typical children as well as individuals with non-specific ID would be valuable. Similarly, it would be interesting to see if domain-specific difficulties are present on tasks that require episodic buffer resources, perhaps after short-term memory skills have been accounted for. On the face of it, the episodic buffer is a modality independent store so perhaps we may not expect domain-related performance differences. However, so little is known about episodic buffer functioning in either typical or atypical development, that such work would be invaluable to specify further the working memory profiles of individuals with Down and Williams syndromes.

Further reading

Down syndrome: Books and chapters

Baddeley, A. & Jarrold, C. (2007). Working memory and Down syndrome. *Journal of Intellectual Disability Research, 51,* 925–931. A very helpful and short review of working memory in individuals with Down syndrome.

Gathercole, S.E. & Alloway, T.P. (2006). Short-term and working memory impairments in neurodevelopmental disorders: Diagnosis and remedial support. *Journal of Child Psychology and Psychiatry, 47*(1), 4–15. A very useful review paper covering several developmental disorders including Down syndrome.

Hulme, C. & Mackenzie, S. (1992). *Working memory and severe learning difficulties.* Hove: Lawrence Erlbaum Associates. This readable book describes a detailed set of studies on short-term phonological memory in individuals with severe intellectual disabilities, including Down syndrome.

Jarrold, C., Purser, H.R.M. & Brock, J. (2006). Short-term memory in Down syndrome. In T.P. Alloway & S.E. Gathercole (Eds.), *Working memory and neurodevelopmental disorders* (pp. 239-266). Hove, East Sussex, UK: Psychology Press. A very useful review chapter in a volume that includes chapters on working memory and a range of developmental disorders.

Rutter, M., Bishop, D., Pine, D., Scott, S., Stevenson, J., Taylor, E. & Thapar, A. (Eds.) (2008). *Rutter's Child and Adolescent Psychiatry*, 5th ed. Oxford: Blackwell Science. An invaluable reference book with chapters/sections on many developmental disorders including Down syndrome.

Down syndrome: Experimental papers

These are listed in the order that they are mentioned in the chapter, rather than in alphabetical order.

Jarrold, C. & Baddeley, A.D. (1997). Short-term memory for verbal and visuospatial information in Down Syndrome. *Cognitive Neuropsychiatry, 2*(2), 101–122. The best single paper to read for discussing phonological short-term memory and visuospatial short-term memory.

Lanfranchi, S., Cornoldi, C. & Vianello, R. (2004). Verbal and visuospatial working memory deficits in children with Down syndrome. *American Journal on Mental Retardation, 6*, 456–466. A very thorough study looking at executive-loaded working memory.

Rowe, J., Lavender, A. & Turk, V. (2006). Cognitive executive function in Down's syndrome. *British Journal of Clinical Psychology, 45*, 5–17. Another thorough study of executive functioning.

Jarrold, C., Baddeley, A.D. & Hewes, A.K. (2000). Verbal short-term memory deficits in Down Syndrome: A consequence of problems in rehearsal? *Journal of Child Psychology and Psychiatry, 41*(2), 233–244. More detail on verbal rehearsal and phonological short-term memory.

Lanfranchi, S., Jerman, O., Dal Pont, E., Alberti, A. & Vianello, R. (2010). Executive function in adolescents with Down syndrome. *Journal of Intellectual Disability Research, 54*(4), 308–319. A broader study of executive functioning.

Carlesimo, G.A., Marotta, L. & Vicari, S. (1997). Long-term memory in mental retardation: Evidence for a specific impairment in subjects with Down's syndrome. *Neuropsychologia, 35*, 71–79. Includes several episodic memory tasks and excellent comparison groups.

Williams syndrome: Books, chapters, reviews

Gathercole, S.E. & Alloway, T.P. (2006). Short-term and working memory impairments in neurodevelopmental disorders: Diagnosis and remedial support. *Journal of Child Psychology and Psychiatry, 47*(1), 4–15. A very useful review paper covering several developmental disorders including Williams Syndrome.

Martens, M.A., Wilson, S.J. & Reutens, D.C. (2008). Williams syndrome: A critical review of the cognitive, behavioral, and neuroanatomical phenotype. *Journal of Child Psychology and Psychiatry, 49*(6), 576–608. A very thorough review and extremely useful background on Williams syndrome.

Rowe, M.L. & Mervis, C.B. (2006). Working memory in Williams syndrome. In T.P. Alloway & S.E. Gathercole (Eds.), *Working memory and neurodevelopmental disorders* (pp. 267–293). Hove, East Sussex, UK: Psychology Press. A very useful review chapter in a volume that includes chapters on working memory and a range of developmental disorders.

Rutter, M., Bishop, D., Pine, D., Scott, S., Stevenson, J., Taylor, E. & Thapar, A. (Eds.) (2008). *Rutter's Child and Adolescent Psychiatry*, 5th ed. Oxford: Blackwell Science. An invaluable reference book with chapters/sections on many developmental disorders including Williams syndrome.

Williams syndrome: Experimental papers

These are listed in the order that they are mentioned in the chapter, rather than in alphabetical order.

Jarrold, C., Baddeley, A.D. & Hewes, A.K. (1999). Genetically dissociated components of working memory: Evidence from Down's and Williams syndrome. *Neuropsychologia, 37*, 637–651. The best single paper to read for discussing phonological short-term memory and visuospatial short-term memory.

Menghini, D., Addona, F., Costanzo, F. & Vicari, S. (2010). Executive functions in individuals with Williams syndrome. *Journal of Intellectual Disability Research, 54*(5), 418–432. A detailed study of executive functioning including executive-loaded working memory.

Rhodes, S.M., Riby, D.M., Park, J., Fraser, E. & Campbell, L.E. (2010). Executive neuropsychological functioning in individuals with Williams syndrome. *Neuropsychologia, 48*, 1216–1226. Another comprehensive study of executive functioning.

Brock, J., Brown, G.D.A. & Bucher, J. (2006). Free recall in Williams syndrome: Is there a dissociation between short-and long-term memory? *Cortex, 42*, 366–375. A well written paper that we have interpreted as providing evidence on episodic memory in individuals with Williams syndrome. You will find additional interesting material here on verbal rehearsal.

Potential exam questions

1 Compare and contrast the working memory skills of individuals with Down syndrome and Williams syndrome in relation to each component of Baddeley's revised working memory model.

2 Critically evaluate whether phonological short-term memory is impaired in individuals with Down syndrome and comment on how this might be related to their language skills.

3 'Working memory difficulties in individuals with Williams syndrome are simply a reflection of their intellectual disabilities.' Critically discuss this statement using experimental evidence to support your arguments.

8

Working Memory in Children with Autism Spectrum Disorders

Learning outcomes

At the end of this chapter, you should have an understanding of what autism spectrum disorders (ASD) are. You should also have a critical knowledge of the strengths and weaknesses of children with ASD in relation to each of the four major components of the revised 'working memory model' (Baddeley, 2007) and be able to support your arguments with research evidence.

With respect to the central executive component of working memory, you should also be able to describe and evaluate the range of executive functioning impairments that are often characteristic of individuals with ASD, and show insight into whether these deficits are causally related to the disorder.

Introduction

Note that children with autism spectrum disorders (ASD) have a known developmental disorder, but they may or may not have an intellectual disability as well. We have looked at several different atypical populations in previous chapters that have varied in terms of whether they have intellectual disabilities

(ID) and/or developmental disorders. ASD are particularly interesting as they can occur with or without an associated ID. Therefore, a proportion of children with ASD have an additional intellectual disability (i.e. IQ in the range 70/75 and below), whereas others have cognitive abilities in the typical range (i.e. IQ 80+). As we will see, much of the research on working memory focuses on one or other of these subgroups.

Autism spectrum disorders (ASD) refer to a range of heterogeneous, life-long developmental disorders of early onset (before 36 months). They are characterised by difficulties in three key areas: (1) reciprocal social interaction; (2) communication; and (3) restricted/repetitive behaviours and interests. Box 8.1 gives further details about these three areas, often described as the 'triad of deficits'.

Box 8.1 The 'triad of deficits' (Wing & Gould, 1979) associated with autism spectrum disorders (ASD)

1   Reciprocal social interaction. Children with ASD seem to lack automatic social responses and show limited interest in other children. The bedrock of social interaction is a shared enjoyment/understanding of events and conversations; this is something that children with ASD have great difficulty with. These problems lead to difficulties in forming social relationships.

2   Communication. Severe language delays are very common in children with ASD. In those children who have language, it is often described as lacking in 'social quality'. In other words, the speech may be repetitive, descriptive and/or stereotypic (copying others) with very little reciprocal social communication. The difficulties with communication extend to non-verbal communication (gestures, eye contact, facial expressions) as well.

3   Restricted, repetitive interests and behaviours. Children with ASD often have very restricted interests, compulsions or rituals and/or unusual preoccupations. For example, they may have an obsession with trains or other forms of public transport, or they may only eat food of a certain colour. Stereotypical movements such as handclapping, bouncing or rocking occur quite commonly. Some children with ASD are very upset by changes in their routines or environments.

The difficulties experienced by those with ASD lead to delayed or unusual development in key psychological and cognitive skills, and are persistent over the life course (van Engeland & Buitelaar, 2008). Autism is often diagnosed in a child's second or third year, but parents may notice abnormalities or delays earlier than this. Parental reports often concern difficulties with language, eating, tantrums or sleeping, rather than more direct indications of the social difficulties associated with ASD; possibly because many early signs of ASD are subtle (e.g. reduction or absence of joint attention). Some children have been noted to show regressions, for example losing language skills between 18 and 24 months, but the reasons for this are currently unclear.

Most individuals with ASD will require some level of support throughout their lives, even those with higher cognitive functioning. There is, however, wide diversity within the range of individuals who have ASD. The key factors that account for this heterogeneity seem to be level of cognitive functioning and language skills. These can vary enormously from extremely low functioning individuals with severe intellectual disabilities, very little or no speech and repetitive or self-injurious behaviour, through to high-functioning individuals who have extremely well-developed skills in particular areas and the ability to obtain employment in 'typical' settings (van Engeland & Buitelaar, 2008). In terms of prognosis for future functioning, having an IQ of lower than 50 and no language by the age of 5 years may be a useful general cut-off point to distinguish those who have a low probability of good social functioning in adult life; in addition, those with better outcomes generally have more support mechanisms (Lord & Bailey, 2002).

A distinction has been made between autism, which refers to a narrower diagnostic range of more severely impaired individuals, and autistic spectrum disorders, which refer to a broader range of less handicapping, but related disorders. An alternative term for ASD is Pervasive Developmental Disorder (PDD). Autism was first described formally by Kanner (1943), based on case histories of several children; and Asperger (1944) described a similar group of children very shortly afterwards (see Frith, 1991). However, Asperger syndrome generally describes individuals who have most of the characteristics of ASD, but not the extensive language difficulties. These individuals may also be intellectually very able, or at least have average or near average IQ. There are difficulties in developing diagnostic criteria that distinguish between autism and Asperger syndrome (see Schopler, Mesibov & Kunce, 1998), although Szatmari et al. (2009) have recently argued that distinguishing between these two disorders based on the absence/presence of a language impairment is helpful in clinical settings. However, it is likely that all of these disorders will simply be referred to as autism spectrum disorders in the future.

Boys are more affected with ASD than girls (a ratio of around 3.5/4.0 to 1); and this ratio may be even higher when we consider individuals in the average intelligence range. As we have seen in other chapters of this book, males are often more vulnerable to developmental disorders, although the reasons for this are not well understood.

The prevalence of ASD is hard to determine with any certainty, because of definitional differences (i.e. narrower definitions versus wider definitions), potential differences in prevalence between those with higher versus lower IQs (ASD may be more prevalent in those with lower IQs), and variations between studies in terms of how they collect information about cases. More recent studies tend to find higher prevalence rates, but this could reflect the fact that the definition of autism and related disorders has broadened in recent years; and/or the methodology for identifying cases in population studies has become more sophisticated. Current estimates are that there are 30–100 cases of individuals with all types of ASD per 10,000 people in the population; although some recent estimates are even higher than this (e.g. Baron-Cohen et al., 2009, estimated 157 cases per 10,000). However, if we look just at cases of autism, the estimate of prevalence is lower, probably nearer 13–30 per 10,000 (see van Engeland & Buitelaar, 2008, for a review of this evidence).

Genetic factors are undoubtedly involved in autism spectrum disorders. Twin studies have demonstrated that there is a high concordance rate for autism in identical twins (60–90%); and among siblings of those with autism, 5% will also have the disorder (van Engeland & Buitelaar, 2008). Atypical brain activity in the fronto-cerebellar areas has also been reported to be characteristic of 'unaffected' siblings on visual attention tasks (Belmonte, Gomot & Baron-Cohen, 2010). Other family studies have indicated that higher rates of milder forms of social difficulties characteristic of ASD and related disorders (for example lack of interest in others, socially odd behaviour, difficulties with executive and planning tasks, language difficulties) are found in the families of those with autism at a rate of approximately 20–30% (e.g. Bailey, Palferman, Heavey & Le Couteur, 1998). However, despite an increasing number of genome scan studies, there is no consistent evidence to link ASD to any particular loci or candidate genes. The majority of cases of ASD seem to have a complex genetic predisposition – and as many as ten different loci may be involved.

The interaction between environmental and genetic factors in ASD is also a fascinating and developing area. A recent study by Auyeung, Baron-Cohen, Ashwin, Knickmeyer, Taylor and Hackett (2009) demonstrated that a higher level of testosterone in the amniotic fluid of the mother during pregnancy was related to the child exhibiting more autistic traits, which could represent either environmental or genetic influences, or a combination of the two. Other environmental factors have been considered including: whether the immune systems in those with ASD are abnormal; whether obstetric risk factors may be higher in individuals with ASD; and whether environmental risks such as toxins, diet or other pollutants might be implicated. However, it is most likely that there are highly complex interactions between environmental and genetic risk factors.

There is also evidence that individuals with ASD show brain abnormalities in terms of functionality and neuropathology (Bailey et al., 1998). Some hypothesise that there is reduced connectivity, together with accelerated overgrowth in the first three or four years of life in ASD, which leads to abnormalities in overall brain size (brains are around 10% larger). It is not yet clear whether there are specific primary abnormalities in brain function, or whether the connections between different brain structures are the cause of the problems (Lord & Bailey, 2002). An emerging area of research looks at brain areas used for a range of cognitive tasks (functional MRI studies) and these suggest there are some systematic differences between those with and without ASD (e.g. Williams, Goldstein, Carpenter & Minshew, 2005). A meta-analysis of functional neuroimaging studies by Di Martino, Ross, Uddin, Sklar, Castellanos and Milham (2009) found unusual patterns of activation in those with ASD on both social (e.g. theory of mind) and non-social processes (e.g. attention, working memory). There is also evidence that the neurochemistry of the brain in those with ASD is somewhat abnormal (van Engeland & Buitelaar, 2008).

ASD can co-occur with other disorders, such as Tourette syndrome, schizophrenia, obsessive-compulsive disorder and ADHD. However, co-morbidity (i.e. having more than one disorder), occurs most often with intellectual disability. Around 50–70% of individuals with autism also have an intellectual disability (ID) of some form (please refer to Chapter 5 for further details about ID). However, it does not appear that autistic traits are strongly related to intellectual disability *per se*. According to recent evidence, ID and extreme autistic traits appear to be 'substantially genetically independent' (Hoekstra, Happé, Baron-Cohen & Ronald, 2009). Similarly, Volkmar, Lord, Bailey, Schultz and Klin (2004) noted that purported associations between autism and other medical conditions/procedures (e.g. genital rubella, immunisation) have not been supported, except in the cases of children with Fragile X syndrome and tuberous sclerosis.

Over the past four decades, much has been written about the possible causes of autism; and the theorising in this area has become immensely sophisticated. We will simply summarise the three main psychological models of autism; but there are plenty of detailed sources that will provide additional information. Potential sources and references are given at the end of the chapter under the heading Further reading. The three main psychological models of autism are as follows:

1 Theory of Mind. This hypothesis attributes the difficulties characteristic of ASD to a core problem with understanding 'mental states'. Those with ASD are not able to understand that they and other individuals have entirely separate and different feelings, intentions, desires and beliefs. Some refer to this difficulty as 'mind-blindness' and it is thought to lead to the range of social and communicative difficulties found in ASD, as well as the characteristic lack of imagination and pretend play. Baron-Cohen (e.g. 1995) has carried out a great deal of research in this area, demonstrating significant ASD impairments on many tasks requiring theory of mind. However, it has been argued that this hypothesis does not offer a full account of the disorder, notably that theory of mind is not a 'core' deficit (van Engeland & Buitelaar, 2008).

2 Central Coherence Theory. This hypothesis attributes the key difficulties found in ASD to a deficit in processing information for meaning. According to this view, individuals with ASD focus on the detail of a situation or stimulus, rather than understanding how context or a more 'global' consideration of all available information will contribute to fuller understanding (Frith, 1991). Although there is considerable evidence that individuals with ASD are better

on tasks requiring the processing of local details as opposed to looking at more global information, this may be a preferred style of processing rather than an impairment as such (Happé & Frith, 2006).

3   Executive Dysfunction. The key argument of this hypothesis is that difficulties in the ability to organise, plan, alter and regulate behaviour to suit the circumstances are the central deficit in individuals with ASD. There is a considerable amount of evidence for executive difficulties in individuals with ASD and we will examine some of this research later in the chapter. Although it has been argued that this hypothesis cannot provide a full explanation for ASD, as executive deficits are seen in other developmental disorders (e.g. Geurts, Verte, Oosterlaan, Roeyers & Sergeant, 2004), it still may be that autism is characterised by a particular profile of executive dysfunction.

Summary

Autism spectrum disorders (ASD) are developmental disorders of early onset that persist throughout life. They are characterised by: difficulties with reciprocal social interaction; communication impairments; and restricted/repetitive behaviours and interests. Many individuals with ASD also have intellectual disabilities, but the genetic basis for these two disorders does not seem to be the same. In this chapter, we will attempt to evaluate whether working memory difficulties in ASD are characteristic of all individuals who have ASD, whether they have an intellectual disability or not, where research evidence makes this possible.

Before moving on to looking at working memory skills in individuals with ASD, it is worth looking briefly at memory skills more generally in children and adults with ASD. Memory skills in those with ASD have been extensively reported in the literature, and some broad findings are relatively well agreed upon.

Brief overview of memory skills in those with ASD

Clinicians often come across individuals with ASD who have excellent memory abilities for specific types of non-social information such as train timetables or dates (Toichi, 2008); or, indeed, other remarkable skills. These are known as savant skills. See Box 8.2 for further information.

Box 8.2   Savant skills

In some individuals with ASD, repetitive or intense interests can be associated with particularly high levels of skill. These are known as savant skills. For example, being able to recall with intricate detail of complex architectural scenes and produce very accurate drawings from memory.

(Continued)

Other savant skills include calendrical calculation (working out on which day in the week someone was born from their birth date), remarkable retention of information such as train timetables and exceptional musical ability.

However, although there are individual cases of remarkable memory skills for particular information, when we look at memory more generally, the picture is rather complex. Some authors have pointed out that although many memory skills may not differ reliably between those with ASD and typical comparison groups, there are nevertheless subtle differences. For example, Williams, Minshew and Goldstein (2008) described a set of comprehensive research studies showing that basic encoding, storage, associative and retrieval processes were not impaired in individuals with high-functioning autism, but once the tasks became more complex, those with autism showed increasingly worse performance, possibly because memory strategies were not employed flexibly or systematically. In addition, there were some specific difficulties with visual and spatial memory tests, including memory for faces.

In general terms, the long-term memory skills of higher functioning individuals with ASD have been described by Salmond, Adlam, Gadian and Vargha-Khadem (2008) as relatively intact with respect to factual memory (often described as semantic memory – this refers to general knowledge and memory for facts); but impaired with respect to memory for particular episodes (often described as episodic memory – this refers to memory for events, often with personal relevance: see also Lind & Bowler, 2008, for further evidence regarding these episodic memory difficulties).

If you would like to read more about memory generally in individuals with ASD, please refer to a recent comprehensive book edited by Boucher and Bowler (2008), cited in Further reading at the end of the chapter.

Here, however, we will now focus on working memory in individuals with ASD, assessing performance in relation to each component of the working memory model, as we have done in previous chapters. If you need a refresher on any of the components of the working memory model, refer to Chapters 1 and 2 or look at the 'aide memoire to the working memory model' at the end of Chapter 2 for a brief reminder.

The phonological loop

Early experiments looking at immediate recall for verbal materials, i.e. phonological short-term memory (PSTM), in individuals with ASD did not use the working memory model as a theoretical framework. However, many of the findings can be interpreted in relation to the working memory model, because the tasks employed included standard measures of PSTM such as digit and word span. The majority of this evidence suggested there were no deficits in immediate verbal recall (in our terminology, PSTM) in individuals with ASD (e.g. Hermelin & O'Connor, 1970).

However, it has been noted that many of the findings upon which these conclusions were based used a methodology that may have affected the results. In many of these studies, the samples of individuals with autism were first matched to comparison participants on their levels of digit span, before other measures of PSTM (for example word span) were administered. This methodological issue, described eloquently by Poirier and Martin (2008), means that the finding of no differences between groups of individuals with and without autism on measures of PSTM may have simply reflected the matching procedure. Digit and word span are regarded as requiring the same mechanisms (the phonological loop), so matching on one is likely to mean that the other will be closely matched as well.

Therefore, it is necessary to look at more recent research that did not adopt this procedure in order to examine more closely PSTM in individuals with ASD.

Bennetto, Pennington and Rogers (1996) carried out a straightforward comparison of PSTM skills in 19 young people with autism (mean age 15 years) and 19 young people with a range of other difficulties, but not autism (e.g. dyslexia, borderline intellectual disabilities). The comparison group was, therefore, a 'clinical comparison' group, which has a key advantage. These are all individuals who regularly see services for their difficulties, so are more comparable to the group with autism who would also be expected to be in regular contact with services. The groups were matched for IQ (autism group = 89; comparison group = 92), age and gender.

This very thorough study included a range of memory tasks, several of which we will come back to in other sections, but for now, the results for a measure of digit span will be considered. Bennetto et al. (1996) found no differences between the groups on digit span, concluding that there was no deficit in PSTM in young people with autism. However, it must be noted that these teenagers were in the relatively high-functioning range, as no participants had an IQ of less than 70.

Russell et al. (1996) carried out a similar study with 33 somewhat younger individuals with autism (mean age 12 years) who had lower levels of functioning (mean mental age 6 years). These authors also included two separate comparison groups, children with moderate intellectual disabilities (MID: mean age 10 years) and children with typical development (mean age 6 years). Each child in each comparison group was matched for verbal IQ to a young person in the group with autism, so the three groups were all of equivalent verbal mental ages (6 years). Note that the most appropriate 'typical' comparison group for children and young people with autism and ID is a mental age level comparison group. This ensures that individuals with autism are assessed in relation to their current cognitive level, which is estimated by using mental age. The comparison group with MID allows comparisons to be made with children who have an ID but not autism. In this way, we are able to see whether having autism and/or ID affects level of performance.

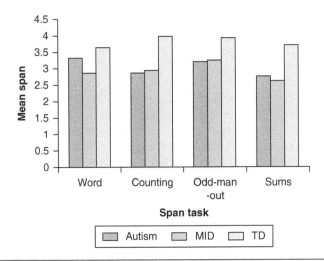

Figure 8.1 Mean span scores for children with autism, moderate intellectual disabilities (MID) and typical development (TD) on a range of memory span tasks

Source: data adapted from Russell et al. (1996)

Figure 8.1 shows the data for word span (averaged over four similar conditions) in each group. For now, just look at the first set of columns, as we will come back to the other measures in a later section on executive-loaded working memory. As can be seen, there were no differences between the children with autism and the typically developing comparison group on word span. However, those with moderate intellectual disabilities (MID) obtained significantly lower scores than both of the other groups. Therefore, deficits in PSTM did not appear to be characteristic of individuals with autism and ID, although they did seem to be characteristic of individuals who just had ID (see Chapter 5 for more information about working memory in children with ID).

Therefore, we have seen evidence that individuals with autism, whether or not they have additional ID, do not show difficulties with PSTM. Similar findings of no differences in PSTM between samples of typical children and those with autism have been reported in several different studies. If you would like to read more, please refer to Joseph, Steele, Meyer and Tager-Flusberg (2005) and Ameli, Courchesne, Lincoln, Kaufmann and Grillon (1988), for relevant findings using digit span tasks in samples of children with high-functioning autism. Similarly, you can refer to Williams, Goldstein and Minshew (2006) for a study using a mixed number and letter span task, again in a sample of children with high-functioning autism. Joseph, McGrath and Tager-Flusberg (2005) found no word span differences between a mixed sample of high and low-functioning children with autism and an age and IQ matched comparison group. However, see Poirier, Martin, Goigg and Bowler (2011) for an alternative view in a study of high-functioning adults with ASD: here difficulties with temporal order recall were reported.

Summary

There is no strong evidence that children with either high- or low-functioning autism have a deficit in phonological short-term memory (PSTM). Performance reaches chronological age level in the case of those with high-functioning autism; whereas performance reaches mental age level in the case of those with low-functioning autism. However, despite the consistency of the findings, it must be noted that there is less evidence in relation to individuals with low-functioning autism; and recent adult work suggests some difficulties with temporal order recall.

The role of verbal coding and verbal rehearsal

This is an interesting issue to examine, because it might be expected that individuals with autism, who generally have speech and communication impairments, might have difficulties with verbal/phonological coding and verbal rehearsal. These processes are carried out using the phonological loop and are defined as follows. Verbal/phonological coding refers to converting pictorial or written information into speech-based material, for example naming pictures or printed words. Verbal rehearsal refers to reciting speech information over and over again to keep it in mind so that it does not decay. Both of these processes, verbal coding and verbal rehearsal, are carried out by one of the subcomponents of the phonological loop, the articulatory rehearsal mechanism. They do, therefore, place demands on speech planning and output mechanisms (refer to Chapters 1 and 3 for further information).

On the other hand, we have just reviewed evidence suggesting that there are no obvious phonological short-term memory (PSTM) difficulties in children with autism. Many would argue that the processes of verbal coding and verbal rehearsal are crucial for having good levels of PSTM, so any child that did not use these processes would be expected to show weak or reduced PSTM performance. Therefore, perhaps the use of verbal coding and rehearsal strategies may be unimpaired in those with autism/ASD?

Several recent studies have examined directly whether children with autism/ASD show evidence for using verbal coding and verbal rehearsal. These skills are sometimes described under the broader term of 'inner speech' and many argue that inner speech has a further role to play in mediating performance on executive control tasks (Russell, Jarrold & Hood, 1999). We will come back to this issue later in the chapter in the context of executive functioning and autism. For now, we will examine the rather more specific issue of whether there is evidence for inner speech difficulties in those with ASD, in the context of phonological short-term memory tasks.

Whitehouse, Maybery and Durkin (2006) investigated the use of inner speech among children with autism using a variety of methods, but we will concentrate on their PSTM task. For this, they presented series of pictures for children to remember (a picture memory span task – see Chapter 2 for further details); but the key manipulation was that these pictures had either short names or long names. Children who were using verbal coding and verbal rehearsal (i.e. inner speech) should find the long-named pictures more difficult. This is the classic word length effect which, although somewhat controversial, does provide an index verbal coding and may also reveal the use of verbal rehearsal when used in the context of a picture memory span task (see Chapter 1 for further details regarding the word length effect and the working memory model; and Chapter 3 for the controversies surrounding word length effects in typical development).

Whitehouse et al. (2006) included a sample of 23 children with autism and 23 comparison children with no known neurological or developmental disorders. The groups were well-matched on verbal and non-verbal abilities, reading ability and gender, although the children with autism were slightly older (exact details of ages were not provided, but those with autism were around 10 years and the comparison children were around 8 years, which means that those who had autism were relatively high-functioning). The pictures were presented on a computer screen, consecutively from left to right, and children were asked to recall the pictures in serial order.

The results indicated that both groups of children showed significant word length effects, but that those with autism showed smaller effects. The authors concluded that both groups of children used inner speech, but children with autism did not use inner speech to the same degree as their typically developing comparisons.

However, not all studies have found the same results. For example, in an earlier study we have already mentioned (Russell et al., 1996), no differences in the size of word length effects were found between typically developing children and children with autism, using measures of word span that carefully controlled for method of recall. In order to control for recall method, Russell et al. (1996) ensured that children heard lists of words and repeated them back in order verbally, or pointed to their responses on a picture board. Results were very similar regardless of output method and the fact that there were no differences in the degree to which the two groups showed word length effects suggested that there were no differences between the groups in terms of how much they used inner speech.

Clearly, the two studies differ in that one presented pictures and the other presented spoken words and this could explain the differing results. Perhaps inner speech processes are more natural and more easily implemented when the input is spoken material? With pictures, one must name the picture first, i.e. verbal coding, which is an extra stage of processing. In any case, there are considerable uncertainties concerning the differences between auditory presentation and visual presentation in respect of word length effects in children (Henry et al., 2000), so differing results are not necessarily unexpected.

However, a later study by Williams, Happé and Jarrold (2008) casts doubt on this explanation. Williams, Happé and Jarrold (2008) also used a picture memory span task to investigate inner speech in children with ASD. Rather than focus on word length effects, these authors looked at 'phonological similarity effects', which are rather less controversial indicators of verbal coding and, hence, the use of inner speech to convert pictorial material into a verbal code (please refer to Chapter 1 for further details about phonological similarity effects). They also examined 'visual similarity effects' to check for the stage prior to verbal coding, i.e. the visual coding stage (for further information on the development of visual and phonological similarity effects in typical development, please see Chapter 4).

Williams, Happé and Jarrold (2008) started with the proposition that there is a developmental shift towards the use of inner speech at around the age of 6 or 7 years in typically developing children. Recall from Chapter 4 that there is evidence that children move from using visual strategies to remember lists of pictures, towards the use of verbal strategies requiring inner speech after the age of about 6 years (e.g. Hitch, Woodin & Baker, 1989; Palmer, 2000a). Therefore, Williams, Happé and Jarrold (2008) hypothesised that, if there were differences between individuals with and without autism in the use of inner speech, we should find a delay in, or absence of, a shift towards verbal coding in the children with autism.

Participants included 25 children with ASD ranging in age from 4 to 15 years (mean age 12 years). The comparison group of 20 children included 18 with moderate to borderline intellectual disabilities and two with average abilities, such that the two groups had the same age range and were matched on IQ. The mental ages of both groups were, on average, around 8½ years, but included 32 with mental ages above 7 years (18 ASD; 14 ID) and 13 with mental ages below 7 years (7 ASD, 6 ID). Therefore, this study included largely low-functioning individuals with ASD who had intellectual disabilities (ID).

Figure 8.2 illustrates the results, which are presented in terms of those who had mental ages above 7 years, versus those who had mental ages below 7 years. This is because there were no differences between those with and without ASD, hence, no evidence that verbal coding (inner speech) was delayed in those with ASD.

The key finding using the mental age 'split' was that those with higher mental ages used verbal coding (phonological similarity effect), whereas those with lower mental ages used visual coding (visual similarity effect), in line with the literature on typical development. Hence, children with ID and ASD both showed the developmental shift towards verbal coding at broadly the mental age that would be expected. This study, therefore, offered no evidence for a deficit in inner speech among those with ASD.

Therefore, two studies found no evidence for deficits in inner speech in those with ASD, whereas one study did. The differences between these studies may reflect the comparison groups employed. Whitehouse et al. (2006) used a comparison group of younger typically developing children who were

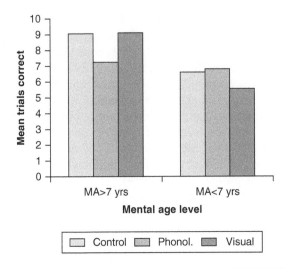

Figure 8.2   Mean trials correct for visually similar pictures, phonologically
similar pictures and control pictures for children (ASD and ID
groups combined) with mental ages over 7 years and under 7 years

Source: data adapted from Williams, Happé and Jarrold (2008)

matched for mental age but not chronological age, whereas Russell et al. (1996)
and Williams, Happé and Jarrold (2008) used comparison groups of children
with intellectual disabilities who were matched on both chronological and
mental age. Williams, Happé and Jarrold (2008) speculate that this could
account for the differences in findings, because the children with autism in
Whitehouse et al.'s study may have shown poorer performance as a result of
their lower verbal IQ, rather than their autism.

This debate continues, and if you would like to read more about it, please
refer to the following articles listed in the full reference section at the end
of the book: Lidstone, Fernyhough, Meins and Whitehouse (2009); Wallace,
Silvers, Martin and Kenworthy (2009); and Williams and Jarrold (2010). This
area would make a good topic for an optional/open choice coursework essay
and details are included at the end of the chapter.

Summary

At present, firm conclusions cannot be drawn regarding the presence or
absence of inner speech difficulties in individuals with autism, as the literature is somewhat contradictory. However, all three studies reported here
have found evidence consistent with at least some use of inner speech among
those with autism/ASD in phonological short-term memory tasks. This is a
rapidly growing area in the literature, which will no doubt produce more
definitive findings in the near future. We will come back to the issue of inner
speech and executive skills in a later section.

The visuospatial sketchpad

Surprisingly, there is relatively little research looking specifically at visuospatial short-term memory (VSSTM) in individuals with autism, as much of the current work has tended to focus on executive-loaded working memory measures, which we will cover in the next section. In keeping with previous chapters, visual and spatial components of the visuospatial sketchpad will be discussed separately in the review below.

One relevant study was carried out by Ameli et al. (1988). These authors examined visual memory processes in 16 high-functioning young adults with autism (mean performance IQ 91) and 16 comparison participants (mean performance IQ 98) who had no history of developmental or learning disabilities. Although performance IQ was not perfectly matched, Ameli et al. (1988) ensured that gender and age were matched between the groups, and they statistically controlled for the differences in performance IQ.

The visual memory task used by Ameli et al. (1988) required participants to view a series of five nonsense shapes for ten seconds. The authors ensured that participants attended to each stimulus by requiring them to match a duplicate set of cards to each item. Following this, the items were re-presented with an extra item inserted randomly in the array. Participants had to identify the new item. (Note that there was also a version of this task using nameable pictures, but we will not consider these results for two reasons: (1) there was the ceiling effect; (2) the nameability of the items means that we cannot be sure this was a test of visual memory.)

As is illustrated in Figure 8.3, individuals with autism performed significantly more poorly than those in the comparison group, indicating that their short-term memory for visual items was impaired. In addition, those with autism performed more poorly on the Benton Revised Visual Retention Test, which requires individuals to recall (and draw) from memory a geometric design that has been viewed for ten seconds. Therefore, Ameli et al.'s (1988) findings suggested that the visual component of the visuospatial sketchpad may be impaired in young adults with autism.

Williams et al. (2005) provided data on the spatial component of the visuospatial sketchpad. These authors, in fact, examined mainly executive-loaded verbal and spatial working memory, so we will come back to these aspects of their study in the next section. However, they included the Corsi blocks task (or spatial span), which was used for the portion of their sample of high-functioning individuals with autism who were children and adolescents (ages 8 to 16, n = 24), as well as for a comparison group of typical children/adolescents matched for IQ (ages 8 to 16, n = 44).

Williams et al. (2005) found that the children and adolescents with autism showed poorer performance on the spatial span task than the comparison group. These results suggested that the spatial component of the visuospatial sketchpad may also be impaired in individuals with autism.

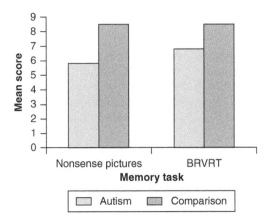

Figure 8.3   Mean performance on a nonsense picture remembering task
(maximum score 12) and the Benton Revised Visual Retention Test
(BRVRT) (maximum score 10) for individuals with autism and a
typical comparison group

Source: data adapted from Ameli et al. (1988)

In a study looking at both visual and spatial aspects of VSSTM, Williams
et al. (2006) administered a comprehensive battery of memory tests to 38
11-year-old high-functioning children with autism (carefully determined
using expert interviews and clinical evaluation, mean IQ = 104); and a comparison group of medically healthy typical children of the same age and overall
IQ level (n = 38). Participants in the autism group were excluded if they had
associated disorders such as tuberous sclerosis or Fragile X syndrome.

Williams et al. (2006) found that the children with autism obtained significantly lower scores on several measures of visual and spatial memory: these
included immediate recall of geometric designs; picture scenes; and spatial
sequences (rather like spatial span). Thus, it appeared that VSSTM might be
impaired in children with autism, in relation to both its visual and spatial
components.

However, Joseph, McGrath and Tager-Flusberg (2005) did not replicate at
least some of these findings. They assessed a sample of 37 school-age children with mixed high- and low-functioning autism, as well as 31 comparison
participants matched for age and IQ. This time, no group differences were
found on a measure of spatial span.

Therefore, we are left with a set of somewhat contradictory findings
regarding visual versus spatial short-term memory. Unfortunately, Joseph,
McGrath and Tager-Flusberg (2005) did not evaluate any potential differences there might have been between low-functioning and high-functioning
children with autism. Such a comparison may have been instructive, as it is
possible that those with high- and low-functioning autism differ in their visual
versus spatial STM abilities.

Therefore, before firm conclusions can be drawn regarding the performance of those with autism/ASD on VSSTM, further research is required. At present, there are two major outstanding issues that need investigation: (1) there is little research comparing visual and spatial short-term memory abilities using comparable stimuli that cannot be verbally coded; and (2) there is no research comparing the performance of individuals with both high- and low-functioning autism/ASD.

Given the findings just reviewed, it is likely that in respect of point (1) there may be significant visual and spatial short-term memory difficulties in those with autism, although the research is not entirely consistent. It is difficult to comment further on point (2) as none of the studies reviewed above compared participants with low- and high-functioning autism. Detailed research examining the theoretical and practical implications of potential deficits in visuospatial short-term memory among high- and low-functioning individuals with autism/ASD would, therefore, be highly desirable.

Summary

There is a limited literature on visuospatial short-term memory (VSSTM) in children with autism/ASD, but several studies have suggested that both the visual and spatial components might be impaired. This area would, however, benefit from further research in order to confirm whether there are indeed visual and spatial short-term memory difficulties in children with both high and low-functioning autism/ASD, as the findings are not entirely consistent.

The central executive

In the following two sections on higher order processing supported by the central executive, we will consider executive-loaded working memory (ELWM), and then 'other' measures of central executive processing including planning, switching, fluency and inhibition.

Executive-loaded working memory

In relation to executive-loaded working memory (ELWM), there is no strong agreement about whether children with autism have difficulties or not.

For example, Williams et al. (2006) noted that our understanding of many aspects of memory in those with autism is currently unsatisfactory, but that this is particularly true for ELWM. The inconsistency of research findings that we will encounter in this section may be related to variability in the population of individuals with ASD, i.e. the fact that ASD covers individuals with the full range of cognitive functioning from low to high (Williams et al., 2006). As in previous sections, therefore, we will attempt to evaluate whether there are impairments in ELWM in those with both high- and low-functioning autism/ASD. Several of the studies mentioned in the following section have already been described under 'the phonological loop'.

Bennetto et al. (1996), for example, compared young people with high-functioning autism to clinical comparison group (see earlier for details). The ELWM measures included sentence span and counting span, both of which required participants to carry out processing (judging sentences or counting dots), whilst at the same time maintaining the results of these processes in working memory (storage). Bennetto et al. (1996) predicted that ELWM would be impaired in their sample of young people with autism, whereas a number of other memory measures without a high executive load, including cued recall and recognition memory, would not. This was exactly the result they found: individuals with autism obtained significantly lower scores on sentence and counting span, but not on the non-executive memory measures. Bennetto et al. (1996) argued that a general impairment in ELWM could be a core deficit in ASD.

Russell et al. (1996) included three measures of ELWM in a study described earlier, with children who had low-functioning autism. Please refer to Figure 8.1 in an earlier section, which includes the data for counting, odd-man-out and sums span relevant to the current discussion. For all three measures of ELWM, those with autism performed more poorly than typically developing children of comparable mental age. These results supported the claim that there is an ELWM deficit in those with autism.

However, Russell et al. (1996) included an important additional comparison group of children with general intellectual disability. These children also showed poorer ELWM. This means that, although there may be a deficit in ELWM in children with autism, it is not confined to or specific to autism and may be present in other more generalised forms of intellectual disability (note that this result is not without controversy, see Chapter 5).

Ozonoff and Strayer (2001) revisited the issue of ELWM in individuals with autism, but failed to find the same results as the two previous studies. They looked at 25 young people with high-functioning autism (age range 7 to 18 years, mean IQ 96) and 15 comparison participants with broadly similar ages (mean IQ 107). Several ELWM measures were employed: a running memory task which required participants to remember coloured shapes from trials either one or two items previously; a spatial working memory span task requiring participants to maintain the locations of one, three or five coloured shapes over a delay; and a box search task which involved finding items 'hidden' within boxes, but not revisiting earlier locations. Regardless of whether reaction time or accuracy was taken as the dependent measure, Ozonoff and Strayer (2001) found no group differences on any ELWM tasks.

These conflicting results are difficult to reconcile. Joseph, Steele et al. (2005) suggested that there may be differences in verbal ELWM but not non-verbal ELWM. They wondered whether individuals with autism were particularly impaired when they had to use 'verbal mediation' during ELWM tasks, in other words when they had to produce verbal labels in order to remember a series of items.

Accordingly, Joseph, Steele et al. (2005) used two versions of the self-ordered pointing test. In the non-verbal version, a set of between 4 and 12 abstract designs was presented repeatedly, in different spatial locations, on a sheet of paper. On each trial, the child was asked to point to a different item, so he or she needed to keep in mind the items that had already been pointed to and avoid touching them again. The task was executive-loaded, because it required concurrent processing (search for a 'new' item) and storage (remember items that have already been pointed to). In the verbal version, items were easily nameable pictures, to test whether the individuals with autism were able to use this strategy of 'verbal mediation' (using the picture names to aid memory). The reasoning was that if the pictures were labelled, participants would be able to utilise the phonological loop to maintain and rehearse the items that had already been pointed to.

Participants included 24 5- to 14-year-old children with autism (mean IQ 96) and a comparison group of 24 mostly typically developing children of the same age and IQ (note that a few children in both groups had measured IQ levels below the average range, so this sample can be described as broadly high-functioning with a few individuals with mild or borderline intellectual disabilities). The authors carefully matched the groups on language skills in order to rule out language differences as possible explanations for their results (individuals with autism generally have some degree of language difficulty).

The data are illustrated in Figure 8.4. There were no differences between the groups on the non-verbal self-ordered pointing task, whereas there were group differences on the verbal task. Joseph, Steele et al. (2005) concluded that children with autism had a specific difficulty in using verbal mediation strategies when carrying out ELWM tasks.

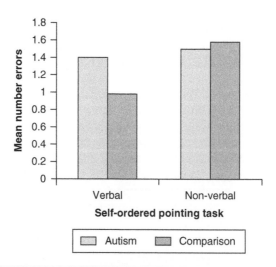

Figure 8.4   Mean performance on verbal versus non-verbal self-ordered pointing span tasks for children with autism and age/ability-matched typical comparison children

Source: data adapted from Joseph, Steele et al. (2005)

How did Joseph, Steele et al. (2005) account for the differences between their results and earlier studies? After all, the earlier studies had used a combination of verbal and non-verbal measures and found differences (or not) on both.

Joseph, Steele et al. (2005) speculated that the ELWM tasks used by Russell et al. (1996) may have caused difficulty for participants with low IQs, because of deficits in speed of information processing. The argument is that these tasks are particularly sensitive to slow speed of information processing, and Russell et al.'s participants were likely to have had both low IQ and low speed of information processing (see Chapter 5 for evidence that children with intellectual disabilities generally have slow speeds of information processing, e.g. Anderson, 2001). By contrast, Joseph, Steele et al. (2005) argued that Ozonoff and Strayer (2001) may have failed to find significant impairments in their autism group because the working memory demands of their tasks were not sufficiently high.

However, these arguments do remain speculative, and, unfortunately, a further study failed to support them. Williams et al. (2005) examined executive-loaded verbal and spatial working memory, this time in 55 high-functioning adults and young people with autism. There were also 69 comparison participants of the same age and IQ. The majority of the participants had ability levels in the average range (mean IQ scores were 109/110).

The first verbal working memory task was the N-back task, where a continuous stream of letters is presented and the participant must match the current item to an item 1-back or 2-back in the list. A second measure was the letter-number sequencing subtest from the Wechsler Memory Scale (Version 3). Spatial working memory was assessed using backwards Corsi span, which is analogous to backward digit span and, therefore, can be regarded as assessing ELWM. A similar forward spatial span measure was used for children. (Note that one can criticise the child measure as being a straightforward visuospatial working memory measure rather than an ELWM measure.)

Williams et al.'s (2005) results are illustrated in Figure 8.5. They found no significant differences between the groups with autism and the comparison groups (adults and children) on the verbal ELWM measures. However, there were significant differences on the spatial ELWM measures (again, for both adults and children). There was some evidence that adults outperformed children as would be expected. Based on these results, Williams et al. (2005) argued for intact verbal working memory alongside impaired spatial working memory in individuals with autism, quite the opposite argument to that of Joseph, Steele et al. (2005).

Therefore, we have one set of authors arguing for verbal ELWM deficits, and another arguing for spatial ELWM deficits (see also Luna et al., 2002). This debate will continue, as it represents a key point of interest in assessing the range of cognitive strengths and weaknesses in those with autism.

At present, some further evidence seems to favour the spatial working memory deficit, but perhaps only when task demands are relatively high. For example, Steele, Minshew, Luna and Sweeney (2007) replicated the finding

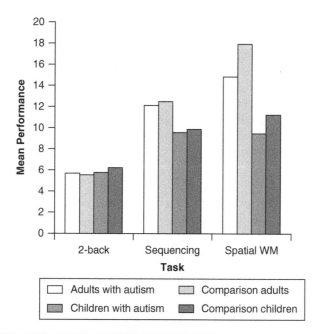

Figure 8.5   Mean performance on the N-back task (response times for the most demanding 2-back condition), letter-number sequencing and spatial working memory for adults and children with autism; and relevant age and IQ matched comparison groups

Source: data adapted from Williams et al. (2005)

of a spatial working memory deficit in a sample of high-functioning individuals with autism, using a demanding spatial working memory measure from the CANTAB battery (a large set of executive and other computerised tests). However, this study did not include a verbal working memory condition, so it cannot address the issue of differential verbal and spatial performance. Similarly, Joseph, McGrath and Tager-Flusberg (2005) examined performance on backwards word span and backwards spatial span, in samples of 37 school-age children with mixed high- and low-functioning autism and 31 comparison participants matched for age and IQ. Joseph, Steele et al. (2005) found that their participants with autism showed deficits on the spatial measure, but not the verbal measure.

However, one of the key difficulties in drawing conclusions regarding relative performance on verbal versus spatial ELWM tests is ensuring that the two types of tasks have been matched for difficulty level. If not, any significant differences between the measures could simply reflect task difficulty and not true modality differences (Williams, Minshew & Goldstein, 2008).

Many have argued that we should expect to see ELWM deficits in those with autism/ASD, given some of the difficulties that are characteristic of this disorder.

However, further research is required to settle the debate regarding verbal/ spatial working memory impairments. It is equally important to examine whether any such impairments are *specific* to autism, rather than ID. Another important issue is to look at visual measures of ELWM, as most of the studies we have reviewed focused on spatial tasks and there may be differences between executive-loaded visual versus spatial measures.

We finish this section with an interesting finding in relation to verbal ELWM and brain activation in adults with high-functioning autism (see Debates and Issues 8.1 box below).

Debates and Issues 8.1 Brain activation and executive-loaded working memory (ELWM)

Koshino, Carpenter, Minshew, Cherkassky, Keller and Just (2005) were interested in the brain regions that were activated when young adults with high-functioning autism (n = 14) carried out a verbal ELWM task, the 'N-back task'. Their version of this task required participants to listen to sequences of letters (20 in this case, presented on a viewing screen one at a time for 500 ms each with a 1000 ms gap between each one). Participants were given three conditions in which they: (1) responded to one particular target letter (0-back); *or* (2) responded when any two consecutive letters matched (1-back); *or* (3) responded when any letter matched that of two letters ago (2-back). Clearly, the working memory demands are negligible in the 0-back condition, modest in the 1-back condition, but higher in the 2-back condition. The comparison group included 14 community volunteers matched for IQ, age, gender, race and socio-economic status.

Koshino et al. (2005) found that neither reaction times nor error rates were different between the two groups, supporting the view that *verbal* ELWM did not differ in those with high-functioning autism (see above). However, *brain activation* did differ between the groups. First, although the comparison adults showed activation in both left and right frontal regions, those with autism showed *less* activation in the left frontal regions. Second, adults with autism showed *greater* activation than comparisons in the right hemisphere parietal regions.

Koshino et al. (2005) speculated that individuals with autism might be less likely to use *verbal processing* strategies (e.g. verbal coding of letters, left hemisphere) and more likely to use visuospatial processing strategies (e.g. visualisation methods, right hemisphere), based on these brain activation differences.

Therefore, there may be differences in *cognitive processing* style in those with autism, in relation to ELWM tasks. Even if the actual scores on such tasks are similar, the brain regions recruited to carry them out may differ in those with and without autism. Do keep in mind, however, that we must take care in generalising these conclusions; similar work needs to be done with children and those with lower functioning ASD.

Summary

With respect to executive-loaded working memory (ELWM), the safest conclusion to draw at present is that individuals with autism/ASD may have difficulties with more demanding tasks, particularly in the spatial domain. However, the findings in this area are contradictory, so caution must be used in making strong claims. In relation to high- versus low-functioning individuals with autism/ASD, there was no particular evidence in the studies reviewed here to suggest notable differences in relation to specific deficits (or not) in ELWM. However, as noted in previous sections, there is less research on low-functioning individuals with autism. It remains possible that some differences between findings in relation to ELWM could be accounted for by level of cognitive functioning.

Other measures of the central executive

In contrast to the contradictory evidence for ELWM impairments in ASD, there is strong evidence for a range of deficits in several other areas of executive functioning (EF). We will consider a few studies that investigate the areas of planning, switching (or set shifting/mental flexibility), fluency and inhibition.

Pennington and Ozonoff (1996), in a now classic review of executive impairments and developmental disorders (very useful for essays – see Further reading at the end of the chapter), noted that 13 of the 14 well-controlled studies they examined found better executive performance in comparison groups than in individuals with autism (this amounted to 25 tasks out of the 32 reported). The effect size, an indication of how large the differences were overall, was nearly one standard deviation, indicating large and 'clinically meaningful' differences.

However, a weakness in some of the studies reviewed by Pennington and Ozonoff (1996) was the failure to account for the co-morbidity of autism/ASD with other disorders. If an individual has two disorders, it is not easy to distinguish whether any deficits that are found are due to autism, the other disorder, or having both disorders together. Another issue concerns high- versus low-functioning individuals with autism. One of the goals of this chapter is to examine whether research findings differ in relation to whether or not autism is accompanied by an intellectual disability. Therefore, we will now look at some of the key studies from the Pennington and Ozonoff (1996) review, as well as more recent work, and attempt to assess the research findings in relation to high- versus low-functioning individuals with autism. A very good additional source of information in this area is Hill (2004), listed in the Further reading at the end of the chapter.

Planning/problem-solving and switching (set shifting/mental flexibility)

Overall, there is robust evidence for impairments in planning and switching among individuals with autism (please refer back to Chapter 2 for details about these and other executive tasks). Several relevant studies will be reviewed in this section.

For example, Rumsey and Hamburger (1988) looked at ten men with autism who had average IQs. By including only those with average IQs (i.e. high-functioning individuals with autism), the authors avoided one potential problem, that poor performance on the EF tasks may simply be a result of intellectual disability and not autism. There were ten comparison participants, broadly matched for IQ, reading, spelling, maths ability and educational level. Note that this was quite a small sample, containing only men, but the participants were well-matched.

A detailed battery of tests thoroughly examined visual and perceptual abilities, sensory perceptual abilities, motor skills, language skills and memory skills. These were all control, or 'non-executive' tasks. The executive function tasks were the Wisconsin Card Sorting Test (WCST), the Trail Making test and a selection of problem-solving tests. These measures, therefore, examined switching (mental flexibility/shifting) and problem solving. Figure 8.6 illustrates the results, namely that those with autism showed dramatic difficulties on all three EF measures (note that longer times on the Trail Making Test represent poorer performance). There were also small deficits in language skills (as we would expect), but visual perception, motor skills, sensory perceptual skills and memory were all largely intact.

Even though these were high-functioning adults with autism, they still showed clear and relatively specific deficits in EF. This study supported the view that there were difficulties with planning and switching in adults with autism.

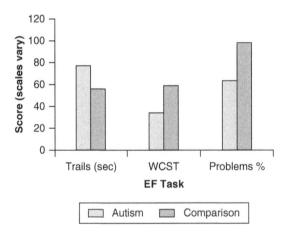

Figure 8.6   Mean performance of individuals with autism and matched comparison groups on three executive functioning measures (WCST, Trail Making Test, problem-solving)

Source: data adapted from Rumsey and Hamburger (1988)

Prior and Hoffman (1990) carried out a similar study, extending these findings to children. They looked at 12 children with autism (IQ = 88, age 13 years) and 12 comparison children of the same average age and IQ (IQ = 100). A range of EF tasks were administered including: the Milner Maze (planning); a simplified version of the WCST (switching); and the Rey-Osterrieth Complex Figure Copying Test (a test of visual memory and organisational abilities).

Children with autism performed more poorly on the Milner Maze (more errors, longer time to complete) and on the WCST (more perseverative errors and fewer correct responses). They were also less able to recall the Rey figure from memory, although other aspects of their performance were intact (e.g. copying the figure). Prior and Hoffman (1990) noted of their children with autism: 'for the most part, they were unable to learn effectively by their mistakes' (p. 588).

Note, however, that there was a mean IQ difference between the groups in the Prior and Hoffman (1990) study of 12 points. Therefore, later research was careful to closely match the children with and without autism for IQ to avoid the criticism that any differences on EF performance between groups could be accounted for by differences in IQ.

For example, Ozonoff, Pennington and Rogers (1991) examined 23 young people with autism (IQ = 90) and used 20 carefully matched comparison children (IQ = 91) from a special education department (children had specific learning disabilities, dyslexia, mild ID, ADHD). In particular, 25% of the controls had co-morbid ADHD, which the authors had to control for as this disorder is also associated with EF deficits. Many tests were administered, but for simplicity, we will focus only on the EF tests that were used, the Tower of Hanoi (a measure of planning) and the WCST (a measure of switching).

As can be seen in Figure 8.7, there were clear differences between the two groups on EF performance: efficiency on the Tower of Hanoi was lower in those with autism; and on the WCST, those with autism made more perseverative responses (failures to switch set when appropriate).

Even taking account of the 25% of the comparison sample who had ADHD (using statistical controls), those with autism were still poorer on the EF tasks. Therefore, this study provided strong evidence for specific EF difficulties in children with autism, with both switching and planning. To check these findings, Ozonoff and McEvoy (1994) followed up the same samples after three years, finding that the (now) adolescents with autism showed no evidence of improving on the EF tasks, whereas, those in the comparison group had improved slightly. The authors concluded that 'Deficits in executive function persist with time and improve little as MA (mental age) increases' (p. 422) and that '... executive function impairment may be a good candidate for a primary deficit of autism' (p. 423).

Finally, Hughes, Russell and Robbins (1994) pointed out that many of the studies of EF difficulties in autism had used predominantly or exclusively high-functioning participants. Therefore, Hughes et al. (1994) carried out a study involving 35 children with autism (7–18 years) who had a range of abilities, but were mainly lower functioning (mean mental age of the sample was 8 years).

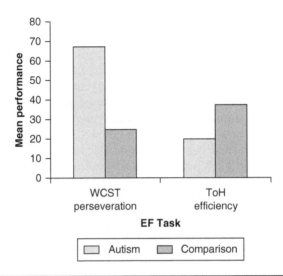

Figure 8.7   Mean performance of children with autism and matched clinical comparison groups on two measures of EF performance

Source: data adapted from Ozonoff et al. (1991)

Two comparison groups included: 38 young people with moderate intellectual disabilities (MID; age 7–18 years; mean mental age 8 years); and 45 typically developing children (mean age 8 years). These comparison groups allowed the authors to test whether having an intellectual disability *per se* might lead to problems with executive functioning, or whether executive difficulties were specific to autism, regardless of intellectual disability.

There were several control tasks to check whether impairments might be specific to EF (these included discrimination learning, visual attention, sensorimotor coordination). The two EF tests assessed planning (Tower of London) and switching ('Intra-dimensional/Extra-dimensional shift' or IED task). Using a pass-fail criterion, Hughes et al. (1994) found that:

- 67% of those with autism failed both EF tests
- 27% of those with MID failed both tests
- 7% of the typically developing comparisons failed both tests

Therefore, having MID lowered performance on EF tests a little, but those with autism were even more impaired. Children with autism showed perseveration and difficulty in transferring their learning to new situations, whereas children with MID were more likely to have difficulty in sustaining attention. The difficulties were not found on the control tasks, they were specific to switching and planning. Therefore, this study supported the view that EF weaknesses were a core difficulty in autism and, therefore, present in those with low- and high-functioning autism.

Therefore, there is good evidence from the studies we have reviewed that individuals with both high- and low-functioning autism have difficulty with two key executive tasks: switching (particularly with respect to 'perseveration', which means returning to the same response over and over again); and planning. If you would like to read about more recent studies that have found similar results, please refer to the following papers in the overall reference section at the end of the book: Geurts et al. (2004); Joseph, McGrath and Tager-Flusberg (2005 – planning only); Ozonoff and Jensen (1999); Robinson, Goddard, Dritschel, Wisley and Howlin (2009).

One final point concerns the question of whether family members of those with autism show evidence of impaired EF skills. Hughes et al. (1999) found that siblings of those with autism were more likely to perform poorly on an attentional flexibility task (ID/ED). Similarly, fewer siblings of those with autism performed perfectly on a 5-item Tower of London task. This suggests that there is a wider 'cognitive phenotype' for autism. In other words, very mild forms of EF difficulties may persist in family members of those with autism, which supports the notion of genetic transmission.

Summary
Experimental evidence suggests that individuals with autism, whether high- or low-functioning, have difficulties with switching and planning. There is relatively good agreement about this in the literature (e.g. see Liss et al., 2001).

Fluency

There is a small body of literature on fluency tasks, and it largely points to those with autism having difficulties. One of the most thorough studies was carried out by Turner (1999). Groups of 22 high- and low-functioning individuals with autism (ages 6–32 years) were compared to similar numbers of high- and low-functioning clinical comparison children and adults (referred to psychiatry services, but without autism; note that the low-functioning comparison group had intellectual disabilities). Both groups were closely matched for age and IQ. The measures of fluency included: category and letter fluency (see Chapter 2); ideational fluency (e.g. think of as many uses for 'newspaper' as possible); and design fluency (see Chapter 2). Turner (1999) found that individuals with autism at both levels of ability (high- and low-functioning) showed marked impairments in performance on the fluency tasks, compared to the comparison groups.

Geurts et al. (2004) also examined fluency, among a number of other areas of executive functioning, in a large study that we will come back to in the next section. Children in three clinical groups were rigorously defined and diagnosed: high-functioning autism (n = 54, mean IQ 98); ADHD with some co-morbid conduct disorder (n = 41, mean IQ 100); and a typically developing comparison group (n = 41, mean IQ 112). All participants were between the ages of 6 and 13 years with IQs in the average range. Geurts et al. (2004) included measures of verbal fluency (for letters and categories), and found that the children with autism (and ADHD) performed more poorly on these tasks than the typical comparison group (even when group differences in IQ were statistically controlled).

Bishop and Norbury (2005a) obtained similar findings. They assessed 14 6- to 10-year-old boys with high-functioning autism (non-verbal IQs of 80 or greater) on two ideational fluency measures (thinking about the possible uses for objects and describing meaningless line drawings). These children were compared with 18 typically developing children who did not differ significantly in terms of IQ (111 versus 107). Bishop and Norbury (2005a) found that the children with autism obtained significantly lower scores in terms of percentage correctly generated responses than the typical comparison group, replicating previous findings of a fluency difficulty among children with autism.

Finally, Robinson et al. (2009) assessed a large sample of children and young people with Asperger syndrome or high-functioning autism (n = 54). All participants were between the ages of 7 and 18 years with IQs between 70 and 130. They were compared to individually matched typically developing children who had the same age, gender and IQ (n = 54). On a verbal fluency measure (generating names of animals, fruit/vegetables, clothes), the number of correct responses did not differ between the groups. However, those with autism made significantly more perseverations, indicating that they were more likely to repeat their responses.

Summary

There is reasonably consistent evidence, using a variety of measures, that fluency is impaired in children with autism. Although there is relatively little research comparing those in the low- and high-functioning range, the one study to date to have done so (Turner, 1999), found no evidence that findings varied according to cognitive level. Therefore, we may tentatively conclude that there are difficulties with fluency in both high- and low-functioning children with autism.

Inhibition

The presence or absence of impairments in inhibition among those with autism is somewhat unclear at present, as will be seen from the review below.

One study to have found no evidence for inhibition difficulties was carried out by Ozonoff and Jensen (1999). These authors compared the profiles of executive functions in children with three different developmental disorders: autism; Tourette syndrome; and ADHD. Based on existing research, it was hypothesised that those with autism would have specific difficulties with switching and planning (see earlier section), but would not show difficulties with inhibition (the inhibition of prepotent responses). By contrast, those with ADHD were predicted to show difficulty in sustaining attention and inhibiting behaviour, whereas, those with Tourette syndrome were predicted to show difficulties only with inhibition.

Ozonoff and Jensen (1999) included children with high-functioning autism (n = 40); children with Tourette syndrome (n = 30); children with ADHD (n = 24); and typically developing comparisons (n = 29). All had mean ages of 11–12 years and IQs in the normal range, but there were small IQ differences between groups (the groups with autism and Tourette syndrome had slightly lower IQs), which were statistically controlled in the analyses. Three EF tests were used: the WCST to measure flexibility/switching; the Tower of Hanoi to measure planning; and the Stroop Colour-Word Test to measure inhibition of prepotent responses.

We have already seen that there is good evidence for planning and switching difficulties in those with autism, and the authors replicated these findings. However, Ozonoff and Jensen (1999) did not find any evidence for impairments in inhibition. Although there were no controls for co-morbid disorders in this study, this may well have acted to make the results even more compelling. This is because co-morbid disorders might themselves have made it more likely that impairments in inhibition were found (e.g. ADHD is associated with inhibition difficulties and some children with autism also have ADHD). Ozonoff and Jensen (1999) did in fact find that the ADHD sample showed difficulties with inhibition.

Similarly, Russell et al. (1999) assessed the performance of children with low-functioning autism on two measures of inhibition, and found no evidence for difficulties. The first task used by Russell et al. (1999) was the 'tubes' task in which children had to track a ball that travelled through an opaque tube from top to bottom, rather like a marble run game. The tube was not straight, but followed a meandering path such that the ball would never drop directly down vertically in a straight line. The child was required to search for the ball in one of three 'catch' trays at the bottom. This task required inhibition, because the temptation would be to assume that the ball would drop vertically, straight down into the catch tray directly below, yet this never happened.

Russell et al. (1999) reported that the performance of 24 children with low-functioning autism (chronological ages 6:1–16:10; mental ages 1:8–5:6) on the tubes task did not differ from typically developing 3-year-olds tested in a previous study. A second study using the 'day/night task', in which children had to say 'night' when they saw a picture of 'day' and vice versa, found similar results. Children with low-functioning autism (n = 19, CA = 13; MA = 7) showed similar performance to typical children matched for verbal mental age (n = 19, CA/MA = 7).

These two studies seemed to provide a consistent picture of unimpaired performance on inhibition tasks among those with both low- and high-functioning autism.

Unfortunately, Geurts et al. (2004) did not replicate these findings. These authors examined inhibition, among a number of other areas of executive functioning, in a study mentioned earlier. Recall that there were large samples of children in three clinical groups: high-functioning autism; ADHD; and a typically developing comparison group. Geurts et al. (2004) included a well-established measure of inhibition (the 'opposite worlds test' from the TEA-Ch: see Chapter 2), as well as measures of working memory (self-ordered pointing), planning (Tower of London), switching/mental flexibility (WCST) and verbal fluency.

The findings were that children with high-functioning autism showed difficulties with inhibition (there were also difficulties with planning, switching and verbal fluency, but no difficulties with working memory – consistent with our earlier sections). Therefore, Geurts et al.'s (2004) findings of impairments in inhibition among children with autism contrasted with the Ozonoff and Jensen (1999) and Russell et al. (1999) studies reviewed earlier.

There are also at least two other studies that reported evidence for some difficulties with inhibition in high-functioning children with autism. Robinson et al. (2009), in a study mentioned earlier, found that children and young people with Asperger syndrome had more trouble filling in 'incongruent' (nonsensical) words on the Hayling Sentence Completion task and made more errors on the Stroop task. However, Joseph, McGrath and Tager-Flusberg (2005) found impairments on one measure of inhibition (like Luria's hand game), but not on another (the Day-Night task) in a sample of 37 schoolchildren with autism.

How might we resolve these conflicting findings? The Debates and Issues 8.2 box below considers one possible explanation.

Debates and Issues 8.2 The role of verbal 'self-reminding' or inner speech in executive tasks

Russell et al. (1999) argued that there is a difference between the Day-Night task and other measures of inhibition such as Luria's hand game. In the Day-Night task, the person must make a verbal response, saying 'day' in response to a picture of night, and 'night' in response to a picture of day. The requirement to make verbal responses, according to Russell et al. (1999) prevents the person from using inner speech, or verbal 'self-reminding', *during* the task to keep in mind the rules of the task.

By contrast, Luria's hand game requires the participant to copy one of two hand gestures; or to produce the opposite hand gesture in each case. There is no verbal response, so the person is able to use inner speech, or verbal self-reminding, as a method of keeping the rules of the game constantly in mind.

Russell et al.'s argument is that individuals with autism do not use verbal self-reminding. Therefore, those with autism perform no worse than comparison participants without autism on the day-night task, because *neither* group can use self-reminding. Conversely, on Luria's hand game the individuals with autism are at a disadvantage, because they are not able to use self-reminding and, therefore, show poorer performance on this task.

This is a very interesting perspective, but it is by no means conclusive. It is not yet entirely clear whether verbal self-reminding or inner speech is routinely used in executive tasks. However, recent work has begun to test the role of inner speech in executive tasks in more detail. For example, see Lidstone, Meins and Fernyhough (2010) in relation to the Tower of London task with typical children.

Therefore, some of the contradictory results in relation to inhibition may be accounted for by the use or otherwise of verbal self-reminding (inner speech). However, as we saw earlier, there is considerable debate over whether individuals with autism use inner speech in a typical manner, with some arguing that they do. In future research, it would be desirable to include several different measures of inhibition in the same study, some that encourage or facilitate the use of inner speech, and some that prevent the use of inner speech to directly test Russell et al.'s proposals. Another important issue is to evaluate whether difficulties with verbal self-regulation/inner speech and inhibition vary in terms of those with high- versus low-functioning autism. Inner speech develops with age in typical children (see Chapter 4), and may do so in relation to mental age in children with autism (Williams, Happé and Jarrold, 2008).

Summary
There is no real agreement in the literature as to whether children with autism/ASD show impairments in the executive area of inhibition. These findings are equally unclear in relation to both low- and high-functioning individuals; and further research will be required before firm conclusions can be drawn. It may be that differences between inhibition tasks in terms of the extent to which inner speech can be used to guide behaviour account for some of the conflicting findings.

Section Summary
The research evidence is consistent in showing that children with autism/ASD show difficulties with planning, switching and fluency across a range of experimental tasks. The evidence concerning executive-loaded working memory remains somewhat contradictory, although some argue that there may be specific difficulties with executive-loaded measures of spatial memory. With respect to inhibition, the research evidence is also contradictory, such that no strong conclusions can be drawn at present.

Most of these conclusions seem to apply equally to both low- and high-functioning individuals with autism/ASD. However, as far more research to date has focused on high-functioning individuals, differences based on cognitive abilities cannot be entirely ruled out.

How are executive deficits related to autism?

Lopez, Lincoln, Ozonoff and Lai (2005) have argued that the restrictive, repetitive behaviours that are characteristic of individuals with autism can be linked to their performance on executive tasks. Specifically, Lopez et al. (2005) found that three executive skills, namely switching, executive-loaded working memory and inhibition (but not fluency and planning), were highly related to measures of restrictive, repetitive symptoms in adults with ASD. Kenworthy, Black, Harrison, della Rosa and Wallace (2009) carried out a similar study in relation to children with high-functioning ASD, replicating the finding that set shifting/flexibility was related to restricted and repetitive behaviour symptoms; but they also reported that semantic fluency was related to the level of communicative difficulties and to social symptoms (dual task performance was also related to social symptoms).

The question remains, why should executive impairments relate to the types of symptoms and behaviours shown by those with ASD? Some authors have proposed that the executive difficulties experienced by those with autism/ ASD stem from a failure to use internal self-directed speech on complex, novel tasks (e.g. Russell et al., 1999). This means that they do not 'remind' themselves using internal self-talk about the rules and relevant information required to carry out executive tasks. We saw earlier how this theory might apply to the contradictory results concerning inhibition, in the 'debates and issues' box in the previous section.

It is worth briefly considering why individuals with autism might not use inner speech. Russell et al. (1999) argued that individuals with autism have a weak or unusual grasp of self-hood, therefore, they do not show evidence of 'self-monitoring' in many areas, including using inner speech to self-remind during complex tasks. Whether or not individuals with autism use inner speech more generally is a somewhat vexed issue, however. We have already seen that there is considerable debate concerning whether individuals with autism use inner speech in short-term memory tasks, with some studies arguing that they do, and others arguing that they do not (see earlier section on verbal rehearsal). However, in relation to the use of inner speech during complex problem-solving tasks, such as the executive tasks we have been discussing, there are reports of difficulties (e.g. Wallace et al., 2009; Whitehouse et al., 2006).

Liss et al. (2001) considered the issue of whether executive difficulties cause autism. They pointed out that in order to support this conclusion, one must show that:

> executive functioning deficits of the same type and degree are not present in other disorders. (p. 263)

In other words, we need to show that there is a particular range of executive difficulties that are found in autism, but not in other disorders. This is often referred to as the problem of 'discriminant validity'. Many authors have pointed out that executive difficulties can be found in so many developmental disorders, that it becomes difficult to state that having an executive deficit is a distinguishing feature of any one particular disorder. One partial answer to this question is to focus on profiles of executive impairment, carefully delineating the types of executive skills that are impaired (or not) in each developmental disorder examined. In the case of autism, difficulties with switching, planning and fluency seem to be most consistent executive difficulties, as we have seen.

Another approach to addressing the discriminant validity problem is to compare two or more different developmental disorders in order to test whether their profiles of executive skills are comparable or not. Liss et al. (2001) did just that, comparing 34 9-year-old children with specific language impairment to 21 children with high-functioning autism (groups were matched for age, socio-economic status, full-scale IQ and non-verbal IQ, but a difference in verbal IQ remained).

Clearly, both of these groups are expected to have difficulties with language and communication, and this is one good reason for choosing to compare these two developmental disorders. Might there be common difficulties that are related to language problems, rather than other aspects of these developmental disorders? In fact, a measure of communication did demonstrate that both groups were equally impaired in terms of communication (Vineland Communication Scale).

As illustrated in Figure 8.8, the groups did not differ in their performance on a planning measure ('Mazes' from the WISC-R), whereas there were differences in the number of perseverative errors on the Wisconsin Card Sorting Test (WCST). However, other aspects of performance on the WCST (number of categories correctly sorted and total number correct) did not differ between the groups. More importantly, when the differences in verbal IQ between the groups were statistically controlled, even the perseveration difference disappeared.

Therefore, children with SLI and high-functioning autism were no different in their performance on executive tasks when verbal IQ was controlled. Liss et al. (2001) suggested that the difficulties experienced by children with autism

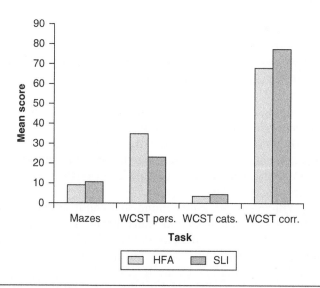

Figure 8.8   Mean performance on a range of executive measures by children with specific language impairment (SLI) and high-functioning autism (HFA)

Source: data adapted from Liss et al. (2001)

on executive measures might be accounted for by their language problems. Joseph, McGrath and Tager-Flusberg (2005), similarly, argued that individuals with autism simply do not use inner speech to mediate problem-solving (this is, after all, almost a defining feature of their disorder), so that the quality of their language skills *per se* was irrelevant.

Other authors have examined the links between executive difficulties and other characteristics of ASD such as theory of mind (see Hill, 2008). Finally, it is worth bearing in mind that not all individuals with ASD have weak executive performance. Hill and Bird (2006) found that some individuals with Asperger syndrome showed good EF performance, so EF difficulties may not be universal in individuals with ASD.

Summary

Executive skills seem to be linked to the symptoms of autism, i.e. repetitive restrictive behaviour. Some have argued that those with autism show weak performance on executive tasks, because they have poor language skills and/or fail to use inner speech to help them in problem-solving tasks. This area requires further research, however, as the role of inner speech in various different executive tasks needs further clarification. Also, the use of inner speech by children with autism is still a matter of debate, as we have seen in an earlier section. Therefore, the issue of whether executive tasks can discriminate between different types of developmental disorders (and why) is not yet resolved.

The episodic buffer

One of the more well-established findings in the literature on memory in those with autism is that remembering 'episodes' or connected information is impaired. We referred to this in our overview on memory and ASD at the beginning of the chapter, and there are many demonstrations of this effect. Two brief examples will be described, taken from studies of children with high-functioning autism/ASD. This work is argued to be relevant for the proposed episodic buffer, because binding information from different working memory systems with existing knowledge is required for remembering coherent episodes.

Firstly, Williams et al. (2006) found that children with autism were less able to remember sentences and short stories than comparison children with typical development (despite the fact that they were equally good at remembering unconnected words). Secondly, Bruck, London, Landa and Goodman (2007) found that children with ASD were less able to remember details of personally experienced events from 'autobiographical memory' (for example, an event that happened to them two years ago); or details about a staged magic show they witnessed 12 days previously. Children with autism did not necessarily make more errors, they simply left more information out.

Another relatively well-established finding is that individuals with autism begin to struggle on memory tasks when the level of complexity is increased. These two findings may be linked; clearly, remembering coherent episodes is far more complicated than remembering unrelated information. (See also chapters by Salmond et al., 2008; Lind & Bowler, 2008; and Williams, Minshew and Goldstein, 2008, in *Memory in Autism* referenced under Further reading at the end of this chapter).

However, another implication of these findings is that the functioning of the episodic buffer in those with ASD/autism may be impaired. After all, this is the component of working memory that helps integrate or bind information from long-term memory with the results of current processing in other components of working memory, to produce memories of 'coherent' episodes and possibly the experience of conscious awareness. Alternatively, working memory processes in individuals with autism may be intact, but hampered by a cognitive processing style that does not lend itself to remembering coherent episodes. For example, the way in which information is 'bound' together in the episodic buffer may not be typical in those with ASD/autism. We will have a look at one study that may support this conclusion.

Mottron, Morasse and Belleville (2001) examined episodic memory in 14 high-functioning (mean IQ 103) individuals with autism (age 11–40 years), comparing them to 14 typically functioning individuals matched for age and verbal IQ. The task was to remember lists of 15 concrete nouns (e.g. BROCCOLI) that were presented on a computer screen in a 5 x 3 matrix. There were three separate conditions with different lists of words; but each word list contained one item from each of 15 taxonomic categories (e.g. vegetables, transport, furniture, drinks etc.).

Participants were shown the 15 words from each list, in differently ordered matrices each time, and asked to find each word individually. The experimental manipulation concerned how they were asked to search for each word. They could simply be asked to find the word (no encoding); they could be asked to find an example from a particular category (e.g. transport – semantic encoding); or they could be asked to search based on the initial syllable (syllabic encoding). To give a concrete example, participants might be asked to (1) find the word 'broccoli' in the no encoding condition; (2) find the name of a vegetable in the semantic encoding condition; and (3) find the word starting with 'BRO' in the syllabic encoding condition.

This manipulation means that for some lists the processing of the items is at a semantic level (enabling us to examine the extent to which semantic information is used in memory – i.e. giving us some insight into the operation of the episodic buffer). It is based on an approach known as 'Levels of Processing' (Craik & Lockhart, 1972) which states that items processed at 'deeper' levels (i.e. semantic as opposed to visual or syllabic) will be better remembered.

The question was, would individuals with autism show this 'Levels of Processing' effect? In fact, they did. Both groups were better at recalling words after semantic encoding (around nine words) than no encoding

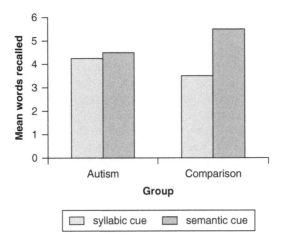

Figure 8.9   Mean extra words recalled after semantic or syllabic cues for those with autism and comparison individuals

Source: data adapted from Mottron et al. (2001)

(around seven words). Therefore, individuals with autism utilised semantic information to support episodic memory to the same extent as comparison participants. Moreover, those with autism showed no deficit in their levels of free recall compared to the comparison group, supporting a second conclusion that there was no overall episodic memory deficit in those with autism. This is a result also found by others including Tager-Flusberg (1986).

The next question was, could they get the participants to recall some of the words they had not managed to remember first time round by giving them extra clues? Here, we would expect that semantic cues (e.g. 'Can you remember which word in the list was a vegetable?') should operate more efficiently than syllabic cues (e.g. 'Can you remember which word started with 'BRO'?'), because semantic coding is 'deeper' and more effective. The results showed that this was the case for the typical comparison participants, but not for those with autism as illustrated in Figure 8.9.

Therefore, individuals with autism showed equal benefit from syllabic (lower level) and semantic (higher level) cues; unlike the comparison group participants who derived more benefit from higher level cues. Note that overall levels of recall did not differ between the groups, just the responsiveness to different cues. This finding ties in with the known bias towards lower-level processing in ASD, which forms part of the 'Central Coherence' theory (Frith, 1989). It may be, therefore, that there is no actual deficit in episodic memory (or the functioning of the episodic buffer to bind information together from long-term memory and current processing) in those with autism. Rather, individuals with autism may show a preference towards lower level processing that sometimes leads to differences in their utilisation of long-term memory knowledge.

Summary

It is possible that individuals with autism/ASD may show a preference towards lower level processing, which has an impact on their episodic memory. It does, however, remain methodologically challenging to demonstrate the difference between an impairment in the functioning of the episodic buffer versus a difference in processing style. Another issue that needs research attention is the potential differences between individuals with high- and low-functioning autism/ASD. The studies reviewed in this section have not included participants with low-functioning autism, so conclusions are necessarily limited.

Overall summary

Autism spectrum disorders (ASD) refer to a range of heterogeneous, lifelong developmental disorders of early onset that are characterised by difficulties in three areas: (1) reciprocal social interaction; (2) communication; and (3) restricted/repetitive behaviours and interests. In considering whether children with low- and high-functioning ASD showed difficulties with working memory, we encountered several areas of considerable debate. However, there were some areas of more consistent agreement, and each are summarised below.

The phonological loop

There was little evidence that children with either high- or low-functioning autism showed deficits on phonological short-term memory (PSTM) tasks, compared to typical comparison children matched for mental age. However, there was much less agreement when we moved on to considering how children with autism/ASD might carry out PSTM tasks (i.e. do individuals with ASD use 'inner speech'?). Inner speech in this context refers to verbal coding and verbal rehearsal, and these skills are closely associated with the phonological loop. It was not possible to determine with any certainty whether impairments in inner speech were present or not, because of the contradictory nature of the findings. Given the language weaknesses of most individuals with ASD, the debate surrounding their use of inner speech in PSTM (and other) tasks is likely to continue.

The visuospatial sketchpad

Although there was relatively little research into visuospatial short-term memory (VSSTM) in children with autism/ASD, a handful of studies suggested that both its visual and spatial components might be impaired. If corroborated, this would be a very interesting finding, as there is other evidence that individuals with ASD might prefer to use non-verbal strategies in carrying out working memory and other cognitive tasks. We would then face something of a conundrum: the preferred cognitive style of individuals with ASD might reflect a working memory weakness. However, much more research into both performance levels and strategic approaches to VSSTM tasks in those with ASD is necessary before such a speculation can be assessed properly.

The central executive

In terms of central executive functioning, there was a large and reasonably consistent literature showing that children with autism/ASD had difficulties with three key executive skills: planning, switching and fluency. The evidence concerning executive-loaded working memory (ELWM) and inhibition was, unfortunately, contradictory. This may, in itself, suggest that even if there are impairments in these areas, they could be less marked. The findings in relation to measures of ELWM were particularly strongly contested, with some arguing that there are modality specific difficulties in relation to spatial but not verbal ELWM tasks. Again, however, further research will be necessary before defininte conclusions in this area can be drawn.

The episodic buffer

With respect to the episodic buffer, individuals with autism/ASD have been reported to find remembering 'episodes' or connected information more difficult than typical comparison groups matched for mental age. This could be a sign of difficulties in binding information together into coherent episodes. However, it is also possible that such difficulties could reflect a preference for lower over higher level processing, consistent with the Central Coherence theory. This is another area that would, therefore, benefit from more detailed research.

Clearly, there are many interesting areas of controversy and agreement in relation to working memory in individuals with autism/ASD. One key area for future research is to look carefully not only at performance levels on working memory tasks, but also to consider the strategies and resources that have been used. In particular, it will be worth investigating both verbal and non-verbal strategic processes in relation to both verbal and visuospatial working memory tasks. A longitudinal approach that tracks children through development would also be helpful, as maturational changes in strategic processes may differ in those with and without ASD.

Finally, although most of the conclusions reached in this chapter seemed to apply equally to both low- and high-functioning children with autism/ASD, most research to date has concentrated on high-functioning individuals. Therefore, possible differences between low- and high-functioning individuals cannot be entirely ruled out at present, and more research including individuals with a range of abilities would be extremely valuable.

Further reading

Chapters, books and reviews

Boucher, J. & Bowler, D. (2008). *Memory in autism: Theory and evidence*. Cambridge: Cambridge University Press. This edited volume contains numerous useful papers on a wide range of aspects of memory in individuals with autism. Chapters 7 and 12 are particularly relevant.

Hill, E.L. (2004). Evaluating the theory of executive dysfunction in autism. *Developmental Review*, 24, 189–233. A very well-written review of the area.

Hill, E.L. (2008). Executive functioning in autism spectrum disorder: Where it fits in the causal model. In E. McGregor, M. Núñez, K. Cebula and J.C. Gómez (Eds.), *Autism: An integrated view from neurocognitive, clinical, and intervention research* (pp. 143–165). Oxford: Blackwell Publishing Ltd. A very helpful chapter that reviews executive functioning and links it with other skills.

Pennington, B.F. & Ozonoff, S. (1996). Executive functions and developmental psychopathology. *Journal of Child Psychology and Psychiatry, 37*(1), 51–87. This is a great paper that reviews EF in four developmental disorders including autism. Very useful background reading for essays and good for comparing different disorders (ADHD, Tourette syndrome, conduct disorder).

Van Engeland, H. & Buitelaar, J.K. (2008). Autism spectrum disorders. In M. Rutter, D. Bishop, D. Pine, S. Scott, J. Stevenson, E. Taylor & A. Thapar (Eds.), *Rutter's child and adolescent psychiatry*, 5th ed. (pp. 759–781). Oxford: Blackwell Publishing Ltd. A thorough and in-depth chapter about ASD generally.

Volkmar, F.R., Lord, C., Bailey, A., Schultz, R.T. & Klin, A. (2004). Autism and pervasive developmental disorders. *Journal of Child Psychology and Psychiatry, 45*(1), 135–170. An in-depth, research-focused general review of the disorder.

Experimental papers

These are listed in the order that they are mentioned in the chapter, rather than in alphabetical order.

Geurts, H.M., Verte, S., Oosterlaan, J., Roeyers, H. & Sergeant, J.A. (2004). How specific are executive functioning deficits in attention deficit hyperactivity disorder and autism? *Journal of Child Psychology and Psychiatry, 45*(4), 836–854. A thorough study of executive functioning.

Bennetto, L., Pennington, B.F. & Rogers, S.J. (1996). Intact and impaired memory functions in autism. *Child Development, 67*, 1816–1835. Thorough and useful for phonological short-term memory as well as executive-loaded working memory.

Russell, J., Jarrold, C. & Henry, L. (1996). Working memory in children with autism and with moderate learning difficulties. *Journal of Child Psychology and Psychiatry, 37*, 673–686. Also useful for phonological short-term memory as well as executive-loaded working memory.

Joseph, R.M., Steele, S.D., Meyer, E. & Tager-Flusberg, H. (2005). Self-ordered pointing in children with autism: Failure to use verbal mediation in the service of working memory? *Neuropsychologia, 43*, 1400–1411. More demanding, but looking at executive-loaded working memory.

Williams, D.L., Goldstein, G. & Minshew, N.J. (2006). The profile of memory function in children with autism. *Neuropsychology, 20*(1), 21–29. Looking at visuospatial short-term memory.

Williams, D.L., Goldstein, G., Carpenter, P.A. & Minshew, N.J. (2005). Verbal and spatial working memory in autism. *Journal of Autism and Developmental Disorders, 35*(6), 747–756. Also quite demanding, looking at executive-loaded working memory with an alternative view to the paper above.

Ozonoff, S., Pennington, B.F. & Rogers, S. (1991). Executive function deficits in high-functioning autistic individuals: Relationship to theory of mind. *Journal of Child Psychology and Psychiatry, 32*(7), 1081–1105. Outlining difficulties with switching and planning.

Hughes, C., Russell, J. & Robbins, T.W. (1994). Evidence for executive dysfunction in autism. *Neuropsychologia, 32*(4), 477–492. More on difficulties with switching and planning.

Turner, M.A. (1999). Generating novel ideas: Fluency performance in high-functioning and learning disabled individuals with autism. *Journal of Child Psychology and Psychiatry, 40*(2), 189–201. A very thorough paper on fluency in high- and low-functioning individuals with autism.

Mottron, L., Morasse, K. & Belleville, S. (2001). A study of memory functioning in individuals with autism. *Journal of Child Psychology and Psychiatry, 42*(2), 253–260. A very interesting paper relevant to the episodic buffer.

Optional or extended essay topic for a piece of coursework

'To what extent do children with ASD use inner speech?'

Use the current chapter for background understanding and setting the scene. Then, read the first two papers to get the 'story' in more detail. Finally, read the last three papers to see how the research has moved on since then. You should also search for more recent papers using your library's Psychology databases.

Whitehouse, J.O., Maybury, M.T. & Durkin, K. (2006). Inner speech impairments in autism. *Journal of Child Psychology and Psychiatry, 47*(8), 857–865.

Williams, D., Happé, & Jarrold, C. (2008). Intact inner speech use in autism spectrum disorder: Evidence from a short-term memory task. *Journal of Child Psychology and Psychiatry, 49*(1), 51–58.

Wallace, G.L., Silvers, J.A., Martin, A. and Kenworthy, L.E. (2009). Evidence for inner speech deficits in autism spectrum disorders. *Journal of Autism and Developmental Disorders, 39*, 1735–1739.

Lidstone, J.S.M., Fernyhough, C., Meins, E. and Whitehouse, A.J.O. (2009). Inner speech impairment in children with autism is associated with greater nonverbal than verbal skills. *Journal of Autism and Developmental Disorders, 39*, 1222–1225.

Williams, D.M. & Jarrold, C. (2010). Predicting the inner speech use amongst children with autism spectrum disorder (ASD): The roles of verbal ability and cognitive profile. *Journal of Autism and Developmental Disorders, 40*(7), 907–913.

Potential exam questions

1   Do children with autism/ASD show working memory difficulties? Illustrate your answer with research evidence relating to all four components of Baddeley's revised working memory model.

2   Critically evaluate whether central executive processing is impaired in individuals with autism/ASD.

3   What is the relationship between the 'triad of impairments' in children with autism/ASD and their profile of working memory strengths and weaknesses?

9

Concluding Comments

Learning outcomes

At the end of this chapter you should have an understanding of how the chapters in this book contribute to our understanding of working memory in typical and atypical populations of children. You should also have an appreciation of the importance of looking at individuals and their unique paths of development, rather than assuming that all children with a particular developmental disorder show the same difficulties over time. Finally, you should have a brief insight into recent work looking at how to improve 'weak' working memory skills in children with typical and atypical development.

Introduction

In this book, we have covered three broad areas. The first part of the book introduced the four-component revised working memory model (Baddeley, 2000, 2007) and gave details on how to measure working memory in typical and atypical populations of children. The second part of the book described how the working memory model has been used to account for typical children's memory development. A number of strengths and weaknesses of the working memory account were discussed in relation to each component of working memory. Finally, the third part of the book posed a simple question about children with atypical development: do children with various different developmental disorders show impairments in some or all of the components of working memory? Children and young people with six developmental disorders were considered: those with intellectual disabilities (ID); dyslexia; specific language impairment (SLI); Down syndrome; Williams syndrome; and autism spectrum disorders (ASD).

The working memory model was used to structure the discussion of memory development in typical and atypical children for three reasons: (1) it has become a major account of memory and thinking in recent years, receiving wide support; (2) comparing memory development in children with typical and atypical development is much easier using a unified theoretical framework; and (3) the clear four-part structure of the revised working memory model provides a theoretical and practical underpinning that is helpful for considering many key aspects of memory development and executive functioning.

Throughout the book, the emphasis was on the methodological adequacy of the studies under discussion. We will now summarise and reflect on some broader issues in relation to the research findings on working memory in typical and atypical children.

How successful was the working memory model in accounting for typical memory development?

We saw in Chapter 3 that the working memory model provided an elegant and simple account for the development of phonological short-term memory in children. The conceptualisation of the 'phonological loop' put forward by Baddeley and Hitch (1974) in their original working memory model successfully dealt with a vast array of experimental findings in adults; and it also provided a good explanation for at least one important aspect of memory development in typical children – the development of 'memory span'. However, there were a number of problems with the phonological loop account in relation to typical children, which were explored in detail throughout Chapter 3. Nevertheless, aspects of the working memory model were still helpful in explaining the development of memory span in typical children, and several authors offered revised versions of the working memory model that accounted for some of the difficulties.

In Chapter 4 it became apparent that although the working memory model was less detailed in relation to the visuospatial sketchpad, the central executive and the episodic buffer, it still offered a good starting point for integrating a wide body of research on memory development and executive functioning in typical children. By taking a detailed look at working memory in both children and adults, researchers have found that the overall structure of working memory in terms of the four major components is very similar throughout development. The addition of the new episodic buffer component of working memory is particularly promising. Although the proposed episodic buffer has not yet been extensively researched, it seems to offer a solution to one of the most pressing issues in relation to memory development: how to understand the crucial links between existing knowledge and working memory development.

What may be missing from the working memory account at present, however, is a full consideration of several important 'other' factors. The 'big four' factors referred to in traditional accounts of memory development in children (e.g. Kail, 1990; Schneider & Pressley, 1997) are as follows: capacity limitations; the knowledge base; memory strategies; and metamemory ('knowledge about memory'). All of these factors have been found to be important in accounting for the child's developing memory skills; and whilst some of them were explicitly considered in the original and revised working memory models (capacity limitations, the knowledge base), others were not addressed (metamemory) or were not addressed in depth (memory strategies).

There remains, therefore, scope for future research to consider how some of these factors can be related to the various working memory systems. In particular, it would be fruitful to examine the relationships between metamemory and executive functioning. The interrelationships between the child's knowledge base, his/her metamemory and his/her ability to use increasingly sophisticated memory strategies has long been of interest, but the concept of an 'episodic buffer' to act as a link between strategy knowledge, strategy implementation and executive control could benefit theorising in this area.

A more nuanced approach to the development of memory strategies, particularly verbal rehearsal, would also enhance the explanatory power of the working memory model. Increasingly, it has become apparent that development of memory strategies is a complex and involved process. Children may use different strategies on different trials of the same memory task; they may even use two or more strategies at the same time (Lehmann & Hasselhorn, 2007). Currently, there is relatively little detailed work tracking the development of strategies with age in a variety of remembering situations; and this type of research would contribute to our understanding of these important processes.

How successful was the working memory model in accounting for atypical memory development?

One of the strengths of the working memory perspective was that it allowed many areas of literature on children with a range of developmental disorders to be summarised and evaluated in relation to the same theoretical perspective (see also Gathercole & Alloway, 2006). Although we were asking a relatively simple question – whether or not children with a particular developmental or intellectual disability showed working memory difficulties – answering this question required a detailed consideration of important methodological factors such as appropriate types of comparison groups, sample sizes, the nature of the tasks used and definitional issues in relation to classification of developmental disorders. In many cases, the working memory model provided not only a theoretical underpinning for the research, but a set of testable predictions in relation to working memory performance in children with intellectual and developmental disabilities, leading to new avenues of research.

It is worth considering how children and young people in each of the six atypical populations we considered in Chapters 5 to 8 performed overall in relation to the four components of working memory. This provides a direct answer to our question of whether there were working memory difficulties in each population of children. Without repeating the extensive discussions in relation to appropriate comparison groups, we will simply summarise here by saying that most comparison groups included children matched for 'mental age' (general cognitive ability). Hence, the conclusions described below are broadly in relation to this type of comparison.

The phonological loop

There was good evidence for impairments in phonological short-term memory (PSTM) in children and young people with several different disorders. Children with ID showed weak PSTM, as did children with dyslexia, specific language impairment (SLI) and Down syndrome. There were no impairments in PSTM, relative to appropriate comparisons, for children with Williams syndrome or children with autism spectrum disorders (ASD).

This set of findings suggests that PSTM is vulnerable in many populations of children with developmental or intellectual disabilities, particularly when language is implicated (e.g. those with Down syndrome and specific language impairment in particular). However, this link with language is not inevitable, because individuals with ASD generally have weak language skills, yet the evidence was that they did not show impairments in PSTM. Interestingly, there was relatively little 'mixed' evidence in the area of PSTM, with the research literature generally in good agreement as to whether there were or were not deficits. This could reflect the fact that PSTM is heavily researched and the measures of this component are well-agreed upon and reliable.

The visuospatial sketchpad

The evidence was somewhat more mixed with respect to visuospatial short-term memory (VSSTM). It was impossible to say with any degree of certainty whether children with ID showed difficulties in this area; and this was also true for children with SLI and ASD. Clearly further research will be required before conclusions about VSSTM can be reached for these populations of children.

However, the research literature was much more emphatic in relation to children with dyslexia and Down syndrome: there were no difficulties with VSSTM reported for children in either of these groups. Taken together with the findings in relation to PSTM, we can conclude that individuals with Down syndrome and dyslexia might have rather specific problems with the simple storage of language/speech material. The findings for children with Williams syndrome were equally clear, but this time they indicated a significant degree of VSSTM difficulty, particularly with spatial tasks. Such findings are in line with the known visuospatial difficulties characteristic of individuals with Williams syndrome.

The central executive

In relation to the central executive, research evidence in respect of individuals with ID, Down syndrome and Williams syndrome was very inconsistent, with some studies finding difficulties and others not. In these disorders, all of which involve intellectual disability of some degree, tasks with executive demands might have been expected to cause difficulties, yet the research evidence has not produced consistent findings to this effect.

However, there were clear executive difficulties reported for children with dyslexia, SLI and ASD. These varied somewhat in terms of detail, lending support to the view that it is possible to develop profiles of strengths and weaknesses in executive functioning for different developmental disorders (e.g. Geurts et al., 2004; Ozonoff & Jensen, 1999). It may also be possible to link particular executive difficulties with the characteristic impairments seen in particular disorders. For example, those with autism showed clear difficulties with 'switching', which could be related to their restricted and repetitive interests/behaviours. However, more research is required to flesh out these profiles and link them in more detail to specific types of cognitive, emotional or social impairments in particular disorders. Additionally, it remains the case that many executive difficulties overlap between groups of children with different developmental disorders, making it challenging to discriminate between disorders on the basis of executive functioning. We will come back to this issue shortly.

The episodic buffer

Conclusions about the episodic buffer must remain extremely tentative as this is a newly developing research area. The limited research available suggested that there may be difficulties with episodic binding for individuals with ID, Down and Williams syndrome, but the findings varied somewhat depending on whether verbal or visuospatial binding was required. There may also be difficulties with binding for children with ASD, although this could reflect a preference for lower-level processing consistent with the Central Coherence Theory. There was little relevant research for children with dyslexia and SLI, but initial reports have not suggested difficulties in this area.

Table 9.1 Summary of the strengths and weaknesses in working memory for children with six different intellectual/developmental disorders ('Yes' indicates strong research evidence for a deficit; 'No' indicates strong research evidence against a deficit; 'Mixed' indicates no agreement in the literature either for or against a deficit)

Area of working memory/ developmental disorder	Phonological short-term memory	Visuospatial short-term memory	The central executive	The episodic buffer
Intellectual disabilities	Yes	Mixed	Mixed	No (verbal) Yes (non-verbal)
Dyslexia	Yes	No	Yes	No
Specific language impairment	Yes	Mixed	Yes	No
Down syndrome	Yes	No	Mixed	Yes
Williams syndrome	No	Yes	Mixed	Mixed
Autism spectrum disorder	No	Mixed	Yes	Yes

The conclusions concerning each component of working memory in relation to each developmental disorder are summarised above in Table 9.1.

In looking at this table, it is apparent that no two disorders have the same overall pattern of strengths and weaknesses. This does suggest that it may be possible to discriminate between different developmental disorders based on a detailed profile of abilities across all components of working memory. The issue of discrimination between developmental disorders based on profiles of impairment has been extensively discussed in the executive functioning literature; but usually in relation to executive tasks and not other aspects of working memory. The findings reviewed in this book suggest that it would be beneficial to look at the full range of working memory skills, including those referred to as 'executive functions', in order to obtain more fine-grained distinctions between developmental disorders. Such an approach might be consistent with the 'multiple deficits' position (e.g. Bishop, 2006) whereby multiple risk (e.g. deficits in particular skills) and protective (e.g. compensatory strategies) factors, often with different causes, combine to affect the likelihood of clinically significant difficulties presenting as a particular 'developmental disorder'.

Another noteworthy point about Table 9.1 concerns the number of areas in which we cannot reach firm conclusions. This is despite the fact that in at least some of these areas there has been a considerable amount of research carried out. Hence, our question – are there working memory difficulties in children with various developmental disorders – cannot be answered straightforwardly in some cases. These mixed findings were particularly apparent for children and young people with intellectual disabilities, possibly reflecting differences across studies in methods used for sampling and defining individuals with ID. Groups of children with ID are heterogeneous, meaning that such samples inevitably encompass a great deal of variability.

Given the variability in sampling, the differences between methodologies and the countless other small variations that occur between research studies, the following point made in a recent editorial for the *Journal of Child Psychology and Psychiatry* is of particular relevance:

> Real findings will stand the test of time and be convergent across multiple study designs, methods, and research teams. (Ozonoff, 2010: 965)

In this book, we have attempted to search for these 'real findings' to obtain a true picture of working memory performance in children who have a range of developmental disorders.

In concluding this section, we briefly consider whether the working memory model has a 'degree of universality' as any good theory of cognitive development requires (Pennington et al., 2003). In other words, can the model account for both typical and atypical development? The answer, overall, must be a tentative yes. The working model was extremely useful in helping to understand and describe memory performance in both typical children and those with a range of developmental disorders. Adopting a unified theoretical framework made it possible to compare individuals with different developmental disorders and structure the discussions and interpretations of typical and atypical development along very similar lines.

Perhaps the weakness of the working memory account lies in the lack of developmental specification: although developmental changes in the phonological loop have been clearly specified, there is much less detail in relation to how and why working memory develops with cognitive maturity in the other three components of the model. This leads on to the next section, in which we consider what might be a more 'developmental' approach to understanding atypical development.

What are developmental trajectories?

Throughout the book, research looking at group differences in average performance on particular working memory tasks has been emphasised; usually by comparing groups of individuals with a particular developmental disorder to typical children matched for mental and/or chronological age. Although deriving appropriate matched comparison groups can be a complex issue (see Jarrold & Brock, 2004; Mervis & Klein-Tasman, 2004), much of the research evidence that is currently available on working memory in typical and atypical children has adopted this approach.

The presence or absence of group differences in performance is used as the basis for conclusions as to whether development might be delayed in the group with a developmental disorder (development proceeding broadly in line with mental age but delayed compared to chronological age) or different (development not proceeding in line with mental age and so not proceeding along a typical path). This delay versus difference distinction is helpful in try-ing to understand whether the development of the various working memory systems might be relatively unimpaired (usually our benchmark is mental age, but it can be chronological age) in a particular disorder, or whether one or more of the working memory systems might be impaired. It is, therefore, an impor-tant first step in the understanding of typical versus atypical development.

However, even if it can be concluded that particular subsystems of working memory are delayed or different in populations of children with atypical devel-opment, this still does not tell us much about why this has occurred. Thomas, Annaz, Ansari, Scerif, Jarrold and Karmiloff-Smith (2009) argue for an alter-native approach to understanding developmental disorders that they believe gives us more information. They advocate the use of 'developmental trajecto-ries'. In this approach, researchers look at how a particular skill develops across a wide age or mental age range. For example, memory span might be assessed in children with a particular developmental disorder between the ages of 3 to 16 years. Next, memory span performance is plotted against chronological or mental age for every child to see whether there are relationships between the two variables. A line of best fit is calculated to produce a visual representa-tion of the developmental trajectory for the atypical group, which shows how memory span changes with increases in chronological or mental age.

In order to assess whether development is different in this atypical group, the same procedure is used for a typical comparison group. These individuals do not need to be exactly matched to the atypical group, but must encompass participants with the same range of mental age and/or chronological age. In other words, the range for their developmental trajectory should be broadly the same. Again, memory span is plotted against mental or chronological age and a line of best fit is calculated. This graph will show how memory span changes with chronological and mental age in typical children.

The researcher can then compare the developmental trajectories for both groups to see whether development proceeds in a similar manner in the atyp-ical group as it does in the typical group.

With this approach, there are several distinctions between typical and atypical groups that can be made. Thomas et al. (2009) describe them as follows: (1) it is possible to see whether a particular skill begins to develop late (delayed onset) in the atypical group; (2) one can also look at whether the development of a skill might be slower in the atypical group (slowed rate of development); and, finally, (3) it is possible to see whether there might be both delayed onset and a slowed rate of development in the atypical group. Further analyses can reveal even more potential areas for differences in developmental trajectories. For example, it might be that development slows or ceases very early for some children with developmental disorders; equally, development may not proceed at all at some points (i.e. no improvements are seen in relation to chronological or mental age); or there may be no systematic relationships between a particular skill and chronological or mental age.

In short, Thomas et al. (2009) argue that studying developmental trajectories can add to our understanding of developmental disorders by giving a more comprehensive picture of developmental change over time. Another advantage of this approach is that when we sample from our relevant populations, we can use every participant, rather than excluding certain individuals because they do not 'match' in terms of chronological or mental age. This should ensure that samples are more representative of the population that they come from and hopefully lead to more reliable results. In addition, a developmental trajectories approach can be one way of resolving difficulties concerning the best ways of matching groups with developmental disorders to each other or to relevant comparison groups. These issues can be particularly complex for those with Down and Williams syndrome (e.g. Jarrold et al., 2007).

It is also very important that we consider each child with a developmental disorder as an individual. Having a developmental disorder, or a particular 'phenotype', should not be considered definitive. It can only be regarded as indicating that the individual has a greater probability of demonstrating a particular behaviour or cognitive feature (Tager-Flusberg, 1999). Another advantage of the developmental trajectories approach is that the researcher plots the performance of every participant and can instantly see the range and variability in performance at different chronological and/or mental ages.

Currently, there is relatively little research that adopts a developmental trajectories approach in the area of working memory and developmental disorders. Similarly, there is little research that explicitly considers how frequent working memory difficulties are in individual children who have particular developmental disorders. It is quite possible that even when there is good evidence from 'group differences' research that a particular working memory difficulty is characteristic of those with a developmental disorder, many individual children may, nevertheless, not demonstrate this pattern.

Another issue concerns whether children who reach the same level of performance on a task really carry out the task in the same way. Superficially, they may look similar, but a more in depth look at, for example, strategic behaviour may reveal important differences (see Lehmann & Hasselhorn, 2007 for an example of such an approach with typical children; and Koshino et al., 2005 for relevant brain activation data on working memory in those with high-functioning autism). Such approaches to the development of working memory are relatively rare, yet they would add considerably to our understanding of memory performance in both typical and atypical development by beginning to get at exactly how memory tasks are carried out.

In addition, although we can use the developmental trajectories approach by sampling widely from differing age groups in a 'cross-sectional' design (everyone is tested at the same time), there are even more advantages to following up children over several time points to see how development proceeds with age in individual children (a 'longitudinal' design). In the field of working memory, there are few studies that track children over time in order to see how working memory develops and changes with age/ mental age, in relation to either typical or atypical development (although see Hulme & Mackenzie, 1992, for a longitudinal study of children with Down syndrome and severe ID). This is a promising area for future research that could be a powerful way of improving our understanding of working memory development in both typical and atypical populations of children, although it must be recognised that such studies are highly resource intensive.

Therefore, using 'developmental' approaches to study changes over time and focusing on the detail of how tasks are carried out by different populations of children offers a way of enhancing our understanding of how working memory develops in typical and atypical children. We have seen that the working memory model has been enormously helpful in understanding how working memory develops in a range of developmental disorders, but that we still lack understanding of: (1) developmental change in many working memory components; and (2) the detail of how tasks are carried out in relation to the various components of working memory. Using new approaches together with a theoretical perspective based on the working memory model has the potential to answer many important questions.

What can we do for children with weak working memory skills?

We conclude with a brief consideration of what we can do for the many children who have low working memory, regardless of whether they have a particular developmental disorder or not. Recent evidence has presented the exciting possibility that training interventions in working memory can lead to real and lasting gains.

Holmes, Gathercole and Dunning (2009) gave 10-year-old children with low working memory six weeks of training on a range of working memory tasks. The tasks were presented in a game format and attempted to improve performance on all aspects of working memory (this was known as 'adaptive' training). Children spent about half an hour per day on the training tasks at school, in supervised small groups. Improvements in all aspects of working memory were seen: phonological short-term memory; visuospatial short-term memory; and executive-loaded working memory (verbal and visuospatial tasks). By contrast, children who received training that did not tax their working memory levels (all training tasks were set at a very easy standard – this was known as 'non-adaptive' training) did not show so many gains, although there were still slight improvements in phonological short-term memory and verbal executive-loaded working memory.

The important finding was that improvements were significantly greater for the adaptive training group on all measures of working memory, with the exception of phonological short-term memory; and that these remained significant even after a period of six months. Many children went from having low working memory to reaching age-appropriate levels, which was very encouraging for the training procedure. Finally, although improvements in academic skills such as reading and mathematical reasoning were not apparent immediately on completion of the training, the adaptive training group did show significant improvements on mathematical reasoning when they were tested six months later.

Similar findings have been reported for children with intellectual disabilities (Van der Molen, Van Luit, Ven der Molan, Klugkist & Jongmans, 2010)) and research is ongoing into groups of children with a range of other developmental disorders. Interestingly, Van der Molen et al. (2010) also found gains in academic performance that related to mathematics rather than reading at their follow-up test. Such findings imply that improvements in working memory skills may be more beneficial in the short-term for mathematics than reading. These developments, although preliminary and not yet tested in 'randomised' double-blind trials (where participants and testers do not know which treatment they receive/implement), are promising for all children with low working memory.

Another approach to helping children with low working memory is to structure lessons in school to compensate for their difficulties. Gathercole and Alloway (2008) have written a very clear and accessible book outlining how this might be done by teachers. Working memory difficulties are not always detected in the classroom and some children may demonstrate low motivation, high distractibility and/or poor behaviour because they fail to remember instructions and have difficulties with many classroom tasks due to working memory limitations. However, initial assessments of this approach have suggested that it does not directly improve academic attainment or working memory (Elliott, Gathercole, Alloway, Holmes & Kirkwood, 2010). Nevertheless, these authors did find some evidence that teachers who were particularly sensitive to their students' working memory difficulties were more likely to apply strategies that improved academic performance (Elliott et al., 2010).

Research in this area is a real priority for the thousands of children who have poor working memory skills, because it offers a direct way of improving academic achievement. Further work comparing and contrasting working memory training schemes will contribute to our understanding of how improvements in working memory might feed directly into better academic achievement. In addition, more research into the application of sensitive adaptations in the classroom to overcome working memory difficulties will be enormously valuable for the many children who find it difficult to access and benefit from learning activities due to working memory limitations.

Using research to improve professional practice is a difficult endeavour, but a number of researchers are making considerable inroads into understanding how to improve and compensate for limitations in working memory in typical and atypical children.

Conclusion

The working memory model successfully dealt with a large number of experimental findings in adults; and it also provided an elegant explanation for the development of 'memory span' in typical children. However, there were a number of difficulties in applying this model to typical development, and several authors offered revised versions of the working memory model that accounted for some of the problems. One of the strengths of the working memory perspective, however, was that it allowed many areas of literature on children with a range of developmental disorders to be summarised and evaluated in relation to the same theoretical perspective. Although we were asking a relatively simple question – whether or not children with a particular developmental or intellectual disability showed working memory impairments – the working memory model provided not only a theoretical underpinning for the research, but a set of testable predictions in relation to working memory performance in children with intellectual and developmental disabilities. Newer approaches to studying development over time using developmental trajectories may add to our understanding of intellectual and developmental disorders by giving a more comprehensive picture of developmental change. Finally, research into interventions that try to improve working memory or adaptations that attempt to overcome working memory difficulties will be a real priority for the thousands of children who have poor working memory skills.

Further reading

Elliott, J.G., Gathercole, S.E., Alloway, T.P., Holmes, J. & Kirkwood, H. (2010). An evaluation of a classroom-based intervention to help overcome working memory difficulties and improve long-term academic achievement. *Journal of Cognitive Education and Psychology, 9*(3), 227–250. Looking at new teachers can compensate for working memory difficulties.

Gathercole, S.E. & Alloway, T.P. (2008). *Working memory and learning: A practical guide for teachers.* London: SAGE Publications Ltd. A very clearly-written book describing how teachers can compensate for poor working memory in the classroom.

Holmes, J., Gathercole, S.E. & Dunning, D.L. (2009). Adaptive training leads to sustained enhancement of poor working memory in children. *Developmental Science, 12*, F1–F7. Very exciting evidence about the benefits of working memory training.

Thomas, M.S.C., Annaz, D., Ansari, D., Scerif, G., Jarrold, C. & Karmiloff-Smith, A. (2009). Using developmental trajectories to understand developmental disorders. *Journal of Speech, Language, and Hearing Research, 52*, 336–358. Outlines the developmental trajectories approach.

Van der Molen, M.J., Van Luit, J.E.H., Van der Molan, M.W., Klugkist, I. & Jongmans, M.J. (2010). Effectiveness of a computerised working memory training in adolescents with mild to borderline intellectual disabilities. *Journal of Intellectual Disability Research, 54*(5), 433–447. More exciting evidence about the benefits of working memory training.

References

Adams, D. & Oliver, C. (2010). The relationship between acquired impairments of executive function and behaviour change in adults with Down syndrome. *Journal of Intellectual Disability Research, 54*(5), 393–405.

Allen, R.J., Baddeley, A.D. & Hitch, G.J. (2006). Is the binding of visual features in working memory resource-demanding? *Journal of Experimental Psychology: General, 135,* 298–313.

Alloway, T.P. (2010). Working memory and executive function profiles of individuals with borderline intellectual functioning. *Journal of Intellectual Disability Research, 54*(5), 448–456.

Alloway, T.P., Gathercole, S.E., Adams, A.M., Willis, C.D., Eaglen, R. & Lamont, E. (2005). Working memory and other cognitive skills as predictors of progress towards early learning goals at school entry. *British Journal of Developmental Psychology, 23,* 417–426.

Alloway, T.P., Gathercole, S.E., Willis, C. D. & Adams, A.M. (2004). A structural analysis of working memory and related cognitive skills in early childhood. *Journal of Experimental Child Psychology, 87,* 85–106.

Alloway, T.P. & Temple, K.J. (2007). A comparison of working memory skills and learning in children with developmental coordination disorder and moderate learning difficulties. *Applied Cognitive Psychology, 21,* 473–487.

Alt, M. (2010). Phonological working memory impairments in children with specific language impairment: Where does the problem lie? *Journal of Communication Disorders, 44*(2), 173–185.

Ameli, R., Courchesne, E., Lincoln, A., Kaufmann, A.S. & Grillon, C. (1988). Visual memory processes in high-functioning individuals with autism. *Journal of Autism and Developmental Disorders, 18*(4), 601–615.

American Psychiatric Association (1994). *The diagnostic and statistical manual of mental disorders (DSM-IV).* Washington DC: American Psychiatric Association.

Anderson, M. (2001). Annotation: Conceptions of intelligence. *Journal of Child Psychology and Psychiatry, 42,* 287–298.

Anderson, P. (2002). Assessment and development of executive function (EF) during childhood. *Child Neuropsychology, 8,* 71–82.

Anderson, V. (1998). Assessing executive functions in children: Biological, psychological and developmental considerations. *Neuropsychological Rehabilitation, 8,* 319–349.

Archibald, L.M.D. & Gathercole, S.E. (2006a). Short-term memory and working memory in specific language impairment. In T.P. Alloway & S.E. Gathercole (Eds.), *Working memory and neurodevelopmental disorders* (Chapter 7, pp. 139–160). Hove: Psychology Press.

Archibald, L.M.D. & Gathercole, S.E. (2006b). Visuospatial immediate memory in specific language impairment. *Journal of Speech, Language, and Hearing Research, 49,* 265–277.

Archibald, S.J. & Kerns, K.A. (1999). Identification and description of new tests of executive functioning in children. *Child Neuropsychology, 5,* 115–129.

Atkinson, J., Braddick, O., Anker, S., Curran, W., Andrew, R. & Wattam-Bell, J. (2003). Neurobiological models of visuospatial cognition in children with Williams syndrome: Measures of dorsal-stream and frontal function. *Developmental Neuropsychology, 23,* 139–172.

Auyeung, B., Baron-Cohen, S., Ashwin, E., Knickmeyer, R., Taylor, K. & Hackett, G. (2009). Fetal testosterone and autistic traits. *British Journal of Psychology, 100,* 1–22.

Avons, S.E. & Hanna, C. (1995). The memory-span deficit in children with specific reading disability: Is speech rate responsible? *British Journal of Developmental Psychology, 13*, 303–311.

Avons, S.E., Wright, K.L. & Pammer, K. (1994). The word-length effect in probed and serial recall. *Quarterly Journal of Experimental Psychology, 47A*, 207–231.

Baddeley, A.D. (1966). Short-term memory for word sequences as a function of acoustic, semantic and formal similarity. *Quarterly Journal of Experimental Psychology, 18*, 362–365.

Baddeley, A.D. (1986). *Working memory*. Oxford: OUP.

Baddeley, A.D. (2000). The episodic buffer: A new component of working memory? *Trends in Cognitive Sciences, 4*(11), 417–423.

Baddeley, A.D. (2007). *Working memory, thought, and action*. Oxford: OUP.

Baddeley, A.D. & Andrade, J. (1994). Reversing the word-length effect: A comment on Caplan, Rochon, and Waters. *Quarterly Journal of Experimental Psychology A, 47*, 1047–1105.

Baddeley, A., Chincotta, D., Stafford, L. & Turk, D. (2002). Is the word length effect in STM entirely attributable to output delay: Evidence from serial recognition. *Quarterly Journal of Experimental Psychology, 55A*, 353–369.

Baddeley, A.D. & Della Sala, S. (1996). Working memory and executive control. *Proceedings of the Royal Society, B, 351*, 1397–1484.

Baddeley, A., Eysenck, M.W. & Anderson, M.C. (2009). *Memory*. Hove, East Sussex: Psychology Press.

Baddeley, A. D., Gathercole, S. E. and Papagno, C. (1998). The phonological loop as a language learning device. *Psychological Review, 105*, 158–173.

Baddeley, A.D. & Hitch, G.J. (1974). Working memory. In G.A. Bower (Ed.), *The psychology of learning and motivation*, Vol. 8 (pp. 47–89). New York: Academic Press.

Baddeley, A.D. & Larsen, J.D. (2007a). The phonological loop unmasked? A comment on the evidence for a 'perceptual-gestural' alternative. *Quarterly Journal of Experimental Psychology, 60*(4), 497–504.

Baddeley, A.D. & Larsen, J.D. (2007b). The phonological loop: Some answers and some questions. *Quarterly Journal of Experimental Psychology, 60*(4), 512–518.

Baddeley, A.D., Lewis, V. & Vallar, G. (1984). Exploring the articulatory loop. *Quarterly Journal of Experimental Psychology, 36A*, 233–252.

Baddeley, A.D. & Logie, R.H. (1999). Working memory: The multiple component model. In A. Miyake and P. Shah (Eds.), *Models of working memory: Mechanisms of active maintenance and executive control* (pp. 28–61). Cambridge: Cambridge University Press.

Baddeley, A. D., Thomson, N. & Buchanan, M. (1975). Word length and the structure of short-term memory. *Journal of Verbal Learning and Verbal Behaviour, 14*, 575–589.

Baddeley, A.D. & Wilson, B. (1985). Phonological coding and short-term memory in patients without speech. *Journal of Memory and Language, 24*, 490–502.

Baddeley, A.D. & Wilson, B. (2002). Prose recall and amnesia: Implications for the structure of working memory. *Neuropsychologia, 40*, 1737–1743.

Bailey, A., Palferman, S., Heavey, L. & Le Couteur, A. (1998). Autism: The phenotype in relatives. *Journal of Autism and Developmental Disorders, 28*, 369–392.

Baker-Ward, L., Ornstein, P. A. & Holden, D. J. (1984). The expression of memorisation in early childhood. *Journal of Experimental Child Psychology, 37*, 555–575.

Ball, S.L., Holland, A.J., Treppner, P., Watson, P.C. & Huppert, F.A. (2010). Executive dysfunction and its association with personality and behaviour changes in the development of Alzheimer's disease in adults with Down's syndrome and mild to moderate learning disabilities. *British Journal of Clinical Psychology, 47*, 1–29.

Ball, S.L., Holland, A.J., Watson, P.C. & Huppert, F.A. (2008). Theoretical exploration of the neural bases of behavioural disinhibition, apathy and executive dysfunction in pre-clinical

Alzheimer's disease in people with Down's syndrome: Potential involvement of multiple frontal-sub cortical neuronal circuits. *Journal of Intellectual Disability Research, 54*(4), 320–336.

Balthazar, C. H. (2003). The word length effect in children with language impairment. *Journal of Communication Disorders, 36,* 487–505.

Baron-Cohen, S. (1995). *Mindblindness: An essay on autism and theory of mind.* Boston, MA: MIT Press/Bradford Books.

Baron-Cohen, S., Scott, F.J., Allison, C., Williams, J., Bolton, P., Matthews, F.E. & Brayne, C. (2009). Prevalence of autism-spectrum conditions: UK school-based population study. *The British Journal of Psychiatry, 194,* 500–509.

Barrouillet, P., Gavens, N., Vergauwe, E., Gaillard, V. & Camos, V. (2009). Working memory span development: A time-based resource-sharing model account. *Developmental Psychology, 45,* 477–490.

Bayliss, D.M., Jarrold, C., Baddeley, A.D. & Leigh, E. (2005). Differential constraints on the working memory and reading abilities as individuals with learning difficulties and typically developing children. *Journal of Experimental Child Psychology, 92,* 76–99.

Bayliss, D.M., Jarrold, C., Gunn, D.M. & Baddeley, A.D. (2003). The complexities of complex span: Explaining individual differences in working memory in children and adults. *Journal of Experimental Psychology: General, 132*(1), 71–92.

Bebko, J.M. (1979). Can recall differences among children be attributed to rehearsal effects? *Canadian Journal of Psychology, 33*(2), 96–105.

Bebko, J.M. & McKinnon, E.E. (1990). The language experience of deaf children: Its relation to spontaneous rehearsal in a memory task. *Child Development, 61,* 1744–1752.

Belmont, J.M. (1978). Individual differences in memory: The cases of normal and retarded development. In M.M. Gruneberg & P.E. Morris (Eds.), *Aspects of memory* (pp. 153–185). London: Methuen.

Belmont, J.M. & Butterfield, C.E. (1969). The relation of short-term memory to development and intelligence. In L. Lipsett & H. Reese (Eds.), *Advances in child development and behaviour,* Vol. 4. New York: Academic Press.

Belmont, J.M. & Butterfield, C.E. (1971). Learning strategies as determinants of mental deficiencies. *Cognitive Psychology, 2,* 411–420.

Belmonte, M.K., Gomot, M. & Baron-Cohen, S. (2010). Visual attention in autism families: 'Unaffected' sibs share atypical frontal activation. *Journal of Child Psychology and Psychiatry, 51*(3), 259–276.

Bennett-Gates, D. & Zigler, E. (1998). Resolving the developmental-difference debate: An evaluation of the triarchic and systems theory models. In J.A. Burack, R.M. Hodapp & E. Zigler (Eds.), *Handbook of mental retardation and development* (pp. 115–131). Cambridge: Cambridge University Press.

Bennetto, L., Pennington, B.F. & Rogers, S.J. (1996). Intact and impaired memory functions in autism. *Child Development, 67,* 1816–1835.

Bernbach, H, A. (1967). The effects of labels on short-term memory for colours in nursery school children. *Psychonomic Science, 7,* 149–150.

Bishop, D.V.M. (2001). Genetic influences on language impairment and literacy problems in children: Same or different? *Journal of Child Psychology and Psychiatry, 42*(2), 189–198.

Bishop, D.V.M. (2002a). The role of genes in the etiology of specific language impairment. *Journal of Communication Disorders, 35,* 311–328.

Bishop, D.V.M. (2002b). Motor immaturity and specific speech and language impairment: Evidence for a common genetic basis. *American Journal of Medical Genetics, 114,* 56–63.

Bishop, D.V.M. (2006). Developmental cognitive genetics: How psychology can inform genetics and vice versa. *Quarterly Journal of Experimental Psychology, 59*(7), 1153–1168.

Bishop, D.V.M. & Edmundson, A. (1987). Language-impaired 4-year-olds: Distinguishing transient from persistent impairment. *Journal of Speech and Hearing Disorders, 52*, 156–173.

Bishop, D.V.M. & Norbury, C.F. (2005a). Executive functions in children with communication impairments, in relation to autistic symptomatology. 1: Generativity. *Autism, 9*, 7–27.

Bishop, D.V.M. & Norbury, C.F. (2005b). Executive functions in children with communication impairments, in relation to autistic symptomatology. 2: Response inhibition. *Autism, 9*, 29–43.

Bishop, D.V.M., North, T. & Donlan, C. (1996). Nonword repetition as a behavioural marker for inherited language disorder: Evidence from a twin study. *Journal of Child Psychology and Psychiatry, 37*(4), 391–403.

Bishop, D.V.M. & Robson, J. (1989). Unimpaired short-term memory and rhyme judgement in congenitally speechless individuals: Implications for the notion of 'Articulatory Recoding'. *Quarterly Journal of Experimental Psychology, 41A*, 123–140.

Bishop, D.V.M. & Snowling, M.J. (2004). Developmental dyslexia and specific language impairment: Same or different? *Psychological Bulletin, 130*(6), 858–886.

Blue, C.M. (1970). Influence of mode of presentation, age, and intelligence on paired-associates learning. *American Journal of Mental Deficiency, 74*, 527–532.

Booth, J.N., Boyle, M.E. & Kelly, S.W. (2010). Do tasks make a difference? Accounting for heterogeneity of performance of children with reading difficulties on tasks of executive functioning: Findings from a meta-analysis. *British Journal of Developmental Psychology, 28*, 133–176.

Borkowski, J.G., Peck, V.A. & Damberg, E.R. (1991). Attention, memory and cognition. In J.L. Matson & J.A. Mulick (Eds.), *Handbook of mental retardation* (2nd edn, pp. 479–497). New York: Pergamon.

Borys, S.V., Spitz, H.H. & Dorans, B.A. (1982). Tower of Hanoi performance of retarded young adults and nonretarded children as a function of solution length and goal state. *Journal of Experimental Child Psychology, 33*, 87–110.

Botting, N. (2005). Non-verbal cognitive development and language impairment. *Journal of Child Psychology and Psychiatry, 43*(6), 317–326.

Boucher, J. & Bowler, D. (2008). *Memory in autism: Theory and evidence.* Cambridge: Cambridge University Press.

Bower, A. & Hayes, A. (1994). Short-term memory deficits and Down's syndrome: A comparative study. *Down's Syndrome: Research and Practice, 2*(2), 47–50.

Brainerd, C.J., Reyna, V.F. & Ceci, S.J. (2008). Developmental reversals in false memory: A review of data and theory. *Psychological Bulletin, 134*, 343–382.

Bray, N.W. & Turner, L.A. (1986). The rehearsal deficit hypothesis. In N.R. Ellis and N.W. Bray (Eds.), *International review of research in mental retardation*, Vol. 14. Orlando, FL: Academic Press.

Broadly, I., MacDonald, J. & Buckley, S. (1994). Are children with Down's syndrome able to maintain skills learned from a short-term memory training programme? *Down's Syndrome: Research and Practice, 2*(3), 116–122.

Brock, J., Brown, G.D.A. & Bucher, J. (2006). Free recall in Williams syndrome: Is there a dissociation between short-and long-term memory? *Cortex, 42*, 366–375.

Brock, J. & Jarrold, C. (2005). Serial order reconstruction in Down syndrome: Evidence for a selective deficit in verbal short-term memory. *Journal of Child Psychology and Psychiatry, 46*(3), 203–316.

Brown, A.L. (1975). The development of memory: knowing, knowing about knowing, and knowing how to know. In H.W. Reese (Ed.), *Advances in child development and behaviour* (Vol. 10, pp. 103–152). New York: Academic Press.

Brown, A.L., Campione, J.C. & Murphy, M.D. (1974). Keeping track of changing variables: Long-term retention of a trained rehearsal strategy by retarded adolescents. *American Journal of Mental Deficiency, 78*, 446–443.

Brown, G.D.A. & Hulme, C. (1995). Modeling item length effects in memory span: No rehearsal needed? *Journal of Memory and Language, 34*, 594–621.

Brown, L.A., Forbes, D. & McConnell, J. (2006). Limiting the use of verbal coding in the Visual Patterns Test. *Quarterly Journal of Experimental Psychology, 59*, 1169–1176.

Brown, R.M. (1974). Effects of recall order, cue placement, and retention interval on short-term memory of normal and retarded children. *Perceptual and Motor Skills, 39*, 167–178.

Bruck, M., London, K., Landa, R. & Goodman, J. (2007). Autobiographical memory and suggestibility in children with autism spectrum disorder. *Development and Psychopathology, 19*, 73–95.

Bull, R., Espy, K.A. & Wiebe, S.A. (2008). Short-term memory, working memory, and executive functioning in preschoolers: Longitudinal predictors of mathematical achievement at age 7 years. *Developmental Neuropsychology, 33*, 205–228.

Bull, R. & Scerif, G. (2001). Executive function as a predictor of children's mathematics ability: Inhibition, switching and working memory. *Developmental Neuropsychology, 19*, 273–293.

Burack, J.A. & Zigler, E. (1990). Intentional and incidental memory in organically mentally retarded, familial retarded, and nonretarded individuals. *American Journal of Mental Retardation, 94*, 532–540.

Bush, E.S. & Cohen, L.B. (1970). The effects of relevant and irrelevant labels on short-term memory in nursery school children. *Psychonomic Science, 18*, 228–229.

Byrnes, M.M. & Spitz, H.H. (1977). Performance of retarded adolescents and nonretarded children on the Tower of Hanoi problem. *American Journal of Mental Deficiency, 81*, 561–569.

Campoy, G. (2008). The effect of word length in short-term memory: Is rehearsal necessary? *Quarterly Journal of Experimental Psychology, 61*(5), 724–734.

Cantor, G.N. & Ryan, T.J. (1962). Retention of verbal paired-associates in normals and retardates. *American Journal of Mental Deficiency, 66*, 861–865.

Caplan, D., Rochon, E. & Waters, G.S. (1992). Articulatory and phonological determinants of word length effects in span tasks. *Quarterly Journal of Experimental Psychology A, 45*, 177–192.

Carlesimo, G.A., Galloni, F., Bonanni, R. & Sabbadini, M. (2006). Verbal short-term memory in individuals with congenital articulatory disorders: New empirical data and review of the literature. *Journal of Intellectual Disability Research, 50*(2), 81–91.

Carlesimo, G.A., Marotta, L. and Vicari, S. (1997). Long-term memory in mental retardation: Evidence for a specific impairment in subjects with Down's syndrome. *Neuropsychologia, 35*, 71–79.

Carretti, B., Belacchi, C. & Cornoldi, C. (2010). Difficulties in working memory updating in individuals with intellectual disability. *Journal of Intellectual Disability Research, 54*(5), 337–345.

Case, R., Kurland, D.M. & Goldberg, J. (1982). Operational efficiency and the growth of short-term memory span. *Journal of Experimental Child Psychology, 33*, 386–404.

Castro-Caldas, A., Petersson, M.M., Reis, A., Stone-Elander, S. & Ingvar, M. (1998). The illiterate brain: Learning to read and write during childhood influences the functional organisation of the adult brain. *Brain, 121*, 1053–1063.

Catts, H.W., Adlof, S. M., Hogan, T. P. & Ellis Weismer, S. (2005). Are specific language impairment and dyslexia distinct disorders? *Journal of Speech, Language, and Hearing Research, 48*, 1378–1396.

Ceci, S.J., Fitneva, S.A. & Williams, W.M. (2010). Representational constraints on the development of memory and metamemory: A developmental-representational theory. *Psychological Review, 117*(2), 464–495.

Chapman, R.S. & Hesketh, L.J. (2000). Behavioral phenotype of individuals with Down syndrome. *Mental Retardation and Developmental Disabilities Research Reviews, 6*, 84–95.

Chein, J.M., Moore, A.B. & Conway, A.R.A. (2011). Domain-general mechanisms of complex working memory span. *NeuroImage, 54*, 550–559.

Chi, M.T.H. (1978). Knowledge structures and memory development. In R. Siegler (Ed.), *Children's thinking: What develops?* Hillsdale, NJ: Erlbaum.

Clegg, J., Hollis, C., Mawhood, L. & Rutter, M. (2005). Developmental language disorders – a follow-up in later adult life. Cognitive, language and psychosocial outcomes. *Journal of Child Psychology and Psychiatry, 46*(2), 128–149.

Cohen, J. (1988). *Statistical power analysis for the behavioral sciences* 2nd ed. Hillsdale, NJ: Erlbaum.

Conners, F.A., Carr, M.D. & Willis, S. (1998). Is the phonological loop responsible for intelligence-related differences in forward digit span? *American Journal on Mental Retardation, 103*(1), 1–11.

Conners, F.A., Rosenquist, C.J., Arnett, L., Moore, M.S. & Hume, L.E. (2008). Improving memory span in children with Down syndrome. *Journal of Intellectual Disability Research, 52*(3), 244–255.

Conrad, R. (1964). Acoustic confusions in the immediate memory. *British Journal of Psychology, 55*, 75–84.

Conrad, R. (1971). Chronology of the development of covert speech in children. *Developmental Psychology, 5*, 398–405.

Conrad, R. & Hull, A.J. (1964). Information, acoustic confusion and memory span. *British Journal of Psychology, 55*, 429–432.

Cornoldi, C. & Vecchi, T. (2003). *Visuo-spatial working memory and individual differences.* Hove: Psychology Press.

Cowan, N. (1999). An embedded-process model of working memory. In A. Miyake & P. Shah (Eds.), *Models of working memory: mechanisms of active maintenance and executive control* (pp. 62–101). Cambridge UK: Cambridge University Press.

Cowan, N. (2005). *Working memory capacity.* New York and Hove: Psychology Press.

Cowan, N., Day, L., Saults, J.S., Keller, T.A., Johnson, T. & Flores, L. (1992). The role of verbal output time in the effects of word length on immediate memory. *Journal of Memory and Language, 31*, 1–17.

Cowan, R., Donlon, C., Newton, E.J. & Lloyd, D. (2005). Number skills and knowledge in children with specific language impairment. *Journal of Educational Psychology, 97*, 732–744.

Cowan, N., Elliott, E.M., Saults, J.S., Nugent, L.D., Bomb, P. & Hismjatullina, A. (2006). Rethinking speed theories of cognitive development: Increasing the rate of recall without affecting accuracy. *Psychological Science, 17*(1), 67–73.

Cowan, N. & Kail, R. (1996). Covert processes and their development in short-term memory. In S. E. Gathercole (Ed.), *Models of short-term memory.* Hove, East Sussex, UK: Psychology Press.

Cowan, N., Naveh-Benjamin, M., Kilb, A. & Saults, J.S. (2006). Life-span development of visual working memory: When is feature binding difficult? *Developmental Psychology, 42*(6), 1089–1102.

Cowan, N., Nugent, L.D., Elliott, E.M. & Geer, T. (2000). Is there a temporal basis of the word length effect? A response to Service (1998). *Quarterly Journal of Experimental Psychology A, 53*(3), 647–660.

Cowan, N., Nugent, L.D., Elliott, E.M., Ponomarev, I. & Saults, J.S. (1999). The role of attention in the development of short-term memory: Age differences in the verbal span of apprehension. *Child Development, 70*, 1082–1097.

Cowan, N., Towse, J.N., Hamilton, Z., Saults, J.S., Elliott, E.M., Lacey, J.F., Moreno, M.V. & Hitch, G.J. (2003). Children's working-memory processes: A response-timing analysis. *Journal of Experimental Psychology: General, 132*(1), 113–132.

Cowan, N., Wood, N.L., Wood, P.K., Keller, T.A., Nugent, L.D. & Keller, C.V. (1998). Two separate verbal processing rates contributing to short-term memory span. *Journal of Experimental Psychology: General, 127*, 141–160.

Craik, F.I.M. & Lockhart, R.S. (1972). Levels of processing: A framework for memory research. *Journal of Verbal Learning and Verbal Behaviour, 11*, 671–684.

Cunningham, J.G. & Weaver, S.L. (1989). Young childrens' knowledge of their memory span: Effects of task and experience. *Journal of Experimental Child Psychology, 48*, 32–44.

Cuvo, A.J. (1975). Developmental differences in rehearsal and free recall. *Journal of Experimental Child Psychology, 19*, 265–278.

Daneman, M. & Carpenter, P.A. (1980). Individual differences in working memory and reading. *Journal of Verbal Learning and Verbal Behavior, 19*, 450–466.

Danielsson, H., Henry, L., Rönnberg, J. & Nilsson, L-G. (2010). Executive functions in individuals with intellectual disability. *Research in Developmental Disabilities, 31*, 1299–1304.

Danielsson, H., Rönnberg, J., Leven, A., Andersson, J., Andersson, K. & Lyxell, B. (2006). The face you recognize may not be the one you saw: Memory conjunction errors in individuals with or without learning disability. *Scandinavian Journal of Psychology, 47*, 177–186.

Darling, S., Della Sala, S. & Logie, R.H. (2007). Behavioural evidence for separating components within visuo-spatial working memory. *Cognitive Processes, 8*, 175–181.

Darling, S., Della Sala, S. & Logie, R.H. (2009). Dissociation between appearance and location within visuo-spatial working memory. *Quarterly Journal of Experimental Psychology, 62*(3), 417–425.

Davidson, M.C., Ambo, D., Anderson, L.C. & Diamond, A. (2006). Development of cognitive control and executive functions from 4 to 13 years: Evidence from manipulations of memory, inhibition, and task switching. *Neuropsychologia, 44*, 2037–2078.

De Cara, B. & Goswami, U. (2003). Phonological neighbourhood density: Effects in a rhyme awareness task in five-year-old children. *Journal of Child Language, 30*, 695–710.

de Jong, P.F. (1998). Working memory deficits of reading disabled children. *Journal of Experimental Child Psychology, 70*, 75–96.

Delis, D.C., Kaplan, E. & Kramer, J.H. (2001). *Delis-Kaplan Executive Function System, Technical Manual (D-KEFS)*. San Antonio: The Psychological Corporation.

Della Sala, S., Gray, C., Baddeley, A.D., Allamano, N. & Wilson, L. (1999). Pattern is span: A tool for unwelding visuo-spatial memory. *Neuropsychologia, 37*, 1189–1199.

Della Sala, S., Gray, C., Baddeley, A. & Wilson, L. (1997). *The Visual Patterns Test: A new test of short-term visual recall*. Feltham, Suffolk: Thames Valley Test Company.

Dempster, R.N. (1981). Memory span: Sources of individual and developmental differences. *Psychological Bulletin, 89*, 63–100.

Depoorter, A. & Vandierendonck, A. (2009). Evidence for modality-independent order coding in working memory. *Quarterly Journal of Experimental Psychology, 62*(3), 531–549.

Detterman, D.K. (1979). Memory in the mentally retarded. In N.R. Ellis (Ed.), *Handbook of mental deficiency: psychological theory and research* (2nd edn, pp. 301–330). Hillsdale, NJ: Erlbaum.

Devenny, D.A., Krinsky-McHale, S.J., Kittler, P.M., Flory, M., Jenkins, E. & Brown, W.T. (2004). Age-associated memory changes in adults with Williams syndrome. *Developmental Neuropsychology, 26*, 691–706.

Diamond, A. & Golman-Rakic, P. (1989). Comparison of human infants and recess monkeys on Piaget's AB task: Evidence for dependence on dorsolateral pre-frontal cortex. *Experimental Brain Research, 74*, 24–40.

Dibbets, P., Bakker, K. & Jolles, J. (2006). Functional MRI of task switching in children with specific language impairment (SLI). *Neurocase, 12*, 71–91.

Di Martino, A., Ross, K., Uddin, L.Q., Sklar, A.B., Castellanos, X. & Milham, M.P. (2009). Functional brain correlates of social and nonsocial processes in Autism Spectrum Disorders: An activation likelihood estimation meta-analysis. *Biological Psychiatry, 65*, 63–74.

Dollaghan, C. A. & Campbell, T. (1998). Nonword repetition and child language impairment. *Journal of Speech, Language, and Hearing Research, 41*, 1136–1146.

Dosher, B.A. & Ma, J.J. (1998). Output loss or rehearsal loop? Output – time versus pronunciation – time limits in immediate recall for forgetting-matched materials. *Journal of Experimental Psychology: Learning, Memory, and Cognition, 24*(2), 316–335.

Duncan, J., Emslie, H., Williams, P., Johnson, R. & Freer, C. (1996). Intelligence and the frontal lobe: The organisation of goal-directed behaviour. *Cognitive Psychology, 30*, 257–303.

Dykens, E.M. (2003). Anxiety, fears, and phobias in persons with Williams syndrome. *Developmental Neuropsychology, 23*, 291–316.

Edwards, J. & Lahey, M. (1998). Nonword repetition of children with specific language impairment: Exploration of some explanations for their inaccuracies. *Applied Psycholinguistics, 19*, 279–309.

Elliott, C.D., Smith, P. & McCulloch, K. (1986). *British Ability Scales* (2nd edition). Windsor, UK: NFER-Nelson.

Elliott, J.G., Gathercole, S.E., Alloway, T.P., Holmes, J. & Kirkwood, H. (2010). An evaluation of a classroom-based intervention to help overcome working memory difficulties and improve long-term academic achievement. *Journal of Cognitive Education and Psychology, 9*(3), 227–250.

Ellis, N.C. & Hennelly, R.A. (1980). A bilingual word-length effect: Implications for intelligence testing and the relative ease of mental calculation in Welsh and English. *British Journal of Psychology, 71*, 43–51.

Ellis, N. R. (1963). The stimulus trace and behavioral inadequacy. In N. R. Ellis (Ed.), *Handbook of mental deficiency: Psychological theory and research* (pp. 134–158). New York: McGraw-Hill.

Ellis, N.R. (1969). A behavioural research strategy in mental retardation: defence and critique. *American Journal of Mental Deficiency, 73*, 557–567.

Ellis, N. R. (1970). Memory processes in retardates and normals. In N. R. Ellis (Ed.), *International review of research in mental retardation*, Vol. 4 (pp. 1–32). New York: Academic Press.

Ellis, N.R. (1978). Do the mentally retarded have memory deficits? *Intelligence, 2*, 41–45.

Ellis, N.R. & Cavalier, A.R. (1982). Research perspectives in mental retardation. In E. Zigler & D. Balla (Eds.), *Mental retardation: The developmental difference controversy* (pp. 121–152). Hillsdale, NJ: Lawrence Erlbaum Associates.

Ellis, N.R. & Meador, D.M. (1985). Forgetting in retarded and nonretarded persons under conditions of minimal strategy use. *Intelligence, 9*, 87–96.

Ellis Weismer, S., Evans, J. & Hesketh, L.J. (1999). An examination of verbal working memory capacity in children with specific language impairment. *Journal of Speech, Language and Hearing Research, 42*, 1249–1260.

Ellis Weismer, S., Tomblin, J.B., Zhang, X., Buckwalter, P., Chynoweth, J.G. & Jones, M. (2000). Nonword repetition performance in school-age children with and without language impairment. *Journal of Speech, Language, and Hearing Research, 43*, 865–878.

Emslie, H., Wilson, F., Burden, V., Nimmo-Smith, I. & Wilson, B.A. (2003). *Behavioural Assessment of the Dysexecutive Syndrome for Children (BADS-C)*. London, UK: Harcourt Assessment/The Psychological Corporation.

Engle, R.W., Fidler, D.S. & Reynolds, L.H. (1981). Does echoic memory develop? *Journal of Experimental Child Psychology, 32*, 459–473.

Estes, K.G., Evans, J.L. & Else-Quest, N.M. (2007). Differences in the nonword repetition performance on children with and without specific language impairment: A meta-analysis. *Journal of Speech, Language, and Hearing Research, 50*, 177–195.

Everatt, J., Weeks, S. & Brooks, P. (2008). Profiles of strengths and weaknesses in dyslexia and other learning difficulties. *Dyslexia, 14*, 16–41.

Fagan, J.F. (1968). Short-term memory processes in normal and retarded children. *Journal of Experimental Child Psychology, 6*, 279–296.

Ferguson, A.N. & Bowey, J.A. (2005). Global processing speed as a mediator of developmental changes in children's auditory memory span. *Journal of Experimental Child Psychology, 91*, 89–112.

Ferguson, A.N., Bowey, J.A. & Tilley, A. (2002). The association between auditory memory span and speech rate in children from kindergarten to sixth grade. *Journal of Experimental Child Psychology, 81*, 141–156.

Ferguson, R.P. & Bray, N.W. (1976). Component processes of an overt rehearsal strategy in young children. *Journal of Experimental Child Psychology, 21*, 490–506.

Fisk, J.E. & Sharp, C.A. (2004). Age-related impairment in executive functioning: Updating, inhibition, shifting, and access. *Journal of Clinical and Experimental Neuropsychology, 26*, 874–890.

Flavell, J.H. (1970). Developmental studies of mediated memory. In H.W. Reese & L.P. Lipsitt (Eds.), *Advances in child development and behaviour* (Vol. 5, pp. 181–211). New York: Academic Press.

Flavell, J.H. (1985). *Cognitive development*, 2nd ed. London: Prentice-Hall.

Flavell, J.H., Beach, D.R. & Chinsky, J.M. (1966). Spontaneous verbal rehearsal in a memory task as a function of age. *Child Development, 37*, 283–299.

Flavell, J.H., Friedrichs, A.G. & Hoyt, J.D. (1970). Developmental changes in memorisation processes. *Cognitive Psychology, 1*, 324–340.

Flynn, J. R. (1987). Massive IQ gains in 14 nations: What IQ tests really measure. *Psychological Bulletin, 101*, 171–191.

Foley, M.A., Johnson, M.K. & Raye, C.L. (1983). Age-related changes in confusion between memories for thought and memories for speech. *Child Development, 54*, 51–60.

Friedman, N.P., Miyake, A., Corley, R.P., Young, S.E., DeFries, J.C. & Hewitt, J.K. (2006). Not all executive functions are related to intelligence. *Psychological Science, 17*(2), 172–179.

Friedman, N.P., Miyake, A., Young, S.E., DeFries, J.C., Corley, R.P. & Hewitt, J.K. (2008). Individual differences in executive functions are almost entirely genetic in origin. *Journal of Experimental Psychology: General, 137*(2), 201–225.

Frith, U. (1989). Autism and 'theory of mind'. In C. Gillberg (Ed.), *Diagnosis and treatment of autism* (pp. 33–52). New York: Plenum Press.

Frith, U. (1991). *Autism and Asperger syndrome* (pp. 37–92). Cambridge, UK: Cambridge University Press. [Translation of Asperger, H. (1944). Die autistischen Psychopathen im kindesalter. *Archiv fur Psychiatrie und Nervenkrankheitan, 117*, 76–136.]

Garon, N., Bryson, S.E & Smith, I.M. (2008). Executive function in pre-schoolers: A review using an integrative framework. *Psychological Bulletin, 134*, 31–60.

Gathercole, S.E. (2006). Nonword repetition and word learning: The nature of the relationship. *Applied Psycholinguistics, 27*, 513–543.

Gathercole, S.E. & Adams, A.M. (1993). Phonological working memory in very young children. *Developmental Psychology, 29*, 770–778.

Gathercole, S.E., Adams, A.M. & Hitch, G.J. (1994). Do young children rehearse? An individual-differences analysis. *Memory & Cognition, 22*(2), 201–207.

Gathercole, S.E. & Alloway, T.P. (2006). Short-term and working memory impairments in neurodevelopmental disorders: Diagnosis and remedial support. *Journal of Child Psychology and Psychiatry, 47*(1), 4–15.

Gathercole, S.E. & Alloway, T.P. (2008). *Working memory and learning: A practical guide for teachers*. London: SAGE Publications Ltd.

Gathercole, S.E. & Baddeley, A.D. (1989). Evaluation of the role of phonological STM in the development of vocabulary in children: A longitudinal study. *Journal of Memory and Language, 28*, 200–213.

Gathercole, S.E. & Baddeley, A.D. (1990). Phonological memory deficits in language disordered children: Is there a causal connection? *Journal of Memory and Language, 29*, 336–360.

Gathercole, S.E. & Baddeley, A.D. (1996). *Children's Test of Nonword Repetition (CN REP)*. Harcourt Assessment: The Psychological Corporation.

Gathercole, S.E., Frankish, C.R., Pickering, S.J. & Peaker, S. (1999). Phonotactic influences on short-term memory. *Journal of Experimental Psychology: Learning, Memory and Cognition, 25*, 84–95.

Gathercole, S.E. & Hitch, G.J. (1993). Developmental changes in short-term memory: A revised working memory perspective. In A. Collins, S.E. Gathercole, M.A. Conway and P.E. Morris (Eds.), *Theories of memory* (pp. 189–209). Hove: Laurence Erlbaum Associates.

Gathercole, S.E., Hitch, G.J., Service, E. & Martin, A.J. (1997). Short-term memory and new word learning in children. *Developmental Psychology, 33*, 966–979.

Gathercole, S.E., Hitch, G.J., Service, E., Adams, A.-M. & Martin, A.J. (1999). Phonological short-term memory and vocabulary development: Further evidence of the nature of the relationship. *Applied Cognitive Psychology, 13*, 65–77.

Gathercole, S.E., Lamont, E. & Alloway, T.P. (2006). Working memory in the classroom. In S.J. Pickering (Ed.), *Working memory and education* (pp. 219–240). London: Elsevier.

Gathercole, S.E. & Pickering, S.J. (2000). Assessment of working memory in six- and seven-year-old children. *Journal of Educational Psychology, 92*, 377–390.

Gathercole, S.E., Pickering, S.J., Ambridge, B. & Wearing, H. (2004). The structure of working memory from 4 to 15 years of age. *Developmental Psychology, 40*, 177–190.

Gathercole, S.E., Pickering, S.J., Hall, M. & Peaker, S.J. (2001). Dissociable lexical and phonological influences on serial recognition and serial recall. *Quarterly Journal of Experimental Psychology, 45A*, 1–30.

Gathercole, S.E., Pickering, S.J., Knight, C. & Stegmann, Z. (2004). Working memory skills and educational attainment: Evidence from National Curriculum assessments at 7 and 14 years of age. *Applied Cognitive Psychology, 18*, 1–16.

Gathercole, S.E., Willis, C., Baddeley, A.D. & Emslie, H. (1994). The children's test of nonword repetition: A test of phonological working memory. *Memory, 2*, 103–127.

Gathercole, S.E., Willis, C., Emslie, H. & Baddeley, A.D. (1991). The influence of number of syllables and word-likeness on children's repetition of nonwords. *Applied Psycholinguistics, 12*, 349–367.

Gaultney, J.F., Kipp, K. & Kirk, K. (2005). Utilisation deficiency and working memory capacity in adult memory performance: Not just for children any more. *Cognitive Development, 20*, 205–213.

Geurts, H.M., Verte, S., Oosterlaan, J., Roeyers, H. & Sergeant, J.A. (2004). How specific are executive functioning deficits in attention deficit hyperactivity disorder and autism? *Journal of Child Psychology and Psychiatry, 45*(4), 836–854.

Glidden, L.M. & Mar, H.H. (1978). Availability and access ability of information in the semantic memory of retarded and nonretarded adolescents. *Journal of Experimental Child Psychology, 25*, 33–40.

Goldstein, K.H. & Scheerer, M. (1953). Tests of abstract and concrete behaviour. In A. Weidner (Ed.), *Contributions to medical psychology*, Vol. 2. New York: Ronald Press.

Gopnik, M. & Crago, M.B. (1991). Familial aggregation of a developmental language disorder. *Cognition, 39*, 1–50.

Gould, J.H. & Glencross, D.J. (1990). Do children with a specific reading disability have a general serial-ordering deficit? *Neuropsychologia, 28*(3), 271–278.

Grammer, J.K., Purtell, K.M., Coffman, J.L. & Ornstein, P.A. (2011). Relations between children's metamemory and strategic performance: Time-varying covariates in early elementary school. *Journal of Experimental Child Psychology, 108*, 139–155.

Grant, J., Karmiloff-Smith, A., Gathercole, S., Patterson, S., Howlin, P., Davies, M. & Udwin, O. (1997). Phonological short-term memory and its relationship to language in Williams syndrome. *Cognitive Neuropsychiatry, 2*(2), 81–99.

Guttentag, R.E. (1984). The mental effort requirement of cumulative rehearsal: A developmental study. *Journal of Experimental Child Psychology, 37*, 92–106.

Hagan, J. W. & Kingsley, P. R. (1968). Labelling effects in short-term memory. *Child Development, 39*, 113–121.

Hale, C.A. & Borkowski, J.G. (1991). Attention, memory, and cognition. In J.L. Matson & J.A. Mulick (Eds.), *Handbook of mental retardation* (pp. 505–528). New York: Pergamon Press.

Halliday, M.S. & Hitch, G.J. (1988). Developmental applications of working memory. In G. Claxton (Ed.), *Growth points in cognition* (pp. 193–222). London: Routledge.

Hamilton, C., Coates, R. & Heffernan, T. (2003). What develops in visuo-spatial working memory development? *European Journal of Cognitive Psychology, 15*(1), 43–69.

Happé, F. & Frith, U. (2006). The weak coherence account: Detail-focused cognitive style in autism spectrum disorders. *Journal of Autism and Developmental Disorders, 36*, 5–25.

Harris, J.C. (2006). *Intellectual disability: Understanding its development, causes, classification, evaluation and treatment*. New York: Oxford University Press.

Hasselhorn, M. & Mähler, C. (2007). Phonological working memory of children in two German special schools. *International Journal of Disability, Development and Education, 54*(2), 225–244.

Hattori, M. et al. (2000). The DNA sequence of human chromosome 21. *Nature, 405*, 311–320.

Henry, L.A. (1991a). The development of auditory memory span: The role of rehearsal. *British Journal of Developmental Psychology, 9*, 493–511.

Henry, L.A. (1991b). The effects of word length and phonemic similarity in young children's short-term memory. *Quarterly Journal of Experimental Psychology, 43A*, 35–52.

Henry, L.A. (1994). The relationship between speech rate and memory span in children. *International Journal of Behavioral Development: Special Issue on Working Memory, 17*, 37–56.

Henry, L.A. (2001). How does the severity of a learning disability affect working memory performance? *Memory, 9*, 233–247.

Henry, L.A. (2008). Short-term memory coding in children with intellectual disabilities. *American Journal on Mental Retardation, 113*, 187–200.

Henry, L.A. (2010). The episodic buffer in children with intellectual disabilities: An exploratory study. *Research in Developmental Disabilities, 31*, 1609–1614.

Henry, L.A. & Bettenay, C. (2010). Measuring executive functioning in children. Child and Adolescent Mental Health, 15(2), 110–119.

Henry, L.A. & Gudjonsson, G.H. (1999). Eyewitness memory and suggestibility in children with mental retardation. *American Journal on Mental Retardation, 104*, 491–508.

Henry, L.A. & Gudjonsson, G.H. (2003). Eyewitness memory, suggestibility and repeated recall sessions in children with mild and moderate intellectual disabilities. *Law and Human Behavior, 27*, 481–505.

Henry, L.A. & Gudjonsson, G.H. (2004). The effects of memory trace strength on eyewitness recall in children with and without intellectual disabilities. *Journal of Experimental Child Psychology, 89*, 53–71.

Henry, L.A. & Gudjonsson, G.H. (2007). Individual and developmental differences in eyewitness recall and suggestibility in children with intellectual disabilities. *Applied Cognitive Psychology, 21*, 361–381.

Henry, L.A. & MacLean, M. (2002). Working memory performance in children with and without intellectual disabilities. *American Journal on Mental Retardation, 107*, 421–432.

Henry, L.A., Messer, D.J. & Nash, G. (2011). Executive functioning in children with specific language impairment. *Journal of Child Psychology and Psychiatry doi: 10.1111/j.1469-7610.2011.02430.x*

Henry, L.A., Messer, D.J. & Nash, G. (in prep.). Working memory in children and young people with specific language impairment.

Henry, L.A. & Millar, S. (1991). Memory span increase with age: A test of two hypotheses. *Journal of Experimental Child Psychology, 51*, 459–484.

Henry, L.A. & Millar, S. (1993). Why does memory span increase with age?: A review of the evidence for two current hypotheses. *European Journal of Cognitive Psychology, 5*, 241–287.

Henry, L.A. & Norman, T. (1996). The relationship between memory performance, use of simple memory strategies and metamemory in young children. *International Journal of Behavioral Development, 19*, 177–199.

Henry, L.A., Turner, J.E., Smith, P.T. & Leather, C. (2000). Modality effects and the development of the word length effect in children. *Memory, 8*, 1–17.

Henry, L.A. & Winfield, J. (2010). Working memory and educational achievement in children with intellectual disabilities. *Journal of Intellectual Disability Research, 54*(4), 354–365.

Hick, R.F., Botting, N. & Conti-Ramsden, G. (2005). Short-term memory and vocabulary development in children with Down syndrome and children with specific language impairment. *Developmental Medicine & Child Neurology, 47*, 532–538.

Hill, E.L. (2004). Evaluating the theory of executive dysfunction in autism. *Developmental Review, 24*, 189–233.

Hill, E.L. (2008). Executive functioning in autism spectrum disorder: Where it fits in the causal model. In E. McGregor, M. Núñez, K. Cebula and J.C. Gómez (Eds.), *Autism: An integrated view from neurocognitive, clinical, and intervention research* (pp. 143–165). Oxford: Blackwell Publishing Ltd.

Hill, E.L. & Bird, C.M. (2006). Executive processes in Asberger syndrome: Patterns of performance in a multiple case series. *Neuropsychologia, 44*, 2822–2835.

Hitch, G.J. & Halliday, M.S. (1983). Working memory in children. *Philosophical Transactions of the Royal Society of London, B 302*, 325–340.

Hitch, G.J., Halliday, M.S., Dodd, A. & Littler, J.E. (1989). Development of rehearsal in short-term memory: Differences between pictorial and spoken stimuli. *British Journal of Developmental Psychology, 7*, 347–362.

Hitch, G.J., Halliday, S. & Littler, J.E. (1989). Item identification time and rehearsal rate as predictors of memory span in children. *Quarterly Journal of Experimental Psychology, 41A*, 321–337.

Hitch, G.J., Halliday, S. & Littler, J.E. (1993). Development of memory span for spoken words: The role of rehearsal and item identification processes. *British Journal of Developmental Psychology, 11*, 159–169.

Hitch, G.J., Halliday, M.S., Schaafstal, A.M. & Heffernan, T.M. (1991). Speech, 'inner speech', and the development of short-term memory: Effects of picture-labeling on recall. *Journal of Experimental Child Psychology, 51*, 220–234.

Hitch, G.J., Halliday, S., Schaafstal, A.M. & Schraagen, J.M.C. (1988). Visual working memory in young children. *Memory & Cognition, 16*, 120–132.

Hitch, G.J. & McAuley, E. (1991). Working memory in children with specific arithmetic learning difficulties. *British Journal of Psychology, 82*, 375–386.

Hitch, G.J., Towse, J.N. & Hutton, U. (2001). What limits children's working memory span? Theoretical accounts and applications for scholastic development. *Journal of Experimental Psychology: General, 130*, 184–198.

Hitch, G.J., Woodin, M.E. & Baker, S. (1989). Visual and phonological components of working memory in children. *Memory & Cognition, 17*, 175–185.

Hodapp, R.M. & Dykens, E.M. (2009). Intellectual disabilities and child psychiatry: Looking to the future. *Journal of Child Psychology and Psychiatry, 50*(1), 99–107.

Hoekstra, R.A., Happé, F., Baron-Cohen, S. & Ronald, A. (2009). Association between extreme autistic traits and intellectual disability: Insights from a general population twin study. *The British Journal of Psychiatry, 195*, 531–536.

Hoffman, L.M. & Gillam, R.B. (2004). Verbal and spatial information processing constraints in children with specific language impairment. *Journal of Speech, Language, and Hearing Research, 47*, 114–125.

Holmes, J., Gathercole, S. E. & Dunning, D. L. (2009). Adaptive training leads to sustained enhancement of poor working memory in children. *Developmental Science, 12*, F1–F7.

Howes, N.L., Bigler, E.D., Lawson, J.S. & Burlingame, G.M. (1999). Reading disability subtypes and the test of memory and learning. *Archives of Clinical Neuropsychology, 14*, 317–339.

Howlin, P., Davies, M. & Udwin, O. (1998). Cognitive functioning in adults with Williams syndrome. *Journal of Child Psychology and Psychiatry, 39*, 183–189.

Hughes, C., Plumet, M-H. & Leboyer, M. (1999). Towards a cognitive phenotype for autism: Increased prevalence of executive dysfunction and superior spatial span amongst siblings of children with autism. *Journal of Child Psychology and Psychiatry, 40*(5), 705–718.

Hughes, C., Russell, J. & Robbins, T.W. (1994). Evidence for executive dysfunction in autism. *Neuropsychologia, 32*(4), 477–492.

Huizinga, M., Dolan, C. & van der Molen, M. (2006). Age related change in executive function: Developmental trends and a latent variable analysis. *Neuropsychologia, 44*, 2017–2036.

Hulme, C. & Mackenzie, S. (1992). *Working memory and severe learning difficulties.* Hove: Lawrence Erlbaum Associates.

Hulme, C., Maughan, S. & Brown, G.D.A. (1991). Memory for familiar and unfamiliar words: Evidence for a long-term memory contribution to short-term memory span. *Journal of Memory and Language, 30*, 685–701.

Hulme, C. & Muir, C. (1985). Developmental changes in speech rate and memory span: A causal relationship? *British Journal of Developmental Psychology, 3*, 175–181.

Hulme, C., Neath, I., Stuart, G., Shostak, L., Surprenant, A.M., & Brown, G.D.A. (2006). The distinctiveness of the word-length effect. *Journal of Experimental Psychology: Learning, Memory, and Cognition, 32*(3), 586–594.

Hulme, C., Roodenrys, S., Brown, G.D.A. & Mercer, R. (1995). The role of long-term memory mechanisms in memory span. *British Journal of Psychology, 86*, 527–536.

Hulme, C., Roodenrys, S., Schweickert, R., Brown, G.D.A., Martin, S. & Stuart, G. (1997). Word-frequency effects on short-term memory tasks: Evidence for a redintegration process in immediate serial recall. *Journal of Experimental Psychology: Learning, Memory, and Cognition, 23*(5), 1217–1232.

Hulme, C. & Snowling, M.J. (2009). *Developmental disorders of language learning and cognition.* Chichester, West Sussex: Wiley-Blackwell.

Hulme, C., Silvester, J., Smith, S. & Muir, C. (1986). The effects of word length on memory for pictures: Evidence for speech coding in young children. *Journal of Experimental Child Psychology, 41*, 61–75.

Hulme, C., Surprenant, A.M., Bireta, T.J., Stuart, G. & Neath, I. (2004). Abolishing the word-length effect. *Journal of Experimental Psychology: Learning, Memory, and Cognition, 30*(1), 98–106.

Hulme, C., Thomson, N., Muir, C. & Lawrence, A. (1984). Speech rate and the development of short-term memory span. *Journal of Experimental Child Psychology, 38*, 241–253.

Hulme, C. & Tordoff, V. (1989). Working memory development: The effects of speech rate, word length, and acoustic similarity on serial recall. *Journal of Experimental Child Psychology, 47*, 72–87.

Im-Bolter, N., Johnson, J. & Pascual-Leone, J. (2006). Processing limitations in children with specific language impairment: The role of executive function. *Child Development, 77*(6), 1822–1841.

Iscoe, I. & Semler, I.J. (1964). Paired-associate learning in normal and mentally retarded children as a function of four experimental conditions. *Journal of Comparative and Physiological Psychology, 57*(3), 387–392.

Issacs, E.B. & Vargha-Khadem, F. (1989). Differential course of development of spatial and verbal memory span: A normative study. *British Journal of Developmental Psychology, 7*, 377–380.

Jarrold, C. & Baddeley, A.D. (1997). Short-term memory for verbal and visuospatial information in Down Syndrome. *Cognitive Neuropsychiatry, 2*(2), 101–122.

Jarrold, C., Baddeley, A.D. & Hewes, A.K. (1998). Verbal and nonverbal abilities in the Williams Syndrome Phenotype: Evidence for diverging developmental trajectories. *Journal of Child Psychology and Psychiatry, 39*, 511–523.

Jarrold, C., Baddeley, A.D. & Hewes, A.K. (1999). Genetically dissociated components of working memory: Evidence from Down's and Williams syndrome. *Neuropsychologia, 37*, 637–651.

Jarrold, C., Baddeley, A.D. & Hewes, A.K. (2000). Verbal short-term memory deficits in Down Syndrome: A consequence of problems in rehearsal? *Journal of Child Psychology and Psychiatry, 41*(2), 233–244.

Jarrold, C. & Brock, J. (2004). To match or not to match? Methodological issues in autism-related research. *Journal of Autism and Developmental Disorders, 34*, 81–86.

Jarrold, C., Cocksey, J. & Dockerill, E. (2008). Phonological similarity and lexicality effects in children's verbal short-term memory: Concerns about the interpretation of probed recall data. *Quarterly Journal of Experimental Psychology, 61*(2), 324–340.

Jarrold, C., Cowan, N., Hewes, A.K. & Riby, D.M. (2004). Speech timing and verbal short-term memory: Evidence for contrasting deficits in Down syndrome and William syndrome. *Journal of Memory and Language, 51*, 365–380.

Jarrold, C., Phillips, C. & Baddeley, A.D. (2007). Binding of visual and spatial short-term memory in Williams syndrome and moderate learning disability. *Developmental Medicine & Child Neurology, 49*, 270–273.

Jarrold, C., Purser, H.R.M. & Brock, J. (2006). Short-term memory in Down syndrome. In T.P. Alloway & S.E. Gathercole (Eds.), *Working memory and neurodevelopmental disorders* (pp. 239–266). Hove, East Sussex, UK: Psychology Press.

Jensen, A. (1998). *The g factor*. Westport: Praeger.

Jerman, O. & Swanson, H.L. (2005). Working memory and reading disabilities: A selective meta-analysis of the literature. In T. Scruggs & M. Mastroperi (Eds.), *Advances in learning and behavior disabilities* (pp. 11–31). New York: Elsevier.

Johnston, J. & Ellis Weismer, S. (1983). Mental rotation abilities in language disordered children. *Journal of Speech and Hearing Research, 26*, 397–403.

Johnston, R.S. (1982). Phonological coding in dyslexic readers. *British Journal of Psychology, 73*, 455–460.

Johnston, R.S., Johnson, C. & Gray, C. (1987). The emergence of the word length effect in young children: The effects of overt and covert rehearsal. *British Journal of Developmental Psychology, 5*, 243–248.

Johnston, R.S., Rugg, M.D. & Scott, R. (1987). Phonological similarity effects, memory span and developmental reading disorders: The nature of the relationship. *British Journal of Psychology, 78*, 205–211.

Jones, D.M., Hughes, R.W. & Macken, W.J. (2007). Commentary on Baddeley and Larsen (2007): The phonological store abandoned. *Quarterly Journal of Experimental Psychology, 60*(4), 505–511.

Jones-Gotman, M. & Milner, B. (1977). Design fluency: The invention of nonsense drawings after focal cortical lesions. *Neuropsychologia, 15*, 653–674.

Jonides, J., Schumacher, E.J., Smith, E.E., Kieppe, R.A., Awh, E., Reuter-Lorenz, P.A., Marchuetz, C. & Willis, C.R. (1998). The role of a parietal cortex in verbal working memory. *The Journal of Neuroscience, 18*, 5026–5034.

Jorm, A.F. (1983). Specific reading retardation and working memory: A review. *British Journal of Psychology, 74*, 311–342.

Joseph, R.M., McGrath, L.M. & Tager-Flusberg, H. (2005). Executive dysfunction and its relation to language ability in verbal school-age children with autism. *Developmental Neuropsychology, 27*(3), 361–378.

Joseph, R.M., Steele, S.D., Meyer, E. & Tager-Flusberg, H. (2005). Self-ordered pointing in children with autism: failure to use verbal mediation in the service of working memory? *Neuropsychologia, 43*, 1400–1411.

Kail, R. (1990). *The development of memory in children*, 3rd ed. New York: W. H. Freeman and Company.

Kail, R. (1992a). Processing speed, speech rate, and memory. *Developmental Psychology, 28*(5), 899–904.

Kail, R. (1992b). General slowing of information-processing by persons with mental retardation. *American Journal on Mental Retardation, 97*, 333–341.

Kail, R. (1997). Phonological skill and articulation time independently contribute to the development of memory span. *Journal of Experimental Child Psychology, 67*, 57–68.

Kail, R. & Park, Y.S. (1994). Processing time, articulation time, and memory span. *Journal of Experimental Child Psychology, 57*, 281–291.

Kamhi, A.G. & Catts, H.W. (1986). Toward an understanding of developmental language and reading disorders, *Journal of Speech and Hearing Research, 51*, 337–347.

Kane, M.J. & Engle, R.W. (2002). The role of prefrontal cortex in working memory capacity, executive attention and general fluid intelligence: An individuals differences perspective. *Psychonomic Bulletin and Review, 4*, 637–671.

Kane, M.J., Hambrick, D.Z., Tuholski, S.W., Wilhelm, O., Payne, T.W. & Engle, R.W. (2004). The generality of working memory capacity: A latent-variable approach to verbal and visuospatial memory span and reasoning. *Journal of Experimental Psychology: General, 133*, 189–217.

Kanner, L. (1943). Autistic disturbances of affective contact. *Nervous Child, 2*, 217–250.

Kanno, K. & Ikeda, Y. (2002). Word-length effect in verbal short-term memory in individuals with Down's syndrome. *Journal of Intellectual Disability Research, 46*(8), 613–618.

Karmiloff-Smith, A., Thomas, M., Annaz, D., Humphreys, K., Ewing, S., Brace, N., Van Duuren, M., Pike, G., Grice, S. & Campbell, R. (2004). Exploring the Williams syndrome face-processing debate: The importance of building developmental trajectories. *Journal of Child Psychology and Psychiatry, 45*(7), 1258–1274.

Katz, R.B., Shankweiler, D. & Liberman, I.Y. (1981). Memory for item order and phonetic recoding in the beginning reader. *Journal of Experimental Child Psychology, 32*, 474–484.

Kavale, K.A. & Forness, S.R. (1992). Learning difficulties and memory problems in mental retardation: A meta-analysis of theoretical perspectives. In T. Scruggs & M. Mastropieri (Eds.), *Advances in learning and behaviour* (pp. 177–219). New York: Erlbaum.

Keeley, K. (1971). Age and task effects in short-term memory in children. Perception and Psychophysics, 9, 480–482.

Kenworthy, L., Black, D.O., Harrison, B., della Rosa, A. & Wallace, G.L. (2009). Are executive control functions related to autism symptoms in high-functioning children? *Child Neuropsychology, 15*(5), 425–440.

Kingsley, P.R. & Hagan, J.W. (1969). Induced versus spontaneous rehearsal in short-term memory in nursery school children. *Developmental Psychology, 1*, 40–46.

Kirchner, D. M. & Klatzky, R. L. (1985). Verbal rehearsal and memory in language-disordered children. *Journal of Speech and Hearing Research, 28*, 556–565.

Kittler, P.M., Krinsky-McHale, S.J. & Devenny, D.A. (2004). Semantic and phonological loop effects on verbal working memory in middle-age adults with mental retardation. *American Journal on Mental Retardation, 109*(6), 467–480.

Kittler, P.M., Krinsky-McHale, S.J. & Devenny, D.A. (2008). Dual-task processing as a measure of executive function: A comparison between adults with Williams and Down syndromes. *American Journal on Mental Retardation, 113*, 117–132.

Klein, B.P. & Mervis, C.B. (1999). Contrasting patterns of cognitive abilities of 9- and 10-year-olds with Williams syndrome or Down syndrome. *Developmental Neuropsychology, 16*(2), 177–196.

Klenberg, L., Korkman, M. & Lahti-Nuuttila, P. (2001). Differential development of attention and executive functions in 3- to 12-year-old Finnish children. *Developmental Neuropsychology, 20*(1), 407–428.

Kohlberg, L. (1968). Early education: A cognitive-developmental view. *Child Development, 39*, 1013–1062.

Kongs, S.K., Thompson, L.L., Iverson, G.L. & Heaton, R.K. (2000). *Wisconsin Card Sorting Test – 64 Card Version (WCST-64)*. Odessa, FL: Psychological Assessment Resources, Inc.

Korkman, M., Kirk, U. & Kemp, S. (2007). *NEPSY II: A developmental neuropsychological assessment manual*. San Antonio: Psychological Corporation.

Koshino, H., Carpenter, P.A., Minshew, N.J., Cherkassky, V.L., Keller, T.A. & Just, M.A. (2005). Functional connectivity in an fMRI working memory task in high-functioning autism. *NeuroImage, 24*, 810–821.

Kreutzer, M.A., Leonard, C. & Flavell, J.H. (1975). An interview study of children's knowledge about memory. *Monographs of the Society for Research in Child Development, 40* (Serial No. 159).

Kunzinger, E.L. (1985). A short-term longitudinal study of memorial development during early grade school. *Developmental Psychology, 21*, 642–646.

Lai, C.S., Fisher, S.E., Hurst, J.A., Vargha-Khadem, F. & Monaco, A.P. (2001). A forkhead-domain gene is mutated in severe speech and language disorder. *Nature, 413*, 519–523.

Laing, E., Grant, J., Thomas, M., Parmigiani, C., Ewing, S. & Karmiloff-Smith, A. (2005). Love is... an abstract word: The influence of lexical semantics on verbal short-term memory in Williams syndrome. *Cortex, 41*, 169–179.

Laing, E., Hulme, C., Grant, J. & Karmiloff-Smith, A. (2001). Learning to read in Williams syndrome: Looking beneath the surface of atypical reading development. *Journal of Child Psychology and Psychiatry, 42*(6), 729–739.

Lamb, M., La Rooy, D., Katz, C. & Malloy, L. (Eds) *Children's Testimony: A Handbook of Psychological Research and Forensic Practice* (2nd Edition). Oxford: Wiley-Blackwell.

Lanfranchi, S., Carretti, B., Span, G. & Cornoldi, C. (2009). A specific deficit in visuospatial simultaneous working memory in Down syndrome. *Journal of Intellectual Disability Research, 53*(5), 474–483.

Lanfranchi, S., Cornoldi, C. & Vianello, R. (2004). Verbal and visuospatial working memory deficits in children with Down syndrome. *American Journal on Mental Retardation, 109*, 456–466.

Lanfranchi, S., Jerman, O., Dal Pont, E., Alberti, A. & Vianello, R. (2010). Executive function in adolescents with Down syndrome. *Journal of Intellectual Disability Research, 54*(4), 308–319.

Laws, G. (2002). Working memory in children and adolescents with Down syndrome: Evidence from a colour memory experiment. *Journal of Child Psychology and Psychiatry, 43*(3), 353–364.

Laws, G. & Bishop, D.V.M. (2003). A comparison of language abilities in adolescents with Down syndrome and children with specific language impairment. *Journal of Speech, Language, and Hearing Research, 46*, 1324–1339.

Laws, G., Byrne, A. & Buckley, S. (2000). Language and memory development in children with Down syndrome at mainstream schools and special schools: A comparison. *Educational Psychology, 20*(4), 447–457.

Laws, G. & Gunn, D. (2004). Phonological memory as a predictor of language comprehension in Down syndrome: A five-year follow-up study. *Journal of Child Psychology and Psychiatry, 45*(2), 326–337.

Leather, C. & Henry, L.A. (1994). Working memory span and phonological awareness tasks as predictors of early reading ability. *Journal of Experimental Child Psychology, 58*, 88–111.

Lehmann, M. & Hasselhorn, M. (2007). Variable memory strategy use in children adapted into a task learning behaviour: Developmental changes and working memory influences in free recall. *Child Development, 78*(4), 1068–1082.

Lehto, J.E. (1996). Are executive function tests dependent on working memory capacity? *Quarterly Journal of Experimental Psychology, 49A*, 29–50.

Lehto, J.E., Juujärvi, P., Kooistra, L. & Lulkkinen, L. (2003). Dimensions of executive functioning: Evidence from children. *British Journal of Developmental Psychology, 21*, 59–80.

Leonard, L.B., Ellis Weismer, S., Miller, C.A., Francis, D.J., Tomblin, J.B. & Kail, R.V. (2007). Speed of processing, working memory, and language impairment in children. *Journal of Speech, Language, and Hearing Research, 50*, 408–428.

Levin, H.S., Culhane, K.A., Hartmann, J., Evankovich, K., Mattson, A.J., Harward, H., Ringholz, G., Ewing-Cobbs L. & Fletcher, J.M. (1991). Developmental changes in performance on tests of purported frontal lobe functioning. *Developmental Neuropsychology, 7*, 377–395.

Liberman, I.Y., Mann, V.A., Shankweiler, D. & Werfelman, M. (1982). Children's memory for recurring linguistic and nonlinguistic material in relation to reading ability. *Cortex, 18*, 367–375.

Lidstone, J.S.M., Fernyhough, C., Meins, E. & Whitehouse, A.J.O. (2009). Inner speech impairment in children with autism is associated with greater nonverbal than verbal skills. *Journal of Autism and Developmental Disorders, 39*, 1222–1225.

Lidstone, J.S.M., Meins, E. & Fernyhough, C. (2010). The roles of private speech and inner speech in planning during middle childhood: Evidence from a dual task paradigm. *Journal of Experimental Child Psychology, 107*, 438–451.

Lind, S. & Bowler, D. (2008). Episodic memory and autonoetic consciousness in autistic spectrum disorders: The roles of self-awareness, representational abilities and temporal cognition. In J. Boucher & D. Bowler (Eds.), *Memory in autism: Theory and evidence*. Cambridge: Cambridge University Press.

Liss, M., Fein, D., Allen, D., Dunn, M., Feinstein, C., Morris, R., Waterhouse, L. & Rapin, I. (2001). Executive functioning in high-functioning children with autism. *Journal of Child Psychology and Psychiatry, 42*(2), 261–270.

Lloyd, M.E., Doydum, A.O. & Newcombe, N.S. (2009). Memory binding in early childhood: Evidence for a retrieval deficit. *Child Development, 80*(5), 1321–1328.

Lobley, K. J., Baddeley, A. D. & Gathercole, S. E. (2005). Phonological similarity effects in verbal complex span. *Quarterly Journal of Experimental Psychology, 58A*(8), 1462–1478.

Logie, R.H. (1995). *Visuo-spatial working memory*. Hove: Lawrence Erlbaum Associates Ltd.

Logie, R.H., Della Sala, S., Wynn, V. & Baddeley, A.D. (2000). Visual similarity effects in immediate serial recall. *Quarterly Journal of Experimental Psychology, 53A*, 626–646.

Logie, R.H. & Marchetti, C. (1991). Visuo-spatial working memory: Visual, spatial or central executive? In R.H. Logie & M. Dennis (Eds.), *Mental images in human cognition* (pp. 105–115). Amsterdam: Elsevier.

Logie, R.H. & Pearson, D.G. (1997). The inner eye and the inner scribe of visuo-spatial working memory: Evidence from developmental fractionation. *European Journal of Cognitive Psychology, 9*(3), 241–257.

Longoni, A., Richardson, J.T.E. & Aiello, A. (1993). Articulatory rehearsal and phonological storage in working memory. *Memory & Cognition, 21*, 11–22.

Longoni, A.M. & Scalisi, T.G. (1994). Developmental aspects of phonemic and visual similarity effects: Further evidence in Italian children. *International Journal of Behavioral Development, 17*, 57–71.

Lopez, B.R., Lincoln, A.J., Ozonoff, S. & Lai, Z. (2005). Examining the relationship between executive functions and restricted, repetitive symptoms of autistic disorder. *Journal of Autism and Developmental Disorders, 35*(4), 445–460.

Lord, C. & Bailey, A. (2002). Autism spectrum disorders. In M. Rutter and E. Taylor (Eds.), *Child and adolescent psychiatry*, 4th ed. Oxford: Blackwell Science Ltd.

Lovatt, P.J., Avons, S.E. & Masterson, J. (2000). Output decay in immediate serial recall: Speech time revisited. *Journal of Memory and Language, 46*, 227–243.

Lovatt, P.J., Avons, S.E. & Masterson, J. (2002). The word length effect and disyllabic words. *Quarterly Journal of Experimental Psychology, 53*, 1–22.

Lukose, S. (1987). Knowledge and behavior relationships in the memory ability of retarded and non-retardant students. *Journal of Experimental Child Psychology, 43*, 13–24.

Luna, B., Minshew, N.J., Garver, K.E., Lazar, N.A., Thulborn, K.R., Eddy, W.F. & Sweeney, J.A. (2002). Neocortical system abnormalities in autism: An fMRI study of spatial working memory. *Neurology, 59*, 834–840.

Macaruso, P., Locke, J.L., Smith, S. & Powers, S. (1996). Short-term memory and phonological coding in developmental dyslexia. *Journal of Neurolinguistics, 9*(2), 135–146.

Majerus, S. & Van Der Linden, M. (2003). Long-term memory effects on verbal short-term memory: A replication study. *British Journal of Developmental Psychology, 21*(2), 303–310.

Majerus, S., Van der Linden, M., Mulder, L., Meulemans, T. & Peters, F. (2004). Verbal short-term memory reflects the sublexical organization of the phonological language network: Evidence from an incidental phonotactic learning paradigm. *Journal of Memory and Language, 51*, 297–306.

Mammarella, I. C., Pazzaglia, F. and Cornoldi, C. (2008), Evidence for different components in children's visuospatial working memory. *British Journal of Developmental Psychology, 26*, 337–355.

Manly, T., Robertson, I.H., Anderson, V. & Nimmo-Smith, I. (1999). *The Test of Everyday Attention for Children (TEA-Ch)*. Bury St Edmunds, UK: Thames Valley Test Company.

Mann, V.A., Lieberman, I.Y. & Shankweiler, D. (1980). Children's memory for sentences and word strings in relation to reading ability. *Memory and Cognition, 8*, 329–335.

Marcel, M.M. & Weeks, S.L. (1988). Short-term memory difficulties and Down's syndrome. *Journal of Mental Deficiency Research, 32*, 153–162.

Marinosson, G.L. (1974). Performance profiles of matched normal, educationally subnormal and severely subnormal children on the revised ITPA. *Journal of Child Psychology and Psychiatry, 15*, 139–148.

Martens, M.A., Wilson, S.J. & Reutens, D.C. (2008). Williams syndrome: A critical review of the cognitive, behavioral, and neuroanatomical phenotype. *Journal of Child Psychology and Psychiatry, 49*(6), 576–608.

Martin, C., West, J., Cull, C. & Adams, M. (2000). A preliminary study investigating how people with mild intellectual disabilities perform on the Rivermead Behavioural Memory Test. *Journal of Applied Research in Intellectual Disabilities, 13*, 186–193.

Marton, K. (2008). Visuo-spatial processing and executive functions in children with specific language impairment. *International Journal of Language and Communication Disorders, 43*(2), 181–200.

Marton, K. & Schwartz, R.G. (2003). Working memory capacity and language processes in children with specific language impairment. *Journal of Speech, Language, and Hearing Research, 46*(3), 1138–1153.

Maughan, B., Messer, J., Collishaw, S., Pickles, A., Snowling, M., Yule, W. & Rutter, M. (2009). Persistence of literacy problems: Spelling in adolescence and at mid-life. *Journal of Child Psychology and Psychiatry, 50*(8), 893–901.

McArthur, G.M., Hogben, J.H., Edwards, V.T., Heath, S.M. & Mengler, E.D. (2000). On the 'specifics' of specific reading disability and specific language impairment. *Journal of Child Psychology and Psychiatry, 41*(7), 869–874.

McCarver, R.B. & Ellis, N.R. (1972). Effect of overt verbal labelling on short-term memory in culturally deprived and non-deprived children. *Developmental Psychology, 6*, 38–41.

McDougall, S., Hulme, C., Ellis, A. & Monk, A. (1994). Learning to read: The role of short-term memory and phonological skills. *Journal of Experimental Child Psychology, 58*, 112–133.

McGilly, K. & Siegler, R.S. (1989). How children choose among serial recall strategies. *Child Development, 60*, 172–182.

McLeod, P. & Posner, M.I. (1984). Privileged loops from percept to act. In H. Bouma & D.G. Bouwhuis (Eds.), *Attention and performance X: Control of language processes.* (pp. 55–66). Hove: Lawrence Erlbaum Associates.

McNeil, A.M. & Johnston, R.S. (2004). Word length, phonemic, and visual similarity effect in poor and normal readers. *Memory & Cognition, 32*(5), 687–695.

Menghini, D., Addona, F., Costanzo, F. & Vicari, S. (2010). Executive functions in individuals with Williams syndrome. *Journal of Intellectual Disability Research, 54*(5), 418–432.

Mervis, C.B. & Klein-Tasman, B.P. (2004). Methodological issues in group-matching designs: Levels for control variable comparisions and measurement characteristics of control and target variables. *Journal of Autism and Developmental Disorders, 34*(1), 7–17.

Metsala, J.L. (1999). The development of phonemic awareness in reading-disabled children. *Applied Psycholinguistics, 20*, 149–158.

Michas, I. & Henry, L.A. (1994). The link between phonological memory and vocabulary acquisition. *British Journal of Developmental Psychology, 12*, 147–163.

Milgram, N.A. (1973). Cognition and language in mental retardation: Distinctions and implications. In D.K. Routh (Ed.), *The experimental psychology of mental retardation* (pp. 157–230). London: Crosby Lockwood Staples.

Miller, C.A., Kail, R., Leonard, L.B. & Tomblin, J.B. (2001). Speed of processing in children with specific language impairment. *Journal of Speech, Language, and Hearing Research, 44*, 416–433.

Miller, P.H. & Seier, W.L. (1994). Strategy utilization deficiencies in children: When, where, and why. In H.W. Reese (Ed.), *Advances in child development and behaviour* (Vol. 25, pp. 105–156). San Diego: Academic Press.

Milner, B. (1964). Some effects of frontal lobectomy in man. In J.M. Warren & K. Akert (Eds.), *The frontal granular cortex and behavior* (pp. 313–334). New York: McGraw-Hill.

Minear, M. & Shah, P. (2006). Sources of working memory deficits in children and possibilities for remediation. In S.J. Pickering (Ed.), *Working memory and education* (pp. 273–307). London: Elsevier Academic Press.

Miyake, A., Friedman, N.P., Emerson, M.J., Witzki, A.H., Howerter, A. & Wager, T.D. (2000). The unity and diversity of executive functions and their contributions to complex 'frontal lobe' tasks: A latent variable analysis. *Cognitive Psychology, 41*, 49–100.

Montgomery, J.W. (1995). Sentence comprehension in children with specific language impairment: The role of phonological working memory. *Journal of Speech and Hearing Research, 38*, 187–199.

Montgomery, J.W. (2002). Understanding the language difficulties of children with specific language impairments: Does verbal working memory matter? *American Journal of Speech and Language Pathology, 11*, 77–91.

Mottron, L., Morasse, K. & Belleville, S. (2001). A study of memory functioning in individuals with autism. *Journal of Child Psychology and Psychiatry, 42*(2), 253–260.

Murphy, K., McKone, E. & Slee, J. (2003). Dissociations between implicit and explicit memory in children: The role of strategic processing and the knowledge base. *Journal of Experimental Child Psychology, 84*, 124–165.

Murry, D.J. (1968). Articulation and acoustic confusability in short-term memory. *Journal of Experimental Psychology, 78*, 679–684.

Nadel, L. (1999). Down syndrome in cognitive neuroscience perspective. In H. Tager-Flusberg (Ed.), *Neurodevelopmental disorders* (pp. 197–221). Cambridge, MA: MIT Press.

Nagai, C., Inui, T. & Iwata, M. (2011). Fading-figure tracing in Williams syndrome. *Brain and Cognition, 75*, 10–17.

Nation, K. (2005). Children's reading comprehension difficulties. In M.J. Snowling & C. Hulme (Eds.), *The science of reading*. Blackwell Publishing.

Nettlebeck, T. (1987). Inspection time and intelligence. In P.A. Vernon (Ed.), *Speed of information-processing and intelligence* (pp. 294–346). Norwood, NJ: Ablex Publishing Corporation.

Nicolson, R. (1981). The relationship between memory span and processing speed. In M.P. Friedman, J.P. Das & N. O'Connor (Eds.), *Intelligence and learning* (pp. 179–183). New York: Plenum Publishing Corporation.

Nicolson, R.I. & Fawcett, A.J. (1990). Automaticity: A new framework for dyslexia research. *Cognition, 35*, 159–182.

Nimmo, L.M. & Roodenrys, S. (2004). Investigating the phonological similarity effect: Syllable structure and the position of common phonemes. *Journal of Memory and Language, 50*, 245–258.

Norman, D.A. & Shallice, T. (1986). Attention to action: Willed and automatic control of behaviour. In R.J. Davidson, G.E. Schwarts and D. Shapiro (Eds.) *Consciousness and self-regulation, Advances in research and theory*, Vol. 4 (pp 1–18). New York: Plenum Press.

Numminen, H., Lehto, J. E. & Ruoppila, I. (2001). Tower of Hanoi and working memory in adult persons with intellectual disability. *Research in Developmental Disabilities, 22*, 373–387.

Numminen, H., Service, E., Ahonen, T., Korhonen, T., Tolcanen, A., Patja, K. & Ruoppila, I. (2000). Working memory structure and intellectual disability. *Journal of Intellectual Disability Research, 44*(5), 579–590.

Numminen, H., Service, E., Ahonen, T. & Ruoppila, I. (2001). Working memory and everyday cognition in adults with Down's syndrome. *Journal of Intellectual Disability Research, 45*(2), 157–168.

Numminen, H., Service, E. & Ruoppila, I. (2002). Working memory, intelligence and knowledge base in adult persons with intellectual disability. *Research in Developmental Disabilities, 23*, 105–118.

O'Hearn, K., Courtney, S., Street, W. & Landau, B. (2009). Working memory impairment in people with Williams syndrome: Effects of delay, task and stimuli. *Brain and Cognition, 69*(3), 495–503.

Ornstein, P.A., Naus, M.J. & Liberty, C. (1975). Rehearsal and organisational processes in children's memory. *Child Development, 46*, 818–830.

Ornstein, P.A., Naus, M.J. & Stone, B.P. (1977). Rehearsal training and developmental differences in memory. *Developmental Psychology, 13*, 15–24.

Ozonoff, S. (2010). Proceeding with caution – the importance of negative findings in the science of psychopathology. *Journal of Child Psychology and Psychiatry, 51*(9), 965–966.

Ozonoff, S. & Jensen, J. (1999). Specific executive function profiles in three neurodevelopmental disorders. *Journal of Autism and Developmental Disorders, 29*(2), 171–177.

Ozonoff, S. & McEvoy, R. E. (1994). A longitudinal study of executive function and theory of mind development in autism. *Development and Psychopathology, 6*, 415–431.

Ozonoff, S., Pennington, B.F. & Rogers, S. (1991). Executive function deficits in high-functioning autistic individuals: Relationship to theory of mind. *Journal of Child Psychology and Psychiatry, 32*(7), 1081–1105.

Ozonoff, S. & Strayer, D.L. (2001). Further evidence of intact working memory in autism. *Journal of Autism and Developmental Disorders, 31*(3), 257–263.

Palmer, S. (2000a). Working memory: A developmental study of phonological recoding. *Memory, 8*(3), 179–193.

Palmer, S. (2000b). Development of phonological recoding and literacy acquisition: A four-year cross-sequential study. *British Journal of Developmental Psychology, 18*(4), 533–555.

Palmer, S. (2000c). The retention of a visual encoding strategy in dyslexic teenagers. *Journal of Reading Research, 23*, 28–40.

Paulesu, E., Frith, C.D. & Frackowiak, R.S.J. (1993). The neural correlates of the verbal component of working memory. *Nature, 362*, 342–345.

Pennington, B.F., Moon, J., Edgin, J., Stedron, J. & Nadel, L. (2003). The neuropsychology of Down syndrome: Evidence for hippocampal dysfunction. *Child Development, 74*, 75–93.

Pennington, B.F. & Olson, R.K. (2005). Genetics of dyslexia. In M.J. Snowling & C. Hulme (Eds.), *The science of reading: A handbook* (pp. 453–472). Oxford: Blackwell.

Pennington, B.F. & Ozonoff, S. (1996). Executive functions and developmental psychopathology. *Journal of Child Psychology and Psychiatry, 37*(1), 51–87.

Peoples, R., Franke, Y., Wang, Y., Perez-Jurado, L., Paperna, T., Cisco, M. & Francke, U. (2000). A physical map, including a BAC/PAC clone contig, of the Williams-Beuren syndrome deletion region at 7q11.23. *American Journal of Human Genetics, 66*, 47–68.

Petrides, M. & Milner, B. (1982). Deficits on subject-ordered tasks after frontal and temporal lobe lesions in man. *Neuropsychologia, 20*, 249–262.

Pickering, S. (2006a). Assessment of working memory in children. In S.J. Pickering (Ed.), *Working memory and education* (pp. 241–271). London: Elsevier Academic Press.

Pickering, S. (2006b). Working memory in dyslexia. In T.P. Alloway & S.E. Gathercole (Eds.), *Working memory and neurodevelopmental disorders* (pp. 7–40). Hove: Psychology Press.

Pickering, S. & Gathercole, S. (2001). *Working memory test battery for children, WMTB-C.* London: Psychological Corporation.

Pickering, S. & Gathercole, S. (2004). Distinctive working memory profiles in children with special educational needs. *Educational Psychology, 24*, 393–408.

Pickering, S., Gathercole, S.E., Hall, M. & Lloyd, S.A. (2001). Development of memory for pattern and path: Further evidence for the fractionation of visuo-spatial memory. *Quarterly Journal of Experimental Psychology, 54A*, 397–420.

Pickering, S.J., Gathercole, S.E. & Peaker, S.M. (1998). Verbal and visual spatial short-term memory in children: Evidence for common and distinct mechanisms. *Memory & Cognition, 26*(6), 1117–1130.

Pinker, S. (1994). *The language instinct: How the mind creates language.* New York: HarperCollins.

Piolino, P., Hisland, M., Ruffeveille, I., Matuszewski, V., Jambaqué, I. & Eustache, F. (2007). Do school-age children remember or know the personal past? *Consciousness and Cognition, 16*, 84–101.

Poirier, M. & Martin, J.S. (2008). Working memory and immediate memory in autism spectrum disorders. In J. Boucher & D. Bowler (Eds.), *Memory in autism: Theory and evidence.* Cambridge: Cambridge University Press.

Poirier, M., Martin, J.S., Gaigg, S.B. & Bowler, D.M. (2011). Short-term memory in Autism Spectrum Disorder. *Journal of Abnormal Psychology, 120*(1), 247–252.

Porter, M.A., Coltheart, M. & Langdon, R. (2007). The neuropsychological basis of hypersociability in Williams and Down syndrome. *Neuropsychologia, 45*, 2839–2849.

Prior, M. R. & Hoffman, W. (1990). Neuropsychological testing of autistic children through an exploration with frontal lobe tests. *Journal of Autism and Developmental Disorders, 20*, 581–590.

Purser, H.R.M. & Jarrold, C. (2005). Impaired verbal short-term memory in Down syndrome reflects a capacity limitation rather than atypically rapid forgetting. *Journal of Experimental Child Psychology, 91*, 1–23.

Reitan, R.M. & Wolfson, D. (1992). *Neuropsychological evaluation of older children*. Tuscan, AZ: Neuropsychology Press.

Reiter, A., Tucha, O. & Lange, K.W. (2004). Executive functions in children with dyslexia. *Dyslexia, 11*, 116–131.

Reynolds, C.R. & Bigler, E. (1994). *Test and memory and learning*. Austin, TX: Pro-Ed.

Rhodes, S.M., Riby, D.M., Park, J., Fraser, E. & Campbell, L.E. (2010). Executive neuropsychological functioning in individuals with Williams syndrome. *Neuropsychologia, 48*, 1216–1226.

Rice, M.L. & Wexler, K. (1996). A phenotype of specific language impairment: Extended optional infinitives. In M.L. Rice (Ed.), *Toward a genetics of language* (pp. 215–237). Mahwah, NJ: Lawrence Erlbaum Associates.

Robertson, E.K. & Köhler, S. (2007). Insights from child development on the relationship between episodic and semantic memory. *Neuropsychologia, 45*, 3178–3189.

Robinson, B., Mervis, C.B. & Robinson, B.W. (2003). The roles of verbal short-term memory and working memory in the acquisition of grammar by children with Williams syndrome. *Developmental Neuropsychology, 23*(1 & 2), 13–31.

Robinson, S., Goddard, L., Dritschel, B., Wisley, M. & Howlin, P. (2009). Executive functions in children with Autism Spectrum Disorders. *Brain and Cognition, 71*, 362–368.

Roizen, N.J., Wolters, C., Nicol, T. & Blondis, T.A. (1993). Hearing loss in children with Down syndrome. *The Journal of Pediatrics, 123*, S9–S12.

Romani, C., McAlpine, S., Olson, A., Tsouknida, E. & Martin, R. (2005). Length, lexicality, and articulatory suppression in immediate recall: Evidence against the articulatory loop. *Journal of Memory and Language, 52*, 398–415.

Roodenrys, S. & Stokes, J. (2001). Serial recall and nonword repetition in reading disabled children. *Reading and Writing: An Interdisciplinary Journal, 14*, 379–394.

Rosenquist, C., Conners, F.A. & Roskos-Ewoldsen, B. (2003). Phonological and visuo-spatial working memory in individuals with intellectual disability. *American Journal on Mental Retardation, 108*(6), 403–413.

Rowe, J., Lavender, A. & Turk, V. (2006). Cognitive executive function in Down's syndrome. *British Journal of Clinical Psychology, 45*, 5–17.

Rowe, M.L. & Mervis, C.B. (2006). Working memory in Williams syndrome. In T.P. Alloway & S.E. Gathercole (Eds.), *Working memory and neurodevelopmental disorders* (pp. 267–293). Hove, East Sussex, UK: Psychology Press.

Rumsey, J. M. & Hamburger, S. D. (1988). Neuropsychological findings in high-functioning autistic men with infantile autism, residual state. *Journal of Clinical and Experimental Neuropsychology, 10*, 201–221.

Russell, J., Jarrold, C. & Henry, L. (1996). Working memory in children with autism and with moderate learning difficulties. *Journal of Child Psychology and Psychiatry, 37*, 673–686.

Russell, J., Jarrold, C. & Hood, B. (1999). Two intact executive capacities in children with autism: Implications for the core executive dysfunctions in the disorder. *Journal of Autism and Developmental Disorders, 29*(2), 103–112.

Rutter, M., Kim-Cohen, J. & Maughan, B. (2006). Continuities and discontinuities in psychopathology between childhood and adult life. *Journal of Child Psychology and Psychiatry, 47*, 276–295.

Salmond, C.H., Adlam, A-L.R., Gadian, D.G. & Vargha-Khadem, F. (2008). A comparison of memory profiles in relation to neuropathology in autism, developmental amnesia and children born prematurely. In J. Boucher & D. Bowler (Eds.), *Memory in autism: Theory and evidence*. Cambridge: Cambridge University Press.

Schneider, W., Körkel, J. & Weinert, F.E. (1989). Domain-specific knowledge and memory performance: A comparison of high- and low-aptitude children. *Journal of Educational Psychology, 81*, 306–312.

Schneider, W. & Pressley, M. (1997). *Memory development between two and twenty*, 2nd ed. Mahwah, NJ: Lawrence Erlbaum Associates.

Schopler, E., Mesibov, G.B. & Kunce, L.J. (1998). *Asperger syndrome or high-functioning autism?* London: Plenum Press.

Schuchardt, K., Gebhardt, M. & Mähler, C. (2010). Working memory functions in children with different degrees of intellectual disability. *Journal of Intellectual Disability Research, 54*(4), 346–353.

Schweickert, R. (1993). A multinomial processing tree model for degradation and redintegration in immediate recall. *Memory & Cognition, 21*, 167–175.

Schweickert, R. & Boruff, B. (1986). Short-term memory capacity: Magic number or magic spell? *Journal of Experimental Psychology: Learning, Memory, and Cognition, 12*, 419–425.

Schwenck, C., Bjorklund, D.F. & Schneider, W. (2007). Factors influencing the incidence of utilisation deficiencies and other patterns of recall/strategy-use relations in a strategic memory task. *Child Development, 78*(6), 1771–1787.

Service, E. (1998). The effect of word length on immediate serial recall depends on phonological complexity, not articulatory duration. *Quarterly Journal of Experimental Psychology A, 51*, 283–304.

Service, E. (2000). Phonological complexity and word duration in immediate recall: Different paradigms answer different questions. A comment to Cowan, Nugent, Elliott and Geer (2000). *Quarterly Journal of Experimental Psychology A, 53*, 661–665.

Seung, H.-K. & Chapman, R. (2000). Digit span in individuals with Down syndrome and typically developing children: Temporal aspects. *Journal of Speech, Language, and Hearing Research, 43*, 609–620.

Seung, H.-K. & Chapman, R. (2004). Sentence memory of individuals with Down's syndrome and typically developing children. *Journal of Intellectual Disability Research, 48*(2), 160–171.

Shallice, T. (1990). *From neuropsychology to mental structure*. New York: Cambridge University Press.

Shankweiler, D., Liberman, I.Y., Mark, L.S., Fowler, C.A. & Fischer, F.W. (1979). The speech code and learning to read. *Journal of Experimental Psychology: Human Learning and Memory, 5*(6), 531–545.

Shing, Y. L., Werkle-Bergner, M., Li, S-C. & Lindenberger, U. (2008). Associative and strategic components of episodic memory: A life-span dissociation. *Journal of Experimental Psychology: General, 137*(3), 495–513.

Shue, K.L. & Douglas, V.I. (1992). Attention deficit hyperactivity disorder and the frontal lobe syndrome. *Brain and Cognition, 20*, 104–124.

Siegel, L.S. & Linder, B.A. (1984). Short-term memory processes in children with reading and arithmetic learning disabilities. *Developmental Psychology, 20*(2), 200–207.

Siegel, L.S. & Ryan, E.B. (1989). The development of working memory in normally achieving and subtypes of learning disabled children. *Child Development, 60*, 973–980.

Simonoff, E., Pickles, A., Chadwick, O., Gringas, P., Wood, N., Higgins, S., Maney, J-A., Karia, N., Iqbal, H. & Moore, A. (2006). The Croydon assessment of learning study: Prevalence and educational identification of mild mental retardation. *Journal of Child Psychology and Psychiatry, 47*(8), 828–839.

Skuse, D.H. & Seigal, A. (2008). Behavoral phenotypes and chromosomal disorders. In M. Rutter, D. Bishop, D. Pine, S. Scott, J. Stevenson, E. Taylor & A. Thapar (Eds.), *Rutter's child and adolescent psychiatry*, 5th ed. (pp. 359–376). Oxford: Blackwell Publishing Ltd.

Sluzenski, J., Newcombe, N.S. & Kovacs, S.L. (2006). Binding, relational memory, and recall of naturalistic events: A developmental perspective. *Journal of Experimental Psychology: Learning, Memory, and Cognition, 32*(1), 89–100.

Smith-Spark, J.H. & Fisk, J.E. (2007). Working memory functioning in developmental dyslexia. *Memory, 15*(1), 34–56.

Smyth, M.M. & Pendleton, L.R. (1989). Working memory for movement. *Quarterly Journal of Experimental Psychology, 41A*, 235–250.

Snowling, M.J., Chiat, S. & Hulme, C. (1991). Words, nonwords and phonological processes: Some comments on Gathercole, Willis, Emslie, and Baddeley. *Applied Psycholinguistics, 12*, 369–373.

Snowling, M.J. & Hulme, C. (2008). Reading and other specific learning difficulties. In M. Rutter, D. Bishop, D. Pine, S. Scott, J. Stevenson, E. Taylor & A. Thapar (Eds.), *Rutter's child and adolescent psychiatry*, 5th ed. (pp. 802–819). Oxford: Blackwell Science.

Spitz, H.H. (1966). The role of input organisation in the learning and memory of mental retardates. In N.R. Ellis (Ed.), *International review of research in mental retardation*, Vol. 2. New York: Academic Press.

Spitz, H.H. & DeRisi, D.T. (1978). Porteus Maze test performance of retarded young adults and nonretarded children. *American Journal of Mental Deficiency, 83*, 40–43.

Spitz, H.H., Webster, N.A. & Borys, S.V. (1982). Further studies of the Tower of Hanoi problem-solving performance of retarded young adults and nonretarded children. *Developmental Psychology, 18*, 922–930.

Spring, C. & Capps, C. (1974). Encoding speed, rehearsal, and probed recall of dyslexic boys. *Journal of Educational Psychology, 66*(5), 780–786.

St Clair-Thompson, H.L. & Gathercole, S.E. (2006). Executive functions and achievements in school: Shifting, updating, inhibition, and working memory. *Quarterly Journal of Experimental Psychology, 59*, 745–759.

Standing, L. & Curtis, L. (1989). Subvocalisation rate versus other predictors of the memory span. *Psychological Reports, 65*, 487–495.

Stanovich, K.E. & Siegel, L.S. (1994). The phenotypic performance profile of reading-disabled children: A regression-based test of the phonological-core variable-difference model. *Journal of Educational Psychology, 86*, 24–53.

Steele, S.D., Minshew, N.J., Luna, B. & Sweeney, J.A. (2007). Spatial working memory deficits in autism. *Journal of Autism and Developmental Disorders, 37*, 605–612.

Sternberg, R.J. & Spear, L.C. (1985). A triarchic theory of mental retardation. In N. R. Ellis & N. W. Bray (Eds.), *International review of research on mental retardation*, Vol. 13 (pp. 301–326). London: Academic Press.

Sternberg, S., Monsell, S., Knoll, R.L. & Wright, C.E. (1978). The timing of rapid movement sequences. In G.E. Stelmach (Ed.), *Information processing in motor control and learning*. (pp. 117–152). New York: Academic Press.

Stigler, J.W., Lee, S.Y. & Stevenson, H.W. (1986). Digit memory in Chinese and English: Evidence for a temporally limited store. *Cognition, 23*, 1–20.

Stokes, S.F. & Klee, T. (2009). Factors that influence vocabulary development in two-year-old children. *Journal of Child Psychology and Psychiatry, 50*(4), 498–505.

Stromme, P., Bjornstad, P.G. & Ramstad, K. (2002). Prevalence estimation of Williams syndrome. *Journal of Child Neurology, 17*, 269–271.

Stroop, J. R. (1935). Studies of interference in serial verbal reactions. *Journal of Experimental Psychology, 18*, 634–662.

Swanson, L. (1978). Verbal encoding effects on the visual short-term memory of learning disabled and normal readers. *Journal of Educational Psychology, 70*(4), 539–544.

Swanson, H.L. (1993). Executive processing in learning disabled readers. *Intelligence, 17*, 117–149.

Swanson, H.L. (2003). Age-related differences in learning disabled and skilled readers' working memory. *Journal of Experimental Child Psychology, 85*, 1–31.

Swanson, H.L. (2006). Working memory and reading disabilities: Both phonological and executive processing deficits are important. In T.P. Alloway & S.E. Gathercole (Eds.), *Working memory and neurodevelopmental disorders* (pp. 59–88). Hove: Psychology Press.

Swanson, H.L. (2008). Working memory and intelligence in children: What develops? *Journal of Educational Psychology, 100*(3), 581–602.

Szatmari, P., Bryson, S., Duku, E., Vaccarella, L., Zwaigenbaum, L., Bennett, T. & Boyle, M.H. (2009). Similar developmental trajectories in autism and Asperger syndrome: From early childhood to adolescence. *Journal of Child Psychology and Psychiatry, 50*(12), 1459–1467.

Tager-Flusberg, H. (1986). The semantic deficit hypothesis of autistic children's language. *Australian Journal of Human Communication Disorders, 14*, 51–58.

Tager-Flusberg, H. (1999). (Ed). *Neurodevelopmental Disorders*. Cambridge MA: MIT Press/ Bradford Books.

Tallal, P. (1980). Auditory-temporal perception, phonics and reading disabilities in children. *Brain and Language, 9*, 182–198.

Tam, H., Jarrold, C., Baddeley, A.D. & Sabatos-DeVito, M. (2010). The development of memory maintenance: Children's use of phonological rehearsal and attentional refreshment in working memory tasks. *Journal of Experimental Child Psychology, 107*, 306–324.

Thomas, M.S.C., Annaz, D., Ansari, D., Scerif, G., Jarrold, C. & Karmiloff-Smith, A. (2009). Using developmental trajectories to understand developmental disorders. *Journal of Speech, Language, and Hearing Research, 52*, 336–358.

Thomson, J.M., Richardson, U. and Goswami, U. (2005). Phonological similarity neighbourhoods and children's short-term memory: Typical development and dyslexia. *Memory & Cognition, 33*(7), 1210–1219.

Toichi, M. (2008). Episodic memory, semantic memory and self-awareness in high-functioning autism. In J. Boucher & D. Bowler (Eds.), *Memory in autism: Theory and evidence*. Cambridge: Cambridge University Press.

Torgesen, J.K. & Burgess, S.R. (1998). Consistency of reading related phonological processes throughout early childhood: Evidence from the longitudinal, correlational and instructional studies. In J.L. Metsala & L.C. Ehri (Eds.), *Word recognition in beginning literacy* (pp. 161–188). London: Erlbaum.

Towse, J. N., Cowan, N., Horton, N. J. & Whytock, S. (2008). Task experience and children's working memory performance. A perspective from recall timing. *Developmental Psychology, 44*(3), 695–706.

Towse, J.N. & Hitch, G.J. (1995). Is there a relationship between task demand and storage space in tests of working memory capacity? *Quarterly Journal of Experimental Psychology, 48A*, 108–124.

Towse, J.N. & Hitch, G.J. (2007). Variation in working memory due to normal development. In A.R.A. Conway, C. Jarrold, M.J. Kane, A. Miyake and J.N. Towse (Eds.), *Variation in working memory*. (pp. 109–133). Oxford: Oxford University Press.

Towse, J.N., Hitch, G.J. & Hutton, U. (1998). A re-evaluation of working memory capacity in children. *Journal of Memory and Language, 39*, 195–217.

Towse, J.N., Hitch, G.J. & Hutton, U. (2002). On the nature of the relationship between processing activity and item retention in children. *Journal of Experimental Child Psychology, 82*, 156–184.

Turner, J.E., Henry, L.A., Brown, P. & Smith, P.T. (2004). Redintegration and lexicality effects in children: Do they depend upon the demands of the memory task? *Memory and Cognition, 32*, 501–510.

Turner, J.E., Henry, L.A. & Smith, P.T. (2000). The development of the use of long-term knowledge to assist short-term recall. *Quarterly Journal of Experimental Psychology, 53A*, 457–478.

Turner, M.A. (1999). Generating novel ideas: Fluency performance in high-functioning and learning disabled individuals with autism. *Journal of Child Psychology and Psychiatry, 40*(2), 189–201.

Turnure, J.E. (1991). Long-term memory and mental retardation. In N.W. Bray (Ed.), *International review of research in mental retardation*, Vol. 17 (pp. 193–217). London: Academic Press.

Udwin, O., Yule, W. & Martin, N. (1987). Cognitive abilities and behavioural characteristics of children with idiopathic infantile hypercalcaemia. *Journal of Child Psychology and Psychiatry, 28*, 297–309.

Ullman, M. T. & Pierpont, E. I. (2005). Specific language impairment is not specific to language: The procedural deficit hypothesis. *Cortex, 41*(3), 399–433.

Vakil, E., Shelef-Reshef, E. & Levy-Shiff, R. (1997). Procedural and declarative memory processes: Individuals with and without mental retardation. *American Journal on Mental Retardation, 102*(2), 147–160.

van der Lely, H.K.J. (2005). Domain-specific cognitive systems: Insight from grammatical-SLI. *Trends in Cognitive Sciences, 9*(2), 53–59.

van der Lely, H.K.J. & Howard, D. (1993). Children with specific language impairment: Linguistic impairment or short-term memory deficit? *Journal of Speech and Hearing Research, 36*, 1193–1207.

Van der Molen, M.J. (2010). Working memory structure in 10- and 15-year-old children with mild to borderline intellectual disabilities. *Research in Developmental Disabilities, 31*, 1258–1263.

Van der Molen, M.J., Van Luit, J.E.H., Jongmans, M.J. & Van der Molan, M.W. (2007). Verbal working memory in children with mild intellectual disabilities. *Journal of Intellectual Disability Research, 51*(2), 162–169.

Van der Molen, M.J., Van Luit, J.E.H., Jongmans, M.J. & Van der Molan, M.W. (2009). Memory profiles in children with mild intellectual disabilities: Strengths and weaknesses. *Research in Developmental Disabilities, 30*, 1237–1247.

Van der Molen, M.J., Van Luit, J.E.H., Van der Molan, M.W., Klugkist, I. & Jongmans, M.J. (2010). Effectiveness of a computerised working memory training in adolescents with mild to borderline intellectual disabilities. *Journal of Intellectual Disability Research, 54*(5), 433–447.

van der Sluis, S., de Jong, P.F. & van der Leij, A. (2004). Inhibition and shifting in children with learning deficits in arithmetic and reading. *Journal of Experimental Child Psychology, 87*, 239–266.

van der Sluis, S., de Jong, P.F. & van der Leij, A. (2007). Executive functioning in children, and its relations with reasoning, reading, and arithmetic. *Intelligence, 35*, 427–449.

Van Engeland, H. & Buitelaar, J.K. (2008). Autism spectrum disorders. In M. Rutter, D. Bishop, D. Pine, S. Scott, J. Stevenson, E. Taylor & A. Thapar (Eds.), *Rutter's child and adolescent psychiatry*, 5th ed. (pp. 759–781). Oxford: Blackwell Publishing Ltd.

Varnhagen, C.K., Das, J.P. & Varnhagen, S. (1987). Auditory and visual memory span: Cognitive processing by TMR individuals with Down syndrome or other etiologies. *American Journal of Mental Deficiency, 91*(4), 398–405.

Vellutino, F.R., Fletcher, J.M., Snowling, M.J. & Scanlon, D.M. (2004). Specific reading disability (dyslexia): What have we learned in the past four decades? *Journal of Child Psychology and Psychiatry, 45*(1), 2–40.

Vellutino, F.R., Pruzek, R.M., Steger, J.A. & Meshoulam, U. (1973). Immediate visual recall in poor and normal readers as a function of orthographic-linguistic familiarity. *Cortex, 9*, 370–386.

Vellutino, F.R., Steger, J.A., DeSetto, L. & Phillips, F. (1975). Immediate and delayed recognition of visual stimuli in poor and normal readers. *Journal of Experimental Child Psychology, 19*, 223–232.

Vicari, S., Bellucci, S. & Carlesimo, G.A. (2000). Implicit and explicit memory: A functional dissociation in persons with Down syndrome. *Neuropsychologia, 38*, 240–251.

Vicari, S., Bellucci, S. & Carlesimo, G.A. (2001). Procedural learning deficit in children with Williams syndrome. *Neuropsychologia, 39*, 665–677.

Vicari, S., Bellucci, S. & Carlesimo, G.A. (2003). Visual and spatial working memory dissociation: Evidence from Williams syndrome. *Developmental Medicine & Child Neurology, 45*, 269–273.

Vicari, S., Bellucci, S. & Carlesimo, G.A. (2006). Evidence from two genetic syndromes for the independence of spatial and visual working memory. *Developmental Medicine and Child Neurology, 48*, 126–131.

Vicari, S., Brizzolara, D., Carlesimo, G. & Pezzini, G. (1996). Memory abilities in children with Williams syndrome. *Cortex, 32*, 503–514.

Vicari, S., Carlesimo, G., Brizzolara, D. & Pezzini, G. (1996). Short-term memory in children with Williams syndrome: A reduced contribution of lexical-semantic knowledge to word span. *Neuropsychologia, 34*, 919–925.

Vicari, S., Carlesimo, G.A. & Caltagirone, C. (1995). Short-term memory in persons with intellectual disabilities and Down's syndrome. *Journal of Intellectual Disability Research, 39*(6), 532–537.

Vicari, S., Marotta, L. & Carlesimo, G.A. (2004). Verbal short-term memory in Down's syndrome: An articulatory loop deficit? *Journal of Intellectual Disability Research, 48*(2), 80–92.

Vicari, S., Verucci, L. & Carlesimo, G.A. (2007). Implicit memory is independent from IQ and age but not from etiology: Evidence from Down and Williams syndrome. *Journal of Intellectual Disability Research, 51*(12), 932–941.

Visu-Petra, L., Benga, O., Țincaș, I. and Miclea, M. (2007). Visual-spatial processing in children and adolescents with Down's syndrome: A computerized assessment of memory skills. *Journal of Intellectual Disability Research, 51*, 942–952.

Volkmar, F.R. & Dykens, E. (2002). Mental retardation. In M. Rutter & E. Taylor, *Child and adolescent psychiatry*, 4th ed. (pp. 697–710). Oxford: Blackwell Science.

Volkmar, F.R., Lord, C., Bailey, A., Schultz, R.T. & Klin, A. (2004). Autism and pervasive developmental disorders. *Journal of Child Psychology and Psychiatry, 45*(1), 135–170.

Walker, P., Hitch, G.J. & Duroe, S. (1993). The effect of visual similarity on short-term memory for spatial location: Implications for the capacity of visual short-term memory. *Acta Psychologia, 83*, 203–224.

Wallace, G.L., Silvers, J.A., Martin, A. and Kenworthy, L.E. (2009). Evidence for inner speech deficits in autism spectrum disorders. *Journal of Autism and Developmental Disorders, 39*, 1735–1739.

Wang, P.P. & Bellugi, U. (1994). Evidence from two genetic syndromes for a dissociation between verbal and visual-spatial short-term memory. *Journal of Clinical and Experimental Neuropsychology, 16*, 317–322.

Waters, G.S., Rochon, E. & Caplan, D. (1992). The role of high-level speech planning in rehearsal: Evidence from patients with apraxia of speech. *Journal of Memory and Language*, 31, 54–73.

Watkins, M.J. (1977). The intricacy of memory span. *Memory & Cognition, 5*, 529–534.

Weiss, B., Weisz, J.R. & Bromfield, R. (1986). Performance of retarded and non-retarded person on information-processing tasks: Further tests of a similar structure hypotheses. *Psychological Bulletin, 100*, 157–175.

Wellman, H.M. (1977). Preschoolers' understanding of memory-relevant variables. *Child Development, 48*, 1720–1723.

Welsh, M.C., Pennington, B.F. & Grossier, D.B. (1991). A normative-developmental study of executive function: A window on prefrontal function in children. *Developmental Neuropsychology, 7,* 131–149.

Weyandt, L.L. & Willis, W.G. (1994). Executive functions in school-aged children: Potential efficacy of tasks in discriminating clinical groups. *Developmental Neuropsychology, 10*(1), 27–38.

Whitehouse, J.O., Maybury, M.T. & Durkin, K. (2006). Inner speech impairments in autism. *Journal of Child Psychology and Psychiatry, 47*(8), 857–865.

Wicks-Nelson, R. & Israel, A.C. (2006). *Behavior Disorders of Childhood*, 6th Ed. Upper Saddle River, New Jersey: Pearson Education Inc.

Williams, D.L., Goldstein, G., Carpenter, P.A. & Minshew, N.J. (2005). Verbal and spatial working memory in autism. *Journal of Autism and Developmental Disorders, 35*(6), 747–756.

Williams, D.L., Goldstein, G. & Minshew, N.J. (2006). The profile of memory function in children with autism. *Neuropsychology, 20*(1), 21–29.

Williams, D., Happé, F. & Jarrold, C. (2008). Intact inner speech use in autism spectrum disorder: Evidence from a short-term memory task. *Journal of Child Psychology and Psychiatry, 49*(1), 51–58.

Williams, D.L., Minshew, N.J. & Goldstein, G. (2008). Memory within a complex information-processing model of autism. In J. Boucher & D. Bowler (Eds.), *Memory in autism: Theory and evidence.* Cambridge: Cambridge University Press.

Williams, D.M. & Jarrold, C. (2010). Predicting the inner speech use amongst children with autism spectrum disorder (ASD): The roles of verbal ability and cognitive profile. *Journal of Autism and Developmental Disorders, 40*(7), 907–913.

Wilson, J.T.L., Scott, J.H. & Power, K.G. (1987). Developmental differences in the span of visual memory for pattern. *British Journal of Developmental Psychology, 5,* 249–255.

Wing, L. & Gould, J. (1979). Severe impairments of social interaction and associated abnormalities in children: Epidemiology and classification. *Journal of Autism and Developmental Disorders, 9,* 11–29.

Winters, J.J., Attlee, L.C. & Harvey, F. (1974). Paired-associate learning of EMR adolescents and nonretarded children as a function of methods of presentation and training. *American Journal of Mental Deficiency, 79*(1), 70–76.

Wisniewski, J.M. & Silverman, W. (1998). Ageing and dementia of the Alzheimer's type in persons with mental retardation, *Advances in Experimental Medicine and Biology, 446,* 223–225.

World Health Organisation (1992). *The ICD-10 classification of mental and behavioural disorders.* Geneva: World Health Organisation.

Young, A.R., Beitchman, J.H., Johnson, C., Douglas, L., Atkinson, L., Escobar, M. & Wilson, B. (2002). Young adult academic outcomes in a longitudinal sample of early identified language impaired and control children. *Journal of Child Psychology and Psychiatry, 43*(5), 635–645.

Yuzawa, M. (2001). Effects of word length on young children's memory performance. *Memory & Cognition, 29*(4), 557–564.

Zigler, E. (1969). Developmental versus difference theories of mental retardation and the problem of motivation. *American Journal of Mental Deficiency, 73,* 536–556.

Zigler, E. & Balla, D. (1982). Introduction: The developmental approach to mental retardation. In E. Zigler & D. Balla (Eds.), *Mental retardation: The developmental difference controversy* (pp. 3–8). Hillsdale, NJ: Lawrence Erlbaum Associates.

Index

Page references to Figures or Tables will be in *italics*